Sing In Me, Muse, and Through Me Tell the Story

Greek Culture Performed

by

Maria Hnaraki

Zorba Press
Ithaca, NY

Published by Zorba Press in Ithaca, New York, USA

Zorba Press
http://www.ZorbaPress.com

The book includes a bibliography of references, a glossary, and an index.
For more information about this book, see the book's web page at:
http://zorbapress.com/?page_id=1052

Release date: October 2013

ISBN: 9780927379168

Library of Congress Control Number: 2013952238

For sales, permissions, and all other inquiries, contact Zorba Press by email at:
books@zorbapress.com

Printings: 0102030405060708091011121314151617181920

Contents

Acknowledgments 5

Introduction 7

Chapter 1: Greece through the Looking Glass 9

Greek Folklore 11
An Ethnographic Approach to Folk Music 20

Chapter 2: Music Mythologies and Identities 25

At the Crossroads of East and West 27
St. Romanos the Melodist 43
Cretan-Turkish Musicians 45
Stratis Kalogeridis 48
Nikos Xylouris 51
Zeus Performed 54
Bridging the Local with the *Glocal* 60
Dimitri Mitropoulos 60
Maria Callas 64
Ross Daly 66

Chapter 3: The Poetics and the Ecology of Greek Singing 77

Musings 79
From Homeric Poetry to Cretan Balladry 86
Songs of the Foothills 93
Songs of the Plains 104
Singing the Tree 109

Chapter 4: Speaking without Words 115

Wedding Dance as Expression, Dialogue and Communication 117
Revisiting Zorba's Dance 127
Raising Ecological Awareness through Dance 134
Resistance through Dancing 144

Contents (continued)

Chapter 5: Greek Literature and the Other Arts 159

Beyond *Zorba* and *Captain-Michael*: Music Tradition and Globalization through the Work of Nikos Kazantzakis 161
The *Masterbuilders* 168
Captain Michael 179
Melissa & Periander 182
Amor Fati 188
Iphigenia's Sacrifices 191

Chapter 6: Tasty Greece 201

A Hungry Bear Does Not Dance 203
Baked Realities 204
We Speak What We Eat: My Big Fat Greek Language 223
A Sample Greek Meal 227

Chapter 7: Re-Discovering Greece 231

The Amphitheater "Greece" 233

Endnotes 237
Bibliography 261
Glossary 279
Transliteration 285
Index 287

About the Author, Maria Hnaraki 306
About the Publisher, Zorba Press 307

Acknowledgments

The author perceives the present endeavor as a collaborative work. She deeply appreciates the opportunities provided to her for various and multidisciplinary discourses on diverse facets of Greek culture and people's understanding of it at several parts of the world (other than her native Greek and Cretan ones): from the Caspian Astrakhan in Russia, the Ankara-capital of Turkey, the Balkan Belgrade in Serbia, and the Eternal City of Rome, to the island communities of Malta, Sicily, Prince Edward and New Zealand, to name a few.

The courtesy of the following publishers should be particularly acknowledged for her own entries:

ABC-CLIO (Greek Folklore)

Bulletin of the Ethnographic Institute *(Revisiting Zorba's Dance)*

Crete University Press *(The Masterbuilders)*

Folklor Edebiyat *(Wedding Dance as Expression, Dialogue and Communication)*

Greek Composers' Union *(Beyond Zorba and Captain-Michael: Music Tradition and Globalization through the Work of Nikos Kazantzakis)*

Greek Ethos *(St. Romanos the Melodist & Maria Callas)*

Greek National Opera *(The Masterbuilders)*

Hellenic Music Centre *(Amor Fati)*

Institute of Ethnography SASA *(Ross Daly; The Poetics and the Ecology of Greek Singing; From Homeric Poetry to Cretan Balladry; Resistance through Dancing)*

Modern Greek Studies Yearbook *(At the Crossroads of East & West)*

Music Library of Greece "Lilian Voudouri"; The Friends of Music Society *(Melissa & Periander)*

Pax Sonoris; The State Folk Center "Astrakhan Song" *(Ross Daly & Iphigenia's Sacrifices)*

Petis Propos Cullinaires; Prospect Books *(Baked Realities)*

Scarecrow Press Inc.; A Member of The Rowman & Littlefield Publishing Group *(Songs of the Foothills)*

Taylor and Francis Group LLC Books *(A Hungry Bear Does Not Dance & A Sample Greek Meal)*

The Smart Set; Drexel University *(We Speak What We Eat: My Big Fat Greek Language)*

As any mosaic preserves the individual qualities of each of its units, so does this book: You may read it piece by piece or treat it as a whole entity. It is a performance dedicated to a) the island of Crete, that pathway of knowledge toward unraveling mental paths, b) my family, who constantly provides me with the appropriate balance, calmness and patience necessary so as to be able and go on in life, and c) the still- and still-to-be-born ones.

Introduction

Sing In Me, Muse, and Through Me Tell the Story: Greek Culture Performed is a collection of ethnographic essays that meditate on Greece through the looking glass method. The book investigates how ancient mythologies shape modern identities at the crossroads of East and West while it also provides an ample description, both broad and deep, of various aspects and incarnations of Greek folklore performance, such as song, literature, music and dance.

In an era of globalization, Greeks insist upon going local by proudly celebrating their multifaceted past as they carry it into a turbulent present. From the time of Homer to contemporary forms of resistance, the poetics of Greekness provide an excellent ground for investigating the ecology of expressive behaviors that may inhabit any mountain or plain. When Greeks, for instance, sing the olive tree and speak without words through music and dance, performance becomes a means of dialogue and communication that raises ecological awareness of one's place by also creating a strong sense of belonging.

In a part of the world where life revolves around the centripetal idea of freedom in opposition to any form of tyranny, a community is willing to be sacrificed for a slice of bread. As the Greek future is predicated upon a stubbornly unfinished past, ultimately, one is at the same time exalted and despondent, grounded and soaring, rationale and passionate — elements in counterbalance that define the very essence of being Greek.

All in all, being Greek in the 21st century offers fertile territory for re-discovering the fundamental nature of life by actually experiencing Greece's truly rich, "baked" realities that have been so much stigmatized as being in "crisis." By building bridges and understanding the wealth and uniqueness of Greek culture, the clues to our own identities may unfold, albeit via labyrinthian pathways, capable of leading us to a catharsis, by realizing that, after all, nothing in our cosmos is … Greek.

Chapter 1

Greece through the Looking Glass

Greek Folklore

Greece & Folklore

Awash by the Mediterranean Sea, Greece serves as a crossroads for three continents. Its climate, typical of the Mediterranean, is marked by warm summers and relatively mild winters. Variations occur between the north and south and between the mainland and islands. Greek economy relies mostly on agriculture. Greece produces cereal grains (such as maize, millet, rice, and wheat), olive oil, grapes, wine, and tobacco. Its animal husbandry consists mostly of cattle, goats, and sheep. Settlements are compact, relatively permanent, densely populated, usually nucleated villages or towns. Local prefects and mayors rule them. Squares and neighborhoods constitute sociopolitical networks, where Greeks gather to socialize, discuss, and gossip.

The performative character of Greek folklore varies depending on age and gender. The traditional ritual protocol of group activities usually calls upon the participation of elderly men first, then younger men, followed by elderly women and then younger women, with children coming in last of all. In addition, different traditions exist for men, women, and children. Regionalism is strong in the country, as individual communities create and celebrate traditions that reflect their own understanding of "being Greek." Everything is local. Yet nationalism and regionalism do not compete as much as they inform each other. Traditional heritage and historical remembrance are often identical.

The Greek word for "folklore" is *laographia*, namely a composite of the noun *laos* – meaning "nation, people," and the verb *grapho* – meaning "to write." Throughout Greece several foundations and museums focus on the research, preservation, study, and presentation of Greek folklore. They publish books and scholarly journals. Their activities include the production of recordings of Greek folk music, usually from field recordings. In the field of research, they try adding to the understanding of the ethnographic wealth of Greece. They promote traditional cultural events and ethnographic interests by the revival of folk rituals and customs.

The study of folklore developed as Greece was trying to establish itself as an independent nation after years of foreign domination by Slavs, Franks, and – for the longest period – Turks. The early Greek folklorists saw the task of establishing a discipline based on an undeniable cultural continuity between the modern Greeks and their linguistic ancestors.

Using folklore as the vehicle for political nationalism, they tried to define cultural identity. In this spirit, they demonstrated continuity in the Greekness from antiquity to modern times. Greek folklore attempted not only to preserve a tradition but also to defend it against everybody who doubts its indissoluble unity with its ancient predecessors. Specific ideology was transmitted through literature, while philosophical nationalism was interpreted as patriotism. Oratory allowed no words of Turkish origin, for example. Instead, ancient Greek terms were used to express imported ideals (usually labeled as neo-Classical purism). The folklorists supported the demotic Greek, the language of the people, their ultimate goal being the consolidation of a nation-state while creating a national discipline of folklore studies.

Greek Identity: An Interesting Twin

Looking in from the outside, we might view Greek people as simultaneously ancient and modern. This is because Greece has an extraordinarily ambiguous, complex historical relationship to the idea of Europe itself and, more generally, to the stereotyped entity we call "western culture."[1] It has been argued that Greeks have a confused identity: Western Europe asked them to be European, while the foreign Greek lovers asked them to be ancient Greek.[2] Let us not forget that only in the early nineteenth century did Greece enter the modern world as an independent nation, freeing itself from four hundred years of Turkish rule. What followed was a debate over what exactly it meant to be Greek. It seems imperative that the name "Greece" be prefixed with the word "modern" or "contemporary" in order to convince its "admirers" that one can still find people living there.[3] Yet today, the ancient Greek tradition seems still to be prominent.

To comprehend the Greek nation's identity, we have to look at its parents. Its father is ancient, strong, heroic, a classical statue in white marble, with fine details and precise dimensions. On the contrary, its mother seems relaxed, magical, erotic, a belly dancer in the blurred harem of fate. The two parents represent allusions to two different periods of Greek history, one recalling the glories of the classical era and the other the more recent Byzantine and Turkish periods. On one hand, the father's image captures what Michael Herzfeld terms the "Hellenic thesis." This thesis, based on Europe's perception of ancient Greece, views modern Greek culture – especially folk culture – as the survival of ancient Greek ideals and denies oriental influences. On the other hand, the "Romeic thesis" represents the mother's image, most characteristically exemplified by linguistic demoticism and reflecting the familiar self-image which Greeks entertain about themselves when conversing with each other.[4]

However, "modern" Greeks still suffer a crisis of identity.[5] As novelist Nikos Kazantzakis put it: "What has the double-descended modern Greek taken from his father, what from his mother? He is clever and shallow, with no metaphysical anxieties, and, yet, when he begins to sing, universal grieving leaps up from his oriental bowels and breaks the crust of Greek logic…"[6]

Greece is symbolically both holy and polluted. It is holy in that it is the mythic ancestor of all European culture, and it is polluted by the taint of Turkish culture, a taint that late medieval and Renaissance Europe views as the embodiment of barbarism and evil.[7] The history of European culture is permeated by references to its sacred roots in ancient Greece. Yet, what happened in Greece after the collapse of the Byzantine Empire, that is, under the long dominion of the Ottoman Empire, has been generally overlooked, as if the "contamination" endured, places Greece outside "our" world.[8] The "barbarians" controlled Greece, but they were not able to eradicate its fundamentally secular and humanistic values.

So, what happens to a nation when all these "sins" encircle it? It reacts and decides to dress up its eastern elements with western clothes. From now on, it does not drink "Turkish" but "Greek" coffee. It looks for the roots of *tsifteteli* (belly dance), a mainly solo female (often characterized as "erotic") dance that relies on the movement of the upper body, at ancient Greek fertility dances.[9] In other words, as a modern nation-state, it encourages an identity with the West, which represses connections to all things non-Greek, especially Turkish, and female.[10]

After the Turkish occupation, studies of all kinds go back to ancient Greece. In their turn, Greek folk song collections – that start in the past and continue in our day – aim at preserving and disseminating a music culture that is Greek. To that end, the Society for the Dissemination of National Music actively records music from throughout Greece, while the Greek Folklore Research Center of the Academy of Athens publishes collections of song texts and music transcriptions.

Thus, it is clear why the identity question was and still is of such paramount importance for the Greeks. The Greek painter Yannis Tsarouchis[11] recalls an inscription on the wall of Kazantzakis' house on the island of Aegina: "one extreme."[12] Kazantzakis replies: "I am an Arab, not a Greek." In his entertaining dictionary, Nikos Dimou defines a Greek by using thirty-one substantives: twenty-five Turkish, three Albanian, two Italian, and one Slavic.[13]

Greek Folk Elements

Being Greek Orthodox is the secular lifestyle for most Greeks. Religiously based events, such as weddings, baptisms, and saints' days define many annual festivities lasting for days, even months, where folklore is being performed at its best. Many pagan elements become prevalent at those occasions, a peculiar and unique characteristic which can certainly be traced to the Greek past. Many rituals take place during Carnival, Easter and Christmas time as well as during specific holidays. In Greece, naming procedures are also religiously defined as Greeks get their first names by actually being baptized.

Superstitions are prevalent, though not dominant, within the Greek culture. Particularly important is the evil eye. Both prayers and spells may keep it away. People carry or decorate their belongings with folk objects, usually in the shape of a blue eye, a pomegranate, or garlic, which they believe will protect them. To exorcize the evil, they spit three times.

Many herbs used as folk remedies grow on the Greek slopes and plains. Local drinks, usually white alcoholic distilled spirits such as the Cretan *raki* or the Macedonian *tsipouro*, are the best cure for sore throats, stomach trouble, and toothaches. In local markets one finds a variety of medicinal herbs, each one prescribed for different medical conditions. Bookstores sell books which explain their therapeutic properties.

Greek language belongs to a subfamily of the Indo-European linguistic family. Regional dialects such as the Cretan, the Pontic Greek, and the Cypriot exist as well as many varieties of folk speech. Predominant in the language are hand gestures and facial expressions. After all, Greek is a high-touch culture. Well-known is the expression "It's all Greek to me," which suggests the difficulty particularly of the ancient form of the Greek language.

Ancient Greek mythology elicits universal admiration. Greek myths constitute core narratives of a larger ideological system set outside historical time. The Aesopian fables educate youth and are expected to mold their ethos and character. Myths about Greek gods and demigods are popular themes for even contemporary television shows and films worldwide. At the same time, legends also prevail, as Greeks like to narrate them artfully in regular conversations to reflect many of the hopes, fears, and anxieties of our time. Older legends refer to episodes considered miraculous and bizarre, such as enclosing in the foundation of a bridge the masterbuilder's wife in order to prevent the structure from crumbling.[14] Common legends also refer to miraculous situations involving saints, such as specific Byzantine icons weeping.

Greek children grow up with not only myths and legends, but also folktales. Telling them is traditionally the grandmother's task, the grandfather usually being the one to tell stories from the wars or the older times. Tales are related and received as fiction or fantasy. As is true of other cultures, famous tales from the international repertoire have been adopted by the Greeks and thus have obtained "Greek" motifs and patterned figures of speech.

"What walks on four legs in the morning, two legs at noon, and three legs in the evening?" The riddle posed to Oedipus by the Sphinx is perhaps the first wisdom question Greeks have an account of. In Greece, riddles are used to educate the youth, who particularly enjoy testing each other's abilities in answering them. Certainly, many riddles are blended into folk narratives as well.

In addition, proverbial speech is very common in Greece. On specific occasions such as in the village of Olympus on the island of Karpathos, everyday communication may be based on the exchange of such expressions. Oftentimes locals organize contests, known as "jousts," which test the inhabitants' abilities to stretch their improvisatory skills by composing and performing proverbial phrases.

Jokes take the form of fictional narratives and end in unpredictable and surprising outcomes for humorous effects. Greeks enjoy ethnic jokes, which may refer to their neighboring countries, such as Italy and Turkey, or to local communities such as jokes about the Cretans and the Pontic Greeks. Such jokes are based on stereotypes whereas joke telling is an entertaining activity. Popular too are jokes that play with the etymology of specific Greek words.

In 776 B.C., Hercules, the older Kouritis, moved to Olympia, where he began the first Olympic Games. According to others, the originator was Pelops, from whom Peloponnese takes its name. However, the modern Olympic Games date from 1896. The Olympic folk culture consists of various folk items such as logos, advertisements and songs, which are especially designed to please the participants and spectators. More importantly, they wish to emphasize the inherent Greekness of the sporting ideal. Delegates to the contemporary Games are two children, Phoebus and Athena, the god of music and light and the goddess of wisdom and protector of the city of Athens. An ancient Greek doll inspired the creation of the 2004 mascots, since dolls have been perhaps the most desirable toys since antiquity. In them we see two children who, through the joy of playing, reveal that the real value of participating in the Games is the sole enjoyment of competition, without necessarily winning. Two siblings, a boy and a girl, are the ambassadors of collaboration, equality and brotherhood.

Children in rural Greece still play on the streets, devising games based on the materials they have at their disposal such as tree branches, balls and rope. They enjoy playing pranks and impersonating legendary heroes. Oftentimes, they perform songs most of which are associated with a specific game such as finding a hidden ring or kerchief. Teasing is always at the center of their activities, which also include competitions and acting.

They favor *Karagiozis*, a form of a shadow theater usually performed in open-air theaters on large white screens erected at the far side of the place, overhung by the dark blue sky and the shadows of trees. Often a small orchestra of musicians sits in front of the screen. Among them is the singer who is going to perform folk poetry and songs. In some cases, though, the singer and the puppet player are the same person. The puppets used in *Karagiozis* are usually made from animal skin and represent figures of history and romance, of nature and fantasy. They are designed, constructed and mechanically operated by human beings. Like the stage upon which they perform, they are usually limited in size but not in imaginative quality. They can be anything their creator desires: people, animals, pieces of furniture, rocks or legendary monsters. Thus, objects become animated on the stage as well. Puppets tend to be far more plausible than human actors, costumed and made up to represent them. Today, the repertory of *Karagiozis* is being renewed always aiming in bringing children into contact with tradition. As folk comedy, *Karagiozis* portrays the essence of life. The performers express themselves with originality. They create their own stories and characters upon folk roots. They mingle elements of tradition with those of their era.

Greek folk architectural style depends on landscape, so there are island and mainland, sea and mountain house styles. White and blue are the prominent colors of island houses, while contours of ocher, claret, and brown dominate the mainland. Roofs may be tile-red, traditionally with a chimney. Island houses are whitewashed, while those in the mountains are paved with stones. Cobblestone roads are a marvel in both the Aegean and mainland Greece. Iron doors in bright colors, such as the ones at the village of Koskinou on the island of Rhodes, are remarkable. So are also Greek pottery and woodcraft products. Churches exist everywhere in Greece. On the mainland, the Byzantine architectural style – that is, basilica with cupola – is prominent. Inside those churches we find many decorations and Byzantine iconography. On the islands, churches are plain, white buildings with a blue sea in the background and with a few icons and a candelabrum. Mainly in Thrace, Crete and the islands across the western coast of Turkey, many examples of Islamic architecture exist. On the Ionian islands, Crete and Rhodes, on the contrary, many are the Venetian-style buildings. The maritime provinces have ports of scenic character, functioning as poles for socializing and strolls.

In Greece, one comes across villagers relaxing in chairs in front of picturesque coffee houses, whiling away their time, enjoying their coffee at their own pace. Between fingers calloused from years of farm work, they click their ever-faithful companions, their worry beads *(komboloi)*.

Festive Greece

Mythology places the birth of music and dance in Greece. Music making where singing, instrument playing and dancing are central activities is very much alive. Elaborate collective rituals and celebrations punctuate the yearly calendar. Greek community feasts belong to a category of events *(glendia)* which include dancing, drinking, singing, eating, talking, and, more generally, people in high spirits *(kefi)* who are willing to share such moments with others in their community. In those events, music, dance, and song constitute a triad. Thus, the researcher of Greek folk music should not only observe the music per se, but also the lyrics and the dances that accompany them as, in the Greek folk tradition, sound is not separated from song and movement.

Since the 1930s, many Greek and foreign researchers have investigated Greek songs. Some recorded and transcribed folksongs.

Many recordings have also been and are still being produced for public use. Among the first to distinguish folk songs into cycles for the purpose of easier study and presentation was Nikolaos Politis. In a 1914 book, he categorizes them as follows: historical, *kleftika* (of the klephts, or brigands), *akritika* (of the borders), *paraloges* (long narratives), love songs, bridal songs, lullabies, carols, of the exile, *moirologia* (mourning songs), songs of the nether world and the angel of death, gnomic, work songs, *vlachika* (country songs) and *perigelastika* (mocking) songs.

As for Greek folk music, one could certainly distinguish between the music of the mainland and the music of the islands. Within those two very broad zones, however, many more distinctions exist. So, for instance, one talks of the music of the island of Crete and within it differentiates between a western and an eastern musical style. In all cases, however, the functions of folk music are similar: to be performed during traditional, ritual contexts and for communal purposes.

Throughout Greece, playing instruments is an almost exclusively male activity (as mourning is strictly female). In different parts of Greece we find different instruments. The basic instrumental music family consists of two components, the melodic and the rhythmic. Traditionally, the most popular Greek wind instruments are the *klarino* (type of clarinet), the *gaida* (type of bagpipe) and the *zournas* (type of oboe). String instruments are the *laouto* (type of lute), the *violi* (violin), the *lyra* (different from the lyre, three-stringed), the *kanonaki* and the *santouri* (plucked and struck zithers, respectively). Usually the *defi* (tambourine) and the *daouli* (type of drum) are used as percussion. Depending on the part of Greece, different combinations of the above create various folk music idioms.

The third member of the triad, dancing, is an integral part of Greek life. An event may not be considered proper if dance is not a basic component. During those events, dancing improvisation may follow the music whereas song lyrics might provoke a dancer's emotions. Spectacular dancing figures carry meaning related to something communal or personal. Everyone who dances holds a specific role as part of the group she or he belongs to. She or he speaks through dancing and without words.

Cretan dancing: Breaking the circle so as to improvise. Photo by Yiannis Bromirakis.

Greek dances are mostly taught informally, through observation and participation. Usually, before each dance takes place during a feast, the person who expects to lead it throws a bill or two in front of the musicians. One of the musicians, basically the leader of the group, picks up this money. This practice is not considered payment. It is called "gifting money" for "ordering a dance." Most of the time, only men are culturally allowed to do that. And every man has to do that in order to represent his name, family, and clan.

Through such music and dance events, both public and social in nature, the people of Greece articulate their community beliefs and represent their identity. Because music and dance are languages, forms of communication through which Greek people express ideas about their culture and society, their analysis provides another mode through which to understand social processes.

We listen to Greek music and we see Greek dances. At the same time, we taste drinks and foods from the traditional Mediterranean cuisine that allows one to enjoy lengthy lifespans. Musicians in Crete perform live music in combination with freshly made local variations of traditional, symbolic foods which accompany various events that take place outdoors during the summer and indoors during the winter.

Festivals and celebrations may be wine feasts as well. At the sounds of traditional music, Greeks open their wine barrels to honor saints (such as St. George the Inebriant) or merely to socialize and have fun. Women offer Greek cuisine, and specialists talk about wine and its history. The many wine presses found by archeologists point to the presence of wine throughout the Greek civilization.

Famous all over Greece are weddings, arenas within which aspects of social identity are represented and reflected. They are "big" and "fat." The preparations for those events start months before the specific day of the actual religious wedding ceremony. An important custom at traditional weddings is the dowry exchange and the decoration with money of the couple's soon-to-be marriage bed. Mothers mourn in anticipation of separation from their daughters and/or perform wedding songs.

Greek costumes, mostly worn today by men and women on special occasions, are very elaborate. They vary from place to place, even within a specific region. Their basic colors are black, red and white. A visit to the museum of the history of the Greek costume (Lyceum Club of Greek Women) is worthwhile. Kerchiefs and scarves as well as jewelry, usually gold coins, spread all over the female chest are important paraphernalia.

Natural threads, used in the making and elaborating of regional costumes and household textiles (such as carpets, blankets and curtains), are produced in Greece. Young girls learn orally, oftentimes through their grandmothers, how to embroider, crochet and knit. Laces decorate many households. Knowing how to make them is considered a special artistry. Looms may be used in specific regions, such as several Cretan mountain villages.

Greek Folklore in the 21st Century

Today, Greek folklore is circulated, for instance, through folksong books with accompanying CDs. It is also officially taught by folk dance troupes and other cultural associations. In addition, Greek folklore keeps being produced for outside consumption. Representations of folk events take place specifically for tourists. Greek immigrants perform their own interpretations of folklore whereas multimedia folk productions are also becoming more and more frequent.

Yet, the identity question is still prominent for Greeks. The dream of a unified Europe, which started officially in 1980, finds Greeks once more puzzled and confused. The present era of globalization very intensively asks Greece for a brave look into the mirror where they are supposed to see not only the heroes of the past but current realities as well.[15]

An Ethnographic Approach to Folk Music[16]

Music as/in culture

Both Alan Merriam in 1964 through "his" *Anthropology of Music* and John Blacking in 1971 through his essay "How musical is man?" coined the study of music as human behavior, a phenomenon, namely, not isolated but rather shaped and created through/by a society. Since then, when studying music, we look for various contexts and functions, realizing that, musical meaning – like language – differs from place to place. Namely, as an art, music is universal but its meaning is not whereas different cultures adhere to it different values. At the same time, people are music activists who define the uniqueness of each performance as an audience constituting music a dynamic, non-static art, which flows and adapts to time by occasionally transcending boundaries as well.[17]

This is how ethnomusicology and its scholars, namely the ethnomusicologists, came to be the ones who study the music of an *ethnos*, namely a nation. In order to successfully do so, they build on an interdisciplinary study that consists of, amongst others, the fields of anthropology, musicology, folklore, ethnology and sociology. On top of that, ethnomusicologists have to be curious researchers, who develop case studies, while trying to identify symbols, images, representations and meanings that will assist them in both understanding diversity and communicating it. Some of their findings may show how all cultures or ways of living around the world may be valid, how each culture is a complex system of behaviors, an expressive and interpretive system, how through culture humans express their experience(s) of the world, as well as how all these, after all, enrich the understanding of ourselves.

Due to recent development in terms of traveling, ethnomusicologists do not rely on an armchair, veranda type of research, but rather actually go to the place they are interested in studying further so as to both learn its music from the inside out and to "honest I-witness" it. For example, folklorist Henry Glassie embraces ethnographic study as bearing (i.e. writing, bringing forth without hiding, direct) honorable (i.e. no lies, truthful, factual) witness (i.e. "I myself have seen") to something human (i.e. for people: a gift from one person to the other). As a result, he looks at ethnography[18] as a wonderful challenge to make a truthful art.[19]

Upon selecting a problem and formulating a design, ethnographers collect and analyze data (via appropriate data-gathering techniques)[20] which they will in turn interpret, understand, organize and present. Through participation-observation, they attempt to immerse in the culture and life under study, though their presence might affect what is being looked for. However, as long as they are genuine and proceed with slow, careful steps, it is highly expected that credibility will be established and that their results will be sufficient.

Moreover, the ethnomusicologists must cope with the feelings of being both an outsider and an insider of the culture they are studying, and should be able to understand how to operate within a local political structure. In addition, they have to be willing to reevaluate their findings in the light of new evidence, namely be flexible and welcome the unexpected. As a result, ethnomusicologists are not the same after completing a fieldwork project as the process through which they learn about others reflects on their own "who is who" as well.

Though dealing with music as an academic, scholarly activity sounds fun, the work of the researcher is quite responsible: to the people studied, the public, the discipline, the students, the sponsors, one's own and the host governments. Giving back and being genuine – even if one does not agree – are important virtues of one's work. After all, the dilemmas of what is ethical to be shared are several, as it is hard to know whether one's ethnography is beneficial for all along with how much one is involved in the lives studied.

Archiving & Documenting Folk Music

A common problem for music researchers is that collections of music are difficult to classify and visualize, music archives being a distinct type of ethnographic representation shaped by an intersection of practice and theory. A theoretical basis so that we can better understand our archives and build better collections is necessary along with understanding what the act of preserving those sorts of materials means.[21]

Physical collections that had (and continue to have) long-ranging, historical scope for the study of Greek folk music are "The American Folklife Center" (AFC) at the Library of Congress, particularly their "Traditional Music and Spoken Word Catalog" (materials dating to the 1890s), the "Archives of Traditional Music" (ATM) at Indiana University, particularly their EVIA Digital Archive Project – Ethnographic Video for Instruction and Analysis, (materials dating to the early 1890s), the "Musical Routes: Digital Ethno-musicological Collections of Crete" (IMS-FORTH), the "Musical Folklore Archives 'Melpo Merlie'," the "Music Library of Greece," the "Hellenic Institute of Byzantine and Post-Byzantine Studies" in Venice and the "Lautarchiv: Humboldt-Universität zu Berlin."

Regarding the last collection, it is worthy to note that it includes the oldest recordings of Cretan music. More specifically, during the First World War, the 4th order of the Greek Army under Colonel Hatzopoulos was besieged by Bulgarians and Germans and therefore captured in the town of Kavala. 6,500 men with their officers were transferred to Görlitz in Germany. At that same time, the Royal Prussian Phonographic Commission decided to visit the military camps so as to record the languages and the music pieces of the foreign captives, under the ultimate goal to create a "Museum of Sound." The leader of that recording group that arrived at Görlitz was the famous Byzantinist August Heisenberg, student of Karl Krumbacher at the University of Munich, who, between July and August of 1917, created a total of 70, 78 rpm recordings, which are today part of the Sound Archive of the Humboldt University, Berlin. 7 of those discs include recordings by Greek captives (4 of them coming from the island of Crete).[22]

Documentation is the key to the usefulness of any field collections. Researchers should develop a form that would include the information they judge appropriate and adequate for classifying their materials. Several recordings usually have problems as there are issues with interruptions, broken sequences, worn out materials which need special boosting or specific software enhancement for advanced noise reduction. An important thing to consider is whether one is willing to notate one's documents and, if so, in what type of notation.

An analysis of folk music may follow, consisting of the documentation's preliminary details but also the musical and pedagogical treatment of the materials that would prepare them so as to be presented and practiced. Let us not forget that the "traditional triptych" in music education consists of listening, performing and composing. That last part can be interdisciplinary, comparative and worked out in collaboration with staff members of museums, libraries and other sorts of educational institutions.

Computational Music Analysis of Folk Music: A Cretan Case Study[23]

A long tradition of computational studies of folk tunes exists. Many of those studies involve the clustering or grouping of pieces by similarity and are driven by the need to represent and predict geographic localization and diachronic evolution of folk tune styles in an attempt to come up with distinctive patterns in folk music.

A set of transcribed Cretan folk songs has been encoded and, as a result, several melodic patterns emerged. This provided researchers with the ability to describe subgroups of folk songs. The corpus of the study consisted of various Cretan music scores from archives, scientific publications and field transcriptions as MIDI files.[24] The method of the analysis used was a computational approach called "pattern discovery" that assisted in locating significant repeated patterns in each type of songs.[25]

What is important to keep in mind, is the musicological evaluation of the statistical results that follows such efforts, and which, in the aforementioned case, underlined the limitations of such an analysis. For example, music transcriptions deviate from live performances. Furthermore, there are microtunings and rhythmic novelties that are difficult to transcribe into notation while the exportation into MIDI files entails a loss of information. In addition, there may be ornamentation and/or fluidity of melodies across styles, especially when different lyrics are sung to the same melody, whereas melodies go beyond the boundaries of their origin and can also be found in other areas with possible variations.

Improvisation should be taken into consideration, as each artist has a unique style of playing, adding small characteristic turns and motives, along with discrepancies in the opinions between the informants and the researchers. Information about the performer might be taken into account but would require more data collection whereas one should not forget the triad observed in Greek folk music, namely that of music-dance-poetry, which demands that scholars treat music compositions as events that include a wealth of ethnographic and anthropological elements and not isolated performances.

Ethnographic Conclusion

All in all, the researcher of Greek folk music should keep in mind its oral nature versus its written, notated presentation. In addition, oftentimes, within Greek culture, the boundaries between speech and song are sensitive such as, for example, in the cases of proverbial speech, animal or church bells sounds that could be easily studied as music.

It will always be hard to decide what is worthy to keep and what to throw away and/or, due to the multidimensional nature of our work, whether our collections will merely consist of purely music or other sort of archival materials as well. For sure, larger repertories are necessary for more objective analyses along with better music scores that embody the nuances of Greek folk music. As a result, our work should rely mostly on audio and at least initially focus on case studies of musicians and certain regions so as to later allow comparative approaches particularly with neighboring countries.

Ultimately, ethnographic approaches to folk culture are lifelines to reality, links to the real world from which we witness and gain information: they allow us to improve our lives and teach us how to be better in the world. They are capable of traveling us there from here. They simply tell us stories of and about real people, like you and me. As life-processes, there is not *one* way to do them, or *a single* rule to follow.

Chapter 2

Music Mythologies and Identities

At the Crossroads of East and West

Cultural Crossroads

The Greek island of Crete is a peculiar place. At the southernmost edge of Greece and as a crossroads for three continents, it preserves several traditions. It has also accepted multiple influences from both East and West. During the Hellenistic era and until the Roman conquest, Crete abandoned its introversion and became energetically involved in the historical fermentations particularly of the eastern Mediterranean area. There, fermentation produced a complex sociopolitical, historical and cultural backdrop, against which scholars find the Mediterranean music areas ideal for study.[26] In this regard, they view Greece as a particularly challenging region of the Mediterranean.

Anthropological interest in southern Europe has often been submerged in a more generalized Mediterranean culture area. However, in the United States, the rise of interest in Europe as a political entity as well as the founding of the Society for the Anthropology of Europe appear to have re-centered the area focus to a significant degree. Recent studies, therefore, of moral and symbolic systems have taken for granted the concept of a "Mediterranean culture area."[27]

More specifically, Greece is a country that offers to scholars, such as Michael Herzfeld, many opportunities for the shaping of a culturally anthropological thought.[28] According to Herzfeld, Europe has been traditionally excluded from ethnography. The ethnography of Greece, however, provides a rich source of material for investigation:[29]

> Ethnographic work in Greece provides special challenges of its own. This country, though politically young in European terms, lays claim to a history said to be the very source of Europe itself, and the Greeks of today have derived both pride and discomfort from the intense preoccupation of their leaders with the status of this ancient heritage.[30]

Crete in Time

Greece is known as the birthplace of music. Evidence shows that music had a significant place in the everyday life since the Minoan era. For example, "The Harvester Vase," a *rhyton* (drinking horn or libation vessel pierced at the bottom) of black steatite from Agia Triada depicts a procession of 26 men led by a man in a mantle or robe. Most of them are harvesters, as it appears from their dress and the tools they carry on their shoulders. In the middle, a *sistrum* (musical rattle) player holds up his instrument and three singers sing from wide-opened mouths. The foremost group of harvesters walks in step; the group behind the musicians is much less organized. The musicians themselves are shown as a different physical type from that of the harvesters. The different positions of the singers' heads may be the artist's way of suggesting the different timbres of their voices. The positions of the legs imply that the rhythm is march-like.

During the Neolithic and Minoan Cretan era (6100 B.C. to 1000 B.C.), Crete flourished on overseas trade. Relationships between the island and nearby countries, such as Syria, Cyprus, and Palestine, were welcomed and encouraged. Pirates and sailors went out from and to the island, which is referred to by Egyptian sources from 3000 B.C. as Keftiu.[31]

From the first century B.C. until the fifth century A.D., Crete was part of the Roman Empire and then became part of the Roman (Byzantine) Empire. During the third decade of the ninth century (826-828), Arabs originally from Andalusia, Spain, conquered the island.[32] A monk advised the Arabs to move their stronghold and described a place in Crete where, after they had fortified it with a defensive ditch *(handaki,* in Arabic, *al-khandaq),* they built their capital, Handax.[33]

On 7 March 961, Handax fell, and Crete reverted to the Byzantine Empire for another 250 years. Many Russians, Slavs and Armenians established themselves on the island. This is evidenced by various surviving place-names, such as Rousochoria, Sklavopoula and Armenoi.[34] In August 1204, the Venetians and Boniface I, Marquis of Montferrat, signed an agreement, known as the Refutation of Crete, whereby Boniface ceded Crete to the Venetians. In October 1204, when the Partitio Romaniae was signed, the Venetians officially "owned" Crete.[35] Finally, in 1206, Enrico Pescatore, the so-called count of Malta, disembarked with a small force on Crete and took control of large parts of the island but was pushed out a few years later by the Venetians. Thus, a period of Venetian rule in Crete began that lasted approximately 450 years.[36]

During this period, many Italian and Jewish merchants inhabited Cretan cities, whereas the population in the villages was almost purely Greek.[37] In 1862, Crete was multi-cultural, a place where the Greek element tried to coexist with Turks, Jews, Arabs and Africans. Crete was also multiracial, a crossroads of peoples that left their mark on the long history of the island. The architecture of the buildings on the island reveals this melting pot as well.[38] Handax is mentioned in Venetian manuscripts either as the *anima* (soul) of Venice or *alia civitas Venetiarum apud Levantem* ("the other Venice of the East"):[39] Venetians "converted" to "Cretanness." On 16 September 1669, Crete fell to the Turks. Under Turkish occupation,[40] more than 60,000 Cretans were forced to convert to Islam.[41] Thus, a population was created that was Cretan in origin, language and customs, but Muslim by faith. Those were the famous *Tourkokrites* or *Tourkokritikoi* (Cretan-Turks), who proved to be many times more fierce and harsh than the original Muslim conquerors. Some of them, the so-called *Cryptochristianoi* (Crypto-Christians), accepted Islam but secretly kept their Christian faith.[42]

Having inherited a rich spiritual and artistic treasure, Cretans assimilated foreign influences and succeeded in composing and combining innovative techniques from Europe with Byzantine forms. In the process, they became the bearers of another Cretan civilization,[43] one that featured major figures who became influential in this period of Cretan history: in literature, Hortatsis and Kornaros; in painting, Michail Damaskenos, Theophanes the Cretan and Domenikos Theotokopoulos, known as El Greco (the Greek); and, in music, Francisco Leontaritis.[44]

During the Venetian domination (1204-1669) and particularly during its last two centuries, a special and unique music style was created, which combined the melodic, eastern music with the polyphonic one of the West. This style was the product of the co-existence of the aforementioned peoples, despite the dogmatic differences between the orthodox and the catholic elements on the island. That style was also cultivated on places where Cretan inhabitants had migrated to due to the Ottoman occupation, such as the Ionian islands (Zakynthos in particular). That is why, after the 17th century, a polyphonic chanting style was established there, usually referred to as "Cretan."

During the period when the Ottomans were in Crete, important Cretan musicians left for Mount Sinai and Constantinople, both significant centers of the Greek Orthodox world. One of the most important teachers and music theorists of the Byzantine School of Music was Yeoryios o Kris, who blossomed between 1790 and 1814, and who taught music at Constantinople, a region of Ephesus called Kydonies as well as on the island of Chios.

That tradition continued to later generations. For instance, of Cretan descent Nikolaos Daskalakis (1897-1988) born in Halki, master chanter at the Chania Metropolitan Church dedicated to the Presentation of the Virgin Mary, was distinguished as a par excellence graduate of the Patriarchate School of the Constantinople Music Union. He was teaching gratis, with a goal to preserve "our" traditional music. In 1976, he was honored by the Patriarchate with the "Office of the Master Chanter of his Holiness Archbishop of Constantinople." He has both set to music several Byzantine hymns and composed others, such as those performed during the funerals of politicians Eleftherios Venizelos (on March 27 1936) and later during that of his son's Sophocles (on February 9 1964).[45]

The brief Egyptian rule in Crete (1830-40) was impartial from the beginning and treated both Muslims and Christians with equality.[46] In 1840, the island reverted to the Ottoman Empire. After a period of bloody and heroic revolutions, the Turks gave up the island in 1898. Crete then became an independent state under a high commissioner, Prince George, the younger brother of the new king of Greece. Nobody was satisfied with this compromise. In 1905, Eleftherios Venizelos, the Cretan prime minister, forced Prince George to retire. Venizelos became national leader and spoke for the need of concord and harmony between Christians and Muslims, and of peace and unity as the ultimate goal. Finally, on 30 May 1913, Crete became part of Greece.

In 1923, the island took part in the exchange of populations, whereby its Turkish inhabitants left and Greek refugees from Asia Minor came in. In 1941, Crete stood once more in the limelight of world history. In May, German parachutists landed in Maleme, Chania, and in other places. After ten days of desperate and bloody fighting by British and Greek troops, the Germans took control of and occupied the island until 1944.

Syncretistic Thesis

> There has been much speculation about the connection and relationship between today's various Greek music idioms and those of much older times, such as Byzantine or even ancient Greek. As it has been wisely observed, it would seem to me to be very unlikely that everything from ancient music has been lost. It would seem to me to be equally unlikely, however, that ancient music has come down to us intact unaltered; the truth would be somewhere in between. Some things have been lost, some things have been preserved at least in spirit if not in form, and many new elements are continually being introduced to a music tradition that is anything but a fossilized relic from older times.[47]

Cretan music accepts elements coming mainly from traditions of the eastern Mediterranean, the Balkans, and North Africa. Due to their long presence on the island, the Ottomans also left elements and sounds of their music culture. Syncretism is the attempt to reconcile disparate, even opposing, beliefs and to meld practices of various schools of thought. It is especially associated with the effort to merge and draw parallels among several originally discrete traditions, especially in philosophy and religion, thereby asserting an underlying unity. The term owes its meaning to ancient Cretans, who, in spite of their differences among themselves, united in the face of external dangers: the word per se is a compound of *syn* (together) and "Crete."[48]

Cretans believe that, in the production of music, there is one who gives (the musician) and others who accept (the audience). Everyone deposits his energy in this action and the focus is the music, not the musician. The musician, who is able to grasp all this energy and transform it into music, is gifted by nature and works in service of all the people. She/he is a professional who knows well how to do his job.[49]

Art can be viewed in different ways. Pottery, for example, can be viewed as something that comes from the land in which the potters live.[50] In the same spirit, music and dance events can be viewed as artistic expressions of the people who participate in them. While music and dance occur all over the world, the many variations provide a way of understanding a specific community, society or culture, by looking at the ways in which its people express themselves through performance.

As in other fields, focusing on case studies of musicians points out the role played by individual men and women in the process of transmission and transformation of oral repertories and music style.[51] This way, we become aware that what we study as a "genre" or "repertory" is the cumulative outcome of musicians' interacting accomplishments, framed in personal life histories, in specific social and historical backgrounds.

Musicians are extremely important in determining the character and dimension of all music production.[52] They are, in a sense, historians, since they all live in a specific time, experiencing and sharing major music practices. The diversity among musicians, but, at the same time, their common engagement with a certain type of music, helps one see how identities are constructed on local bases.

Cretan Literature

Now, let us attempt to understand how we defend and adopt the identity with which the place or region we live in nurtures us, in this case, the Cretan one. In one way, identity is shaped by sociocultural ideas. After all, "culture is the way the mind is molded through interaction with the world."[53]

Georgios Hortatsis composed the theatrical play *Erofili* around 1595: Panaretos grows up at a friend's palace after his father is killed in a war with Erofili, the princess of Egypt. They fall in love and secretly get married. The king decides to invite young men to court his daughter; she refuses. Her secret relationship is revealed. Very upset, the king kills Panaretos and, as a dowry, offers to his daughter Panaretos' hands, heart and head. Erofili, disgusted by the spectacle, grasps a knife and commits a suicide.[54]

Having a strong Cretan personality himself, through this play, he wished to remind the Greeks who they all were. With the very first words he wrote, he made *Erofili* resemble the prevalent, prominent Cretan school of painting of sacred icons (*agiografia*). Simultaneously, he praised Crete through a hymn, with references to both the glorious Minoan past and the ancient Greek past. For example, he suggested that the chorus asks Zeus for help, which is reminiscent of ancient Greek drama, especially Greek tragedies. Hortatsis partially shaped what he thought the Cretan identity was or should be. Giving his work the name Erofili and letting "her," the heroine's voice sound strongly throughout his drama, he empowered the female presence. He used to believe that "fame is vain, and the good fortune doesn't last for long, because of fate's games. Freedom is our greatest virtue, and tyranny our worst enemy. More than anything, we should feel and be free to love what we want."[55]

Interestingly, however, looking into diaries and other accounts from Hortatsis' life, we can see that the main source of inspiration for *Erofili* is the Italian tragedy *Orbecche*, written in 1543 by Giambattista Giraldi, whereas Hortatsis himself seemed to be of Anatolian descent.[56] More specifically, he came from Asia Minor. Possibly his last name denotes a Byzantine-Anatolian descent of a family that, according to local tradition, came to Crete when the well-known settlement of wealthy men and old soldiers of the Byzantine army took place in 961. The Cortazi (from the Latin *saturo*; to fill, satiate, satisfy, saturate) were among the first "Roman," Constantinopolitan families that settled in Crete on land given by Emperor Nikiforos Fokas.[57] Thus, Hortatsis' identity and, by extension, Erofili's identity, were shaped not only by the Cretan but also by various other idioms.

Let us bear in mind that Hortatsis lived during the great literary and language revival of Crete. As a result, his live contact with the Cretan audience helped toward a conscious "turn" of the Cretan idiom and dialect. Hortatsis managed to form a lingual instrument of the Cretan literature by rejecting the use of the mixed language form, which belonged to the middle- and late-Byzantine tradition of the early Cretan production.[58] Thus, the language he used was the everyday Cretan dialect, which he himself spoke, a mixture of eastern and western elements traced on the island of Crete.

Erofili influenced the birth of Erotokritos, the main hero in the homonymous book, an archetypical long epic romance composed by Vitsentzos Kornaros in the early 17th century Crete, consisting of approximately 10,000 fifteen-syllable rhymed verses in the local dialect:[59] Erotokritos, a charming *laouto* player, is in love with Aretousa, daughter of Hercules, king of Athens. Because of his descent, son of the king's advisor, their love has to be kept secret. In a race arranged by the king, Erotokritos wins. His father asks the king to grant Erotokritos Aretousa's hand in marriage. The king refuses; he banishes Erotokritos and invites young royal suitors to the palace as possible husbands for Aretousa. She refuses, and her father imprisons her. The king gets involved in a war. His life is threatened. Erotokritos disguises himself as an African, wins the battle, and saves the king's life. When the king asks what he wants in exchange, Erotokritos requests that he gets married to Aretousa. The king worries that Aretousa will once more disappoint him. Indeed, when Erotokritos, in disguise, asks Aretousa, herself, to marry him, she strongly refuses: Though having suffered greatly in prison, she remains faithful to him. Eventually, she finds out the truth, and the play ends with their wedding.

Kornaros composed a poetic mythical world, shaped by the elements that were purposefully and consciously chosen from different historical eras: classical Athens, Byzantium, and the medieval chivalric life of the Frankish Peloponnese and the Greek islands. Scholars note the Homeric character of Erotokritos. Through him, time becomes diachronic and confirms an identity which traces its sources in a glorious past, but also in the present, to give life to a bright future.

Erotokritos defends his renaissance qualities and spreads a message for freedom as a means for reaching personal happiness. This is mainly the demand of the young woman he is in love with, Aretousa, who gives the final solution through bright images, psychological and real collisions. In their love relationship we see, in all its greatness, the triple ideal and eternal passion of bravery, beauty, and wisdom. All these ideals expressed by Erotokritos stem from the nature of Greek identity. For example, when Erotokritos fights, the Cretan nation (under the empire) sees in him the symbol of its own battles for freedom from Turkish rule.

Kornaros – born in Sitia, Crete, in the beginning of the seventeenth century – came from a Venetian-Cretan royal family. There is no doubt that the official language of the "Nobili Veneti" was Greek and, more specifically, the Cretan dialect. By choosing to speak that language and teach it to Erotokritos, Kornaros emphasized his Cretan identity. Thus, though he was born in Venice in 1793, Erotokritos spoke a language which was a mix of eastern and western Cretan dialects. In addition, Erotokritos was inspired by the French novel *Paris et Vienne* (Pierre de la Cypede, 1432). Thus, the hero of the novel is a mixture of Italian, French, and Greek elements and qualities.

Both names, Erofili and Aretousa, have been given to young girls or places all over Greece. People memorize passages from the two works and recite them to the accompaniment of a plain, repetitive melody, not only in Crete, but also in other areas – for instance, in Cyprus. Even the Cretan-Turks read or listen to Erotokritos and his *laouto* music. Ross Daly and Chris Williams were amazed when, on the western coast of Turkey, they met Cretan-Turks who had moved from Crete in the 1920s, after the exchange of populations, who still remembered parts of the Erotokritos and wept while singing them. All in all, this epic has influenced several Greek poets, such as Solomos (1798-1858), Sikelianos (1884-1951) and Seferis (1900-1971).

Nikos Kazantzakis has also attempted to address the issue of identity through his writings. Cretan in origin, the author of *Zorba*[60] chose his eternal *Ellinas* (Hellene) to represent the Greek race itself, thus, a marvelous synthesis of both East and West. In his books, Kazantzakis evokes Homeric themes. He creates his own epic poem *Odyssey*, a vision of homeland.[61] Through this work, he reunites the individual Greek Odysseus to the eternal elements of his country: sun, sea, traveling.

Mikis Theodorakis composed the soundtrack of the film that made *Zorba* famous worldwide. Until then, Theodorakis was known as a "political" composer who explored the question of what it means to be Greek. Of Cretan descent, he worked like a historian to create ideological images through his music.[62] Though Zorba carried his *santouri* wherever he went, he, at the end, became known as a dancer to *bouzouki* (plucked instrument of the lute family) music. Zorba's national identity is ambiguous. He wanders in many of the regions north of the contemporary Greek borders, around the Balkan countries, as well as near the Asia Minor coasts. He also often travels to and lives in Crete for a specific period of time. So, although he definitely feels Greek, he cannot identify himself with all the characteristics that Greece shares with the so-called West as part of a European geographical and political entity.

For example, his ability to dance with another man in a spirit of uninhibited camaraderie – throwing pain and care into a passionate dance – is something lost to the European. Through dancing, he expresses ecstasy, sure of his manhood.[63] Kazantzakis did not nurture him with the western dream of organizing and governing a renewed Byzantine Empire. Instead, he urged him to favor and listen mostly to his heart, rejecting the mind.

Zorba feels neither merely European traits inside him, nor pure, classical, ancient Greek elements, nor the anarchist chaos and the "without will" perseverance of the East. He breathes, rather, another air, a composite of all these forces and its components that empower and make him at once proud and brave, without getting lost and disassembled into an abyss. Kazantzakis calls this view Cretan,[64] a composite of Greece and the East. In this context, Kazantzakis seems constantly to be asking himself the questions: what is Greekness and what Cretanness? How should a Greek act when faced with evil? How can we be patient? How can Greece have a nationalism rooted in both its ancient heritage and its contemporary reality, yet avoid the rhetoric, callousness, and romantic megalomania of the Great Idea? What does being human mean?

Kazantzakis was born in 1883, when the Turks dominated Crete and the monuments of the Venetian presence were still prevalent. He recalled the muezzin's voice, dragging and eastern, coming out of the mosques. He saw Muslims and Christians drinking together.[65] From this world, he moved to a French school, where he met with the West. Back in Crete, he lived and fought in his own unique way. The village where his house was changed its name; instead of *Varvaroi* (barbarians), it is now called *Mirtia* (myrtle).

Blood is the basis of the Greek *ratsa* (race). The Cretan Kapetan Mihalis cuts his finger. So does the Turkish pasha. They exchange blood drops and become "brothers." From now on, their friendship is based on blood, and nothing should stand as a hindrance between them.[66] In Kazantzakis' *Buddha* (1983) and *Askitiki (The Saviors of God: Spiritual Exercises;* 1971), eastern religious and spiritual ideas prevail: there is nothing. For Kazantzakis, the forms of human dignity are two, the oriental and the occidental – as everyone and everything in his life is overwhelmed by an inexorably destructive fate. We are a modest letter, a syllable, one word from the gigantic Odyssey. All we do is fight, struggle, and get burnt. Our "new" ten commandments[67] as well as our "new" credo urge us to believe in one God, *Digenis Akritas.* And who is that Digenis Akritas? The main hero in the Greek folk song, in whom, during the Turkish occupation, the Greek nation saw its savior.[68]

In his 1991 book,[69] Herzfeld examines a particular city in Crete. Focusing on the Cretan town of Rethymno, once a center of learning under Venetian and later Turkish rule, he considers questions confronting conservators and citizens as they negotiate the "ownership" of history: Who defines the past? To whom does the past belong? What is "tradition," and how is it determined?

Exploring the meanings of the built environment for Rethymno's inhabitants, Herzfeld finds that their interest in it has more to do with personal histories and the immediate social context than with formal history, which attracts the conservators. He also investigates the inhabitants' social practices from the standpoint of household and kin group, political association, neighborhood and gender ideology, as well as the effects of all these on attitudes toward home ownership. In the face of modernity, where tradition is an object of both reverence and commercialism, Herzfeld's book emerges as an important ethnographic window onto the ambiguous cultural fortunes of Greece.

As people in Rethymno care about the fate of buildings that both house living individuals in the present and preserve the past of the Greek nation, those writings also examine Cretan music as a way for Cretan people to express themselves and preserve their nationality as well as exhibit and disseminate it. Herzfeld's individuals, in a debate about the relationship between Greek culture and the idealized entity called Europe, claim that Greece is an ancestral land. Those words also assert that Cretans maintain they are the bearers of a great ancient past and struggle through music to show their particularity as a place.

The battle described by Herzfeld is one over the possession of identity. That battle is over the future of a past. Rethymno not only belongs to its citizens; it is also part of a modern nation-state with a monumental conception of history. Those two aspects and identities come into frequent conflict.[70] Cretans fight for their identity, trying to keep a continuous thread with their past, through their present and future. As time changes, there is conflict between who they used to be and who they currently are.

Finally, Herzfeld's study is indeed one of how people negotiate their sense of place.[71] Through music, Cretans show where they come from; in other words, they make a statement of what their place is and how they view it, shaped by individual and social factors. Multiple pasts and multiple presents, choices of pasts negotiated in shifting presents, all those games of time shape for Herzfeld what a Rethi(e)-mni-otis (man from Rethymno) is,[72] and for our purposes, through the lenses of performance, what a Cretan is.

Echoing Herzfeld, this study concludes that Crete is a lived place, and that its people must deal with the realities of social existence. Buildings or music become "ours," meaning that they are Greek, they are Cretan, but also reminders of the Arabic, Venetian, or Turkish domination. Tourists may admire them, but locals praise or condemn them. They embody different pasts for different actors. Monumental history has its place in Crete, but Crete has and is a place of many histories.

Today, Cretans publish books of *mandinades* (traditional folk rhyming distiches). They choose lyrics and compile CDs to accompany them. Such an example is the book *Emine* (the Turkish name of the protagonist) by the contemporary Cretan folk lyricist Karatzis. Written in the Cretan dialect, *Emine* talks about the same virtues that Cretans do, such as honor, humanity, beauty, faith, freedom.

Moreover, *Emine* brings one memories of Digenis, Erotokritos and Aretousa. One of its main messages is that modern man should respect the traditions of the past. In this book, Karatzis builds a love story between a Cretan hero and the daughter of a Turkish *pasha* (2000). On the CD that accompanies the book, Vasilis Skoulas and Spyridoula Toutoudaki sing excerpts from a "Cretan love song," published by Aerakis, and music by Christos Stivaktakis, a local *lyra* and *laouto* player.

Cretan Performance

> I do not accept Crete without *lyra*, *glendi*, without dance. Crete is *man-dinades, parees, kouzouloi* (crazy) people![73]

Cretan music itself is rich and complex, encompassing a variety of types and genres. In all cases, Cretan music "behaves" socially. To exist, it needs the Cretans. We cannot hear it without imagining all kinds of interaction among the participants: dancing-singing, eating-drinking, chatting-reflecting. Moreover, Cretan music is mostly vocal: it does not exist in isolation from the traditional Cretan proverbial poetry. Scholars have studied how specific musical identities and aesthetics are shaped as well as negotiated in particular communities. Anna Caraveli deals with the symbolic village community born in performance, the notions of *glendi* and *kefi* (high spirits). Steven Feld shows transitions from sound to community. John Blacking depicts how musical processes are based on patterns of interaction and cultural forms.[74]

Such performance studies explore cases where *kefi*, ecstasy, repetition, and other forms of expression through music are manifested. Those cases are indeed related to music identity and aesthetics because of the common expression of *kefi* that can be traced between the Cretan and other cultures. For example, *kefi*, the Greek word for high spirits, is the same for both Turks and Arabs *(keyf)*.

An arena for the expression of individual identity and the negotiation of community boundaries in Crete is the *glendi*.[75] The Cretans capable of experiencing and conveying true *kefi* in the *glendi* are usually called *meraklides, levendes, palikaria* (braves, the human heroes who always stand ready to defy death in order to obtain liberty). Thus, *meraklis, levendis, palikari* refer to the passion and skill displayed in performance, combining aesthetic, moral, and ritual elements.[76] This is what Cretans aim for in life, what many of their songs talk about, such as, for example, "A bird with *meraki* (yearning)" and "*Levendoyenna Kriti* (Crete: Giving birth to gallant men)."

As already mentioned, Crete was under the Venetian rule for 465 years prior to the Turkish occupation. The word *mandinades* comes from the Italian *mattinate*.[77] *Mandinades* are an integral part of the Cretan music tradition. More importantly, they are the essence of Cretan culture. They shape Cretan identity powerfully and symbolically.[78] Many of them used to have Islamic contexts in the past. Now, instead, locals have both "purified" and amplified them with words such as "my Christian," "my Cretan girl," and so on.

Ross Daly plays on the *lyra* the modal music of Greece, the Balkans, Turkey, the Middle East, North Africa and North India, and believes that, despite the difference in terminology, there are distinctive similarities in the way virtually all these cultures approach improvisation and rhythm, as well as in the way they perceive the relationship between tradition and originality.[79] Let us mention here that Cretan music employs a modal structure. The concept of absolute pitch does not exist, and a pitch designation does not indicate an absolute, but rather an approximate pitch. A musician may tune his instrument higher or lower so that the range of the instrument more closely matches the range of his voice.

Cretan Music

Today, the established trademark of music on the island of Crete is the *lyra*, a pear-shaped, three-stringed bowed instrument.

The noun is feminine, hence, the relationship between the *lyra* player and this instrument is an erotic one. Vasilis Skoulas, a famous *lyra* player from the village of Anogia, traces his musical progress to his love relationship with his instrument.[80] Antonis Psarantonis, another famous *lyra* player from the same village, sees reflected on the *lyra* the heart of all the people.[81] Many Cretans talk about *lyra* as their greatest love, the instrument which, as Erotokritos' *laouto*, speaks to their souls and comforts their sorrows. It is the voice of Crete. "*Lyra* is my life," the *lyra* player believes; "*lyra* music is my life," the Cretan agrees.

The sound coming from the *lyra* – a quiet little instrument – is unique, even though the music being played on it can be clearly recognizable as eastern Mediterranean, with obvious resemblance to other traditions belonging to the same geographical area. However, on closer observation, an interesting detail concerning its playing manifests itself. The fingering technique of the left hand is rather different from that of the vast majority of string instruments. Instead of pressing the string with the tips of the fingers to produce the different notes, the strings are touched lightly by the back of the nails, producing a very strong, sharp tone, and facilitating a wide range of embellishments which considerably enrich the melodies being played.

In this respect, resemblances to the Bulgarian *gadulka* (Bulgarian type of *lyra*; three-stringed, pear-shaped folk fiddle) and the Turkish *kemenche* (*lyra*-like instrument played especially in the Black Sea region of Turkey) become more concrete, given that both instruments make use of the same technique. The only other region in the world where such a peculiar technique is used is north India, especially Rajasthan, where instruments such as the *sarangi* are found.

Beginning in 1955, performing Cretan music on a violin was forbidden, because of a nationalistic policy and purism adopted by Greek folklorists.[82] The violin, imported to Crete from Italy during the Venetian domination, was interpreted as a foreign instrument unrelated to Cretan music tradition, and was banned, while the

Antonis Fragakis (Cretan *lyra*, vocals). Photo by Yiannis Bromirakis.

lyra was chosen as the heir and symbol of uncontaminated music folklore. In this process of remodeling Greek music folk culture, the *lyra*, which was present during the Byzantine period and whose name evokes ancient classical Greece,[83] could be accepted, while the violin was regarded as a symbol of foreign domination and "pollution."[84]

Therefore, to remodel Cretan culture, people chose a music symbol to reconnect the present reality of the island to a remote past. The insistence with which the stereotype of the *lyra* player was and is still presented in documents about Crete reveals that what is evoked by this image is considered necessary to disseminate a new sense of the history of Crete.[85] Since then, *lyra* has become the music symbol of Cretan ethnic identity and the *lyra* player a hero.

Studying abroad in Crete-Greece: Relief wall painting of the sacred Minoan bull at the west bastion of the Knossos Palace (Heraklion-Crete).

"Greekness: language, tradition, landscape."[86] *Aroma Kritis* (Scent of Crete) is the title of a CD by Mihalis Kallergis.[87] Its cover consists of a composite image in an orange background. The *lyra* player is on the left, in black clothes, playing his instrument, on his knees, standing. On his right, there is an image of a *lyra* and a wooden knife, traditionally symbol of bravery and manliness.[88] On the right side of the cover, in front of a background of a windmill and coastal, whitewashed houses, we distinguish the ruins of the Knossos palace and the Phaistos Disc. That cover speaks of a juxtaposition that easily joins the Minoan past and the present to imply an expected and welcomed continuity as well as a "tension between homegrown identity and mobile cosmopolitanism."[89]

Next to the *lyra* player are oftentimes two other men who play the *laouta*. Those instruments – like most of the large-bodied lutes found in the eastern Mediterranean – are clearly related to the very old Arabian lute known as the *oud*. Even the name *laouto* is quite obviously a derivative of the Arabic word *al'oud*, namely, "the wood." The *laouta* have four double strings, a very low tuning, and are played with long plectrums, originally made from the feathers of a type of buzzard commonly found on Crete. They also have movable frets, indicating that non-tempered intervals must have been in use at some time, even though most contemporary renditions of Cretan music tend to limit themselves to the use of the western-tempered scale.

The Cretan *laouto* is a larger and deeper version of the *laouto* found elsewhere in Greece. Until quite recently, however, the most widespread Cretan *laouto* appears to have been the *boulgari*, a long-necked lute with a flat soundboard and a hole in the body, essentially very similar to, if not the same instrument as, the *saz* (a long-necked type of lute). Under the influence of the Greek *laouto*, the *boulgari* eventually died out. Stelios Foustalierakis played that instrument, and we have many fine recordings of his playing style, which seems to owe more to the *bouzouki* than the Turkish *saz*.[90] Though well-known through recordings, the *boulgari* is not encountered often as part of traditional Cretan music ensembles.

As Chris Williams maintains,[91] improvisation in the Cretan context is firmly anchored to the social function of the music. The *lyra* player or violinist must vary the melodies to sustain interest. A *lyra* or violin player who cannot improvise is simply *not* a musician. Williams points out that the *taximi* (improvisation) appears in a varied form in Crete. Cretan musicians learned fixed introductions to tunes. Now, a freer introduction is played. However, that is not quite like a *taximi*, being less an exploration of the mode than a kind of stage setting for the tune to come. It is often theatrical in spirit and would rarely involve modulation.[92] At the same time, William argues, the performer must conform to the strict rules of the music so that the dance can continue in time and in step with the performer's playing:

> Playing Cretan music is being part of a group. And when I say group, I mean not only the instrumental and vocal ensemble, but the whole society and community that participates in the event as well. Viewed in this regard, Cretan music brings forth a social idea and, by extension, a social ideal, in opposition to the western classical tradition, where the performer's ego is usually at the center. If anything, the Cretan example provides a socialist model.[93]

Giorgos Manolakis (Cretan *laouto*, vocals). Photo by Yiannis Bromirakis.

What sort of madness comes over us? What sort of madness comes over us to make us throw ourselves on another man? There was a time when I used to say: 'That man's a Turk, or a Bulgarian, or a Greek.' Now, when I look at people, I say: 'This one's a good fellow, that one's a bastard.' They can be Greeks, or Bulgarians, or Turks – it doesn't matter. Is he good? Or is he bad? That's the only thing I ask nowadays. And as I grow older…I feel I shan't even go on asking that! Whether a man's good or bad, I'm sorry for him, for all of them.[94]

Our songs express our sorrows, our struggles and the agonies of our people. The Mediterranean functions as the uterus of all the peoples who live around it. There are many common aspects in the way these people create and express themselves. The purpose of this discussion of music is to show these similarities – the common points that link these peoples – and to contribute to communication through the common language of music, which is the language of the soul. It is apparent that the music of the people in the Mediterranean touches and moves each of us.[95]

Cretan localism expresses persistence for freedom. Like the character of Zorba in Kazantzakis' novel and the homonymous movie with which they daily come to experientially and repeatedly live, Cretans choose to dance instead of cry. The essence of the Cretan uniqueness is formulated by geography, intercultural effect, history and tradition as a means of expression. Contemporary ethnographers should make use of history to show how identities are shaped. The cultures around the Mediterranean are complex, because there, various idioms are intermingled.

Cretans' creativity is inspired by the past and by their neighbors. Through the ages, Cretan music has expressed the influences of all its colonizers-inhabitants. It may be erotic when speaking in the romantic language of the Venetian literary forms of the fifteenth to the seventeenth centuries. It may also express sorrow and pain, it may be a cry for freedom, bursting out in *aman-aman* (woe is me!) when recalling memories from the period of the Turkish domination.

Because of its geographical position and its historic cultural base, Crete acts as an example of a living organism in continuous motion, inspiring and encouraging, designating a deep meaning regarding the idea of country and homeland. Because of this position, Crete can also become the educational and research center of the area, as well as the intermediary among Europe, Africa and the Middle East, a central bridge of communication and cooperation at artistic, cultural and other levels. As the best ambassador and, at the same time, as a modern peaceful conqueror, ages after the Minoans, the rulers of the seas, Crete stands poised to play that role, once more, today.

St. Romanos the Melodist

Most people are familiar with the Greek folk music but not the Byzantine, ecclesiastical music tradition which was coined and performed throughout the Byzantine Empire, namely between 330-1453. When the Fall of Constantinople took place, that tradition continued to flourish in monasteries. It is survived in manuscript sources with a musical notation that is phonetic and syllabic, making use of formulae while, at the same time, paying particular attention to the syntactical structure and the proper accentuation of the text.

Byzantine chants are melodic, florid, liturgical recitatives. Their composition is based on 8 basic modes ("sounds") while their singing is traditionally antiphonic, consisting of two choruses of well-trained chanters. The development of major, hymnographic forms began in the fifth century with the rise of the *kontakion*, a long and elaborate metrical sermon, which found its acme in the work of St. Romanos the Melodist (6th century).

St. Romanos is one of the giants of "our" sacred music, one of the pillars of the "Golden Epoch of Byzantine hymnography," which includes personalities such as Ephrem the Syrian, John Damascene and Andrew of Crete. He is venerated by both the eastern and western churches. He was born in Emesa-Syria (Homs, in Arabic) and became Christian at an early age. He served as deacon at a church in Beirut before moving to be a sexton *(neokoros)* in Hagia Sophia in Constantinople, where he died in 560 AD.

Favored by the Patriarch for his virtues and piety, the legend has it that he was assigned to chant even though he had not been trained as a chanter. During the pre-Christmas all-night vigil, Romanos prayed hard in front of the icon of the Theotokos in the church of the Blachernae. Miraculously, the Theotokos appeared and gave him a paper scroll to eat. Not only was he able to chant but he amazed both the Patriarch and the Emperor with his enchanting lyrics: "Today the Virgin bears Him who is transcendent."

His fame and subsequent contributions earned him the honorary title "The Melodist." He became a teacher of chanting contributing significantly not only to ecclesiastical psalmodies but also to music, in general. In particular, he perfected the genre called "Hymn," which is based on equal, harmonic numbers of syllables and accents. Moreover, he is considered the foremost composer of *kontakia*, which are characterized by a rich poetic style expressing grandiloquence and pathos, chanted in liturgical services during the entire year.

One of the most renowned and loved services in the Orthodox Church, the "Salutations to the Theotokos" *(Heretismi)*, is attributed to St. Romanos. They are divided into four parts: "The Annunciation," "The Nativity," "Christ" and "The Theotokos." They are intonated during the first four Friday evenings of the Easter Lent period. The entire "Akathist Hymn" is performed on the fifth Friday. The hymn forms an alphabetical acrostic as each of the twelve long and short stanzas begins with a letter of the Greek alphabet. Moreover, it is made up of praises directed to the Mother of God beginning with the salutation of the Archangel Gabriel "Rejoice" *(Here)*. Each short stanza ends with the "Alleluia" and each long one with the refrain "Rejoice, O Bride Unwedded!" *(Here Nimfi Animfefte!)*.

When barbaric hordes sailed into the Marmara Sea and set a siege on Constantinople, the Patriarch toured the great walls of Constantinople holding an icon of the Theotokos, bolstering the faith of the defenders. Unexpectedly, a great storm destroyed most of the invading fleet, and thus the siege was lifted. Thankful faithful filled the Church of the Theotokos at Vlachernae on the Golden Horn and prayed all night long chanting salutations to the Virgin Mary without sitting. Hence the title of the Hymn "Akathistos," in Greek meaning "not seated," which is the reason why when performed the audience remains standing.

St. Romanos is considered "the Pindar" of ecclesiastic poetry and the Patron Saint of "our" Choirs and Chanters. He is the author of thousands of prayers and hymns. His compositions are known for their originality and wealth of ideas. Throughout them, the Saints, Christ and the Virgin Mary are portrayed lively and in a humane manner. He was not only writing the lyrics but was also setting them into music, following a simple, comprehendible language, so as to reach all audiences; yet his music is full of meaningful substance and his technique impeccable.

Cretan-Turkish Musicians[96]

Cretans and Turks lived together and moved back and forth between Crete and the western coasts of Turkey (Asia Minor) for many years. Thus, their singing and dancing repertories combined Greek and Turkish elements. In the past, this was very conscious. It was mostly recognizable in Rethymno in the 1920s and 1930s especially due to three musicians: Andreas Rodinos,[97] Harilaos Piperakis[98] and Stelios Foustalierakis[99] (known as Foustalieris).[100] Their songs spoke of love and life, with all its negotiation games and fatal outcomes.

Speaking of amalgams: St. Nicholas Church in Splantzia-Chania (Crete-Greece).

Cretan-Turkish people were Cretans who converted into Islam either violently or voluntarily (in order to acquire privileges). They made up approximately 1/3 of the population on the island of Crete till approximately 1880. The unique culture of the co-existence of Muslims and Christians on the island of Crete particularly in terms of its music expressions only recently has started being researched.[101] For instance, the Italian ethnomusicologist Magrini was engaged in the study of such a song genre, the *tabachaniotika*, an urban type of Cretan music played in years past mostly in coffee shops and restaurants in the harbor districts of Chania and Rethymno.[102]

Researchers claim that many of the *tabachaniotika* can be traced to Foustalieris and, more generally, to the period after the 1923 Treaty of Lausanne. Interestingly, though, some of those tunes are termed as *Paleoi Skopoi tis Kritis* (Old tunes of Crete.) The tunes are not old at all, but the phrase is telling. In general, the whole process of adoption and adaptation of "oriental" features into Cretan music is interesting. Indeed, in one case, Foustalieris adapted the Turkish song, "Ada sahillerinde bekliyorum" (I am waiting at the coast of the island), usually performed at the Pringiponisa near Constantinople, to the Cretan one, "Everybody asks me why I cry."[103]

In Crete, the piece just mentioned is called "Halepianos amanes." There are at least two more songs that share the same melody with it. One is an old song of Antonis Diamantidis or Dalgas called "Matia mou" (My eyes)," and the other a Syrian song called "Qadduka 'al-mayyaas (Your flirtatiously swaying figure)". Because of its Arabic roots, that song has various elements that make it sound not exactly like a typical Turkish song. Daly asserts it belongs to a group of songs called *muwashahat*, a musical form that originated in Al- Andalus (medieval Spain and Portugal).[104] Regarded as the oldest Arabic songs, today they are preserved mainly in the Syrian city of Halab (Aleppo), even though it is believed that they originated with the Moors. Obviously, by naming their version "Halepianos Amanes," Cretans refer to Halepa, a region in Chania. However, it is an interesting and intriguing coincidence that this piece comes from Aleppo in Syria and not from Chania.

The singing that accompanies this music is definitely of an oriental nature, with a specific and deliberate use of a certain nasal quality, and highly embellished. *Aman-aman* (for mercy's sake!; woe is me!) is an exclamatory expression Cretan singers oftentimes use to denote, among others, sorrow, pain, misfortune. Wonderful melodic improvisations *(amanedes)* are based on the word *aman*. In synchronization with the singers, dancers may translate them into movement as well.

Vasilis Stavrakakis, for instance, a famous Cretan singer and mandolin player, officially began his singing career by participating at a singing contest in the village of Anogia. His performance of a *tabachaniotiko* song won him a prize. Daly composed the song "Black Sea," which we can find in *Dreamlands*,[105] but also in many of his other recordings. For this composition, he used "the melody of Ali," traced somewhere to the prefecture of Lasithi. Cretans say that Ali was a Turkish violinist. Daly, however, believes that he was not a Turk, but a local Cretan who had converted to Islam.[106]

Cretans gave Patrick Leigh Fermor, a British agent in Crete during the German occupation, the nickname Filedem, because of his love for the well-known Cretan homonymous song. The American movie *Meeting over Midnight,* about Fermor's kidnapping of German general Heinrich Kreipe, uses that song's melody in its soundtrack. Stelios Foustalieris had learned it from the Turkish crew of a ship in the port of Rethymno. The song refers to a bloody, warlike Turk named Edem who was sarcastically nicknamed "*file* Edem" ("friend Edem") in his slaughter of Cretan

Christians. Foustalieris gave other lyrics to the song – which he considered to be very serious – while later, it was recorded by Thanassis Skordalos,[107] and still later, by the Cretan singer Nikos Xylouris, with the well-known verses, "Filedem, *aman-aman!* I'm in love with a Turkish girl in the mosque," and so on.

Williams talks about the rehabilitation of the demotic song in Greece. He cites the example of Yannis Markopoulos, a contemporary Greek composer of Cretan origin, and, specifically, his 1972 recording with Xylouris, *Ithagenia* (Citizenship, Nationality). He views this work as far more than a political statement against the Greek military junta of 1967-1974. He observes that the songs on this record are suffused with Cretan styles, and the whole work arguably anticipates later attempts to combine Cretan and oriental styles, containing, for instance, some interesting use of the *saz* (a long-necked type of lute).[108]

Descriptions of the existence of Cretan-Turkish musicians can be traced in several novels (e.g. by Nikos Kazantzakis), folk song lyrics (such as the "The song of Memetakas"),[109] CD liner notes,[110] regional conference proceedings[111] as well as personal information provided by local musicians.[112] Lastly, more information on Cretan-Turkish musicians one may find in several sources such as the following: a) The 2008 Dermitzakis book which provides us with several folklore elements for the Cretan Turks that resided in the capital of the island of Crete, namely Heraklion, during the era of the *Kritiki Politeia* (1896-1913), b) the 1999 Zaimakis study which reports on several Cretan Turks musicians who sang and/or performed on the violin, the *lyra*, the *bouzouki*, the *boulgari* and the *tambouras* (string instrument of Byzantine origin), c) the 1993 Tsivis book which refers to the Cretan Turks musicians from that area (such as the *lyra* player Mehmet Bey Stafidakis (1878-1908), composer of the popular melody called "Stafidianos"), and d) the 1999 Diktakis book which, amongst others, also mentions violin player Moustafas Karagioules (1845-1930) from the village of Kallergiana at Kissamos who composed the well-known "Karagioule *sirtos*."

Stratis Kalogeridis[113]

One of the greatest music personalities within the Cretan music tradition is the violin player and composer from eastern Crete, Efstratios or Stratis Kalogeridis. Kalogeridis was born at the town of Sitia in 1883. When he was ten years old, he started performing on the mandolin and then proceeded with the violin while being exposed to local, traditional sounds of that area performed by both *lyra* and violin players. In 1903, he went to Toulon so as to study chemistry, but he quickly switched to music, which resulted to two years of studies at the Odeum of that French town.

He returned to his hometown in 1905, where he remained till 1907, and then moved to Heraklion where he worked as a photographer. While at the capital of Crete, he continued to compose and perform music. At the same time, after 1951, he became an active member of the artistic committee of the Municipality of the Heraklion Philharmonic which he also occasionally directed. He died in Athens in 1960.

His composition known as "The Kalogeridis *condylies*" along with his unique violin playing technique became a point of reference as well as grounds of competition, imitation and inspiration for the next generation of Cretan artists, both to the east and the west part of the island. However, it is his contribution to the music tradition on the eastern part of Crete that was catalytic not only because he preserved and re-formed older melodies, but because, at the same time, he created and performed with great dexterity new ones.[114]

Another important contribution of his was the foundation of a violin school at the Heraklion region. Many musicians who wanted to learn classical music were influenced by his teachings. Because of his background in western classical music, Kalogeridis also led the way to the harmonization of folk music which he mainly performed at coffee and other public spaces at Heraklion.[115]

It is important to mention that Kalogeridis was notating folk music on scores that could be shared with other classical musicians. This way, western-trained musicians could learn and play the traditional music tunes, particularly the ones who were not able to do so by merely listening. In addition, due to him, several areas of eastern Crete, such as the regions of Viannos and Pediada along with that of Mirabello, that where, traditionally, *lyra* predominated, switched to violin playing.[116]

Kalogeridis' work is twofold, consisting of both compositions and music recordings (which started in Athens in 1933). His compositions were recorded on western staff notation along with several folk music pieces that he also transcribed. The Vikelaia Municipal Library of Heraklion has published parts of it[117] whereas the recordings are included in eight 2-sided 78 rpm discs, totaling to 16 music pieces.

All in all, Kalogeridis must be viewed as a music bridge that has united the past with the future of Cretan music. He was innovative in that he transcribed, created and performed the patrilineal music heritage of eastern Crete in a unique way.

**Kostis Kotronakis from the region of Gazepi Windmill-Crete on the violin.
Photo by Yiannis Bromirakis.**

Moreover, he transformed the folk music tunes into artistic ones, bringing Cretan music closer to the western classical prototypes, which, in turn, familiarized classical lovers with their roots. This added variety with diachronic value onto the Cretan *condylia* genre particularly in terms of its interpretation at the region of Sitia.

Nikos Xylouris[118]

Greeks honor Nikos Xylouris as the ambassador of Cretan music to the rest of the world, representing it with all of the dignity and the ethos worthy of such a glorious tradition. On Nikos Xylouris they see an "archangel" who, with distinctive vocal timbre, together with timeless expressive quality, gave an entirely new dimension to singing. Although very traditional in his approach, Nikos Xylouris was also highly innovative. He has come to be regarded as a symbol, indeed as an embodiment of the virtues of the archetypal Cretan spirit. His unique personality incorporated and balanced the attributes of pride and humility, nobility and simplicity.

"Psaronikos" was his nickname, "psaros," being an adjective "adopted" from his grandfather who was stealing the Turks, running as fireball, seizing them as fish (*psaria,* in Greek). A rare phenomenon for today's world, where the most popular songs get totally forgotten in a year or so, why do people still remember Nikos Xylouris' songs and perform them, even though they neither saw nor witnessed him perform live?

Xylouris was born on July 7 1936, at the village of Anogia.[119] His parents had 6 children, 3 girls and 3 boys, and he was the 4th child. After the Germans destroyed his native village, he was placed at a boarding school. There, he first publicly showed his interest in music by performing at school feasts. At the age of 12, the teacher of the village convinced his father to buy him a *lyra*. He insisted on knowing how to play that instrument without having even touched it. He would attend the village feasts and observe the *lyra* player. He would then grasp pieces of wood and pretend performing on them. Of course, he was just making mouth sounds. However, he soon became one of the most wanted instrument players and singers of the region for weddings, baptisms, and other social events.

When he was 17 years old, he went to the capital of the island, Heraklion, where he performed at the Music Club "Kastro" ("Fortress"). He would deliberately avoid the central avenues so as not to be made fun of because he played the instrument of the "uncouth" villagers. At that time, everyone was pretending to be "European," namely "modern."

In 1956, during a Carnival feast at the village of Venerato, he met with Ourania Melabianaki. He kept performing serenades under her balcony till 1958, when he eventually "abducted" her. In 1960, their first child, Giorgos, was born, followed 6 years afterwards by their 2nd, Rinio. Ourania paid for the production of Xylouris' first record which featured "his" song to her, "My Cretan Woman" ("Kritikopoula mou" or "Mia mavrofora otan perna").

In 1966, Nikos won the 1st price at a San Remo competition for his music-*lyra* composition called "Sirtaki." In 1967, he operated the first Cretan-music Club in Heraklion, "Erotokritos." Between 1969 and 1980, Xylouris moved to and lived at the capital of Greece, Athens. While there, he performed at "Konaki," an Athenian-Cretan music club, but also at several other music halls.

In 1970, Xylouris met with the Director of the Columbia-EMI Takis Lambropoulos who asked him to work on non-Cretan music traditions. In 1971, he won the famous song price "Charles Cros" in France. The producers went after him. He learnt his songs "on foot" as he had no time for rehearsals. He would listen to the tape while at home or in the car. He would then sing long and learn them. Composers found this authentic and thus invited him to the studio and recorded him "on spot." As a result, he worked with Greek popular musicians such as Stavros Xarchakos, Christos Leontis, Elias Andriopoulos and Yannis Markopoulos. In fact, Xylouris made a crucial turning point in the Greek recording industry with his Cretan *rizitika* (mountain) songs as orchestrated by Yannis Markopoulos.

During the Greek military regime (1967-1973), Xylouris' voice became a flag of resistance. His music got forbidden at the mass media. His songs made political statements while he insisted performing wearing the Cretan warrior attire. Besides performing the traditional repertory of songs, he lent his voice to the creations of contemporary composers. This way, the authentic Cretan expression and the traditional song of Crete gained a panhellenic respect, a power they never had in the past. That is why he has been placed primarily in the hearts of the Greek people and secondarily in their memories.[120] He was not only a nightingale but also a loyal friend and good company.

Although very traditional, Xylouris was also highly innovative. He always gave a fresh, personal sound to whatever he sang. He listened very carefully to all of the great players prior to himself and absorbed the essence of their music, never simply copying what they were doing. "Once this essence became part of his very being, he was able to use it in his own unique and creative way. Essentially, this is the way in which all great traditions grow and develop through the medium of remarkable individuals such as Nikos Xylouris."[121]

Since 1973, Xylouris had been bitter about the music networks and the money profits and making: "I do not sing for money. I sing for the people. Singing means love, passion." In 1979, he started having pains in the head and the thorax, thus he traveled to New York where several medical tests were conducted at the Memorial Hospital. When operated and told that he had not many hopes, he immediately jumped out of his room and started performing the *"Agrimia"* ("Wild beasts") *rizitiko* song.

On February 8 1980, as the lyrics by Nikos Gatsos set to music by Stavros Xarchakos attest, "God aimed at a brave man… My generation's king, don't go down the stairs. Drink the immortal water so as to defeat time."

One still hears the sounds of Nikos Xylouris and cannot forget the voice of the man who struggles and finally manages to be heard in difficult political times. Xylouris was a devoted patriot, a free man who characteristically used to say that he was proud of three things: "That he is Greek; that he is a Cretan; that he votes for

Venizelos!" That is why he is still alive among us: he "owns" songs and is an idol, a prototype for the majority of Cretan performers.[122]

Zeus Performed[123]

Memoryscapes

Mountains are "tangible signs of ancient time in the landscape, perceived and identified with a revisited, living past,"[124] "topographical memory places,"[125] namely sites
evoking a sense of continuity, hybrid places "compounded of life and death, of the
temporal and the eternal, endless rounds of the collective and the individual, the
prosaic and the sacred."[126] They stop the flow of time and inhibit forgetting,[127] resulting to a "mountain theology"[128] which exists in the protracted endurance or resurrection of myth and history, language and text.

On the island of Crete, tall and stable mountains that have been part of the Cretan
civilization since antiquity are associated with local values. Such high mountains are
considered spaces of isolation and ramparts of freedom. Their inaccessible land and
physical isolation offered protection and a place where, during various uprisings,
military equipment could be stored.

Mere looking at such mountains inspired and still reinforces on Cretans power during hardship.[129] For instance, an invocation of Mount Ida, *Psiloritis*, stands
for strength, endurance, honor and pride. Because that mountain has served as a
stronghold of revolution, it is perceived as the soul of Crete. It is the tallest mountain on that Greek island, the place where, according to mythology, Zeus was born
alongside with music and dance.

Kourites

A popular myth on the island of Crete says that, in order to conceal the cries of
baby Zeus, so as his father Cronus not to find and thus devour him, the ancient
inhabitants of Crete, the *Kourites*, performed a vivacious, leaping dance, the *Anogianos pidichtos* (leaping dance from Anogia), still performed at the historic town of
Anogia that is located at the foot of Mountain Psiloritis.[130] Rhyming couplets performances, *mandinades*, namely improvised, fifteen-syllable, in iambic meter, proverbial, rhyming distiches, devoted to Zeus accompany such music and dance rites,
raising monuments in history and memory while simultaneously shaping what "being from Crete" is.[131]

Similarly to how Herzfeld examines the "ownership" of history in relation to what
he calls "social" and "monumental" time,[132] several Cretan music scholars trace in
local dances elements of a "glorious" Greek past.[133] Revolts are oftentimes the main
theme of performances which glorify the strongly ingrained Cretan ideal of gallant
living and dying. Song lyrics that accompany such dances refer to various Cretan
landscapes surrounded by mythologies and histories, ancient and modern and, as a
result, their stories function both ideologically and ideally.

"Zeus or Hymn to Psiloritis": Psarantonis

Coming from that village, Antonis Xylouris – better known as Psarantonis – records in 1999 his album *Ideon Andron*, dedicated to the cave where Zeus grew up. A specific song from that work, track 6, a dragging Cretan dance called *sirtos*, is titled "Zeus: A Hymn to Mount Psiloritis." Psarantonis' vocal timbre, raw and earthy, and his *lyra* playing – accompanied by percussive rhythms on a clay pot and the Cretan *laouto* – embody his unique approach, which alludes to the roughness of the landscape of his native foothills of legendary Mount Ida. The lyrics of the song, in the traditional *mandinades* format, simply witness how the snow never melts on the top of Psiloritis and how Zeus was a shepherd with a house in Anogia.

Psarantonis was born in 1942, in Anogia. He first picked up the *lyra* at the age of 13, and within one month, he played at his first wedding. Brother of the famous Nikos Xylouris, or Psaronikos, in three years, Psarantonis became one of the most renowned musicians in Crete due to "his unique voice, which ranges from mellow whispers to low singing and from cacophonous bellowing to an incomprehensible moaning, and his playing – from simple to beautiful, from wild to painful."[134]

According to him, Zeus met a shepherd who invited him to rest in his mountain home *(mitato)*. He offered him fresh water, milk and cheese. In exchange for his hospitality, Zeus promised him a music instrument that would seduce animals, birds and humans. Therefore, he removed out of his hand-woven bag a turtle shell, animal skin, goat horns, intestine strings, and a bow with male goat hair, and constructed the *lyra*. As soon as the shepherd performed on it, he got enchanted by its sound which he then spread to the rest of the island.[135]

When asked why he performs with closed eyes, Psarantonis, "the cry of gods," responded how he travels to landscapes he loves in order to make his music beautiful and how nature is the god that also gives music to him.[136] For this particular composition, the artist was staring at *Psiloritis* from the cave Zeus was born in, and started quarreling with the mountain using his music instrument and voice. Psarantonis is known for arguing with Greek priests who ignore the presence of Zeus. If he is the essence of Crete indeed, perhaps the secret of his music talent simply resides in his glance toward the mountains, namely the heroic and playful eyes, without hope yet without fear, that dance with the tragic elements of life in both ecstasy and joy.[137]

Xenios: Miltos Paschalides

Art rock musician Miltos Paschalides entitled his most recent, 7th personal album *Xenios: Crete Within Me* (2010), and dedicated the homonymous track to Psarantonis. Paschalides was born in the town of Kalamata and grew up in Athens, where he attended school and also took guitar classes. He went to Crete to study mathematics and philosophy in 1986 and left the island in July 2003.

Xenios, Philoxenon or Hospites are three adjectives for god Zeus, the patron of hospitality and strangers *(xenoi)*. The song that was composed in eastern Crete during the summer of 2009 is dedicated to Psarantonis, whom Paschalides met by accident during spring 1993, on a central street in the capital of Crete, Heraklion. The composer explains how hard it is to speak of such a monumental musician, like Psarantonis. He remembers how Psarantonis recognized him as the musician outside Crete who incorporates Cretan elements in his music, and how this qualifies to being a Cretan as well, and concludes: "Psarantonis is the most convincing story-teller I have ever met, the only one, in fact, Zeus would forgive, if he would ever return to Crete!"[138]

Xenios imagines Zeus today, after 30 centuries, being exiled, alone, bored and forgotten, trying to find out how he could still contribute. The god who used to be a protector of hospitality is now a foreigner, with no thunder in his arms and no love, strolling around to find lost and old Minoan friends. While wandering at the capital of the island and waiting for Ariadne to show up, he also desires to walk on the mountains and the plains of Mount Ida where he grew up, sit on his throne at Mount Juktas, recall the old prophecy and, speechless, watch for the second cataclysm.

In other words, *Xenios* would be … "xenos," namely, a foreigner, in contemporary Crete. He would not have liked a capitalistic, "getting rich" attitude combined with a lack of aesthetics when it comes to instruments and styles used in current music trends. His only redemption would be the sound of the authentic *lyra* players.[139] This is how and also why Paschalides filters within himself the traditional spirits, treating them in a mostly tender way, in critically Cretan terms.

The song rhymes but not in the *mandinades* format, its basic melody being on a *pyrrhic* (warlike) *Anogianos pidichtos* (leaping) dance with the following characteristic refrain in a "classic," dragging *sirtos* from Chania rhythm: "The only thing that saves Zeus is Psarantonis' playing the bow on the *lyra*." The *lyra* performance, the drum *(daouli)* and the *laouto* along with vocals illustrate well how composer and singer Paschalides co-exist in salutary spirits with the Cretan melodies but also how, after all, he, himself, may be one of the most convincing, contemporary storytellers. In fact, the only one Zeus would forgive for the ecological, aesthetic and spiritual crimes committed on and against the island is Psarantonis, a symbol, according to Paschalides, of a Crete that still dreams, resists, creates and preserves pieces of its divine madness.

"Juktas": Kelly Thoma

In her disc *Anamkhara* (2010), which in Gaelic means "friend of the soul," Kelly Thoma, a core member of Ross Daly's *Labyrinth* for the past ten years, "sympathetically" performs on the Cretan *lyra* (a soprano variation of this instrument) a composition called "Juktas," alluding, of course, to Mount Juktas, where the tomb of Zeus is located, one of the most significant summit sanctuaries of the Minoan period. That mountain was a place of worship in the years of Christianity and the Byzantine era as well as during the Turkish period. During the Cretan revolution of 1897, it became a refuge for the rebels.

Another Cretan, not by birth but rather by soul, Kelly was born in 1978, in Piraeus. In 1995, she started studying *lyra* with Daly (also a non-Cretan by birthright but by heart and soul) while traveling with him and his group, *Labyrinth*, participating in concerts in Europe, Asia, Australia and the USA with musicians from various, different traditions.[140] In this composition, Kelly is accompanied by Zohar Fresco (born in Israel to a Jewish family of Turkish origin) on the *tamburello* and the *davul* as well as Daly on the *bendir*. During our 12 May 2011 interview, she explained how Juktas is the mountain she particularly favors and daily faces from her village house in Archanes. From a north-west perspective, Mount Juktas resembles the face of a man lying down, looking at the sky. It is said to be the head of Zeus who died and is buried there. The name of the mountain, which derives from a corrupted form of the Roman word "Jupiter," enhances this view.

The music piece revolves around a basic phrase and is in the rhythm of the Cretan dragging dance *sirtos*. Kelly's performance reflects the rich experience which she has gained as part of the/through her interaction with *Labyrinth* through her collaborations with master musicians from various countries, while her composition reveals a rich imagination, a wise and mature balance between the indispensable discipline and austerity which characterize the traditions she has studied, and free creative expression: "creative expression free of dogmatic attitudes, which is a fundamental need of any young artist."[141] Through her music, her goal is to reach a "meaning that pertains to the ultimate spiritual love, which elevates the soul to a new dimension."[142]

The Abduction of United Europe: Minas Alexiadis

Minas I. Alexiadis' epic comic opera-cabaret in two acts *The Abduction of United Europe* [which was first performed in 2010 at the "Orient Express Music Wagon" (Athens) of "The Train at Rouf Railway Theater"] draws on the ancient Greek myth related to Zeus' coupling with young Princess Europa, which thus gave birth to the so-called "European civilization." Along with traditional music elements, it also compositionally combines songs in tango, rumba, samba, Latin, as well as other ethnic and Greek mainland, island and urban-style tunes with jazz melodies and rhythms, all in rhyming verses, satirizing the current European sociopolitical and economic issues.

Alexiadis, assistant professor of Music Theatre and Opera at the Department of Theatre Studies, University of Athens, holding degrees in law and musicology, studied piano, theory and composition in Greece as well as in Germany. Since 1984, most of his works have been commissioned whereas many of his varicolored compositions have been performed, broadcasted through TV and radio stations, and internationally awarded. Next to his compositional career stands a bright academic one, with several scholarly presentations, publications as well as many administrative and educational positions at various music institutions.[143]

Five talented performers interpret all songs of *The Abduction,* which borrows elements from genres such as the comic opera, the variety show, the musical and the cabaret, playfully and lively directed by Tatiana Lygari. Thanasis Vlavianos in the role of Zeus the Olympian performs on the electric bass and the *baglamas* (a long necked, plucked bowl-lute), Tina Yotopoulou as Europe plays the recorder and the percussion, Evangelia Tsiara fulfills her role as the narrator via singing, percussion and castanets, Andreas Stergiou as Apollo performs on the guitar and the mandolin while Andreas Stamatopoulos accompanies all the aforementioned performers on the piano.[144]

The program's cover by famous Greek cartoonist KYR is telling: a bull, whose horns are formed by the word "USA," refers to the President of that superpower country, while blond Europe, "The Old Lady," which alludes to the European Union, shouts "GO HOME." Brilliant not only as a composer but also as a verse-maker, Alexiadis masterfully plays with the popular myth to talk about the contemporary struggles for energy sources, oil, natural gas as well as the diplomatic relationships between the USA and the countries of the European Union. Even though neither the music rhythms nor the instruments are of Cretan origin, some of the inventive and imaginative lyrics do rhyme with the aforementioned *mandinades* format, being purposefully simplistic and childish or sharp and politicized.

Even though, as the composer explains in the program notes, "the typology and the idiomatic characteristics of the comic opera, such as the disguise, the illusion about one's identity, the adventurous couplings and the unexpected plot are followed," we observe that the poetic text is not being instrumented or sung as a classic opera buffa or a childish drama would, whereas predominant are the strophic songs and the performed prose. Similarly to how the ancient myth is bravely transformed into something more comic, the "classic," variable music styles create a uniquely pluralistic music and intercultural amalgam defined, paradoxically, both by stylistic harmony and idiosyncratic autonomy.

Zeuses Performed

All of the aforementioned compositions underline the significance of history for the Greeks as well as their strong connection to a place, the island of Crete. Mythologies surrounding Zeus are reborn through music and dance performances to show the concrete links between past and present through a chronological continuation, preserving one's tradition. Their stories remind us that history repeats itself and it is at the past, therefore, one needs to look back before proceeding further.

"Zeuses performed" allow rare glimpses into the various trajectories that connect a charter myth, so to speak, with detailed references to toponyms and significant sites that map out the island of Crete, according to Papalexandrou, "as an arena that constitutes an integral part of local memory, identity, and morality."[145]

Such references to the natural world are not only meant to reflect the fact that, traditionally, Cretans simply live in harmony with nature, but also to encourage them to do so. Even though each composer draws on different music elements, all works create sound- and memoryscapes that travel one to the island of Crete. They function ecopsychologically, creating a strong sense of place and belonging, which is not only physically and geographically, but also ideologically specified. Conclusively, this deeply felt sentiment also defined as *topophilia*[146] transforms those performed experiences into communal memories, which constitute a rich source of knowledge and identity and profoundly speak for a poetics of Cretanhood.

Bridging the Local with the *Glocal*

Dimitri Mitropoulos[147]

Dimitri Mitropoulos and *Fête Crétoise*

Dimitri Mitropoulos (1896-1960)[148] is mostly known as a conductor though he started off his music career by composing at a young age – his first works dating back to 1911, before he systematically even started studying advanced theory of music at the Athens Conservatory.[149] He left around forty-five compositions that can be divided into three, internally continuous, periods. The first, from 1911 to 1920, includes most of his works along with the composed for piano in 1919 *Fête Crétoise,* a piece where one witnesses his turn to "a more advanced, daring and innovative style that experiments novel ideas in harmony, rhythm and writing."[150]

Between 1916-1920, Mitropoulos served at the band of the Military Guard of Athens.[151] It was the *mandinada* "I will never cook broad beans again, I will never set up a pot," which Mitropoulos as a soldier heard in 1917 via his comrades-in-arms and *lyra* players,[152] that inspired him to compose the *Cretan Feast.*[153] Initially, the work was composed for solo piano, purposefully for his recital exam[154] with the title "For Crete, Feasts and Joys!"[155]

On March 11 1928, Mitropoulos presented that work in Athens, orchestrated by Nikos Skalkottas, via the Athens Conservatory Symphony Orchestra. That same work the Thessaloniki State Symphony Orchestra chose to present years after, on March 5 2010, at the Thessaloniki Concert Hall, and on October 12 2010, at the Konzerthaus Berlin (based on the fact that both composers had lived in Berlin and thus had many admirers there). [156]

Nikos Skalkottas orchestrated this work in Berlin during 1924-1928 and – this being his first orchestration for symphony orchestra – he did so with respect to the original source measure by measure and note by note under a few exceptions. However, in this early orchestration we find common elements that Skalkottas also used in his *36 Greek Dances* (1931-36; new orchestrations of many dances in 1949, and individual numbers arranged for other ensembles) and his ballet music, especially in his last ballets *Four Images* (1948; orchestrated from movements of the ballet *The Land and the Sea of Greece*) and *The Sea* (1948-49). There is a quite moving note where Mitropoulos asks Skalkottas to compose a part for a 3rd trombone and a tuba, something that Skalkottas, in fact, added a posteriori at the lower part of his manuscript.

The aforementioned work Mitropoulos has devoted to at that time Prime Minister of Greece, Cretan-born Eleftherios Venizelos, who then impersonated the Great Idea – meaning the restitution of Greece's former borders – which was marked by the Greek-Turkish 1919-1922 War and the Asia Minor Expedition. Politician Venizelos has oftentimes been associated with Cretan melodies such as the *pentozalis* dance. Mitropoulos also alludes to this Cretan melody through the vivid, initial accelerando of his *Cretan Feast*. Around that same time, composers, such as Marios Varvoglis, relied heavily on Greek folk tradition for their compositions[157] whereas others, like Manolis Kalomiris, had already set the foundation for the creation of a National Music School via ethnic operas like *The Masterbuilder*.

Greek composers, such as the generators and followers of the Greek National School of Music, i.e. Dionysios Lavrangas, George Lambelet, Manolis Kalomiris, Marios Varvoglis, Emilios Riadis, etc., responded to the invitation for re-birth by the Greek intellectual world and immediately connected with the vernacular language movement *(demoticism)* and the wars for liberation. When the First Balkan War (1912-13) started, Manolis Kalomiris and Spyridon Samaras (perhaps the most internationally lauded Greek composer before Dimitri Mitropoulos) were publishing even on newspapers their nationally revolutionary songs.[158] Sixteen-year old Mitropoulos, however, was still "dreaming at the seashore," "closing his eyes" to those national events as his teenage heart would not vibrate by patriotic sentiments that could consequently transform into music.[159]

Several musicians and musicologists have commented on the way Mitropoulos was utilizing Greek "folk music" in his compositions. According to Lambelet, "despite the general trend in Greece which, at that time was looking for its "national composer," Mitropoulos was not captivated by the "Sirens' of National Music"[160] whereas Thurneyssen "locates at Mitropoulos' *Greek Sonata for Piano* the beginnings of the formation of a national music that was methodologically different, however, from the one other composers had followed so far."[161] Lastly, musicologist Kostios observes how in Mitropoulos' *Feast* the element of folk music is upgraded in an attempt not to create a "National Music School" but to follow the path of a "European exoticism." More specifically, he writes:

> The materials borrowed from folk music play a rather decorative role, a procedure which paves a new road to the democratization of music, a democratization involving the non-discriminatory acceptance of elements of a "lower-class" provenance, an inward democratization of music per se, not confined to the ways and means of its dissemination. In this context, Mitropoulos converges with Béla Bartók. Having crossed the narrow straits of neo-classicism and the Vienna School, the overlooked Greek composer emerges not only as a pioneer for his own time but also as a forerunner of a much later era, so that he would appear very much modern even today.[162]

In the *Cretan Feast,* Mitropoulos felt the intense need to express his personal experience under the romantic influence of composers such as Glazunov.[163] Toward this end, he used melodic inspiration, luxuriant late-romantic idioms, daring assonances and intense sound colorings, which reveal his willingness to free himself from the "school regulations" and discover other expressive means. Mitropoulos' setting of the Cretan lyrics to music did take into consideration the character of that poetry: he purposefully dressed them in *pyrrichean* rhythms that evoke the world of a feast and attest to heroic pianism and fervency in an attempt to explore the potentialities of traditional Greek music as a source to be more thoroughly integrated into contemporary compositions. The work's dynamics emphasize the main melodic lines and remind one how poetry would sound like, in quick and tense rhythms. The piano composition is exceptionally demanding, both technically and musically.[164] Let us not forget that Mitropoulos himself was a brilliant pianist, who also brought forth the rhythmic element, essential for the Greek song in its three-dimensional entity, namely speech, music, dance.[165]

A transcription of the music theme Mitropoulos based his composition on can be traced in Georgios Hadjidakis 1958 book *Cretan Music*[166] under the category of comic songs. That song we listen at a popular 1975 recording by legendary Cretan singer Nikos Xylouris "I sing what I remember" under the title "To love me, to love me not." Though both Hadjidakis and Xylouris *mandinades*-lyrics vary, prevalent is the same idea: a girl who, like a devil, keeps driving a guy crazy. According to Hadjidakis, in older times, that song functioned as a theatrical play and a means of entertainment. The leader of the song used to hold a towel or a kerchief and imitate certain words of the poem, whereas the audience would sing and repeat the lyrics.[167] That Hadjidakis transcription composer Nikiforos Nevrakis (b. 1940) has also elaborated in his choral composition *I Don't Cook Broad Beans Anymore* for solo tenor and mixed choir a cappella.[168]

Cretan Feast

Philosophically, Mitropoulos' *Feast* is characterized by optimism which is traced to his youth. It reflects ideals of what it means to be a Cretan as expressed in the folk poetry stemming from that society through a celebration: "Honor life to the fullest!" Mitropoulos, by devoting his work to Venizelos, makes a deliberate choice of Cretan focus.

Furthermore, his composition reveals a spiritual approach, which we could trace on his religious sentiments he was well-known for – let us not forget the tremendous impression St. Francis of Assize had on him. Mitropoulos is using a rather classical approach, which is obvious in both the piano solo work but also the Skalkottas instrumentation, which makes use of the full classical orchestra and its symphonic approach. He is not, however, making use of traditional, Cretan or other Greek instruments, even though he implies dancing rhythms. His work shows a strong preference for the chordophones and aerophones and relies on them to perform several variations of the lyric parts but also for conversing while improvising on basic melodies.

Conclusively, this work derives its nucleus from folk poetry and the Cretan *man-dinada*, more specifically, transforming it, however, from a verbal to a sonic matter. In other words, it purposefully suppresses the words giving unintentional initiative to the sound. Its music language comprises a sound amalgam which blends ethnic pasts, functioning as lingua-franca. The civilization the composer feels nostalgic for is undoubtedly the Cretan – as the selected rhythmic and melodic soundscapes declare.

Classical music composers have frequently looked for music inspiration at folk cultures. Mitropoulos relied on folk poetry from the island of Crete and set that strictly local lore to music by transforming it into sounds, creating, this way, a universal musical language which does not lose, however, its ties with its roots. Ultimately and subconsciously he proposed an alternative way of including verbal materials in music compositions by relying on and viewing one's ethnic past as an original source of creation.

Through such an innovative look at folk music, language barriers can be abolished by transforming words into sounds and thus appealing to a larger audience. Composers are invited to re-invent, re-structure and re-compose traditional music themes, preserving their energy and fineness, the authenticity of their primordial model, their vibration and soul, following the paths of the anonymous folk composers. This way a dialogue between the past and the present is being achieved while a new local-and-global *(glocal)* identity is being created. Potentially, here a tradition of the future lies, at the artful orchestration, namely, of our new *folk* reality, that of multiculturalism, through bridging local and global voices and transcending hard borders via soft, music-poetic ways.[169]

Maria Callas

The legendary Greek-American opera star Maria Callas was the daughter of Greek immigrants to the United States. She was born in New York on December 2 1923 as Cecilia Sophia Anna Kalogeropoulou. Her father set up a pharmacy in New York City and changed the family name to Callas. Callas was a dramatic coloratura soprano and the best-known opera singer of the post-World War II period. She self-willingly transformed from a chubby, painfully shy and awkward girl into the magnificent Callas presence. She combined an impressive bel canto technique with great dramatic gifts, being an extremely versatile singer with a wide range repertoire.

Her mother, with whose ambitions Callas clashed, made her take piano lessons. In 1937, she went with her children to Athens, and got stuck there during WWII. Callas enrolled at the Athens Conservatory in 1940 where the well-known coloratura soprano Elvira de Hidalgo was teaching vocals. When she was barely 16, she began singing in leading roles and gave public concerts during the difficult years that Athens was occupied by the Germans. More specifically, she sang Santuzza in the Athens Conservatory's performance of *Cavalleria Rusticana*. Her first concert in Athens she gave in 1940 as Beatrice in Suppé's *Boccaccio*, in 1942 as Tosca and in 1944 as Leonore in *Fidelio*. Callas became the most famous pupil of that Spanish opera pedagogue.

Even though she received her musical education in Greece, Callas established her career in Italy. Returning to her father in New York in 1945, she was heard by tenor Giovanni Zenatello, who engaged her for her Italian debut, Ponchielli's *La Gioconda* in Verona in 1947, at the famous Verona Arena open air opera stadium, by the foothills of the Alps. Conductor Tullio Serafin directed her in that performance. He too recognized her extraordinary talent. In 1949, when the singer for the leading role of Elvira in Bellini's *I Puritani* fell ill, Serafin substituted Callas, and her ascendancy took off meteorically. In Verona in 1947, another man fell in love with the 23-year old Greek diva: the nondescript, older than her, wealthy industrialist, Giovanni Battista Meneghini. He gave up his brick-making business to marry and manage Callas' career. However, she left him for flamboyant Aristotle Onassis in 1957 (Callas denied this whereas others support she was child barren). They divorced in 1959.

Due to her marriage to Meneghini, whose surname she incorporated with her own during the period of her marriage (1949-59), she added to her repertory Bellini's "Amina," Donizetti's "Lucia" and Verdi's "Leonora," "Violetta" and "Gilda." She was in constant demand whenever rare and vocally taxing operas of the older school were produced, such as Gluck's *Alceste* and *Iphigénie en Tauride* and Cherubini's *Médée*. Her greatest triumphs were won as "Norma," "Medea," "Anne Boleyn," "Lucia," "Lady Macbeth," "Violetta" and "Tosca." Many of those roles she repeated in the major opera houses of the world, where her fame reached a level that recalled the careers of Caruso and Chaliapin. Callas made her Covent Garden debut in 1952 and her American one at Chicago in 1954 and at the New York Met in 1956 (both as Bellini's "Norma").[170]

Callas' voice, especially during the early 1950s, was in itself an impressive instrument. It had a penetrating individual quality, rich variety of color and a great agility in florid music. Her musicianship was impeccable, her insight remarkable and acting ability exceptional, so that she presented her roles as organic wholes. She was hailed as "La Divina"; Leonard Bernstein called her "The Bible of Opera"; Franco Zaffirelli, who directed her in operas and made a movie entitled *Callas Forever*, called her the "Michelangelo of Singers."

Even though she was forced to deal with the exigencies of wartime poverty and myopia left her nearly blind on stage, Callas was an authority in all that she did on the stage and in every phrase that she uttered. She endured a huge weight loss mid-way of her career, and, though the results made her svelte and glamorous, it is thought to have contributed to her vocal decline, causing a premature end of her career.

At a party in Venice hosted by Elsa Maxwell, Callas met Onassis. A man of enormous power and charisma, Onassis charmed the great diva taking her aboard his luxurious yacht and introducing her to world leaders like Churchill. Callas had a 9-year affair with the great tycoon. However, Onassis ended the affair to pursue and eventually marry the newly widowed Jacqueline Kennedy after the assassination of President John Kennedy in 1963. Callas and Onassis were global newsmakers for decades till their tragic end.

Callas is reported to have confessed: "First I lost my weight, then I lost my voice; and then I lost Onassis." She retired from stage in 1965 in the leading role in Puccini's *Tosca* at Covent Garden, London. She continued to record and gave concerts as late as 1974. She also worked as a producer and teacher. After a turbulent life, she became reclusive and died alone in Paris on September 16 in 1977 at the young age of 53, 2 years after the tragic death of Onassis. Her ashes were flown to Greece and scattered in the Aegean Sea. For millions of people, she was the focus of unparalleled fascination, the enigma of a highly publicized and yet intensely private personality. She believed that "you are born an artist or you are not. And you stay an artist, even if your voice is less of a firework." She herself did so!

Ross Daly

Harmonizing the Cretan *lyra*

Tall and thin, with long, gray-white hair and a thick moustache, a sincere smile, plenty of sincere words in a Cretan accent, and armed with a warm heart and lots of kindness, Daly invites us on several journeys of sound and silence, in the realm of music. He welcomes us and offers invitations to meet him at his friends' houses, at his house, at concerts. Based on and acting from Crete, Daly provides us with a good example of a living organism in continuous motion, inspiring and encouraging as well as designating a deep meaning regarding the idea of country and homeland. His work impersonates the goal of music, thus an alternative, philosophical and dialectic worldview, toward human understanding, communicating and cooperating in cultural and other levels.

Although of Irish descent, Daly thinks of himself as an artist of no nation, an eternal traveler. Among the variety of string instruments he plays, he particularly caresses the Cretan *lyra*. A man who espouses no national identity, Daly plays the *lyra* in a style based on all the experiences he gains both from his professional training and travel experiences. As a result, the *lyra*, a musical instrument that is the trademark of Cretan music, functions as a passport to a "non-native" music, played by a non-Cretan musician. At the same time, Daly, a man of no specific national or musical identity, identifies strongly with an instrument of a specific place. This allows Daly to give to the *lyra* his own voice, expanding beyond the local borders of Crete, allowing his music to pass safely through the customs and traditions of "authentic" Cretan music.

During childhood, Daly studied cello and classical guitar; in other words, he had what he calls a "normal classical education on that stuff." However, he thought he was "not particularly talented in cello," that he was "not in that great mood for it," so he abandoned it. "With the guitar, so to say, I became more bonded." But neither the classical guitar nor the cello ever enabled him to fully express himself; this tradition was very "suffocating" for him, "especially the way it used to be taught then."[171]

In the 1960s, he happened to be in San Francisco, "where many interesting sounds of contemporary music existed, thus, rock and all this." He listened to those sounds and liked them: "I myself was playing them on the guitar, starting with blues till I do not know what else." Still, though, something in all that did not much suit him. He remembers: "The first time I listened to Ravi Shankar playing the sitar, I was very impressed and liked it immediately. I saw a music that had all the structure and discipline one finds in classical music, but at the same time had lots of freedom one sees in other kinds."[172]

This was his first contact with Indian music that sparked his interest on non-European music traditions and turned his attention eastward. "I was trying to do with

At Houdetsi, Ross Daly informally improvising on his sympathetic _lyra._

my guitar several things I heard from the sitar and from other eastern instruments.
I was collecting records and was listening to them – Persian, Turkish, Greek, Arabic,
whatever you want," Daly said.[173] Soon he realized that, if he wanted to get himself

seriously engaged with those traditions, he should occupy himself with the instruments they employed, because the guitar was not the proper instrument to render their music.

Daly finished school in England where he was born (29 September 1952) and partially raised,[174] and took his first classes of Indian music at a college there. The classical guitar studies began to subside. He concentrated on the sitar and went to India for sitar lessons. Around that time, at the age of eighteen, he had his first experience with Cretan music:

> [It is] a hot summer evening in August of 1970 when, during the course of a brief stay in Crete, I am taken to a neighboring village to a *paniyiri* (feast) – somewhere in Mesara – to listen for the first time in my life to Cretan traditional folk music. I have no idea what I am going to hear; all I know is that it is not going to resemble the urban *bouzouki* tradition, which is all that I knew of Greek music. I had almost no knowledge of rural Greek folk music to prepare me for the surprise that I was going to experience.[175]

After this musical encounter, Daly continued his classical music studies in England with deep thoughts of abandoning them. He made a stop in Crete again in 1972 and, meanwhile, he also traveled to Turkey, Persia, Afghanistan, thirsty for learning their musics. Around 1973, he felt capable of playing the Indian sitar (plucked stringed instrument) and the Afghan *rabab* (string instrument belonging to the lute family), but he run out of money. He returned to England in 1974 and worked as a street musician.

In 1975, one more trip aimed India. However, Daly recalled the Cretan *lyra* and gave a second thought to his plans: "There things are more resting, relieving. I will stay for some time to engage myself with the *lyra*, to see where things will lead me."[176] He spent time on the island studying but also making money so that he could continue to India. In Chania, he opened a coffee shop with some friends. In the summer, he worked as a fisherman. At the same time, he also started his music wanderings with the *lyra*, entering profoundly into its world. Since then, Crete and Greece became his permanent abode and his "chair" has transferred to Greece, his first encounter with Cretan music proven to be something quite unique:

> My first experience of Cretan music was definitely an experience which surprised, confused and certainly amazed me. I had never heard anything similar, and I remember that I was very much impressed by this listening, because I immediately liked it very much.[177] I never make qualitative comparisons between different music traditions because I believe them to be so subjective as to be without any real meaning, but I would go as far as to say that my first experience of Cretan music is definitely an experience which surprised, confused, and certainly amazed me. I could clearly hear very distinct influences from a wide range of eastern Mediterranean and North Afri-

can sources, but it had a character all of its own, which distinguished it from all of these other idioms.[178]

Daly has researched the rich and varied "classical" and folk traditions with master musicians from all over the world. For example, he studied classical guitar with Brent Knowland and Patrick Benham, sitar with Jachindranath Saha, *rabab* with Mohammad Omar, Cretan *lyra* with Kostas Mountakis and *kemenche* with Ihsan Özgen. While in Crete, he constantly grasped on occasions where he could go and listen to *lyra* music performed live. By time, he started performing with other musicians, gaining experiences but without making this his profession: he did not intend to become a Cretan *lyra* player; his goal was to learn to play the *lyra* well.

Sometime in the early 1980s, Daly came to Heraklion, the capital of Crete, to perform with various musicians (like Psaroyiannis, the brother of Nikos and Antonis Xylouris). He created his first group and music workshop, *Labyrinth*, and started giving traditional music concerts. Initially, he concentrated on the many different traditions and cultures which have influenced the music of Crete in the course of the centuries. In his improvisations and compositions he tried to work out those different cultural tendencies within Cretan music. "Not belonging to anywhere," he claims, is an advantage. But he has never abandoned his education in and experience with classical music.

One of the CDs they then made, *Ross Daly and the Labyrinth: Mitos* (Thread), illustrates some of the music traditions they worked with. For example, the track "Thalassa Mavri" (Black Sea) opens with improvisation in North Indian Rāg Bhairavi, on the Afghani lute, the *rabab*. According to the liner notes, Daly plays it "in the style and technique of an Arab *oud* (pear-shaped plucked lute) and an Indian *sarod* (large string instrument), combined with Greek and Turkish phrasing."[179] Other instruments also featured are the Turkish *kemenche* (string bowed music instrument), the Persian *zarb* (goblet drum) and the Indian *tambura* (or *tanpura*; drone string instrument).

In 1982, he recorded a disc with Vasilis and Mitsos Stavrakakis, *Oneirou Topoi* (Dreamlands), which reflected what he was doing then at concerts. In 1984, they recorded a second disc, under the title *Lavirinthos* (Labyrinth).

Daly went to Athens and returned to Chania, working and teaching at a private music school, while at the same time practicing and playing with other musicians. In 1986, he made a solo recording which included music other than Cretan, such as Ottoman classical pieces as well as some of his own compositions. Daly was welcomed in Athens in 1987-1988 and was offered many jobs. He moved there to collaborate with other musicians and work outside the borders of Cretan music. He continued teaching, recording, performing, learning and traveling.[180]

In the summer of 2003, Daly moved back to Crete and started a music movement at the village of Houdetsi (located in a distance of 20 km south of the city of

Heraklion, in 450m altitude). Today, an old village two-story stone manor hosts and exhibits his music instrument collection, whereas many music meetings, workshops and various concerts of distinguished music leaders from several countries take place at its courtyard in the summers, with Cretan music always in the center. This way, both Daly's inner wish for constant learning and personal growth came true and Crete became the focal point of such a rewarding initiative.

Studying abroad in Crete-Greece: With Ivan Varimezov, master player of the Bulgarian bagpipe (*gaida*), and his students, at the "Labyrinth Musical Workshop" held annually at the village of Houdetsi.

Mobile music customs

Daly's music creates flexible places, harmonizing musicians who are contingently brought together to produce performances in certain places at certain times. His compositions and work prove that places are indeed dynamic – "places of movement."[181] Through the *Labyrinth* world music workshops, seminars and concerts he constantly organizes with the participation of various musicians who gather and perform on the island of Crete, Daly manages to create mobile music macrocosms within a specific societal microcosm, proving that "places are like ships, moving around and not necessarily staying in one location."[182]

A well-known, respected master and an acclaimed virtuoso on a range of string instruments, including the Cretan *lyra*, the *kemenche*, the Greek *laouto* (lute), the Turkish *saz*, the Arab *oud*, the Persian *tar* and the Indian *sarangi*, and always in motion, Daly, started searching for his own sound, wondering:

> I am not Cretan, not even a good sample of Irish I am, as I do not have a country I can say that I was born and raised there. However, I want to play music, I cannot say by definition that I identify with a specific music tradition. I like and I love various traditions, I am seriously engaged with them, so good, all this work, where does it lead me?[183]

Looking for an answer, Daly shapes his own playing of the Cretan *lyra*, where he embodies all he knows (playing technique, instrumentation, formal and rhythmic structure) about *lyras* that belong, for instance, to the Cretan, Turkish and Bulgarian traditions. He comprehends that Mediterranean history is impressively rich and that Hellenism developed into what might be called the first historical experience of "globalization."[184] Moreover, he has realized that the Mediterranean is a mosaic of cultural mixing and borrowing, a privileged and fertile model for various music interchanges,[185] and, thus, he researches the art of music through a "syncretic" attitude.

Daly has also experimented on the construction of "his" *lyra*. For instance, he substituted the metal heads for the long wooden pegs thus allowing the instrument to rest more steadily on the chest and therefore free movement of the left hand. He devised and constructed "sympathetic" *lyras* (his current one having around 18 strings). Unique is his performance on the *tarhu*, an instrument created by Australian Peter Biffin, with 5 playing and 12 long sympathetic strings, capable of playing a large range of styles from both East and West.

Daly recognizes his Cretan *lyra* teacher, Kostas Mountakis, as a "very positive and important person in his development." He comments on a trip where he joined Mountakis to perform Cretan music in London, and specifically the moment they happened to be at a house with Indian musicians, improvising on the *lyra*. During this informal music happening, the Indians heard something, they found common ground, and called Mountakis "great guru."

The aforementioned example showed Daly how Indians, or any good musicians, even when know nothing about Cretan music, they can understand, feel and, at the end, identify with somebody who plays well. It revealed to him how Cretan music can be disseminated, heard and favored by people all over the world and how musicians who have a good relationship with their civilizations are not closed and opposed to different sounds. Instead, they are more open, automatically gaining a sense of respect towards everything which is being created and is genuine.

In his improvisations, Daly uses phrasing that is identifiably Cretan as well as Irish, Indian, even Tuvan. He believes that the *lyra* should enter the Irish, Indian or Tuvan music tradition carrying into each and embracing the uniqueness of this instrument. As a result, he invites Indian musicians, for instance, and gives concerts with them in Crete and elsewhere in Greece.

In musical journeys-experiments of this type, Daly does not think of himself as a characteristic example of a Cretan *lyra* player. For instance, he embodies his own playing into one Indian piece and performs Indian elements on the *lyra*. Simultaneously, he "grasps" popular, traditional Cretan melodies and arranges them in ways that match with that specific Indian piece. As a result, he improvises using phraseology from Cretan pieces, but even from some Irish ones.[186]

Daly views Cretan music as one of many spiritual musical traditions in search of a common origin of nature. He strongly defends that "Crete is unlike any other place in the world" thus has made the island the basis and point of reference for his music travels. Moreover, for him, music is not any man's creation; it is not even the creation of mankind as a whole. Rather, it is a gift to mankind:

> Civilization belongs to the realm of lived experience. Inspiration and initiation do not belong to this realm. Instead, they merely leave imprints in the world of experience, which serve as catalysts for the awakening of the search and the longing for the source of inspiration, of music, of experience. It is through the awakening of this longing that we can see the primary and indeed fundamental difference between this music and any other expressive arts, which utilize the medium of sound.[187]

When Crete meets Tuva

The group Daly initiated and now leads has included at various times musicians from a wide range of different ethnic backgrounds. The members of *Labyrinth* do not necessarily share a common ideology or philosophy; they are rather united in a common spirit and, of course, love for music. For instance, in 2003, Daly invited *Huun-Huur-Tu,* the quartet which is Tuva's unofficial music culture ambassador and representative and which brings to the world the unusual tradition of throat-singing, and gave concerts with them in Crete and elsewhere in Greece and Cyprus.

This collaborative and on-going project is called *White Dragon* and consists of the voices and the instruments from the steppes of Tuva; the vocals of Cretan Giorgos Xylouris and Greek Spyridoula Baka; the Iranian family percussion trio "Chemirani Ensemble" on instruments such as the *zarb*, the *daff*, the *bendir* and the *udu*; and the wide variety of sounds introduced by *Labyrinth* performed on the Cretan *lyra*, the *rabab* (bowed string instrument), the *saz* (plucked string instrument), the *tarhu* (new form of spike fiddle created by Peter Biffin), the *ney* (long, end-blown flute), the *laouto*, the *santouri* and the *clarinet*.

Tuvan throat singers are rock stars in Greece. Their fame started with soccer and a television advertisement for the country's most popular soccer lottery, in which a barber shaves a man's head to resemble a soccer ball, with its black and white patches, to the accompaniment of a soundtrack featuring "Eki Attar" (Good Horses), a popular piece of the quartet Huun-Huur-Tu.[188] The name of that group means "sun-propeller," the vertical separation of light that often occurs just after sunrise or before sunset, an image which illustrates their refraction of sound in their peculiar guttural harmonies.[189] *Huun-Huur-Tu* is an innovative group because all members sing as one ensemble, something not traditionally done in Tuvan music.

The Tuvan *igil* is a type of upright fiddle strung with two thick horse-hair strings. The fingering technique of the left hand is reminiscent of that of the *lyra* with the notes being produced by pressure with the nails being applied to the side of the string. The Tuvan *byzanchi* is a very unusual bowed instrument with four horse-hair strings and a double bow which passes between the 1st and 2nd as well as between the 3rd and 4th strings simultaneously, and which also utilizes the fingernail technique for the left hand. Thus, on both the Cretan and the Tuvan instruments the resulting sound is rich in overtones (although not very loud). The music is not pitch- but timbre- centered,[190] producing, thus, a very strong, sharp tone, and facilitating a wide range of embellishments which considerably enrich the melodies being played.

Daly embodies his own playing into Tuvan pieces and performs Tuvan elements on the *lyra*. He also takes popular, traditional Cretan melodies and arranges them in Tuvan-friendly ways by employing pentatonic scales, the most obvious common ground between Tuvan and Cretan music, along with rhythms that suggest horses. He is not sure "that's what the rhythms initially represented in Cretan music, but there's unquestionably a similarity, and the Iranian *zarb* works very well with Tuvan music, the way it marks the rhythm."[191]

Ecologizing … tradition

Apart from the commonalities in instruments, techniques and blending of sounds, there is a perceptually spiritual element which connects those two traditions as well. For Tuvans, the sounds of nature have been their school, their university.[192] Cretan folk song lyrics use images borrowed from the physical environment too, such as the eagles or the mountains. Tuvans perform this music partially as an offering to spirits,[193] and as pastoralists, use sound mimesis stimulated by perceptual immediacy.[194]

Symbolically speaking, "when you play music, you've taken from nature, and you give back to it; everything passes through you, and in the end, you're back to a zero, a big and beautiful zero.[195] After all, the main influence between musicians is freedom, like water running in the mountains and the birds flying in the clear skies.[196]

Daly has no country, but he feels home at music. If music has the power to bring to life and evoke nostalgia for a place,[197] then, for Daly, this is a space he has not seen or associated himself with, but which, in the world of his sonic imagination, is real.

Perhaps this is the power and enchantment multi-composition imposes on him: the building of a house which no living person has seen, but which, in the intellectual world, acquires material existence and, thus, functions as cultural memory.

"Silent," Syn-cretic Syn-thesis

Daly turns an innovative look into Cretan songs, abolishing language barriers by transforming words into sounds and thus appealing to a larger audience. His music is defined under the premise of silence, or, perhaps, the initiative of the sounds. The lyrics to the music he plays are absent, and even when they are present, the meaning of the performance is located at the sonic result. Consequently, his musical language is an aesthetic and not a verbal amalgam of rich and diverse sonic elements, as he expects musician and listener to resign from their position as artist, creator or individual in order to achieve an internal state of silence and to become the instrument of this music.

His compositions, at the reception level, are esoteric. There are a number of musical components in them which evoke the spiritual, such as the drones, the repetitiveness and the acceleration. Many of them also work in time through a sense of progression via repetition and building up, a central feature in the Cretan musical tradition.

He is (almost) invisible on stage and his message is found on the sound he produces. Paradoxically, perhaps, I perceive Daly's music as a… silent art: the way Daly articulates music sounds is detached from the world of ideas and words, and what, in my view, is the determinant of his prolific compositions is the synergy and coexistence of multiple sounds "in-harmony."

Daly's whole work questions the East-West synthesis and perceives Greek music as part of a wider eastern cultural plateau which stretches as far as Central Asia and North Africa, providing a model to those looking for alternatives to ethnocentric or regionalist narratives. Though often departing from Cretan norms, Daly recasts the Cretan repertoire into a dynamic interaction with relative music vocabularies, suggesting that, if cultures are compatible, so are people. In a sense, he uses his compositions as passports that will enable him to transcend customs and borderlines.

He stops at no borders, performing and creating his own music universe leading his audiences to magic musical voyages beyond multicultural fashions, trying to break down as many boundaries as he can, and so to offer himself as the space of a meeting between the many musics that have deeply influenced him. He is not interested in anyone's ethnic civilization. He believes we all have different aspects of the same thing, with some specialties and variations related to the place:

> The differences are superficial enough and it is, like when we say, that we want to study the plants of a region, then, we definitely have to study the specific form of nature, namely, which plants grow here and which there.

However, we never forget that our subject is the whole nature. The same happens with music: it is something that unites the whole world, but, in different places, it exists in different forms.[198]

Daly's model

Many researchers argue that music can be used as a means of a) transcending the limitations of our own place in the world, b) constructing trajectories rather than boundaries across space,[199] and c) esoteric persuasion. Viewed in those contexts, Daly can be "legally" considered a citizen of a "between world musical aesthetics" which is "based on the concept that intercultural collaboration, hybridization and crossover are not negative experiences if directed from within."[200]

Daly creates soundscapes, musics that exist side by side in the lives and imaginations of so many people. His music invites us to an imaginative travel based on auditory memories. His compositions are flexible, accommodating local detail while allowing for translocal connections. His work shifts the emphasis from the performer to the produced sound, and important, therefore, is its cultural production and the dynamic music dialogue of the past with the present. Stressing the links of an earlier history *in spite* of national histories, Daly's representation seems to conjure up a pre-modern cultural *koine*. In reality, his worldview is post-nationalist in that it proposes a new identity for being in the present.

Moreover, Daly's music "becomes an anchor for understanding diverse human settings" as "what emerges is a narrative that accommodates many musical styles within an inclusive, interactive context."[201] His new musical language is "g-local," because it functions as a connecting bridge amongst diverse neighbors, in a clearly multicultural era. His vision is one of openness and inclusion. Music itself has a unique unifying power and can become the vehicle of deep communion among people despite national boundaries or differences, breaking down dualities such as "us" and "them."

In a sense, Daly reconstructs concepts such as "home," "community" and "locality." Therefore, I view him as an innovator of a local level, who re-creates a reformative, desirable tradition, by adding to it a new dimension, in which the dichotomy of global versus local is more carefully defined.[202]

All in all, Daly coins a music language determined by esoteric persuasion, fluidity, hybridity and multivocality. If mobilities involve complex "hybrid geographies" of humans and non-humans that contingently enable people and materials to move and to hold their shape as they move across various regions,[203] then Daly's model has successfully served as a catalyst for Cretan music to open up to the contemporary era, to meet with its neighbors and with the rest of the world, by simultaneously transcending the limitation of its place and gaining a position in the world. Viewed through contemporary translational, complex, Mediterranean lenses, this example can lead many others to creative synergies and trajectories as well as to the cultivation of soft borders and bridges rather than boundaries across place.

Ross Daly orchestrates our new reality: multiculturalism. He invites us all to become world-citizens, where home is the globe and our heart. He harmonically reminds us that we will survive not by denying the existence of the different, of the other, but by creatively synthesizing it with our heritage and our philadelphic, philanthropic, syncretic, and... critically Cretan hospitality.

Chapter 3

The Poetics and the Ecology of Greek Singing

Musings

Overture

The word "music" is Greek and relates to what the ancient 9 Muses,[204] daughters of Zeus and Memory, were cultivating, namely a variety of arts (e.g. theater, poetry and dance) and sciences (e.g. mathematics and astronomy). "Rhythm" and "melody" are terms that etymologically stem from those times as well, when music was viewed both as art and a subject of scientific-philosophical inquiry.

Music in Greece offered relaxation and entertainment but also had a central role in civic, religious life which, in extension, was believed to influence human behavior. Plato, for instance, in his *Republic* and *Laws* spoke for types of music that should be allowed in an enlightened civilization whereas Aristotle in his *Politics* advocated for the educational function of music which has an apparent effect in the development of "ethics."

In 1859, the Greek scholar Spyridon Zambelios (1815-1881) published a lengthy disquisition on the origins of the modern Greek word *tragoudo*. He argued that it is a derivative of the classical Greek *tragodia*, namely tragedy.[205] One should not forget how and when the study of folklore as a discipline developed so as to understand why Greek folklorists studied songs and compared them to ancient Greek meters, poetic forms, modes as well as to the Byzantine ecclesiastic music.

But, have the songs of the modern Greeks retained the spirit and essence of Attic tragedy? Potential evidence may lie on the view of human happiness which occurs again and again in Greek songs along with insistent reminders of eventual death. Heritage may exist in the wedding village songs that have preserved a tragic essence – where the sophistication of Europe had failed to do so.

Furthermore, there is a formal analogy of ritual and personal passage between marriage and death Greek folk rites. *Moirologia* (dirges) are distinctive by virtue of their special context (funerals, graveside visits and sometimes memorial services), of the behavior associated with them (violent displays of grief), of the performer's sex (almost always female) and of their musical forms. They have ritual dimentions opposed to the verbal texts alone. As such, they generally have both generalized (formal) and particular (person-specific) referents in the social universe of the community.

Wedding songs do conform to patterns associated with dirges. The groom's family provides the couple with a house to live in which entails the bride's physical departure from her natal home. The songs marking the bride's departure often share prosodic, musical and verbal features with the dirges while the iconography of the two genres frequently exhibits similarities. Death may be represented as a marriage with the earth (hence the priest symbolically pours soil over the body of the deceased person). In Crete, the funeral of a young, unmarried person is marked by the wedding symbolism of white sugared almonds. The Greek word for "in-laws" depicts the one who mourns (hence from the verb *pentho*, to mourn, the words *pe(n)theros*, father in law, and *pe(n)thera*, mother in law). It is the female kin of the bride who displays their grief at her departure in the laments they perform.

In Greek singing and lamenting we observe musical performance in opposition to ordinary speech. In English, one can "sing a song" or "sing a lament." In Greek, one can do neither; but one can "say" either genre. The Greek term *kaimos* is used of any intense emotion that is revealed in strongly demonstrative behavior. Such behavior may include enthusiasm as well as intense grief. All in all, dirges are in certain significant respects like wedding songs.

Greek folk songs used to be an indispensable part of daily life, functioning as a means of self-expression. They reflect on the basic philosophies of daily life, the regional traditions and beliefs, the social complexities, while they also express certain beauties of Greek nature, love, happiness, profound sorrow, life and death. Based on their content, folklorists divide them into several categories.

There is great similarity and diversity within Greek folk songs. Vocally, they are mainly monophonic and instrumentally heterophonic. Irregular meters are oftentimes found in the melodies that accompany them. Ornamentation and improvisation are key characteristics of that tradition whereas oral transmission versus memorization is the main means through which that wealth of knowledge has been passing down from older to newer generations. That process has resulted to numerous variations that were created hundreds of years before Greek folk songs even started being collected, edited and published.

Place-conscious Education

Education can serve the social and ecological well-being of particular places. This intervention is important for place-based educational theory and suggests the possibility of broader discussions about education as a means for dealing with interrelated social and ecological issues and for effecting socioecological change wherein the social and ecological are held to be inextricably interdependent.[206]

Poetry and music are important and pervasive in Greek students' everyday life. They have entered technology in many ways, as electronic greeting cards, facebook groups, twitter and text phone messages. Thus, they can constitute a tool in the educators' hands which, in a unique way, holistically develop students' personality. In other words, they are able of promoting the spiritual, moral, social and cultural development of students as well as their mental and physical development. Nowadays, those art forms are a subject of school curricula in different parts of the world, expected to also develop students' skills, knowledge and attitudes that will eventually transform them into responsible and active citizens.

With an eye towards future generations, art and music education aim at raising students' awareness so that the way one lives affects the world around one's *ecos*. It is crucial for students to acknowledge that all aspects of the environment, local and global, living and non-living, relate and influence each other and therefore need to be sustained in harmony. Concurrently, it is equally crucial for students to acknowledge that they constitute part of the environment with which they are "inextricably interdependent."[207] In other words, students and the environment have a symbiotic relationship; they affect the environment and the environment affects them. It is this symbiotic relationship that students need to, first, acknowledge and, secondly, sustain in balance for otherwise the consequences will be disastrous for all.

This way, students are given opportunities to respect their own *ecos* so as to be able and appreciate the *ecos* of others as well. Students' sustainable development also becomes an aid to their intercultural understanding for issues of identity and belonging, similarity and difference, human rights and responsibilities. Thus, all aspects of the students' identity become meaningful for they are connected to several aspects of their environment. Students acknowledge the critical relationship between poetry, music and *ecos* and learn to create opportunities to relate to other cultures. In order to place the aforementioned issues in education practice, educators need to re-conceptualize their pedagogical values, aims, content and practices. This re-conceptualization of education provides the basis for establishing the students' sustainable development.

Greek folk poetry holds a strong potential to sensitize students to the environmental or ecological aspects of a place through which they learn and discuss numerous topics, issues and problems. Specific subject-matters which stem out of Greek rhymes may include human pain and nature, endless love and nature, fate and nature, religion and nature, musical instruments associated with feelings of love and happiness, distant love and color in traditional costumes as well as migration and economic poverty.

Upon reading and analyzing Greek folk poetry, the educator can ask the students to identify and discuss how the symbiotic relationship between nature and man is conveyed as a result of the specific culture and time. For instance, students might be asked to explore how locality influences composing, to comment on the use of natural elements and how they illustrate certain occasions, to compose a song that portrays various feelings, to relate objects from their environment with meaningful aspects of their life, to simulate sounds that portray the sentiments of people from other parts of the world, to specify how certain lyrics have social and economic associations, to talk about the moods of the composer as well as to produce sounds from their local context and relate them with certain emotions.

In short, students' knowledge, skills and understanding towards sustainable development are broadened since Greek poetry conveys the importance that nature plays in local and global cultures but also in personal identity. Educators could create interactive kits through which students learn to value and care for their home by a) identifying lyrics that have social and cultural associations, b) recognizing how locality influences composing, c) commenting on the use of natural elements to express feelings, d) discussing how voices and instruments are associated with certain feelings, e) relating objects from their environment with meaningful aspects of their life, f) simulating sounds that portray feelings of people from other parts of the world in specific time and place, g) producing sounds from their local context related to feelings, and h) composing their own rhymes or songs.

For example, on July 25 2005, I recorded my paternal grandmother, Eleni, composing *mandinades* at her summer house in Tsoutsouros, somewhere in central-south Crete.[208] I entitled and published an excerpt of that project as "Life is an ocean." As we were sitting at the terrace of the house, right in front of the beach, gazing at the endless blue, my grandmother started giving me advice for life, using proverbial speech, all in the Cretan traditional *mandinades* format. Amongst those lyrics were the following: a) "I sit and I meditate, as if I am about to paint a hagiography, why is the sea water salty but the fish saltless?" and b) "I enjoy sitting and crying by the beach, and narrate each one of my burdens per wave."

To the aforementioned example, one could ask one's audience to identify sounds from the natural environment, such as, for instance, the ocean water heard on the background of the recording, and then proceed to comment on the feelings of the composer, which in this case is my grandmother. One could go on further to talk about critical global issues, such as the water situation the Mediterranean, or the rare "*Drosoulites*" (Dew Men) phenomenon that takes place in southwestern Crete's Frangokastello.[209] Moreover, the audiences could be exposed to a geographical specification, as the sea in that part of the world is called Libyan due to its proximity to the homonymous country in northern Africa. Lastly, talking about fish and salt, allusions to the local economy and the salt production as well as the healthy Mediterranean Diet could be made, along with an exposure to the Minoan Sea culture as it's promoted via the unique project "Thalassocosmos" (Sea World) at the "Cretaquarium" and the Hellenic Center for Marine Research.[210]

All in all, the use of Greek folk poetry with nature imagery takes on an ecological dimension and suggests a connection between identity and environmental awareness. Nature has spiritual and moral truths to convey and it is the business of the educator to demonstrate them. Greek folk song lyrics use images borrowed from the physical environment. In extension, this could be interpreted as "ecologizing" and, thus, raising environmental awareness through one's traditions.

Ecologies

Ecopoetry engages what Gilcrest calls a skeptical environmental poetics:[211] it recognizes the power of poetry to help humanity re-envision its relationship to the nonhuman world and its limitations in achieving this awesome role.[212] Greek poetry may function as green plants: "it can arrest energy on its path to entropy and help create a self-perpetuating and evolving system, which revolves around creativity and community."[213]

According to Scigaj, a sustainable poem is the verbal record of the percept, of the poet's originary perception.[214] Greek folk poetry is sustainable as it presents nature as a separate but yet equal other. It offers exemplary models of biocentric perception and behavior, as it neither subordinates nature to a superior human consciousness nor reduces it to immanence.[215] As a verbal record of an interactive encounter in the world of our sensuous experience between the human psyche and nature, Greek lyrics transform themselves into ecopoems, thus a tool for altering the reader's perceptions from the anthropocentric to the biocentric, a purely sustainable practice. They encourage us to understand, respect and cooperate with the laws of nature that sustain us.

Greek land embodies the deeply felt everyday experiences of carrying on agriculture and pastoralism. Names of music genres on the island of Crete denote such relationships, such as the "goat" (gitsikia sousta) or the "sheep" *(provatisios choros)*, the "tree heath-evergreen shrub" *(priniotis)* and the "rose" *(rodo)* dances. Locals refer to the love repertory that stems from the plains or the valleys, in opposition to the one associated with the mountainous, wilder "areas."

Meditative goat.

Landscapes untouched by time remind one of past values which influence strongly and shape present and future. Cretans consider Mesara the crossroad of many civilizations. It is in Gortina, for instance, that, according to myth, Zeus slept with Europa. The name Europe was first used there, where the Minoan civilization blossomed and one can see the double nature of Crete, the face that opens its arms to both Africa and the rest of the world.[216]

Studying abroad in Crete-Greece: Under a resilient olive-tree in Gortina, the place where Europa conceived her first son, Minos, with Zeus.

Timbres of instruments and singing styles also serve to construct and evoke place-based identities. Cretan singers embody the roughness of "their" homelands.[217] Musicians of the mountainous parts add small bells to the bow of their instruments called "hawks-bells" (*gerakokoudouna)* in order to further increase the volume and add rhythmic emphasis to their melodies. They even enlarge the original sizes of their instruments so as to mimic the "thunders" (*vrondolyra*, namely thunder-*lyra*).

According to Magrini, there is a distinction between two ways of performing Cretan mountain songs, the "goat" and the "sheep" style.[218] The first refers to a style widespread in the mountains, characterized by a "head voice," the frequent use of the singer's high register, and particular emphasis on melodic decoration, performed with great dexterity. By contrast, the "sheep" style, which is widespread in the plains, is closer in some respects to the style of the Byzantine chant. It employs a "chest voice," and is less ornamental. Both styles are characterized by their great resonance, which the performers trace to the use of such songs by partisans during their resistance against foreign rules.

All in all, Greek music can provide for us today, our threatened planet, not only inspiration for ecological concern and action but also an ethical base that could strengthen the panoplies for such action. A selection of the best of such poems could become an eco-pulsing gospel in our struggle for survival. It could inspire and nurture committed ecological action, especially if combined with ethical humanism, intended to cultivate environmental consciousness and ecological action.[219]

Eco-awareness

Since the times of Homer, Greek nature and landscape have prevailed in Greek literature. Like Japanese Haikus, Greek rhymes reconcile humans with nature. As Philadelphia's murals, some of which function as "green walls," Greek lyrics possess the power to transform a community space, generate affinity and encourage stewardship with nature while providing an experiential learning opportunity, as well as a healthier, more beautiful environment for its recipients. All in all, Greek folk poetry carries images that can promote ecological preservation.

Moreover, the extensive use of the Greek language and folk imagery through it are themselves expressions of the Greek spirit and promote the importance of developing environmental sensibilities. Traditionally, Greeks were harmoniously connected with nature, a connection that is spontaneously reflected in the generous use of natural imagery in their art forms, one of which folk poetry is. Suggesting the significance for interpreting nature imagery in Greek folk literature teaches contemporary Greeks today to re-become sensitive to their own immediate environment. In extend, it promotes the crucial importance in today's world of all humans being aware of their physical surroundings.

In a turbulent era of global crises, Greek, "green," eco-ways of looking at performances can reconnect us with our roots. Moreover, they remind us that the seeds of a worthy and vital outlet for collectively and soulfully exercising of creativity and imagination via music and dance do spring.

From Homeric Poetry to Cretan Balladry

In the words that follow, I shall discuss "The Daskalogiannis Song," a Cretan oral heroic poem that consists of 1,034 lines, all of which are rhyming couplets, namely distiches of two 15 iambic syllables lines, each one being a completely self-contained statement. The song narrates the 1770 Sfakia rebellion against the Ottoman rulers, prompted by promises of Russian aid, and focuses on the treacherous invitation of Ioannis Vlachos or Daskalogiannis (1722 or 1730-1771) to Heraklion by the Pasha, where he was captured and flayed alive. The composition informs us that Barba-Pantzelios, a cheese maker from the village of Mouri in Sfakia, dictated the song to lector Sifis Skordilis, who wrote it down in 1786.

Typically sung by men only, this historical narrative is intimately wedded to the principal musical repertoires for communal feasts and celebrations. The current study re-visits the formulaic theory[220] and the Homeric epic as Cretan bards – who survive on mountain villages – and their narrative, particularly iconic poems, mediate tradition, refine cultural stereotypes, cultivate notions of home and idealize a heroic past. "The Daskalogiannis Song," in local dialect, allows a rare glimpse into the various trajectories that connect southwestern Crete to the rest of the island.

Village of Askyfou-Sfakia (Crete-Greece), 4 September 2011: Feast following the commemoration of the 1774 events, namely when the Sfakians besieged the tower of and killed the most terrible janissary of Crete, Alidakis Ibrahim.

The story behind the song

The Cretan heroic myth is rooted in several revolts against the Turks. Of those the most magnificent was that of Daskalogiannis, whose grand conception was to re-establish the old order, to restore *romiosini* (namely, Greekness).[221] He failed, but, unlike others who have gone down to history in comparative anonymity, he was lucky in having a chronicler.[222]

Daskalogiannis was one of the wealthiest men in Crete. His nickname translates to "John the Teacher," teacher being a mark of respect to his education (his actual name was Ioannis Vlachos). He spoke foreign languages and wore European clothes. He owned a fleet of ships which traded throughout the Mediterranean, and, in the course of a commercial expedition to the Black Sea, he met with the Russian Count Orlov and became, without realizing it, a pawn in Russia's strategy. The song, however, shows that the Russians deceived Daskalogiannis.[223] The depressing story of retreat before the Muslim army, which outnumbered Daskalogiannis' force by about thirty to one, is told in detail by Barba-Pantzelios.[224]

In Crete, with a population that was historically to a large degree illiterate, "the spoken word and storytelling took on tremendous importance as conveyors of collective memory and local history."[225] In a society governed and defined by the spoken word, history takes on a more fluid, malleable character, and "over time can be subtly reworked and mythologized until it reflects a version of reality that most suits the purposes and desires of its tellers and listeners."[226]

At the same time, on the island of Crete, the persistence of the heroic age into the present, the geographic isolation of villages such as the ones located at the Sfakia mountainous areas, the recitation of old poems such as the long epic romance *Erotokritos* and the creation of new ones, the absence in the heroic poems of supernatural or shamanistic elements and the presence in them of a humanistic epic mentality, all these make Cretan folk poetry an interesting laboratory,[227] even though a fair amount of what the songs tell us can be corrected by documents located, for instance, at the Turkish archives in Heraklion, the capital of Crete.

For instance, our poet, Barba-Pantzelios, exaggerates Sfakia's autonomy and the strength of the Turkish forces used to crush the revolt. In his account, Daskalogiannis offers to give himself up whereas his uncle, Protopappas, appears hostile to the revolt and ends up voluntarily accompanying Daskalogiannis to the Pasha. Lastly, the date of Daskalogiannis' execution is wrong as he was imprisoned for about a year and then put to death, whereas in the poem, his martyrdom immediately follows his defiance of the Pasha.[228] Because of the 16 years between the actual event and the song's composition, several parts of it have taken mythical aspects. However, the departure from those historical facts serves one purpose: to make the story heroic.[229]

"The Daskalogiannis Song" was first published in 1874 by Emile Legrand, based on a copy that was given to him by Iosif Manousogiannakis, and was broadly cir-

Daskalogiannis memorial statue at the village where he was born, namely Anopolis-Sfakia (Crete-Greece).

culated and re-published by various editors soon after.[230] Today, we know of approximately ten shorter variations that have stemmed out from that same epic, the longest one being of 85 verses long. Those versions were the result of the singer's mnemonic abilities but also the audience's expectations.[231] By having been able to read it, several people have also been able to perform by memory parts of the song and thus commemorate the historical events it remarks. The main topics dealt in the song are the preparation of the rebellion, the Turkish expedition, the invitation by the Pasha, the return of the Daskalogiannis' companions to Sfakia as well as the sad devastation of that area.

Daskalogiannis believed that the uprising was possible, so he overcame internal reactions and organized the movement at Sfakia in the spring of 1770. He was counting on Russian help and the fact that the terrain was quite inaccessible made a potential Turkish raid difficult. However, the Turkish reaction was formidable. Sfakia was destroyed whereas no Russian assistance came. Some women and children managed to get to other parts of Greece (such as the Peloponnese and the island of Cythera) whereas others managed to escape to the Samaria Gorge. Daskalogiannis, in order to calm the Turkish rage, handed himself over on 17 June 1771 and suffered a horrific death (he was skinned alive in front of his brother who was driven insane) at Heraklion, the capital of Crete.

Place-based songs

As in Homeric balladry, the characteristics of several heroic Greek folk songs become formulaic tools for carrying meaning. Similarly, "The Daskalogiannis Song" functions as a common identifier of the people who perform it at communal events, employing characteristic melodies, musical rhythmic and metrical structures, calling them to be place-conscious educated human beings, by re-examining the impact of places on culture and identity and embracing one's political role as place maker.

Its lyrics describe specific landscapes. When one is familiar with the place where history has been born, one can feel information and perceive it differently. At the same time, when someone knows the history of one's place, then "spaces" acquire a different substance. Isn't it a pity that at school we don't learn about our microcosms and that we are being taught by urban-trained teachers who aren't aware of those micro-histories? Wouldn't a good history lesson be the one that spoke to us in our own language, of our own land's history and nature? And, wouldn't it best if that was achieved via familiar lyrics and tunes?

The Samaria Gorge

For example, the Samaria Gorge at the Sfakia province, a UNESCO Biosphere Reserve and a Wildlife Refuge of the EU's Natura network of protected areas, has played an important role in the local culture in terms of folk narratives and values.[232] The free and ascetic life of the Samaria wild goat (Capra aegagrus Cretica or *kri-kri*) has acquired an emblematic significance and personifies gallantry and love of freedom, values that represent Crete in general.

The ancient Greek word "*sfax*" means "land of gorges."[233] The role of Samaria in the history of Crete has been leading as it provided refuge, a safe passage and a base for revolutionary activities. Its inaccessible land and physical isolation offered protection and a place where military equipment could be stored, with a natural bay that was used as a point for receiving supplies by sea.[234] It is a living example of a harmonious relationship throughout the centuries between humans and nature. In fact, many of the historical events that defined the course of the island would not have had the same result were it not for the Samaria Gorge.[235]

A Cretan rhyming-couplet characteristically says that "if you wish to learn what the Sfakian land produces, ask the gorges to tell you of Daskalogiannis." Even though the song recounts the Cretan sacrifice, it is also full of toponyms that prove the relationship of place to people.[236] In the Samaria Gorge, every speck of earth, for those who know the place, has its own name (a microtoponym, we may say). For instance, on lines 455-464 of "The Daskalogiannis Song,"[237] Barba-Pantzelios eloquently describes the effort the Sfakians made to save the women and children hidden in the Samaria Gorge, the shelter for life and den of freedom:[238]

> The Turks are capturing many shores, they are heading to Agia Roumeli;
> The families are leaving, they are exiting at Linoseli.
> At an attempt to enter the ravine, at the bottom of Samaria,
> At the Portes they met with Yannis Bonatos.
> So they battle with him and he makes them turn back.
> They passed Eligia and yet he draws near them.
> Others also came straight in from Xyloskalo,
> Turning upside down any families they found.
> Few were guarding and suddenly fell upon them;
> They only manage to arrive at Neroutsiko where they are shored up.

Homeric poetry & Cretan balladry

Several researchers assume Cretan songs were created by the Dorians who settled on mountainous areas of Crete around 1000 BC. Evidence proves songs were composed during the Venetian and Turkish occupation, as they relate to the Byzantine and Frankish poetry of the Middle Ages. More specifically, the number of syllables in a song's verses witnesses which were composed during the Venetian occupation, which were imported from Italy and which were created after the fall of Crete to the Turks.[239] The characteristic style of Cretan poetry itself, the *mandinades*, can be traced back to fifteenth and sixteenth centuries manuscripts.[240]

More specifically, in Crete, we come across songs which take us back to the days of the Byzantium and the 9th century that are pre-Venetian, semi-religious songs that are also pre-Venetian, a few narratives that may be pre-Venetian, and several others distributed between the thirteenth and the seventeenth centuries, clearly from the pre-Turkish era.[241] It is interesting to observe, therefore, that the proportion of songs that can be proved to come after 1669 is very small indeed, even though our records of the Turkish period are richer than those of the Venetian.

The Venetian fortress of Goule or Rocca al Mare (1523-1540) guarding (and sealing) the harbor of Heraklion-Crete (Greece).

Several Cretan scholars trace in those songs elements of the "glorious" Greek past. For example, we know that Cretan nobility was proud of its descent from the twelve Byzantine lords whom Alexius I Comnenus had sent out to possess the island. Thus, the use of Byzantine motifs in Cretan songs, such as the love of strange compound adjectives, is not surprising.[242] Baud-Bovy recognizes similarities amongst religious melodies he found on Mount Athos manuscripts and Cretan folk songs he collected[243] and explains how Cretan songs were very powerful and thus performed and passed down by the monks.[244]

In many of the Cretan songs that deal with revolts, Apostolakis detects the Homeric questioning concerning the worlds of the living and the dead.[245] Notopoulos argues how Cretan bards – who still survive on the mountain villages of Sfakia and Psiloritis – and their narrative poems are imbued with the same code of honor that characterizes Homer and his warriors.[246] He goes on further to show how these revolutionary ballads accompanying contemporary Cretan feasts (the so-called "songs of the table") relate to the ancient Greek symposia. "The audience cannot tell whether the story imitates life or life the story," he claims,[247] depicting how the formulaic texture found in Cretan songs agrees with the way epic Homer was performed at communal gatherings and the songs were passed down from generation to generation via minstrels. For example, Daskalogiannis' response to the Pasha King Leonidas had also given. The farewell scene with his wife reminds us of the one between Hector and Andromache. Moreover, the hero's self-sacrifice also identifies with that of the Greek Orthodox Christian belief.

In addition, "The Daskalogiannis Song" has retained the formulaic prologue with the invocation to a higher being and the announcement of the hero and the theme of the poem followed by the narration of the event. It concludes with a quite long epilogue which gives us information not only about the bard but also the circumstances of the composition and a description of his poet friend who dictated the poem to him under the Holm-oak.[248] The structure of the poem is permeated with parataxis with approximately 40% of it devoted to speeches that make the story dramatic.[249] The similes and metaphors reveal the beauty of nature, contrasting its eternity with the transience of mortality.

Collective Singing

All in all, Cretan folk poetry is capable of cultivating both a sense of place and ecological awareness along with a duty to one's home. Its environmental themes can function as cultural vehicles, keeping alive the distinctive nature and culture, the "scent" of Crete. After all, "hearing" who we are through folk poetry makes everything around us become part of our life stories. Learning to listen to what places are telling us is the pedagogical challenge of place-conscious education.[250]

Collective memories turn the singer into an organic historian. The ritualized process of remembering historic facts through songs inspires and encourages us to recall our past not only in an attempt to preserve it but, most importantly, in order to prepare for the future. Through tough periods of crises not essentially financial but mostly ideological and ecological, the notions of the Homeric *"arete"* (virtue), the Christian *"thisia"* (sacrifice) along with the modern Greek *"levendia"* (gallantry) can and should be re-visited through songs like the "Daskalogiannis" one (755-8), where the "We" stands before the "I":

Firstly for my fatherland, and secondly for my faith,
Thirdly for the Christians who live in Crete.
For even if I am from Sfakia, I am also a child of Crete,
And to see the Cretans in torment hurts me.

Songs of the Foothills

"The power of place will be remarkable."
    Aristotle, *Physics*

"The good *mandinada* isn't randomly built;
It must contain stone, soil and water from Crete!"
    Cretan rhyming distich (*mandinada*)

Claiming Land

Cretan forms of musical expression have been interpreted historically and connected to the fight, the resistance and the numerous rebellions against the Turks (particularly in reference to a "tainted" Ottoman past), who landed on the island in 1645, conquered it in 1669 and controlled it until 1898. In more recent times, an active resistance was endeavored against the German invasion during the Second World War. During such periods, in order to claim land, Cretans sang.

Crete became part of Greece only in 1913, its inhabitants having managed to remain autonomous through a "rebel" attitude. The Cretan mountain-dwellers are particularly famous for their sustained resistance to "foreign" occupation. Cretan music performances consolidate *is-land* (in the sense of "being one with one's land") identity: certain lyrics suggest Cretans have to protect their land and be strong because their ancestors fought for it as well. Stokes' main argument that music informs our sense of place[251] is also the case with Cretan songs. Here I argue how Cretan singing is a social activity that still provides a means by which people recognize identities and how places, such as the island of Crete, through singing become "ours."[252]

Songs of the Foothills

The genre of the Cretan mountain songs called *rizitika* is place-based because it recognizes value in the Cretan folk and their language, its co-inhabitants and the Cretan landscape itself. The songs were created by the inhabitants of western Crete who dwell in the White Mountains (Lefka Ori or Madares) shepherds' lands, in the so-called "domain of Mousouroi" areas. Their name derives from the Greek word "*riza*," which means root (as in the English word "rhizome"). Thus, *rizitika* are the "songs of the foothills." According to Cretans, these songs are perceived as the cultural heritage, the basis of life, similarly to how the roots of a tree are the source of its nutrition, in other words, a direct and solid link to Mother Earth. As such, the *rizitika* are the basis of Cretan culture and carry on the traditions, beliefs and legends of the Cretan land.

The *rizitika* have diverse lyrical functions and contexts. For example, they may refer both to death and the underworld, speak of friendship, hospitality and love, zeal for freedom, admiration of the brave, pastoral life, family ties, evoke the preparation for political rebellion, resistance to oppressors or belong to the heroic song genre. Most importantly, they make symbolic use of nature images, which convey meanings of independency and freedom in an allegoric, yet obscure to an outsider way. This is exactly what enabled partisans throughout different periods of occupation (such as Turkish and German) to organize resistance: their serious and austere nature, intricate melodies and performative complexity.

Through that local pathway, language carries its own ecology as well. Cretan dialect takes its audience to the villages where various idioms unique from place to place exist. As the poetic texts promote an ethic of "the wild" and reinterpret Cretan rebellious identity in the service of environmentally-minded place awareness,[253] Cretan rhymes are judged in relation to the larger social and historical context of each community. The use of the local dialect in them and their context represent the everyday Cretan life "in place," lending that art form social and natural dimension. Thus, via music-poetic performances, experiences are transformed into living memories of an ecological realm, which also constitutes a rich source of knowledge and identity.

Rizitika researchers agree that the presence of Turkish words in the Cretan songs' lyrics cannot prove late date; those which have Turkish words have them nearly always in positions where they are demonstrably not part of the original texture.[254] They also describe specific words that belong to a "noble," Venetian tradition. In opposition, songs of the Cretan insurrections are full of Turkish words or words of Turkish roots with Greek endings.[255] Baud-Bovy, in specific, comments how the Turkish influence on Cretan songs is apparent in the use of exclamatory phrases such as "*aman-aman*" (woe is me), scales with augmented second and disaccentuation of the so-called "political" (namely, from Constantinople) verse.[256]

Taking the aforementioned linguistic questionings into consideration shows that the "quality" and "dimension" of place for a Cretan are definitely more than just aesthetic or affectional; it is also moral.[257] As American Indian literatures promote and teach the interdependence and connectedness of all living things, likewise Cretan songs centralize landscape and place its recipients within an environmental context. After all, place is not only physical, but ideological as well.[258] Beside its geographical specification, it carries deep meanings.

Heterophonic Melodies of Homophone Ideas

When listening to Cretan mountain songs one can immediately relate them to Byzantine chanting. Because Cretans communed with donkeys or horses, the song rhythms follow the pace of those animals sounding like "horse marching." The melodies are many and the singers never achieve unison for each man sings in his own pitch and in such a way that his own voice is not lost in the group singing. These songs might be raucous to the western ear but are full of the gusty vitality of the Cretan mountaineers.[259] Traditionally, women are not solo singers; however, they know the lyrics and occasionally join the chorus by repeating them "silently."

The Cretan poet, subject to history participated in or witnessed by the self and the audience, avoids the marvelous and the improbable; though occasionally listeners come across speaking horses and birds. The poems are sung to a basic narrative melody – indeed, many lyrics share the same melodies – which extends over the entire distich. If any dramatic quality exists in the poems, it is due mostly to the events themselves, rather than to the poet himself.

The songs are mainly vocal and male. A soloist usually leads such performances and introduces each stanza, whereas an informal choir repeats them similarly enough to responsories. Their verses are made up of a variable number of syllables. A stanza consists of an entire line and the first hemistich of the following one; all the stanzas except the first one begin with the repetition of the last hemistich of the previous one, so that they are all interconnected, thus making the song strophic.

I witnessed the performance of the following lyrics on July 24 2010 at the Cretan village of Meskla as part of the memorial activities held in honor of late Drexel University President Constantine Papadakis, a native of that village. As the religious services and officials' speeches came to an end, a group of local men stood by the bust of Dr. Papadakis, which now overviews the central square of Meskla, singing:

Oh golden world, oh silver world, oh gilded globe of beauty,
Who, liar, managed to enjoy, exhaust and outwear you?
I, liar world, enjoyed you; but will not win you over!
On foot I walked on mountains, riding a horse on plains,
A passer-by…

During the performance, each stanza is sung by a soloist repeated by a second group (choir 2), as might occur in smaller convivial gatherings, or a group (choir 1) repeated by a second group (choir 2), as in the case of a larger gathering such as a local feast, with no variation of the verbal text; by contrast, minor variations in the musical interpretation of the melody are common. The style of choral singing is heterophonic: the performers carry the same basic melody with some individual melodic or rhythmic variations.

The iterative technique seems to be connected with the group partaking in a common psychological condition and with the necessity of reaching and manifesting emotional contact and accord. It is an expression of one of the most basic forms of interpersonal relationship and for its structure it may be named "iteration in consonance," to emphasize the search for a group relationship through the members' collective resonance in a common action. It is of course a form of communication which stresses the emotional value of joining together in a symbolic behavior.

In contrast to other forms of iterative singing, what is peculiar to the performance of the *rizitika* is that, when performers sing the lines, they elaborate them according to a particular technique called *apogaermata* or *andigaermata*. That is, they split the lines into fragments, breaking up words as well, and proceed to repeat incomplete parts of lines in a kind of "stammering." Baud-Bovy parallels this technique to the function of "salt" in food: namely the essence of that art form.[260]

Magrini posits that these pieces may represent a *musica reservata*, accessible only to cultural insiders, an idea that leads us to consider Cretan society as a warrior culture which honors and inspires both creative individualism and community loyalty, and protects its identity.[261] As a reaction to occupation which threatened geographic and cultural boundaries, Cretans attempted to reinforce borders through various means. Thus we find responsorial performances of songs that alternate between idiosyncratic solos and prescribed choral responses whose rules of performance practice are known only by insiders.

Social Music Making

Cretan songs are integral to the principal repertory for communal rituals and family or friendly celebrations. In all cases, such songs are orally presented and performed by many people from memory. They form the main means of common entertainment as all members of the village take part in these festivities ideal for communal communication. Based on the type of performance occasion, they can be divided into two repertoires: the *tavla* repertoire (songs for the table or "feast-songs") and the *strata* repertoire (songs for the road). The *tavla* repertoire is reserved for convivial occasions, mainly wedding banquets. The *strata* repertoire is strictly reserved for parts of the wedding rites other than the banquet, which include the transfer of the dowry to the bridegroom's house, the ceremonial welcome by the bridegroom's mother of the bride, and the gathering of the gifts.

A basic form of communication consists when men sing together. What is enacted and created through musical activity is the collective interaction which develops in the group's socialization, and which, through the performance, activates the thick web of social relationships synthetically expressed with the term *parea* (namely, group of friends). Through the feast, the *parea* celebrates itself and its members, developing, through the chosen practice of call-and-response singing, a relationship shaped according to an ideal of cooperation and socialization of the group's values.[262]

The performance requires extreme precision in the processes of memorization and rendition of the verbal and musical arrangement specific of individual songs. Such a complexity emphasizes the ritual character of performing the *rizitika*, implying that their particular communicative code is shared by the singers. They, in turn, find in this musical genre a performative outlet for their own collective identity, which cannot easily be accessed by others, as it requires an in-depth knowledge of the oral tradition of the group.

Ultimately, music-making in Crete is more than simply an activity: rather, being "good at making music" is a fundamental aspect of being "good at being a man."[263] Viewed through Dawe's lenses, Cretan songs are socially constructed and made meaningful within the Cretan island society.[264] As a result, a man's ability to sing a song has an importance which is being evaluated. Even though women are not actively participating to the performance of that genre of songs, they do have a voice when it comes to judging the singing abilities of the performers as part of the local group, the society that produces them. Let us also mention that women are performers of other types of songs, such as lullabies and laments, where men remain "silent." When the singers perform together, in unison, they may sound cacophonic as each one is acting "egoistically" but for the common good, in loud, unison voices of personal caliber.[265]

Natural Topologies

The inhabitants of Crete believe that their traditions have been preserved as well as kept alive due to the harsh land that was tough to be accessed and conquered. The *rizitika* songs assist them toward this direction by dynamically expressing and confirming the relationship between Cretans and their predecessors as well as between their environment and their history.

Similar to how Tuvan singing was born in Tuva, a Russian republic situated on the Mongolian border, out of the culture of sheep and reindeer herders using mimesis of horses, rhythms and other metaphors taken mostly from the natural environment,[266] Cretan folk song lyrics use images borrowed from the physical environment. By doing so, they reassure that Crete, an island at the periphery of the Greek world, is capable of protecting the borderlines of the country it belongs too, Greece, from its "hostile" neighbors, alluding to contemporary disputes over the Aegean Sea.

For instance, according to Greek mythology, the golden eagle was Zeus' friend, a symbol of strength, courage and justice, and a good omen, which he kept by his side at all times. In Byzantine heraldry, the double-headed eagle represented the dual sovereignty of the Emperor (secular and religious) and the dominance of the Byzantine Emperors over both East and West. According to a Greek folk song, an eagle grasped the head of the last Byzantine Emperor, Constantine Palaiologos, so that the Turks wouldn't loot it. Cretan eagles are unique to the Mediterranean, biologically strong birds, that reside on steep rocks, harsh mountainous and gorge-type areas. They are endangered species, protected under the LIFE Program of the European Union.

An example of a Cretan song that refers to an eagle describes that bird seated on a high mountain, at the edge of a cliff, all wet and covered by ice, asking for the sun to rise, so that the snow melts away from its wings and the frost from its fingernails. That song has been performed several times at wedding celebrations I was present. It was also performed on November 4 2009, for the 80th birthday of the Archbishop Anastasios of Tirana, Durrës and All Albania by his former student, Cretan-born and currently the Pope and Patriarch of Alexandria and all Africa, Theodore the 2nd.

According to Hadjidakis, the aforementioned song describes the activities of rebel Michail Vlachos, a Cretan guerilla who was eventually captured by the Turks and executed on the central common of Heraklion on February 1857.[267] In the song, he is impatiently awaiting spring so that can once again ascend the mountains of the Omalos region, and, from that height, announce the island's liberty and stir up national sentiment. The author of the poem is reported to be the fighter Stefanos Dalis, a participant in the 1821 Greek war of independence.[268]

Another image, that of the wild goat *(kri-kri)*, comprises a hymn to freedom and the will to live. Cretan-born Zeus, after all, was nourished by the milk of the wild goat Amalthea. That animal had sacred significance for the Minoans, something attested on several wall paintings, vessels, seals and coins. In Cretan poetry, the wild goat, also an endangered species unique to the island, serves as a metaphor for the rebel heart that does not succumb to any yoke and breaks free even from the prison of the mind.[269]

Take for instance the popular Cretan song which talks of wild goats and kids, tamed deer, where the singer is asking the animals to provide him with information on "where they live, where they are staying at during the winter." The response by the "wild" flock is that "they live in the precipices, the cliffs; the steep peaks are their winter quarters, the caves in the mountains are their ancestral home." Apart from being performed at private and communal feasts, that song has been identified with different periods in Greek history that deal with guerilla- and anti-totalitarian feelings.

Let me underline here that Cretan-Turks, namely the Muslim inhabitants of Crete until 1923, listened to the music of the Cretan instruments, danced the same dances with the Greeks of Crete and sang (almost) the same tunes. However, they avoided the performance of "rebel songs" because they knew most of them included anti-Turkish symbolisms and nature or love metaphors purposefully misleading.

Other allegoric songs, though they do indeed describe notable events in history, they generally cloud or replace the historical events by Cretan poetic symbolism: "The Eagle," mentioned earlier, is one such example, where the bird symbolizes the Cretan rebel of that time and the rebellious heart in general. Though the origin of that song is uncertain, it depicts the misfortunes of a group of Cretans who were trapped in a cave in Russia during a severe snow storm. When the reports of the incident reached Crete, an inhabitant of the Sfakia region of Crete wrote this poem in tribute to the victims.[270]

"When Will the Sky Be Clear"

> When will the sky be clear, when will it be February,
> So that I can grab my gun, the beautiful cartridge belt,
> And walk down to Omalos, on the Mousouroi road,
> To deprive mothers of their sons, and wives of their husbands,
> To make babies cry without mothers,
> To cry for water at night, and for milk in the morning,
> And, when the sun rises, for their poor mother...

Greek ideals have survived in time but also in space. Today, Cretan songs are still performed in the villages of the area they were created at. Numerous Greek composers have recorded albums that include them using both western orchestras and local, traditional instruments such as the trademark of Cretan music, the three-stringed *lyra*. Famous Cretan musicians, such as Nikos Xylouris, have recorded and made such songs popular throughout Greece. This way, Cretan songs have exceeded the island borders and have thus become mainland hymns and sources of inspiration to liberty and independence.

At the same time, Cretan songs have not only become a strong symbol of identity for all the people of Greece, but have even exceeded Greece's political borders, coming to function as a common language amongst Greeks globally. For example, during the spring of 2009, we performed in unison "When Will the Sky Be Clear," a song which simply asks for better weather, at the Greek Embassy in Washington DC. For the former Greek Ambassador to the USA Alexandros Mallias that song evoked recollections of his tenure in Geneva as Press officer during the 1970s Greek military regime.

Morgan argues that the aforementioned song was performed against the Venetians and only later against the Turks.[271] His evidence relies on the fact that the Mousouroi family mentioned had disappeared in the Turkish period: indeed, they had disintegrated under the force of internal vendettas.[272] The song, known to all Cretans, is the inspiration and rallying cry of their ancestors in the revolts against the Turks. However patriotic it became in the Turkish era, it was originally a vendetta song of the Venetian occupation.[273] Today, performed in and outside Greece, "When Will the Sky Be Clear" still expresses passion for freedom and represents the Greek fighter soul.

"When Will the Sky Be Clear" has become like a second anthem to the Greeks, constantly being performed during several occasions in recent times as well. For instance, it has been associated with modern Greek historical events, such as anti-junta student demonstrations during 1973 and the Cypriot "tragedy," namely the Turkish 1974 occupation of that island and all the atrocities that came with it, as well as other activist cases, such as events in support of the Armenian, Kurdish and

Palestinian struggles. "When Will the Sky Be Clear" can be heard recorded or live at Greek stadiums during soccer or basketball games whereas it may also accompany pre-election campaigns.

Recently, that song was performed by demonstrators at major Greek protests against the economic austerity measures imposed on Greece by the Troika but also by famous Greek singers who supported such activities via live music concerts. At the same time, it functioned as the main "soundtrack" of the anti-austerity protestors organized by the "Direct Democracy Now!" movement known as "The Indignant Citizens Movement" at several locations all over Greece, the most popular one being organized around the Athens Constitution Square.

Back to the Roots

The dimensions of places are perceptual, sociological, ideological, political and ecological. In that sense, places are deeply pedagogical, centers of experience and meaning making. Viewed in that context, Cretan folk poetry, such as the *rizitika*, can educate the youth not only via knowledge but through an environmentally sensitive spirit. Because islands, both viewed as geographical entities and physical realities, "attract affection, loyalty, identification (…) They are places: special places, paradigmatic places, topographies of meaning in which the qualities that construct place are dramatically distilled."[274]

For the Kenyan Kikuyu, music is not just for entertainment, it is also used so as to remember history. It reinforces levels of consciousness and an appreciation of one's tradition. It develops ethnic and politic identities, inspires and encourages remembering history.[275] Similarly, Cretan singing brings back memories of "our" land, resistance and liberation. Sound is inseparable from social landscape and music is integral to the geographic imagination, an effective form of resistance to the homogenizing forces of culture history.[276]

In their majority, Cretans wish to be proud, conscious of heritage and history, singing their way blissfully through the challenges of globalization. As more and more immigrants mostly from the Middle East reach Greece through Crete, the "threat" to loose identity becomes stronger. It is precisely in those, not only Greek but, more significantly, in Cretan dialect lyrics that locals find refugee and a strong sense of interconnectedness with their homeland. That is why the performance of mountain songs is respected with an almost religious devoutness and welcomed by the younger generations on the island of Crete and by Cretans all over the world. The fact that such songs are included at the Greek school books and are part of the repertory of national school feasts strengthens the aforementioned idea(l)s.

Through commonly shared phraseology, the individual pain becomes collective and the personal a refraction of the collective. This way, Cretan songs serve as cultural fertilizers, capable of consolidating grounds and cultivating notions of home.

By re-localizing and ecologizing them we can teach our audiences to be responsible to their home and call for Cretan inhabitants to become socially and ecologically aware of their island.[277]

Conceptualizing History & Landscape

Viewed through the aforementioned lenses then, Cretan natural landscapes characterized by powerful mythological, historical, religious, artistic or other cultural meanings invested in natural features become conceptualized. In local memory and identity, such experiences have shaped a very distinct sense of pride, toughness and independence that feeds on centuries-old memories of resistance to foreign invaders and defense of local autonomy and freedom at all cost.

The legacy of these revolutionary times can still be felt a century later through the notion that Crete is somehow quintessentially free, Greek, self-sufficient and "tough." While the songs transmit an interpretation of the past, they are also a tool for learning the central values of Cretanness: the courage, audacity and worth of the braves, the ability to face risk, the strength of character, the wisdom, the shrewdness of reasoning, the resistance against the trials of life, the love of honor (*philotimo*), the hospitality, the importance of friendship and, above all, the sensitivity to the wide range of human emotions vis-à-vis nature, life and death. It would be difficult to separate the qualities of the hero sung about in the *rizitika* from the lifestyle qualities associated with "being a true Cretan."

All in all, through folk poetry, Cretans hear who they are, as everything in their environment becomes part of their life stories. Cretan folk poetry loudly calls on nature and ecologizes the discourse of Cretan tradition out of caring about the physical, natural world. The more we study it, the more clearly we perceive that nature has furnished man with a complete commentary on one's self.

Traditions of the Future

> Compassionately, tranquilly, I squeeze a clod of Cretan soil in my palm. I have kept this soil with me always, during all my wanderings pressing it in my palm at times of great anguish and receiving strength, great strength, as though from pressing the hand of a dearly loved friend…O fierce clay of Crete, the moment you were twirled and fashioned into a man of struggle has slipped by as though in a single flash.
> —Nikos Kazantzakis, *Report to Greco*

Place has been presented as both concept and material reality, representing social and symbolic interrelations between people and their physical environment whereas music reflects social, economic, political and material aspects of the particular place in which it is created. Changes in place thus influence changes in musical sounds and styles.[278]

There are several Cretan music groups who pursue an "authentic" singing of Cretan songs: thus, strictly male and vocal, versus mixed-gender and occasionally instrumental and/or mixed with pop sounds and instruments. Those include the "Rizites" from the village of Karanou I witnessed performing at the foothills of the White Mountains in August 2009 for a reunion of the Pancretan Association of America. That group maintains a webpage and a facebook group, performs regularly, encouraging and promoting the preservation and teaching of such songs to the younger generations. Several also are the Cretan artists who include mountain songs performances in their repertory. Legendary Psarantonis gives to the singing style of those songs a unique, pioneering approach, which embodies the roughness of "his" village, in particular, and the island of Crete, in general, in combination with the timbre of his vocal performances and *lyra* playing.

A recent performance "From the Skies of Crete" at The Odeon of Herodes Atticus in Athens (June 2, 2010) reflected how he is a vivid representation of mountain life in Crete, embodied both in his appearance and music. In fact, Psarantonis, who has garnered both Greek and international recognition,[279] could be compared to a mountain, or a Minotaur hidden in a cave. In his *lyra* playing and singing, he takes all the joy and struggle of being on the foothills and lets it gush out in his performances. His belief is that nature has everything, including music, and looks for inspiration by meditating at length, looking at the Cretan mountains.[280]

Ross Daly who has made Crete his home since the 1970s includes the performance of "The Eagle" *rizitiko* song at his "Music of Crete" 2005 CD (by FM Records). According to him, "the poetic level of the lyrics in these songs is exceptionally high and many connoisseurs of Cretan music consider them to be the most beautiful in the entire repertoire."[281] In that piece, he plays the *lyra* solo, replacing the lyrics with sounds, this way turning a verbal art of communication into a non-verbal one.

Lastly, just as island societies are essentially glocal and mobile, owing their very existence and identities to their (invariably open) window to the outside world,[282] I would like to also mention Greek contemporary composers who have turned an innovative look into Cretan songs, abolishing language barriers by transforming words into sounds and thus appealing to a larger audience. George Koumendakis does so with his "Typewriter tune for marimba solo" which he bases on the Cretan *rizitiko* "I Walk at Night." The piece belongs to a series of compositions called "Unknown Dialects: Eight Music Dialogues" and is an attempt to decipher music letters sent to several recipients by exploring the various dialects of the Greek musical tradition. Through it, Cretan-born Koumendakis approaches Cretan music in abstract, pyrrichean, dance spirits, without the use of a traditionally Greek instrument though as he, himself admits, "during the last couple of years, Greek traditional music has been the moving force of his compositions."[283]

All in all, as Cretans realize that "no man is an island," they are conscientiously returning to their roots, using Cretan songs as a way of doing so, as part of an understanding that Odyssean nostalgia is not an illusion but a valid response to one's identity. Through that pathway, they are confident that, as in the story of Adam and Eve, they are too made out of soil; and that, in order to examine their souls and thus know themselves, they would have to keep performing island songs.

Songs of the Plains

Music on the island of Crete is yet today an important element of everyday life, an amalgam of mythologies and histories. It is a dynamic tradition, continually developing and adapting to current realities, while simultaneously struggling not to lose its ties with its roots. Songs that stem from the plain areas are accompanied by the violin and the *laouto* (lute) or the mandolin, or the Cretan *lyra* with *gerakokoudouna*, or the Cretan *lyra* accompanied by the lute. The Cretan lute has a rhythmic role which allows the violin or the *lyra* to interpret the main melodies.

A principal dance form that accompanies those tunes is the Kastrinos *pidichtos* (namely leaping) also known as *Maleviziotis*. Its name derives from the city of Heraklion and its older name Kastro (fortress), Malevizi referring to a district in the west Heraklion province.[284] It is considered as one of the oldest dances on the island of Crete, stemming from the ancient *orsitis*. As a religious, war dance, it also related to *pyrrichi*.[285]

Throughout this dance, the performers hold hands in the position that resembles the letter W. Their feet move lively, quickly and rapidly in small steps, always facing slightly right, to the front, back or the side. Traditionally, this dance would divide into three music parts: introductory warming up in a slower rhythm that would then proceed with faster beats so as to provoke the dancer till it would decelerate so as to rest her/him.[286] That dance form offers its participants the opportunity to execute difficult movements and various dancing maneuvers.

Mandinades

To be considered a Cretan, one must know both to recite and to compose *mandinades*, namely improvised, fifteen-syllable, in iambic meter, proverbial, rhyming distiches, each divided into an eight- followed by a seven-syllable part, where the fourteenth syllable must be stressed and the fifteenth unstressed. *Mandinades* are an integral part of the musical tradition of oral composition-in-performance. They rely on formulas, thus groups of words under the same metrical conditions that are being repeated.[287] The practice of this technique underlines the linguistic and mnemonic skills members of the creative process possess. Each *mandinadologos* has a repertory of formulas. Composed pieces are created on spot and are thus considered a product of communal participation.[288]

Live traditions of *mandinada* contests to which improvisatory skills are central are still prominent. Cretans call them *kontaromahies*, which translates to "fights with poles," or *drakarismata*, namely "collisions." It is easy to compose the first line. The complementary, the second and rhyming one, requires better skills. Those compositional strategies are important devices the performers use to gain authority and recognition. In addition to serving as entertainment, *mandinades* are a means of expression for masculinity and a forum for discussing local issues, providing an opportunity for Cretans to express and debate their respective philosophies of life.

The *mandinades* performance is accompanied by instruments such as the Cretan *lyra*, the violin, the mandolin, the guitar but also the lute. In opposition to the *riziti-ka* that are performed vocally without instrumental accompaniment, the poetic texts of the *mandinades* are fixed to Cretan melodies or musical forms that support improvisatory singing and verse making, the *condylies*, which have been extremely popular in eastern and central Crete.

Usually, a singer begins the first fifteen-syllable line and the rest of the musicians and/or group of friends (*parea*) repeats it. During that time, the singer has time to think of the second line, which he then sings, and so on. The requirement is that the poems sung are linked thematically. Their meaning is judged for its performing and social appropriateness in relation to the occasion but also the larger social and historical context of the community, transforming music and dance experiences into memories of the island's community.[289]

Cretan *mandinada* contests derive from the social interaction of everyday life. This process is not unique to Crete. Erdener, for instance, examines Turkish song and poetry in the process of creation and attempts to understand how the meaning of the song duel emerges from the social interaction between the performers and the audience. His main question seems to be: "How do the competing minstrels establish, maintain, and rearrange meanings in the process of interaction?"[290]

In the Cretan case too, some of the poetic meanings are directly expressed or implied in the song texts, whereas others are communicated indirectly through actions.[291] In a song dueling context, both the people in the audience and the performers interact with each other on the basis of the meanings that words, music and social behavior have for them. In Crete, the process of learning how to recite poetry is identical to acquiring one's own native tongue. Like Turkish minstrels, Cretans lay the foundation for composing poetry spontaneously after hearing thousands of poems in their childhood and early years of adulthood from those around them. "By hearing, memorizing and imitating poems, a young minstrel absorbs the rhythm of singing and the rhythm of rhyming, and constructs the basic rules of composing poetry."[292]

The *mandinada* verses reveal shared images, ideas, concepts and symbols. They are a culturally determined symbolic behavior and a form of artistic communication in which competitors have the opportunity to demonstrate their creative competence in an artificially constructed game atmosphere. However, during a song duel the performers do not mechanically reproduce the verses, which they have learnt by heart. "Because of the anticipation of people in the audience, a competing minstrel must incorporate an unexpected situation, topic or the presence of an unexpected individual into his poetry."[293]

Serenade performances are nostalgic, romantic as well as poetic ways of expression and communication. Traces of such events one finds in both the ancient Greek and the Byzantine eras. On the island of Crete, serenades became popular when the romance *Erotokritos* appeared. Through it we learn that the lute would accompany those tunes which would take place in the late evening. Etymologically, the word serenade in Greek, namely *kantada*, comes from the Latin "cantare," which stands for reciting while singing, praising in verse, performing a role, soothing or enchanting through singing and/or revealing a secret.[294] In ancient Greek, the verb *katado* stood for singing or entertainment through song.

The Cretan towns of Sitia and Viannos are famous for that genre of music which is either of erotic or entertaining, namely of an amusing character. Amongst the most popular instruments that would accompany the vocals are the violin, the mandolin, the guitar and the lute, as solo instruments or combined in duets. The verses of the *kantades* are typical *mandinades* whereas their basic music tune is that of the *condylies*. On the island of Crete, singing of that style is monophonic.

Melambes village weekly reunion: Manolis Lagoudakis on the *lyra*, Yannakomichalis singing.

In older times, serenades were part of the younger people's lifestyle, who, through them, would confess their feelings to their beloved ones. Though they could not do so profoundly, it was socially acceptable to dress with music notes and therefore present their emotions melodically. A Cretan village where that tradition still survives is that of Melambes in southern Rethymno. There, a unique style of performing that style of music exists, evolving around the notion of *parea* (group of friends).[295] The inhabitants of Melambes and its surroundings who have "migrated" to Heraklion, the capital of Crete, such as Kostas Fotakis and Giorgos Markakis, meet weekly so as to bring forth this tradition. They invite locals to a "sing along together," aiming both to the perpetuation of what they perceive as an ancestral tradition as well as its dissemination to the younger generations (a representative example being mathematician but also *lyra* and mandolin player, and singer Manolis Lagoudakis).

Musicians of the plains

By show-casing local musicians one may both discover and investigate the broad and the multifaceted identity, the species as well as the aesthetics of Greek music. An interdisciplinary committee consisting of medical doctors, teachers, social and cultural anthropologists, music and dance researchers (and lovers) diligently led by Dr. Emmanuel Chnarakis has recently put together and published several materials (such as CDs, DVDs, accompanied by thick, liner notes) on the musicians that follow.

The information those works provide its readers and listeners is of historical, anthropological, cultural and music significance. Its goal is to underline the variety of music idioms that exist on the island of Crete by focusing on the music making and the creations of musicians who perform on a series of instruments that identify mostly with the region called "Pediada" (namely plain). It aims to the preservation of a local music style by case-studying several of its representatives, serving, at the same time, as a research tool with raw materials for further examination. The group of people that worked together so as to compile all these materials shares a passion for their country, culture and music. Their texts present the musicians' biographies, talk about their place of origin, whereas they also negotiate traditional music on the island of Crete.

The publications have so far showcased:[296]

1) Iraklis Stavroulakis (1919-1997) was a legendary musician, violin-player and singer, from the Greek village of Episkopi at the county of Heraklion, capital of the island of Crete. Stavroulakis "harmonized" East-West in his playing in a purposeful decision to create and interpret through his violin melodies from the region of Heraklion but also the village that nurtured him. He was capable of varying the local *condylies* by simultaneously embodying in them "foreign" elements without, however, degrading the local character of Cretan music.

Stavroulakis' playing asked not only for listening but also dancing. His ultimate goal was the substantial communication through performance and its three-dimensional Greek character, that of "music-word-movement." While performing on the violin, he would converse with the dancers, adjusting his playing to the properly "correct" steps.

2) Manolis Chaniotakis (1906-2002) from the "Minoan," famous for its pottery village of Thrapsano, also performed violin music on the island of Crete and, more specifically, the region of Pediada. He extensively performed *condylies* but also the popular dance form on the island of Crete, namely the *Kastrinos pidichtos*. Worthy to mention is his tireless execution of long, demanding melodies for the sake of the local community and the dancers, by, at the same time, evoking the proper mood which enabled participants to keep performing for hours.

3) Giorgis Maravgakis or "Droseros" (b. 1933) comes from the neighboring to Thrapsano village of Mouhtaro (or Evangelismos). "Droseros" " (namely, "Fresh") is known for his keen interpretations on a variety of "plain" music genres, such as the *condylies* and the *Kastrinos* dance, but also other varieties of Cretan dragging and leaping dancing melodies. He has preserved the rarest "tune of the Pelalimata," a characteristic example of a regional melody that, according to locals, was used to accompany serenades and feasts that would take place around the homonymous lake, somewhere between the villages of Thrapsano and Mouhtaro (or Evangelismos).

As "Droseros" himself attests, in older times, when people were not using cars for transportation and had to walk back to their homes when a feast in either village was over, they would be accompanied by music on their way till the region of Pelalimata. There, the finale of the feast would take place by performing the homonymous melody, while the villagers from either group would communicate by exchanging oral, improvised verses, without dancing.

4) Yannis Fragoulidakis or Skarpathiotis (1920-2010), from the village of Kastelli, performed on solo violin representative tunes from the region of Pediada. His tunes reflect local sounds, such as the *condylies* and several interpretations of the Kastrinos dance, but also neighboring traditions from the western (e.g. dragging dances from the region of Chania-Kissamos) and eastern parts of the island (e.g. *condylies* from the Sitia prefecture).

5) The last two musicians performed mainly on the *lyra* and came from the village of Alagni. Giorgis Mathianakis or Psaros (1910-1995) specialized on the playing of the *viololyra*, namely a type of *lyra* that has many common traits with the violin. Manolis Mathianakis or Alagnianos (1908-1988) performed, amongst others, with Kostis Papadakis or the Kostis "of the Priest's Wife (*tis Papadias*)" (1913-1997) on the mandolin and with Yannis Apostolakis on the three-course (*trichordo*) *bouzouki* (a plucked string instrument with three pairs of strings).

Singing the Tree[297]

"Her" Olive Culture in Cretan Folk Poetry & Music

On the island of Crete, images frequently used within its folk songs are the olive and the olive-tree. The music-poetic formulas make use of the olive culture literally, through references to its rich agricultural cultivation since the antiquity, but also metaphorically, by recognizing it as a symbol of pride, global peace and feminine beauty. In fact, the Greek word for "olive," namely, *elia*, also stands for "skin spot," a symbol of beauty but also means of recognition amongst beloved ones. Here I focus on that aspect of the olive within the Cretan culture by looking at specific musi-co-poetic examples as well as by placing it within a broader ecological realm.

Such lyrics are based on conventional thematic, musical and linguistic patterns, often imbued with "gnomic" force, which should possess poetic excellence and co-herent meaning.[298] For example, tradition calls that Cretan women who have several children and are thus considered "successful homemakers" are the first to pick and taste the olives of a tree that gives fruits for its first time so that, in continuation, it also blossoms. A word that is frequently used to symbolically denote and speak of female beauty throughout Cretan poetry is the one for the "olive:"[299]

> Your eyes are like olives on a branch; your eyebrows like a two days old moon.
> I will mill the olive around your lips; with its olive I will light up love's vigil light.
> If I were to become a member of your family, I'd gladly be picking up your body's olives.
> I will turn into a swallow and sit on your neck so as to kiss the olive you have on the cheek.
> An angel drew your arched eyebrow; a drop by his paint brush is the olive on your cheek.
> When picking olives I think of your olive; I love you, Catherine, please, change your stance.
> You have an olive on the cheek and another on the arm; the one on the neck is your secret knife.
> I do not want the fake olives your dad has; I want the real ones you have on your cheeks.

After all, Goddess Athena, according to the Cretan mythology, was born on the shores of river Triton in Crete. She won the contest against God Poseidon about naming the city of Athens, as the popular Greek myth says, by offering to the hu-manity an olive-tree, namely a symbol of peace, wisdom and prosperity. Thus, fertility is perceived as a major attribute of the olive tree. As a result, Greek families who looked to gain fertility in their fields looked particularly to that tree.

As Meneley argues, the olive tree is both the sign of "feminine *techne*," namely the civilized and civilizing domestic crafts, and "masculine *techne*," namely the craftiness on the battlefield. Athena, who is also Odysseus' tutelary goddess, is the goddess of both aforementioned "*techne*," the olive tree being her gift to humankind.[300] Moreover, virginity, a qualisign of value that is used to characterize both people and olive oil, examined within the discourse of women and olive oil, stands for purity. It is perhaps not accidental that not only was Athena the goddess of *techne* but she was also a product of a virgin birth (who also remains a virgin for all the time), springing from the head of Zeus fully grown and clothed.[301]

In order to further illustrate the spread of the systematic cultivation techniques to the rest of Greece, Cretan mythology attests to the following: Anius, Ariadne's grandson, is one of the Cretans that King Minos' brother, Rhadamanthus (son of Zeus and Europe), chose as a ruler of several islands that belonged to the Cretan kingdom. He had three daughters, Oeno, Spermo and Elias. Dionysus correspondingly gave to the three daughters the power to change whatever they wanted into wine, wheat and oil.[302]

The absence of olives from the traditional, Cretan table creates nostalgia for what "home" (*ecos* in Greek) means. Therefore, I suggest a natural, eco-friendly reading of performances, such as the aforementioned, as I assert that the texts of the folk singers negotiate identities and express Cretan ideals and values of an environmentally-minded character. Since folk poetry and ecology are diligently interconnected, the use of folk poetry as a means of education could raise ecological awareness. In that context, the olive culture as negotiated via the texts of the folk poets could function as a "green" message to audiences of all ages.

Cretan folk song lyrics use images borrowed from the physical environment, such as the olive and the olive tree. For Cretans, such environmental imageries evoked through singing produce a sense of belonging to a specific, yet tangible land, which is part of who they are, namely their Cretan identity. Let us not forget that, as archaeologists Renfrew and Margaritis argue,[303] it was in Crete that a true agricultural revolution sparked and its clues grew: olive trees thrived on poor soil where little else would grow, which means land that would otherwise be barren could produce food.

Hamilakis acknowledges that food is culturally defined and acquires immense significance in all societies because it involves the human body.[304] It is (through consumption) an act of incorporation involving senses, feelings and emotions. The Italian philosopher Francesca Rigotti states that "the word is eating, and knowledge is food." "Her" philosophy processes thought as if it were food: it prepares, cooks and serves it in order to be eaten. Her book describes an analogy between food for the mind and food for the body.[305] In fact, food processing, much like thought processing, rests upon the ability of combining the unique with the multiple, the skill of setting off, separating and mixing elements into a universe ordered by precise laws, logic and rituals.

Viewed in that spirit, let's take into consideration the following: The Greek word for olive, *elia*, is, grammatically speaking, of feminine gender. In addition, it rhymes with the Cretan version of the word for girl, namely, *kopelia*. Skin spots, elies, in Greek, on the face or anywhere on the body, were highly perceived as "beauty marks," symbols of femininity, around the mid-nineteenth century and till the 1950s.[306] Moreover, in the Greek language, an olive can have humane attributes and, therefore, be "*stravomita*," namely with a "crooked nose," "*hondrolia*," fat, "*kolovi*," crippled, or... even "wrinkled."

Among the dances most performed on the island of Crete is the *Chaniotis* or *Chaniotiko(s)*, a circular dance performed both by men and women who may use this opportunity of communal, social dancing as a way of flirting and expressing personal emotions. An example of such a tune that makes use of the "olive image" is the one by the popular *lyra* player and folk music composer Kostas Mountakis (1926-1991). The musically elaborate melody revolves around one *mandinada* which asks a girl to explain why she has planted olives on her cheek and, this way, enslaved him forever.

The olive (Olea europaea L.) has a long and venerable history in Greece, and was mentioned by Homer as early as the 900 B.C..[307] When we turn to the Greek world, it seems clear that its cultivation was known in the Early Bronze Age Crete and that oil was being extracted both there and in the Greek islands.[308] After all, the land of Greece is particularly friendly to the olive whereas the Greek word for oil specifies olive oil.[309]

The first inhabitants of Crete, besides other crops, occasionally collected and ate the fruit of the wild olive tree (Olea oleaster), from as far back as the Neolithic Period (6,000-3,000 BC). Later on, during the 3rd millennium B.C., the inhabitants of Crete started the cultivation of the olive-tree and, during the 2nd millennium, proceeded to its systematic exploitation. On Minoan Crete, after 2,000 B.C., the olive assumes prominence in the royal economy of Knossos and is later passed on to the economy and life of Mycenaean Greece.[310]

According to the motto of the innovative Cretan olive-oil company *Terra Creta*, "if the Mediterranean is the world's olive grove, then Crete marks its heart."[311] A valuable information source on the importance of olive tree cultivation for the prehistoric societies is the evidence provided by the Linear B sun-dried clay tablets, unearthed in the Cretan Minoan city of Knossos, and in the palace of Pylos in the Peloponnese. On those tablets, dating back to the 14th-13th centuries B.C., the olive tree and the olive oil acquire their name in the Greek language, and thus, their identity for the economy and for the daily use of their time. It is the first point in history that we have the differentiation of the tree, the crop and the oil, and the three elements are depicted with three different ideograms. More specifically, the Greek words attested in Linear B syllabic script for olive tree and olive oil are "e-ra-wa" (*elea*) and "e-ra-wo" (*eleon*), respectively.[312] After all, the word "oil" in many languages derives from the ancient Greek word.

Plenty are the olive images that are found within Greek music and songs. Before re-turning to them, though, let us travel to the Greek island of Ithaca. The marriage bed of Odysseus and Penelope was made of an olive tree built into the house foundations. If the house is a metonymy of the world, then the bed is the symbol of the house, thus, the "*ecos*." It is not accidental that the bed is the outmost sign of recognition between the Homeric couple. It is not accidental, moreover, that the bed is made by an olive tree which is deeply rooted on the ground. That Homeric scene transforms itself in the Cretan variation of the Greek folk ballad "The Return of the Immigrant."[313] Here, the secret of Odysseus regarding the making of the bed out of the olive tree becomes the "olive," a skin spot, namely, on the body of the immigrant's wife.[314]

Sutton argues that we can understand the evocative power of food by examining some of the properties of synesthetic memory.[315] According to him, "the experience of food in Greece is cultivated synaesthetically and emotionally so that eating food from home becomes a particularly marked cultural site for the re-imagining of 'worlds' displaced in space and/or time."[316] But, isn't the union of senses an embodied aspect of creating the experience of the whole? If so, then, the synesthetic qualities of food are an essential ingredient in ritual and everyday experiences of totality. "Food does not only simply symbolize social bonds and divisions; it participates in their creation and recreation."[317] Olives, besides taste and smell, have a great association with both episodic and semantic memory, both symbolic and linguistic recognition, which explains why they are so useful for encoding powerful memories of vision or words.

In "The Return of the Immigrant," the "foreigner," *xenos*, who returns home after many years, his wife does not recognize, thus she asks for several proving marks.[318] The recognizing marks he offers her first, namely details regarding the garden or the house, are not intimate enough to prove a relationship between "the foreigner" and the woman. It is the last stage of recognition, a basic element of tragedy, according to Aristotle's *Poetics*,[319] that provides the listener with a "catharsis" and, in this variation, the repetition of the imagery confirms it: "You have an olive on your cheek, another on your arm pit, and two more in-between your breast, like the sun and the moon."

All three major Mediterranean religions, Christianity, Islam and Judaism, refer to the sanctity of olive oil, which was widely used in their rituals. The olive tree is the holy tree of all these three religions, the living hymn of God's creation. Its evergreen leaves denote immortality. The use of oil in the Greek Orthodox Church is meant to cure and sanctify the soul and the body, and is used as a weapon on the field of battle against evil and ammunition for eternal life. It is not accidental that one of the cognomens of the Virgin Mary, Panagia, is *eleovrytissa*, namely, she who is the wellspring of oil, the source from which oil springs, after a miracle she performed on Mount Athos (according to which she filled an empty vessel with oil).[320]

The olive harvest period in Greek is called *vendema* or *liomazohto*, and the women who pick the olives *mazohtres*. During the olive picking period, a significant number of workers gather at the olive production areas. The olive groves echo with voices, jokes, teasing and songs of the *mazohtres* and the *ravdistes*, those workers, namely, who climb on the trees and beat the olives till they fall on the ground. There are many distinct songs that refer to olive picking and to how this activity would allow for various social events and love affairs to take place amongst the *mazohtres* and the cultivators or other villagers, who wonder: "When picking is over, what reason will I have to grasp my basket so as to be able and see you?"

Similar to the aforementioned is the Palestinian story award-winning journalist, teacher, radio producer and author Sandy Tolan reports[321] at the National Public Radio: "People here record their history in relation to the olive trees," one of his informants characteristically says and continues: "People feel that every tree has a memory for them." The story ends with a traditional Palestinian harvest song called "Ya Daeiti" ("My Hands"). It is not accidental that the name of the Palestinian town Birzeit literally translates to "Bir," namely well, and "Zeit," namely oil. Hence, it means "well of oil," referring to the wells at which its inhabitants historically stored virgin-pressed olive. In fact, at the town center, stands an old press, with twin one-ton stones of granite that used to crush olives into oil. Similarly, several places in Greece are named after the "olive," such as the villages of Elia or Elea at Heraklion-Crete, Avlon-Euboea or the Laconic Peloponnese.

In *Branches of Memory*, Seremetakis[322] proposes that remembrance can be found in the emotional connection to particular spaces that have their own biographies, in objects that trigger deep emotions and narratives:

> The care and tending of olive trees is their adornment, what connects them to a household and to collectivity. The care and tending of olive trees endows them with affective value in relation to other subsistence crops (…) Each grove of olive trees (…) is the mark of the one on the many…

All in all, the olive tree through its cultivation is invested with feeling and history, and is expressive of the women and men whose hands care for it. After all, its cultivation is a projection to the future that always carries along the signature of a person.

In a way, this both emotional and conscious investment gets realized via Greek traditional music, especially due to its social role. Oftentimes, on the island of Crete, *mandinades* are performed dialogically, face-to-face, usually with the purpose of competing or teasing. They may be sung, set to music, or even spoken. Such a performance occasion could be during olive picking, as the composition "Time Has

Come" by Kostas Mountakis witnesses.

The music piece is a *kalamatianos* dance, originally from the famous – even out-side Greece – for its olives region of Kalamata, nowadays the most popular dance form in Greece. As is the case with most Greek folk dances, it is danced in a circle with counterclockwise rotation, the dancers holding hands, following a 7/8 beat. Depending on the occasion and the dancers' proficiency, certain steps may be taken as jumps or squats. The lead dancer usually holds the second dancer by a handker-chief, this allowing her or him to perform more elaborate steps and acrobatics.

The "Time Has Come" lyrics talk of the implicit outcomes such activities may result to by emphasizing on the presence of young women, *kopelies*, who will start picking olives, *elies*, this way, enabling the millers and the *mazohtres* to chat and, thus, do "golden business." The millers ask for the weather to be friendly so as to en-able the picking and, hence, their meeting with the young girls, who will be holding the baskets, asking them to grind their olives "under proportional payment." And the song concludes: "Please, my beautiful girl, grasp the basket and I will hold the ladder so as to assist you going up the olive-tree but, as soon as you're done, let's kiss each other and 'make... olive-oil' under the olive tree"!

The aforementioned folk songs and dances do not look for a nostalgic revival or preservation of what Crete "is," but rather assert a particular interpretation of Cre-tan identity that suggests ethical responsibilities entailed by living on that island[323] as "the olive trees carry the wrinkles of our fathers" that Mother Earth "teaches us how to study."[324] Musico-poetic creations lead to the transformation of a reality to a new, poetic universe, in which nature and its basic elements gradually tend to lose their real hypostasis and substance, and thus become symbols, in which the element of personal and human experience is crucial and dominant. From Homer's almost naturalistic depiction of the olive tree, combined with adjectives which refer to its productive qualities along with the calm and at the same moment impressive image of its presence, to folk poetry and music, the olive tree justifies its prime position in Greek experience and thought.[325]

For the Greeks, olives are the memory of a strong connection with the land and the taste of earth. Performers and their audience, through ritualized processes, transform natural images into human essences. The olive tree depiction into Greek music and dancing unveils and reflects the aesthetic principles of a civilization, which respects the olive tree as source of life and lavishes on it care and toil. The more the Greeks engage themselves with such efforts, the more clearly they perceive that, should they wish to understand who they are, they would simply have to keep singing the "trees of life."

Chapter 4

Speaking without Words

Wedding Dance as Expression, Dialogue and Communication

Entering the dance[326]

We are about to attend the wedding feast of a Cretan friend. I am thrilled, my companions too. From the windows of the car we see the proud mountain of Psiloritis bathed in sunset colors. A strong afternoon wind wafts to our ears the melodies of the *lyra*. Upon arrival, we park and walk to the lower part of the village. The music sounds and the smell of the grilled meat lead us on.

Our destination is the groom's house. There, with his male friends, after the ceremony at the church, he drinks *raki*, a traditional alcoholic spirit from grapes, the short drink of Crete, the equivalent of the Italian grappa, distilled from the skin and stones of raisins, with a musty flavor, whereas he also treats all of his guests with big pieces of meat and watermelon. He wears a white *sariki* (turban). I congratulate him from a distance. Here we are at the wedding feast, the widest part of this very narrow street where most of the bride's family lives.

Happy faces, smiles and loud voices greet us. By a wall there is a wooden stage where the musicians perform. Around it people dance continuously. Few are sitting on benches. The villagers undertake to treat us. They bring huge pieces of meat and red wine. They honor us with a white handmade handkerchief. Later they bring us a whole watermelon. We "slaughter" it with the knife they hand us.

Old and young men in traditional clothing "occupy" the first dances. The dancing floor is theirs. As I find out, it is the groom's close male relatives, excited and full of joy for the wedding event, who are among the first to give themselves to dancing. The older men perform dragging steps. When improvising or making solo figures, they keep their arms extended, ready to fly. Younger men and women join the dances afterwards.

Meanwhile the musicians accept requests. Men gathered in front of them, ask for particular tunes and songs. A "successful" Cretan wedding feast is achieved through its participants' *kefi* which is arrived at methodically and systematically through drinking, singing and dancing, and through intensive expression of feelings and special relationships among the guests of a wedding feast. Without *kefi a glendi* (feast) cannot exist. After reaching and while reaching it, a wedding feast becomes a means of identifying community members and of establishing identities and roles in it.

Time comes for every request to be played. "How slowly do moments pass when waiting, but how fast sweet moments go by," the *lyra* player sings. The men who know this *mandinada* shake their hands, swing their heads, and clap while dancing.

It is almost midnight and the whole village is still awake. Those who do not dance sing along with the melodies or comment on the ones who are dancing. In the beginning of the event there was just one dancing circle. Now more and more circles of dancers are added, sometimes the one into the other, like a snail, or the labyrinth of King Minos, as Cretans envision it.

Men and women, children too, excited and full of joy, give themselves to dancing. Everybody who dances shares *raki* from the same bottle. "My basil with your curly leaves stand where you are, so that your lovely smells can be spread all over the world," a young man requests. While dancing to it, he also sings and performs acrobatic dancing movements and agile leaps.

The sensation of watching is great. The males' dancing figures tempt my eyes. They are magnetic. The music is hand-clapping and foot-stomping; humming in our ears. People who do not dance wave their heads. The dancers enact their lives in the narrow street. They dance their lives and give us their hearts. There is synchronization, communication between the musicians and the dancers. The sounds convey meanings, and the lyrics are powerful.

Merry people sing along with the melodies or comment on the dancing. On the stage, three *laouto* players and one *lyra* player (who is also the basic singer and the leader of the group) play music through amplifiers. A solo melodic invitation by the *lyra* players invites the dancers to the dancing floor, in the narrow street where the bride lives. It is the *lyra* players who also indicate which group's turn it is. They decide upon the length of the dances too.

The bride and the groom join the dances very late that night. The ground is free for them, their close friends and relatives. Men who carry guns shoot once in a while, to celebrate the wedding event. *Yia sou!* (to your health!), *na zis' i Kriti!* (may Crete live forever!). Hearts are united, the village is united, more and more people are dancing. Our company and friends request a dance and we join them. We hold hands with people we do not know.

Music and dance for joy, as a release of energy and power, expressing a culture, confirming community bonds, representing a family's name. Music is for music and dance is for dance. The night goes on, and the bodies continue moving. It is 4.30 a.m. The *lyra* player performs "Quit Living with Dreams." Dance is never-ending, and life goes on...

> Wherever I go I carry with me soil from Psiloritis,
> To spread it so that the whole world becomes Crete.
>   Cretan rhyming distich (*mandinada*)

The narrow streets of the old, Cretan villages lead to the abrupt hills. While walking through them, one experiences squares with shops and taverns. Many of those restaurants serve traditional Cretan food, such as macaroni with *anthotiros* (a special type of salty white hard cheese, very similar to ricotta), *ofto* (roast), as well as wonderful deserts, including *galaktoboureko* (a sort of milk pastry), *mizithropita-kia* (mizithra cheese pies), and *sarikopites* (another type of cheese pies) with honey syrup and fresh *mizithra* (similar to farmer's cheese and ricotta), while some of the shops sell embroidery, laces, carpets, and colorful handmade pieces of cloth.

Sfakiani pita, namely pancake with cheese kneaded into the dough served with honey at Sfakia-Crete.

Cretans are hospitable and friendly, serving *Xenios* (Hospitable) Zeus. On several occasions, such as small gatherings in restaurants, they do not hesitate to take down instruments that decorate the walls, to play them and sing. They are also willing to share stories from the wars, legends about their village, folk sayings and poetry with visitors.

On the mountains surrounding the village one can observe the bearded vulture and the wild goats. Cretans plant *vasilikos* (basil). Its leaves are curly, numerous, and have an intense aroma. Usually parts of it are put behind the ears of the musicians and the people who dance happily. Many song lyrics refer to this plant and compare it to the female presence and virtues, as *vasilikos* generally stands for beauty and dignity.

Cretans need few excuses for social gatherings with all the merriment, music, dancing, food and drink that constitute a true *glendi*. Being from Crete is an art, a performance. The traditional Cretan life-style allows one to have something of one's own but at the same time to be different from other Cretans, Greeks and the rest of the world.

> I have stopped falling in love – this is, I think, a problem,
> Because one who doesn't love, has nothing to hope for.
>   Cretan rhyming distich (*mandinada*)

In Greece, marriage is of supreme value. It is regarded as a necessary condition of procreation, and therefore of the continuation of life, and, in a more metaphysical sense, of the self through the perpetuation of family names and the persons of the parents. As social institutions, weddings reflect broad patterns of cultural behavior while they also reveal much about a society's values, structure and ethnic conscious-ness.[327] They are large, communal events which address many sorts of understand-ings that community members hold. The "speak of" kinship ties, interfamilial rela-tionships and the distinct stages of the life-cycle through which women and men pass.[328]

In Crete, the whole village participates and has to participate in those events in or-der for the community ties to be upheld and the communal identity to be expressed. Such events bring people together who may, for personal reasons, not talk to each other in everyday discourse. Those wedding events, however, unify the villagers in the name of their place. In Crete, not being able to attend a wedding without a rea-sonable excuse may be considered as an insult not only for the families of the newly married couple, but also for the whole society.

In Greece, one cannot have a wedding without dance. The dance event and the wedding event are integrated, inseparable. Dance begins from the moment one gets married in the church. In the Greek Orthodox church, after the priest gives the newly-weds the Cup to drink three times in a row, in token of their common life together, the entire wedding party walks three times in a circle. This scene has been traditionally called the "Isaiah's dance." Of great importance is also the dance that sometimes takes place at the churchyard, upon the conclusion of the religious cere-mony, symbolizing the "bringing out" of the newlywed couple (the bride, in partic-ular)[329] into society.

The wedding preparations start months before the specific day of the actual cere-mony whereas a traditional Cretan wedding can last from one to ten days. The days before the actual celebration special wedding breads, foods and sweets are prepared by the two families. The animals that are going to be slaughtered on the occasion of that event are selected by the local shepherds. Wine and *raki* are also gathered in great amounts. Honey and walnuts are served to all unmarried women. A few days before the wedding ceremony several smaller feasts are held separately for the groom and the bride. Relatives and friends may also visit the two households and give them their wedding gifts in advance.

The center of the dance event is the celebration of the new couple. This exchange symbolizes the acceptance of the bride and the groom by each family and by the whole society and is being established through dancing. The wedding *glendi* begins late in the evening and dance is its central activity.

Dancing

Since dance is the central activity in Cretan wedding feasts, I shall call them dance events. Wedding feasts include, among other things, dancing as a necessary part for all the participants, of all genders and ages. Dancing is more than knowing the steps; it involves both social knowledge and power. In those Cretan wedding feasts, girls and boys, women and men act in different ways and assume roles that are assigned to them culturally. Celebrants perform in gendered ways and experience themselves as gendered subjects.

In a dance event, all ages take part and play a specific role. The presence of the old men testifies to the continuation of generations and communal tradition. The old women have the right to scorn everything that is considered, according to them, inappropriate. In Crete, behaviors observed in dance events may be criticized for a long period after their actual execution.

Despite the fact that the song and the instrumental playing are "male matters" (instrument players are dominantly male since the lyrics of the majority of songs address a woman) dance cannot be acted without the participation of women. Though men are the ones who start the dancing in the wedding feasts and who take almost all the initiatives while dancing, all dances performed at weddings are mixed, performed by both genders, exactly because they symbolize the presence of the community as a whole in a public place. In this context, the criteria of participation in a dance are not individual but social.

Men in Crete still wear the traditional boots (*stivania*) and the typical scarf (*sariki*), which, at wedding events, is placed around their necks and not around their heads (as they normally do), and which at wedding events is not black but white. Most of them carry knives in their trousers' pockets or in their waists, symbols of masculinity, pride and honor. The whole costume of the male, usually a plain dark (preferably black) shirt and a *vraka*, is still worn by older and younger men in present-day Crete as respect to cultural heritage. The pants of the *vraka* are exaggerated breeches with a fullness of fabric that somewhat resembles a tail. Stuffing the shirt into this contributes added weight and makes for a nice swing while dancing.

Another symbol of masculinity is the mustache that typically men in Crete have. Cretans are also known to be good shepherds. They compete in animal-theft, in which the stronger of the shepherds are engaged. They construct narrations of their male identity and represent their deeds through them. They usually own a gun. They avoid quarreling, but they will do so if someone insults their pride and honor. They will draw the gun and shoot in the air to celebrate a wedding event.

While dancing, Cretan men give the impression of cranes, trying to imitate the flying of the birds they daily see. Flying symbolizes their desire for independence, for freedom (*eleftheria*). Their elder relatives and friends move with slower movements that seem to be simple but which are, in fact, thoughtful and wise. In the vivid dances, they give themselves to dancing. They perform many leaps, showing off their *levendia* (gallantry), strength and agility, that they do not fear anything or anybody who threatens (or has threatened in the past) them and their village. In other words, they feel independent and free because they can dance. The wildness of their dance is a sweet one, self-protecting against any misfortune.

This way, performers and viewers are socially and historically placed individuals. Moreover, this communication involves decoding or making sense out of the process and product of cultural forms that manipulate human bodies in time and space according to the cultural conventions and aesthetic systems of a specific group of people at a specific time and in specific contexts.[330]

The father of the bride usually maintains the first position in dancing for a long time. Because of his age, his steps are heavy. He may wave a kerchief with his right hand. His arms are extended. The emphasis is on his steps. He dances full of joy and pride. He invites others to also join the dance, sharing his happiness.

Women join in the dances later in the evening. Their dancing steps are conspicuously chaste, avoiding the acrobatics of the young males. The older ones walk sedately up and down, minding children or chatting in small groups. Others line up on the wall, watching the general activity but avoiding direct personal contact with individual young men. Women in Crete regard these events as a valued break in the daily routine, a chance to go out and socialize. Such feasts may also be a chance for them to meet with their future husbands.

Women's posture, when dancing, remind one of the ancient Minoan goddesses of fertility, holding snakes on their opened hands and exposed chest. They assume this position when they come in the middle of the circle to perform turns and other dancing figures. They hardly move their torso, while they keep their arms in an open position in opposition to the men, who keep their hands behind their back, especially when dancing as a couple. Generally, women are expected to dance demurely but with a proud posture. Their torso must remain stable and upright, while nothing moves from waist to head.

All ages of women get up to perform, although with varying degrees of skill and grace. Young girls tend to add more swerves and bounces than young adult women do. Stylistically, the foot movements of the older women are differentiated from those of the young ones. Young women tend to take larger steps than older women. Married women may also join in on fast-tempo dances and perform with verve and liveliness. Generally, though, as those women get older, their style of dancing is expected to become more serious and less playful. Older women tend to use walking rather than springing steps.

The bride is the central and most symbolically elaborate figure in the entire wedding ritual. A specific group of people, starting with the close relatives and the family of the bride and the groom "dances her" (what is known as the bridal dance; *o choros tis nifis*). The bride and the groom dance in the first positions to honor their guests. Their dance has a symbolic meaning; it establishes the union of a woman and a man, the male and the female entity.

When dancing, both women and men must be careful on how they move and what they say. Everyone must know what her/his position in the dance is. At the same time everyone must eat, drink, and dance. When outside the circle of dancers, people observe and gossip. They watch and judge who is a good dancer. They applaud the good dancing figures; they shout "nice, opa-opa I'm saying!" (*"oraios, opa-opa leo!"*), or whistle. They give the impression that the important thing celebrated is not the wedding but the dance itself.

Cretans may comment negatively on the people who prefer "foreign" dances instead of the Cretan ones. They recognize Cretan dances as a living history of their place and they refuse to "pollute" their dancing repertoire with "modern" dancing. Women should not shake their chests and hips; these are "immoral" movements. Even men should keep a balance while performing individually acrobatic dancing figures otherwise they become "clowns" and *Karagiozides* (namely, "entertaining shadow-puppet theater figures"). Good dancers are the ones who keep their bodies dignified and upright. Because most of the dances are done in a circular chain formation, arm gestures are practically excluded. When a dancer leads, then she/he may leave the chain and dance singly. Men extend their arms, whereas women place them around, hugging, almost squeezing their waist.

Facial expression is also important. Performers are happy and serious at the same time. Happy because they are dancing, they are celebrating, but also serious because they are being watched, because the community will judge them and, at the end, it is their dancing tradition they must represent in the best way.

Cretan dancing can be of two broad categories, dragging (*sirto*) and leaping (*pidichto*). The first category refers to the movement of the feet over the ground in a dragging or shuffling motion, and the second to a springing, hopping, jumping, stamping, or leaping foot motion. There are also some dances that contain elements of both. The most popular form of those dances is the open circle with the regular handhold position. In this position, and when facing the chain of dancers, the arms of the people who dance resemble the letter W. The hands of the dancers are held out to the side while their shoulders are high with an almost right-angle bend at the elbow. Another popular Cretan dance form is the straight line in which the outstretched arms are placed on the shoulders of the adjoining dancer.[331] Finally,

Cretan dances proceed counter-clockwise.

Most of the Cretan dances follow the traditional ritual protocol with the open circle and the order of participation according to gender and age ranking within the family and the community. Through that gender and age intermingling, the concept of "community" is being fulfilled in the Cretan towns and villages.[332]

The majority of Cretan dancing consists of open, single curved lines or serpentines. Progressive step movements move directly over the advancing foot. Overall, the quality of the movements is clipped and nervous with some smoothness primarily attributable to the fact that the feet are kept close to the ground. There is variation between slow and quick steps with emphasis upon a gradual increase in speed. The great diversity of rhythms and their combinations may result in many types of steps and figures.

Because most Cretan dances are in an open circle, it is the first dancer (*brostaris*) who takes the initiative. The distinctiveness of the community is reproduced in the *egoismos* (ego; pride) of the individual performer. One who is "good at being a man" must also know how to dance the acrobatic steps of the leader of the line.[333] The lead dancers can execute complicated steps consisting of whirls, turns or lively jumps. Their movement is towards the right, leading all dancers around a ground pattern maybe best described as half-moon. When a male leads he is particularly encouraged and expected to indulge in various hand slaps, slaps on thighs, soles and heels, in addition to numerous leaps, turns and acrobatic movements.

His relatives and friends are among the first to join him. People who join the dances later should not join as leaders, this being a rude behavior. When the leaders retire, they move to the rear of the line, passing their position on to the person immediately to their left.

The behavior of the first dancer shows her/his personality, which is being criticized by the whole village. Consequently, while the Cretan circle dance may look like a team dance, it is mostly a dance performed by the first dancer. The first dancer expresses her/his individuality in dancing, while the rest of the dancers convey the communal spirit. Both the first dancer and the rest of the dancers "talk" through dancing about social embodiment. The dancer has to dance throughout the whole music piece because her/his abilities may also be judged in relation to the length of time. In general, Cretans may dance for hours. Often their dances take the form of competition of stamina and bravery.

Cretans learn how to dance by holding hands with elders at feasts, such as weddings, through watching and observing. When in school, they practice Cretan dances as part of their gymnastics classes, at school feasts and national holidays. Outside school, they may also join local dancing troupes. Dancing functions as a means of exhibiting abilities, developing friendships, entertainment and confirmation of gender and communal identity. Its steps are not a mere matter of mimicry. In this context, Cretan dance is a mainly public event that assumes educational dimensions.

When Cretans refer to the feasting experience of dance events they talk about "their" dances. A group of specific dancing forms that are repeated in a cultural unit, such as the village of Crete, could be called its dancing repertory. That repertory in Crete reveals the local tradition of that area and, at wedding feasts, is strictly Cretan. Sometimes, dances of other Greek regions may also be performed but that is not the norm.

All in all, Cretan dance is a double expression of the inner and the outer world: an expression that comes out from the dancer, expressing her/his personality, individual past and emotional situation. Furthermore, the expression that comes out of this environment is the one that her/his surroundings impose upon them, and which unavoidably is being expressed throughout the dance, the music they listen to, the people who dance with them or look at them, the occasion under which they dance, all the past of the social team they belong to.

Certainly, the people of Crete dance with passion. The movements of their feet can be really rapid, while they may also lead them to ecstatic phenomena, also because they dance for a long time. As the dancer loses herself/himself in the dance, as she/he becomes absorbed in the unified community, they reach a state of elation in which they feel themselves filled with energy beyond their ordinary state. And at the same time, feeling themselves in complete and ecstatic harmony with all the fellow-members of their community, the dancers experience a great increase in feelings of amity and attachment towards them.

The kinds of touching in the line dances found throughout Crete and Greece, more generally, convey a sense of camaraderie, unity and strength. Dancing, in this sense, also gives one the feeling of security. By touching, the dance produces a condition in which the unity, harmony and concord of the community are at a maximum, and in which they are intensely felt by every member. Holding hands with people also offers one happiness and security. This feature of Greek music is particularly beneficial for emotional stability as both listening to and performing music in a group setting have been shown to be successful means for emotional self-regulation, expression and relaxation.

Lastly, Cretan dancing at weddings is a moral discourse. One cannot attend a wedding ceremony without also attending the dance event that follows it. And everyone is expected to dance.

After the dance

> As long as Crete is singing songs and dance is never ending,
> Fearless flying like the eagle, it will be forever living.
> Cretan rhyming distich (*mandinada*)

Through the present essay the story of a community, in this particular case, of

Crete, can be told through a wedding dancing feast, where Greeks identify with the way they dance (in the sense of "we are what we dance"). Because dances are an integral part of life, an event is not considered a proper wedding, if dance is not a basic component. Since one cannot have a wedding without dance, the dance event and the wedding event are, in a certain sense, the same thing. Greek weddings offer undoubtedly several opportunities for gathering and merry-making, while they are also the best ground for local dances to be performed and for locals to "speak" about themselves through dancing.

In great part, Greece owes its existence to its dances, a country where islands, such as that of Crete, will be living as long as locals express themselves through dancing. Because it is dancing that makes Greeks, above all, to feel free and bound to one another. This is important for the Greek concept of life. Let us remember the epitaph of the Cretan-born author Nikos Kazantzakis: "I have no fear, I have no hope, I am free." This expresses the essence of being Greek – and this is exactly what the whole discourse of Greek performance is about.

Studying abroad in Crete-Greece: At the Kazantzakis' tomb (in Heraklion-Crete) that bears the epigraph "I have no fear; I have no hope; I am free!"

Revisiting Zorba's Dance

Before the Dance

> My life's greatest benefactors have been journeys and dreams. Very few people, living or dead, have aided my struggle. If, however, I wished to designate which people left their traces embedded most deeply in my soul, I would perhaps designate Homer, Buddha, Nietzsche, Bergson, and Zorba.[334]

The words to follow are on Zorba the Greek and his dance. My goal is to show the importance of dancing in Greek culture and how Greeks talk through their body, as well as how, through body language, Greeks create a dialogue between the western-Apollonian-order with the eastern-Dionysian-chaos. Greeks act life; indeed, as Zorba, their kinsman, they dance it as well. By doing so, Greeks subconsciously and creatively use dancing as a therapeutic means of self- and psycho-analysis, as they manage to liberate themselves by healing their egos. After all, the world of Greece is a world of culture, always with the *anthropos* (human being) centered.[335]

Constantine Cavafy and Nikos Kazantzakis are two modern Greek writers whom non-Greeks are familiar with. The popularity of the novel *Zorba the Greek* is attributed to the fact that it urged American and European intellectuals discover what they were not, what their repressed self was; in other words, it offered westerners a prototype of liberation.[336] Readers got fascinated by the transcendence of the ego that the East was promising them. The Mediterranean eyes of Kazantzakis' work were an attraction for the western society, which, tired from logic and abundance, admired Zorba, a daring, spontaneous hero, who refused conventions and admitted his emotional passions.

In 1964, the film "Zorba the Greek" was released and became even more popular than its "visual" 1960 relative, "Never on Sunday." The film was directed by Michael Cacoyannis with the popular soundtrack composed by Mikis Theodorakis. The final image by which the audience left the cinema was that of Zorba's dance, a scene which became the symbol of Greece and of the Greek spirit represented by Zorba in particular.[337] Mikis Theodorakis comments that the film's music has been turned into a myth.[338] Since that time, Zorba and his dancing have lent their name to restaurants and various other products all over the world. [339]

When in Paris, between 1907 and 1909, Kazantzakis combined his studies about the French philosopher Bergson with a reading of Nietzsche. The German philosopher had a powerful influence on Kazantzakis, who, in turn, wrote a dissertation on him. Clearly, Nietzsche's "process theology" is expressed in Kazantzakis' novel, *Zorba the Greek*. According to Nietzsche's ideas about the sources of religion, god is the result of whatever the most energetic and heroic people value and create.

Peter Bien, indeed, argues how Zorba's actions are immediate reflections of Nietzsche's ideas.[340] To his perception, Zorba is the "superhuman" who knows that there is not a true, reasonable, permanent, ordered, or good world for us.[341] Throughout his works, however, Kazantzakis does not kill "his" God, as Nietzsche would do, but, instead, wishes to save Him, same thing that derives from Kazantzakis' wish to kill the awesome father of his childhood, whom he continued to hate and fear most of his life.[342]

Kazantzakis had an obvious relationship with psychoanalysis. Even though he seemed to despise psychoanalysts, in 1922, in Vienna, he wrote that he is satisfied with Freud's theory for dreams and instincts. He particularly favored the dark subconscious as we see in a 1949 letter to his philhellene Swedish friend Knoes. He visited the Viennese psychiatrist Stekel to consult him regarding his skin disease.[343] Indeed, it was the occasion of that illness which brought him in contact with psychoanalysis and convinced him that the power of the unconscious was stronger than his willful determination to become a religious prophet and a heroic world figure by means of self-discipline and identification with Buddhist principles.[344]

A psychological analysis of Zorba could argue that Kazantzakis' hero who lives everything, every day, as for the first time, is the exact opposite of his biological father, the dreadful, authoritative Captain Michael (Kazantzakis' 1953a novel carries his father's name in its original, Greek version).[345] Indeed, Kazantzakis felt free when the formidable man died, that "heavy lion" who had contributed to the emotional eunuchism of his childhood.[346]

A New Statesman

> If it had been a question in my lifetime of choosing a spiritual guide, a guru as the Hindus say, a father as say the monks at Mount Athos, surely I would have chosen Zorba. For he had just what a quill-driver needs for deliverance: the primordial glance which seizes its nourishment arrow-like from on high; the creative artlessness, renewed each morning, which enabled him to see all things constantly as though for the first time, and to bequeath virginity to the eternal quotidian elements of air, ocean, fire, woman, and bread; the sureness of hand, freshness of heart, the gallant daring to tease his own soul, as though inside him he had a force superior to the soul; finally, the savage bubbling laugh from a deep, deep wellspring deeper than the bowels of man, a laugh which at critical moments spurted redemptively from Zorba's elderly breast, spurted and was able to demolish (did demolish) all the barriers – morality, religion, homeland – which that wretched poltroon, man, has erected around him in order to hobble with full security through his miserable smidgen of life.[347]

An intellectual is writing a manuscript on Buddha. At the port of Piraeus, he meets with Alexis Zorba, an uneducated man, and hires him to superintend the work-men in the abandoned lignite mine on the island of Crete. Zorba values experience and understanding more than scholarly learning: "What's the use of all your damn books? You think too much, that is your trouble. Clever people and grocers, they weigh everything." After a series of victories and failures, the writer leaves Crete, but asks Zorba to teach him to dance.

The story described illustrates the contrast introduced by Nietzsche between the Apollonian and the Dionysian outlook on life. Apollo, the writer, represents the spirit of order and rationality, while Dionysus, Zorba, represents the spirit of ec-static, spontaneous will to live. The whole story is a fable about the mind and the body.[348]

Bien describes the boss' transformation this way: "His Apollonian powers, hither-to either paralyzed or misdirected, can now turn to the task of redeeming Dionysian reality, rescuing Zorba from dissolution."[349] He can now function as a "tragic" artist, fuse his western mentality with Zorbatic barbarism, transform within his womb the barbarian seed, and bear an artistic son: the tragic myth called Zorba the Greek.

Kazantzakis wants his eternal Greek (or, Hellene) to be nothing different than the Greek race itself, a marvelous synthesis of both East and West. Moreover, through "his" Zorba, Kazantzakis embraces both the western as well as the eastern. The pro-tagonist wants to get rich, but, at the same time, acts very irresponsibly. He aban-dons rationality to live in madness. In Bien's view, he rejects the mind in favor of the heart, whereas everyone is overwhelmed by an inexorable, tragic, destructive fate.[350]

Kazantzakis' vision, besides being Greek, is definitely Cretan as well. Crete, for Kazantzakis, is his homeland, an island at the southernmost part of Greece, a cross-roads of many cultures and civilizations, a synthesis that he always pursued. He feels neither European, nor ancient Greek, nor eastern. He breathes another air, a composition of all these forces and their components that empower and make him proud and brave. The syncretic glance that dares to look at life and death nakedly, Kazantzakis names Cretan. It is the exact same look of the Minoan who stares at the scared bull, just before his dangerous leap.[351]

Scholars have traced political connotations on Zorba as well. They comment on how he expresses patriotism by being an internationalist during the Second World War period.[352] Although the homonymous novel was written during the dark days of the Occupation, through it, Kazantzakis' double objective was to examine and project the Greek people's remarkable powers of endurance despite repeated disas-ter, and the artist's need to draw from the unpleasant concreteness of everyday real-ity in order to create abiding archetypes.

Though the film ends rather deliciously with Zorba teaching the boss how to dance, the whole point of the book's end is that the boss is liberated as an artist and is then able to write his "Saint's Life of Zorba." He does not become like Zorba (as the film would have us believe). Instead, the boss converts Zorba's flesh into spirit.[353]

Undoubtedly, Kazantzakis sees Zorba as a teacher, and writes about him in the same spirit Plato "apologizes" for Socrates. For him, Alexis Zorba is a spokesman of wise teachings, who created his biographer, Nikos Kazantzakis, who, in turn, metamorphosed him into Zorba the Greek. Through those writings, Kazantzakis is now the author who applies his authority to control and expand on his hero's personality.[354] By creating such models, he struggles to resemble them, thus, he is also being self-created.

All in all, Kazantzakis creates a myth, as, through Zorba, he emotionally addresses great moral questions of inaction, agency and fate versus free will. He then uses this myth as his own, personal mirror.[355] But, will he dance?

Zorba's Dance

> I do not believe in coincidence; I believe in destiny. This bas-relief divulged the secret of my life with astonishing simplicity, perhaps the secret of Zorba's life as well. It was a copy of an ancient tombstone carving. A naked warrior, who has not abandoned his helmet, not even in death, is kneeling on his right knee and squeezing his breast with both palms, a tranquil smile flitting around his closed lips. The graceful motion of the powerful body is such that you cannot distinguish whether this is a dance or death. Or is it a dance and death together? Even if it is death, we shall transform it into a dance, I said to myself, encouraged by the happy sun falling upon the warrior and bringing him to life. You and I, my heart, let us give him our blood so that he may be brought back to life, let us do what we can to make this extraordinary eater, drinker, workhorse, woman-chaser, and vagabond live a little while longer – this dancer and warrior, the broadest soul, surest body, freest cry I ever knew in my life.[356]

Kazantzakis often feels compelled to describe in details and depth the gradual development of psychological conditions that lead to an imperative necessity for singing or dancing. Such activities represent, for him, the outcome, the climax, and the quintessence of the inner psychological preparation and ascent, often complex and bewildering, of the hero reaching his true liberation through such fundamental acts. Moreover, he also mentions in his writings the use of musical instruments, manipulated by his heroes as symbols of elevation at important moments. All in all, Kazantzakis sees music and dance as means of extreme elevation, often almost a religious one. [357]

Zorba may also be viewed not as a novel, but as a memorial.[358] When Zorba's flesh died, his myth started to crystallize in Kazantzakis' mind. Zorba started to become a fairy tale. Kazantzakis would see him dance, neighing in the middle of the night and calling him to spring up from his comfortable shell of prudence and habit, and to take off with him on great travels. [359] His love (*Eros*) for Zorba, gave life to his death (*Thanatos*). The writer, who is not a dancer, immortalized him in pen.

Zorba's singing and playing on the *santouri* (dulcimer) carries his sorrow and his yearning. It is the dancing, however, which Zorba manages to drag his boss into, which acts as the intensively as well as impressively emotional and passionate act: Kazantzakis sees on the music-dance blaze-up of Zorba the contact with the timeless, a moment that transcends every cultural civilization meaning.[360] Indeed, on the last day in Crete, the boss learns from Zorba a remedial lesson in dancing. But, unlike Zorba, he does not merge with the dance; in Nietzsche's terms, he does not become the work of art.[361]

Zorba is dancing solo, arms extended, ready to fly with the eagles of Crete. He has the freedom to perform improvisational, virtuoso movements, giving himself to dancing. He jumps in the air, performing agile, acrobatic leaps, trying to show his gallantry and pride, demonstrating strength and agility, and that, in fact, he does not fear anything and anybody who threatens his freedom; He feels independent and free because he can dance.

In Greece, the embodied soul can find its release not through logos but through movement. Zorba is the authentic, almost forgotten Greek self, the man who may drink, curse and sleep with women of loose morals but who has an enviable quality that the educated European lacks: he is in tune with himself. The metaphor is one that would have appealed to Plato, for it is through the means of music and dance, a language of the body (*soma*) as well as the mind (*nous*), that Zorba, in contrast to the "boss" (and perhaps to Kazantzakis himself), achieves a secure sense of his place in the universe.[362]

As Kazantzakis states, this novel about his diseased friend Alexis Zorba is more than anything a dialogue between a pen-pusher and an older folk person; a dialogue between a lawyer of the mind and the great soul of the people.[363] It is apparent that Zorba's stories are more connected to the body than to the brain. In such contexts then, folk dancing becomes for Zorba and, in extension for the Greeks, a primal non-verbal behavior, an authentic voice, a "deeper body language."[364]

Savigliano argues how tango is the only place in which she feels comfortable, restless, but at home, especially when not at home.[365] Such is Zorba's story. His dance both hurts and comforts him. It is his changing, resourceful source of identity, his strategic language, a way of talking about, understanding, exercising decolonization.

"Boss, I have never loved a man as much as you. I have hundreds of things to say, but my tongue just can't manage them…So, I will dance them for you." It is when feelings well up to the point where words can no longer suffice that Zorba begins dancing. For Zorba, the impersonator of the folk, or for any Greek, in extension, dance is the ultimate creative act and follows its own, natural laws. Despite the fact that the book does not end with the dance scene, most people continue to see the conclusion as the hero learning to dance and thereby to perceive the world in the manner of his mentor.

Kazantzakis' biological father demanded that his son becomes a fighter, and not a writer. By using folk elements, such as the aforementioned vivid dance scene, Kazantzakis indirectly describes his liberation as a writer, which lies in the discovery of an "authentic" person; the narrator of popular, folk stories. In this sense, Zorba teaches Kazantzakis how to express himself in folk style; he becomes his foster father.[366]

Greeks are passionate people. They adore life and enjoy living. But, as the wise Buddha said, the more you are attached to this world, the more you suffer. From the times of Homer the complaint is the same: life is wonderful, but so short! Let us not forget that the Greek word for song (*tragoudi*) stems etymologically from the ancient Greek word "tragedy."

The original Zorba, the hero of Kazantzakis' novel, is a passionate but not a jovial person. In his depth you can find a lot of despair. His merry-making is tinged with a strong taste of regret. You can hear this in Greek songs. You can feel it in the deep, serious expression of a male solo dancer. He is not having fun. He is expressing the beauty and the agony of living. Indeed, Zorba transforms his metaphysical questionings into structured, rhythmic movement: Who made the world? Why? Why do we die? Where do we come from and where do we go?[367]

Dance, after all, is a body dialogue with the queries. Zorba travels with an open chest and closed eyes. His dancing teaches unity and pride, the take-off. He deals with God; he speaks a language that cannot be interpreted, but felt. Zorba taught Kazantzakis to love life's trouble,[368] and not to be afraid of death. Through movement, with no fear and no hope, the writer shall be free!

Flights

> I experienced great agitation and fellow feeling as I gazed at this flying fish, as though it was my own soul I saw on that palace wall painting which had been made thousands of years before. "This is Crete's sacred fish," I murmured to myself, "the fish which leaps in order to transcend necessity and breathe freedom." Did not Christ, the ICHTHYS, seek the same thing: to transcend man's destiny and unite with God, in other words with absolute freedom? Does not every struggling soul seek the same thing: to smash frontiers? What good fortune, I reflected, that Crete should have been perhaps the first place on earth to see the birth of this symbol of the soul fighting and dying for freedom![369]

Though the boss danced, he did not become like Zorba. He did not wish to pass the remaining of his life in Dionysian enthusiasm. He learnt from him, however, how to face the contradictions in life with happy disposition. He wrote a book on him, creating an Apollonian parable of Dionysian knowledge, succeeding, once more, Greece's mission toward western civilization throughout the ages: to bring together the eastern instinct (*pathos*) with the western reasoning (*logic*).[370]

Kazantzakis was definitely not aware of what we would formally call today "art-" or "dance- therapy." Following, however, a reflective path as a writer, he kept targeting resolution and personal satisfaction through his works. His Zorba is contemporary and universal in that he is both real and constructed, as we all also are. The same way Kazantzakis' Zorba opposes to the "boss," our identity also dissolves into multiple, contradictory forces. We are all many, and full of oppositions, our unity being only a fake structure.[371]

More than 60 years since Kazantzakis wrote Zorba and more than 40 since it became a film, Zorba the Greek is still, worldwide, the recognizable cultural-artistic product of Greece – even the "passport" of modern Greece. It may even symbolize the folkloric Greece that many of us want to get rid of, but its sincere aim is to teach us how to find personal freedom by dancing, by performing a creative act, undergoing a change analogous to creation. After all, it was a friend, Alexis Zorba, who molded Kazantzakis, who, in turn, created Zorba the Greek, and, by extension, all of us modern, dancing Zorbas.

Raising Ecological Awareness through Dance[372]

Wandering

> How can the life of nature, how can all this beauty be drawn into life, into towns? Can the dancers suggest all this and remind men of it in winter time, in the cities?
> —Isadora Duncan[373]

While meditating on Duncan's Greek dances, I questioned myself: How… Greek? Isadora was first and foremost an American! Although she never met with great success by American audiences, she loved America and felt that her dancing, for all its Greek inspiration, was American dancing. Responding to Walt Whitman's – one of the many writers she was inspired by – famous poem "I See America Singing," Isadora wrote an article entitled "I See America Dancing."[374] She proclaimed that "she was a Scotch-Irish-American, perhaps through some affinity nearer allied to the Red Indian than to the Greeks."[375] Yet, her devotion to the Greek ideal was constant, her dancing embodying the spontaneous expression of her soul lifted up by beauty.

More wanderings followed: How would Phidias design his sculptures having seen the Parthenon amidst cloud, smog and dirt? Does the environment reflect art, or is it the art that results from the environment we live in? In other words, is art eco-friendly, and, if so, can Duncan's choreographies, which are making rich use of natural imagery, depict it?

Such are the premises I follow, and my argument is that art, and dance in specific, might be a way to denote ecological and environmental awareness in a "fat free" and "decaffeinated" world. One way of achieving that, is by examining Duncan's Greek choreographies, and applying their spirit to contemporary life.

Isadora Duncan

> Dance is a religion greater daring than ever before.
> —Isadora Duncan [376]

Practically, everybody knows something about Isadora Duncan, how she died in a sports car, her neck snapped by her own trailing scarf; or, how she was one of the original "liberated" women, played in a movie by Vanessa Redgrave. Whatever the case is, Isadora is mostly a product of our own personal and collective projections. Indeed, that is the way she wanted it, from the very beginning. Duncan insisted on mythologizing herself, because she longed to be noticed and remembered.[377] Whenever asked when she started dancing, she invariably responded "in the womb of a mother who could survive only on iced oysters and champagne, Aphrodite's food."[378]

Duncan grew up and was exposed to romantic, Victorian, puritan and modern eras, which overlapped between the mid-nineteenth to early twentieth century. During those times, there was a huge resurgence of interest in the antiquities. Anything Greek was high and noble, thus, by associating dance with Greek art, Isadora moved one step closer to her goal of making dance a high art form. The fact that she set her choreographies to classical composers, such as Chopin, for example, whose music had nothing in common with Greece, led music critics to inveigh against her art, jibing at her reconstructions. Duncan's argument, however, is that we know practically nothing of old Greek music, so she selected "real" music, showing it was possible to dance to the compositions of Chopin, Beethoven, Liszt and Wagner. She knitted music and dance through the compulsion of the heart, unscientific but real. It was the spirit of music which released her, not the form.[379]

First and foremost to Isadora, the dancer was not just a dancing body with its head cut off, but a thinking, expressive individual. She expected dancers to study not only dance, but also art, literature, philosophy and science. She, herself, was incredibly well-rounded. She studied not only the Romantic writers, musicians and artists, but also thinkers from the Enlightenment like Rousseau and Nietzsche, Darwin and Haeckel. She also visited countless museums to study art. She aspired to be a muse of her time, oftentimes called the 10th muse and even Sappho, inspiring many artists in their poems, sculptures, photos and paintings.

Isadora's social views covered a wide field: her vision included everything, from dress reform to vegetarianism, to birth control. Here she is in her own words: anti-puritanical, eros-affirming, libertarian, radical in everything, an authentic free spirit, one of the boldest condemners of miserabilism in all its forms, an inspiration for all who dream a better world, all who strive to make that dream a reality.[380]

"Her" Dance

> For many days no movement came to me. And then one day came the thought: These columns which seem so straight and still are not really straight, each one is curving gently from the base to the height, each one is in flowing movement, never resting, and the movement of each is in harmony with the others. And as I thought this my arms rose slowly toward the Temple and I leaned forward – and then I knew I had found my dance, and it was a Prayer.
> —Isadora Duncan[381]

The Greek word for dance is *choros*, a term initially meaning the choir which sang, spoke and danced with the purpose of intensifying a mood, an essential part of the ancient Greek theater. Ancient Greeks considered dancing as a high art form, alongside drama, music and poetry, the Muse Terpsichore being its protector. The dancing of the chorus revealed the nature of the image of the Hellene: the experience of suffering as a stimulus to a greater affirmation and love of life.

Isadora, wishing to capture the spirit of Greek tragedy, formed a ten boys' chorus, which she used as a background to her performances. She believed that the ancient hymns, such as those for Apollo and Aphrodite, had found their transformation into Byzantine music in the Greek Church. She conceived the dance as a chorus or community expression.[382] Perhaps the most authentically Greek dance Isadora performed was when she and her family laid the foundation in Kopanos, even though she called this folk dancing "primitive."

Duncan is known as the mother of modern dance, founding a way of interpretive dance, blending together poetry, music and the rhythms of nature. She did not believe in the formality of conventional ballet and thus gave birth to a freer form of dance, performing barefoot and in ancient Greek apparel, wearing tunics based on the Greek Ionic chiton, to augment the beauty of the human form and also to enhance the flow of movement. According to her view, Greeks must be made to celebrate the Greek gods and to give up their terrible modern costumes. All in all, Isadora's dances explored the human condition of the artist as an individual rather than a tool of simple storytelling, which was the ballet dancer's role. Many of her works expressed themes such as loneliness, sacrifice, ecstasy, pilgrimage and self-discovery.

Isadora discovered the inner wellspring of dance movement: the breath and the solar plexus, located at the center of the chest. "Her" body was divided into three zones, the head, the torso and the limbs, corresponding to the three essences of human behavior, the mental, the moral and the vital. Action occurred in three corresponding ways, away from the center (ex-centric), balanced (normal) and toward the center (concentric).[383]

The Glory that was Greece

> Other places may belong to different times. Greece is eternal. Beauty belongs to Eternity.
> —Isadora Duncan[384]

In the last decade of the nineteenth century, to link something with Greece automatically dignified it. Everything Greek was the rage. In 1985, a French man, Maurice Emmanuel, had written a treatise on "The Antique Greek Dance" attempting to reconstruct ancient dance steps by analyzing statues and the figures on vases. One of his aims was to link Greek dance with "modern dance," such as French ballet, by pointing out similarities and differences, so as to aggrandize a form temporarily in need of all the justification it could get.[385]

Greece's worship stemmed from a general American interest in (and version of!) an ancient culture, resulting at that time in lecture series, from a highbrow podium in which Americans tended to congratulate themselves as direct heirs of Athenian democracy (mind the name of the historic capital Philadelphia, projected as… an American Athens!). Slides and illustrations of the Acropolis were popular in many homes, though what was known of the real ancient Greece was rather limited.

Duncan's turn to Greece coincided with the epoch when American Universities studied Greece to reincarnate its spirit, in post-philhellenic terms, attributing to Europe a neoclassical flavor. Greek games flourished at Colleges. Greek theaters, civic and commercial buildings in the image of a Greek temple were also being built. This was an attitude which was confronted by many Greek intellectuals as picturesque and individualistic, or nationalistic and even fascist – walking along with several European ethnic movements.

America envisioned itself as the true heir of the great Greek civilization, in all of its political, economic and artistic glory.[386] Isadora Duncan and her family had their own imagination of what was popularly supposed to be derived from the Greek and also what was genuinely Greek.[387] And they were not alone: "No people in the world are as much in need of what Greece has to offer as the American people. Greece is not merely the antithesis of America, but more, the solution to the ills which plague us. Economically it may seem unimportant, but spiritually Greece is still the mother of nations, the fountain-head of wisdom and inspiration," Henry Miller also asserted.[388]

All in all, we are talking about a form of invented Greek nationality, a double distortion:[389] a distortion of ancient Greek reality and modern Greek reality as well. It provided (and to some degree still provides) a sense of connection to something apparently admirable, significant, even eternal. Ancient Greece was thus transformed. It had once been seen as the founding culture of the West; now it became the founding counterculture of the West.[390]

However, Duncan quit the Greeks who were too busy fighting with the Turks, though Constantine Melas[391] attributed to her the fact that she brought to the country again the immortal beauty of Phidias and the age of Greece's greatness. "If I am Greek," Isadora wrote, "it is the Hellenism of Keats' 'Ode to a Grecian Urn.'"[392] Greece, thus, was an idea and an ideal of an alternative mode of valuation, which identified and honored, amongst others, the Dionysian energies of life. Duncan was Greek not by research or imitation but by divine inheritance, for Greece was truly a state of mind.[393] According to her, "it would be wrong to call her art Greek. Her art was more universal. Where Greek art is national in a narrow sense, hers was not. She aimed to speak the language of humanity, and while her dancing owes inspiration to the Greeks, it is not Greek really, but very modern – her own idea."[394]

For Duncan, as for many upper- and middle-class Americans, dealing with the rapidly modernizing world at the turn of the century, this idyllic vision of "Nature," whose origin was traced back nostalgically to the "glory of Greece," represented the romantic values that modernity threatened to destroy. In other words, Duncan's appeal to "Nature" was an anti-modern impulse, which refused to even recognize the modern body's inextricable dialectic with the modern machine, in whose grip, ironically, Duncan and her two children were to die.[395] For her, Greek dances were spontaneous and natural, and she strived to revive them. They were "not mere national dances, but *human* dances."[396]

In sum, Greece was (and is, occasionally) imagined as the inheritor of ancient glory, natural beauty, gaining even supernal meaning. Greek plays were increasingly seen as celebrations of internationalism, pacifism, dissent and women's rights.[397] Ancient Greece was really avant-garde, but perhaps what would really be avant-garde would be to take a closer look at ancient Greece. Greeks represented exuberance and flight – especially for freedom – and such was the spirit Duncan encapsulated with the sternum lifted to the sky, the arms scooping and seeming to hug heaven. The resurrected Olympic Games which debuted in 1896 and asked how fast, high and far the body was capable of projecting itself by simultaneously promoting the classical motto of "a healthy mind in a healthy body," definitely assisted Duncan with her dancing body inquiries who argued that German and Swedish gymnastics have in view only the development of the muscles whereas they also neglect the proper correlation of spirit and body.[398]

The Greek Experience

> It is to Greece that we must turn, because all our dancing goes back to Greece.
> —Isadora Duncan[399]

Duncan entered ancient Greece through the study of its vases, friezes and sculptures, observing them housed in London, Paris and Munich. She concluded that the Greeks accorded a unique value to bodily movement: dancers not only appeared beautiful, they also appeared holy, as gods and goddesses.

Duncan attributed her interest in Greek culture to a reproduction of Botticelli's "Primavera" which hung above her bed. However, the Phidian sculptures and the Elgin Marbles went beyond the delicate, neoclassical tastefulness of Botticelli. They were robust as well as refined, massive as well as buoyant; figures of forces as well as repose. The reclining and the lunging of several figures on the East Pediment as well as other Greek temples soon made their way into the Duncan vocabulary.[400]

In 1902, along with her mother, brothers and sister, Duncan traveled to Greece and purchased Kopanos hill outside of Athens, facing the Acropolis, to construct an elaborate dancing stage, a temple to art, modeled after Agamemnon's palace. As for the material used, red stone from Mount Pentelicus was to be brought in carts drawn by donkeys. When the day for laying the cornerstone for their future home arrived, the Duncans insisted on making it a festive occasion, according to the old Greek tradition. They invited the peasants from the surrounding neighborhood and engaged a priest to perform the ceremony, presumably handed down through the Byzantine priests from the time of the Temple of Apollo. The priest, attired in black robes with a large silver cross hanging loosely on his chest, decapitated a black cock with one stroke of his sacrificial knife.[401] Bare-legged, with sandaled feet and flowing draperies, the Duncans danced from village to village, and the world called them mad. Duncan wished her voyage to resemble that of Odysseus. Villagers came to greet them while Duncan characteristically commented that "the first landing of Christopher Columbus in America could not have caused more astonishment among the natives which grew to speechless curiosity when she and Raymond knelt down and kissed the soil."[402]

Isadora knew she could not imitate the Greeks because the Greeks themselves were not imitators.[403] She was drawn to figures in arrested motion, to poses suggesting action just completed or about to start which, in turn, supplied her with gestures, such as the Nike of Samothrace, the small Tanagra figure, the three headless Fates who once reposed on the East pediment of the Parthenon, a stooping knucklebone player, or a frenzied maenad.[404]

She was exposed to the notion that the fierce Dionysian aspect of Greek tragedy and Greek religion was a necessary balance to the Apollonian aspect that entranced Nietzsche. For her dancing furies and maenads, Duncan experimented with dissonant images such as clawed hands, crouched body and the upward fling of the head that she noticed in moon-besotted dogs as well as in painted bacchantes.[405] *The Birth of Tragedy* was "her Bible" and her vision that of Zarathustra. Her dancing would help persons, especially women, overcome their faith in an otherworldly God by educating them into an awareness of their own bodily being as holy and beautiful as the source of their highest ideals.

All in all, passion played a major role in Duncan's re-productions, and we could draw parallels between her Greek dances and the Argentinean tango, which was constituted as a sophisticated New World exotic, thriving today even in Japan (thus an example of double exoticism).[406] One could also argue how Duncan's dancers resemble "eastern" Zorbas, who, despite "western" logical conventions, travel with an open chest.[407]

Embodying Duncan

On May 14 2008, I attended Isadora Duncan Dance Classes taught by Lori Belilove, artistic director, and Cherlyn Smith, associate artistic director, of the Isadora Duncan Dance Foundation. The classes took place at the McBurney YMCA, in New York City, between 1.00 and 3.30pm (elementary and intermediate levels). Lori "had an early awakening and inspiration living in Greece,"[408] where she studied, right after completing high school, with Mr. Vassos Kanellos.

Students – women of all ages and a man – were encouraged to incarnate Cherubs and Tanagra figurines, and kick the satyrs. Poetically encouraged by softly speaking Lori, they were enforced to place their egos in the front, in a giving-taking mood, practicing extensively the offering gesture. To facilitate those imageries, the instructor shared pictures with them, amongst which were those of Apollo, Alcmene, Nike, the Amazons, the Maenads and several fragments from the Parthenon pediment. Lori kept underlying how sculptures had been made as if the artist processed them under the water.

According to a published lesson plan distributed at the Isadora Duncan Dance Foundation, "the technique followed is a free flowing art form, appropriate for all ages and built on natural movements such as walking, running, jumping, skipping, leaping and tossing." For example, one lesson focuses on "The Bouncy Run," a locomotive step inspired by the mythological story of Atalanta's Race.[409]

The approach I witnessed was system-less. Initially there was a pianist accompanying the moves, later recorded music by Beethoven, Chopin and other "classical" composers followed, in a non-strict way. As the wave movement repeated at least four times, the dancers clarified a sense that their bodies were the waves they were making. "In the Duncan technique, the rhythm of the music is danced by the legs while the melodic line is expressed by upper body movements and gestures, which emanate from the solar plexus."[410]

For a Greek, trained not in ballet but folk dances, particularly the springy, leaping ones from the island of Crete, jumping around and flying freely agrees with Duncan in spirit. However, a Cretan dancer will recall and, thus, embody the flying of the eagles around the mountains, and not Nike's wings; the sea-waves rather than the furious maenads. Which, in a sense, might be what Duncan's general belief was, namely that "it must make a great difference to a child's life whether it is born by the sea or in the mountains."[411]

Ecologizing Duncan

> All true movements possible to the human body exist primarily in Nature.
> —Isadora Duncan[412]

Duncan's dance is not Greek; it is the study of the movements of nature. As a child, Duncan danced on the sea beach by the waves and tried to imitate them. She translated nature's rhythms into human rhythms conceptually.[413] Much of Isadora's days were spent running free in the outdoors (she always hated being in school), and this is where she found tremendous inspiration for the development of her art of dance, studying the movement of trees, wind, snow, waves, birds, storms and rain. Botticelli's painting made the connections among dance, nature, culture and the Greeks.

Flora from "La Primavera" was one of the first Greek figures that Duncan imperson-ated. Isadora even copied Venus' costume as she thought she was born when Venus was in the ascendant.[414]

According to Darwinist, German biologist Ernst Haeckel, whom Isadora passion-ately studied, ecology is the branch of science that studies habitats and the inter-actions between living things and the environment (from the Greek *ecos* meaning house and *logos* meaning knowledge). Thus, Duncan was ecologically dancing, as she created her choreographies based on the interaction and study of anything that had to do with the physical, natural and cultural environment.

More specifically, Duncan recognized that dance rhythms are created by gravity's pull and the body's response to that magnetism.[415] The harnessing of electricity gave her a new framework, a new vocabulary for dealing with nature, no matter how mystically and romantically she set about it.[416] According to her, the waters, the winds, the plants, the living creatures, all these obey a controlling rhythm of which the characteristic line is the wave. In nothing does nature suggest jumps or breaks; between all the conditions of life there is continuity or flow which the dancer must respect in her/his art.[417]

Duncan called one of the commonest figures in the Bacchic dances, the one with the head turned backward, the universal Dionysian movement, and argued that the motive underlying that gesture is in all nature: the animals in Bacchic movement turn back the head. The waves of the ocean form this line under a storm, the trees in a tempest.[418]

In the dance entitled "Water Study" (1900), choreographed to another Romantic era composer, Franz Schubert (Waltz Op. 91, No. 12), the dancer is both represent-ing water while she/he also becomes water. Duncan designed the crashing of waves, the spiral motion of an eddy and the drawing current, but the dancer is simultane-ously a person playing in the water and a seagull skimming its surface. She achieves that effect by dividing the body so that parts simultaneously express different en-ergies or emotions. Renowned second generation Duncan dancer, Julia Levien, de-scribes this difficult element of the Duncan technique as the use of several "voices of the body." [419] The feet follow a standard three beat waltz rhythm, while the arms and torso express the lyrical, flowing melody. The ribs and torso shift away from the center of the body, thereby pulling the dancer off-balance as if she/he has been struck by a wave. The feet follow to catch the body, the dynamic of fall and recov-ery adds more undulations to those of the torso, and the choreography explores all movements related to water. Lastly, the face registers excitement at the thought of a new "game" when the dancer decides to emerge and chase a water bird.[420]

For Isadora, what was natural was good, what was artificial was bad. This was par-tially why she was so profoundly against ballet, also because she thought of women not as a thing apart and separate from all other life but rather a link in the chain. Steichen photographed Isadora as she made a gesture completely related to the Parthenon columns, appearing to intoning her hymn to the eternal rhythms of the universe.[421]

So, Isadora learned from the Greeks how to study nature. As a yogi of the Epicurean School,[422] she tried to adopt a stoic philosophy to alleviate the constant misery which she felt.[423] The ancient Greek philosophers, who underlined the importance of the environment and emphasized the immediate ties between human beings and nature, influenced her profoundly. By deploying the Greeks as a strategy to collapse art and nature, Duncan posited dance as part of the cosmic unity and divinity of nature and thus elevated dance into the realm of "high" art.[424] For Duncan, the body is that curious place where nature and culture – what anthropologist Mary Douglas called the "physical" and the "social" bodies – somehow interpenetrate.[425] Thus, if, according to Duncan, dance never goes against nature, then the dancer is physically aware of her/his culture.[426] All in all, it is the Greek figures that helped Duncan see nature as a primary source of dance inspiration, and, viewed this way, Duncan's dance is Greek.

Environmental Performing

> My idea of dancing is to leave my body free to the sunshine, to feel my sandaled feet on the earth, to be near and love the olive trees of Greece… Two thousand years ago a people lived here who had perfect sympathy and comprehension of the beautiful in Nature, and this knowledge and sympathy were perfectly expressed in their own forms and movement.
> —Isadora Duncan[427]

A united cosmos is manifested in all Greek folk art: Cretan distiches ecologize the discourse of folk literature by teaching audiences to reinterpret certain conventional metaphorical uses of nature imagery as literal messages with an environmental theme.[428] In parallel way, Duncan's choreographies suggest new codes for reading nature, through environmentally significant lenses. In a "globally warmed" reality, such imageries suggest that there is something wrong with humans' violation and pillaging of nature, and that it is an ethical necessity to act. If "green is the new black," then there is a lot to be learned from the reintroduction of folk art in our lives.

If Duncan considered her dances as expressions of the Greek spirit and philosophy, then there is a connection between Greek identity and environmental awareness that could be construed as reproducing the romantic notion that authentic regional identities are tied to land. In a sense, Duncan longed nostalgically for a return to an age when such a relationship ostensibly existed.[429]

We could, thus, make use of Duncan's Greek dances to promote environmental sensibility and ecological aesthetics. Today, attempts to foster environmental education through the use of theater, parades and other forms of performance art to reach large audiences and increase environmental awareness are taking place all over the world.[430] Smith's thesis[431] recognizes that contemporary environmental performance art is simply a relatively recent extension of theater for social change.

Moreover, dance therapists underline the "cathartic" relationship between natural elements and particular places in the environment. They speak of attuning to essential qualities by identifying and interacting with natural objects, by being in and interacting with nature as poetic act and via the creative force of nature as a metaphor which shapes us as if we were a piece of art.[432] Such experiences may "metamorphose" and reconnect us to our own naturally creative energy.

If "An Inconvenient Truth," to borrow the title of Al Gore's eco-friendly film, is today's "Emo" reality, then we may consider of becoming natural bodies. One way of achieving so, is via Duncan's path, who, by connecting dance to Greece, was also integrating dance with Nature and Art.

Resistance through Dancing

Performing Cretanness

Cretan dances function as threads that have fashioned the fabric of Cretan society since ancient times, providing authentic evidence of the continuity of Crete's popular tradition and rhythm. Despite modernization, on one hand, which has impacted many places all over Greece and Crete, and the dances' old history, on the other, folk dancing is still a common means of expression for most Cretans.[433] In fact, Cretan dance performances take on a modern and present significance which remains relevant and fresh and not just a caricature of a distant past. In a sense, dancing is an important representation of Crete's traditional culture; in other words, Cretans are what they dance.

Historian Hobsbawm defines "invented tradition" as "a set of practices (…) of a ritually symbolic nature" that "automatically implies continuity with (…) a suitable historic past."[434] Moreover, according to Nettl,[435] a unique, particular role of music is to reconnect the present reality to a remote past. To achieve this, Cretans choose dance symbols. The persistence with which the revolutionary and historical stereotypes were and are still presented in Cretan documents reveals that the connotations of those images are considered necessary to spread a new sense of Cretan history. In this way, the dances under study become a symbol of Cretan ethnic identity and their dancers heroes. Even though "invented" and/or "re-invented," they take on a life of their own, truly becoming custom and reality in the musical and cultural life of modern-day Crete.

Bottomley suggests that "collectivism is literally embodied in the form of dance and the shared code of communication between dancers."[436] She views Greek circle dances as a ritual of solidarity, offering a "cultural hegemony" opposing Ottoman rule.[437] In fact, dancing performed as cultural survival is an important practice signifying the sense of national identity and independence because it becomes a representation of both the expression of resistance to domination and the expression of freedom.[438] In this context, Greek folk dancing serves to strengthen cultural identity in modern times, especially amongst the Greek diaspora communities. Through performance, the ordinary folk manage to retain their cultural heritage and collectively remember it by commemorating the dances of old as national heroes and celebrating the value of nationhood.[439]

Dance is communicative behavior, a "text in motion" or "body language."[440] For Greeks, dance can be a physical instrument or symbol for feeling and/or thought, a double representation of the inner and the outer world. It is an expression that comes out from the dancers, expressing their personality, individual past and emotional situation. Furthermore, the feeling that comes out of this environment is the one that the dancers' surroundings impose upon them, and which is unavoidably expressed throughout the dance, the music they listen to, the people who dance with them or look at them, the occasion for which they dance, all the past of the social team that they belong to.[441]

Conclusively, what Dawe[442] states for island musics truly stands for Crete as well:

The study of expressive culture in any society provides us with an insight into deeply held values and beliefs passed down over generations. Music, song, dance and drama for instance, registering changes, pressing issues and reconfigurations in the social environment are, therefore, also a means by which society and culture can be shaped, in social action as lives lived musically.

Mytho-musicologies

Nowadays, the predominant belief among Cretans is that the art of dancing originated in "their" island. In fact, Cretans were extolled by Greeks as exceptional artists and acknowledged as masters of dance,[443] a common belief being that the best Greek dancers today are the descendants of those people.[444] Cretans are mentioned in Homer, Hesiod and Euripides as dancers, whereas their mythical role has been much enlarged by later "classical" writers such as Plato and Apollonius of Rhodes.

For example, it is believed that Theseus, while coming back from Crete, performed with his colleagues a dance that resembled the turns and the curves of a labyrinth. Significant also is the description of Achilles' shield in *The Iliad* when Homer, amongst others, remarks that the labyrinth was Ariadne's ceremonial dancing ground, "a dancing-floor where young men and women were dancing" (590-606).

The roots of Cretan dancing are deep. Tradition credits Rhea, the mother of gods (daughter of Uranus, the sky, and Gaia, the earth), as the one who taught dance to the ancient inhabitants of Crete (as a special gift, proper for religious ceremonies). Testimonies coming from the Minoan era prove the general belief that dances were predominant: Cretan people used dancing in order to educate the youth and particularly in order to shape their ethos and character. Notably, after the end of Cretan wars and battles, everyone danced.[445]

Freedom in Unity

Cretan dances are integral to the principal musical repertoire for feasts and celebrations. They are orally passed down from generation to generation though, today, several Cretan dance schools also exist. Dances performed at *glendia* form the main means of common entertainment as all members of the village take part in those festivities. The *glendi* incubates the emotional state which strongly reflects the moods of the participants. During that interplay, feelings of stability and calm reflect a fixed structure of the event.[446]

Amongst Greeks, Crete is famous as the island where events become panegyric. Through revolutions and periods of subjugation, Cretans refined the Greek notion of the *palikari*, who, during times of festive celebrations, displays his gallantry by showing off his dancing skills. It is the concepts of the *levendis* and the *meraklis* who bring *kefi* (high spirits) to a party, turning simple events into festive celebrations of life. A *glendi* starts with slow dragging dances and it gets faster and louder as the *kefi* increases and reaches its pinnacle with the girls dancing with swirls and turns that are fascinating to watch, and goes to the leaping (*pidichtos*) dances and crescendos with men (*palikaria*) dancing, showing off their mastery.

As a result, dancing in Crete is more than simply an activity as Cretan dance is strictly socially constructed. A woman's/man's dance performance as the leader or her/his improvisation has an importance which is being evaluated. In such contexts, music-making requires the possession of a profound perception of various existential issues as well as of the dynamics between individual and group, and between tradition and creativity. The great ability of the Cretans consists in handling these issues through a sophisticated and conscious use of the word and the body, generating forms of musical expression laden with a multiplicity of individual and social meanings.[447] The fame of past times can still be felt through the notion that Crete is resilient and, above all, free as the dances convey diachronic, genuine Cretanness.

All in all, dancing at those festive events is a highly structured social practice with rules that vary from one locality to another. According to Cowan,[448] in addition to striving for exuberant *kefi*, locals in these events a) "perform" gender, class, political and regional identities, b) negotiate power relations and c) express solidarity or rivalry with kin, neighbors and friends. Through dancing, an important part of the Greek perception about life, Cretans feel both free and united. This is what to be Cretan is, and this is how vitally the Cretans through their music, dance and song represent themselves, as, according to a popular *mandinada*, "the branches should never forget their roots, because if the roots perish, the branches will also wither."

Dancing With the Heroes

Today there are five main, clearly distinct types of dances in Crete. Among the most performed is the *Chaniotis* or *Chaniotiko*, a circular dance also called *sirtos*. The name *Chaniotikos Sirtos* indicates that this is a "shuffling" line dance from the city of Chania. The leader of this dance, in interaction with the music, performs various hand-slaps on thighs, soles and heels, does numerous leaps, turns and acrobatic maneuvers, while the line moves smoothly and evenly. According to the feeling of the music, the dancer moves vigorously with sharp, quick steps, or very smoothly, almost daintily. The whole circle may move a little forward, then back. Because of its popularity with composers and musicians, *Chaniotikos sirtos* is among the most musically complex and virtuosic dances.[449]

Cretan women calmly, soberly and gently performing the *sirtos.*

Acrobatic dancing of the *pentozalis,* on blue *vrakas* and black *stivania* that fly off the ground.

Pentozalis (meaning five-stepped dance, five dizzying steps or giddy five step rhythm) is another popular Cretan dance. It is springy and energetic, working up to a great speed. The name of this dance means "*pente*," thus, five, "*zala*," thus, steps, and is typical of tricky, fast-stepping dances.[450] The *pentozalis* is a line dance in which the participants clasp one another's shoulders and perform steps classified as leaping. The dancers move with increasing speed and perform intricate steps on the spot.[451] Frequently, this dance breaks up into smaller groups which perform somersaults while in line, the leader always elaborating on the basic steps and leaping through the air. As the dance draws to a close, the small groups once again take their places on the line.[452]

Both of these dances have been "mythologized" by local history as part of the Cretan musical folklore. Legends related to the origins and birth of Cretan music and dance pertain to the two of the aforementioned dance forms, the sirtos and the pentozalis. More specifically, it is acknowledged that the Cretan sirtos was developed in the Chania province, most likely in the region of Kissamos, and spread to the rest of Crete from there, hence the name of the dance Chaniotikos (namely, in honor of its place of origin). There is one characteristic melody labeled as the protos (first) sirtos (or Chaniotikos, or Kissamitikos, namely from Kissamos) that is considered to be the original one from which the dance sprung and was created.

It is believed that in ancient times the dance served as a necessary means of expression and encouragement in cases of war. Moreover, a local legend says the dance was coined as *protos sirtos* and was composed by Cretan soldiers who participated in the failed defense of Constantinople against the Ottoman Turks in 1453. The Sultan allowed the Cretans to return home due to their bravery, which resulted from their refusal to surrender for several days after the City's fall. They, in turn, settled down in the region of Kissamos and kept performing those melodies till the mid-18th century. That same year, a wedding was organized at the Chania village of Lousakies to gather important local leaders and plan a rebellion against the Turks, which, according to tradition, was discovered by means of treachery and, hence, put down.

In fact, the first musical rendition of the dance is attributed to a violinist from the village of Lousakies-Kissamos, Stefanos Triandafillakis or Kioros,[453] who reworked the three hundred-year old melody, giving the opportunity to the performers to create a dance as both a symbol of the revolt and a way of honoring the memory of the Cretan warriors of 1453.[454] The *Chaniotikos sirtos* became popular in that region and was performed until the Greek revolution of 1821.[455] It then spread to the rest of the island, carrying its revolutionary and epic character, particularly during the two World Wars, by being varied in both style and expression.

The second dance under examination, the *pentozalis*, is perceived as an ancient, *pyrrichean* dance form, namely a war dance that served to test the footwork and agility of the dancers in ancient times. Its present form and name are attributed to the period of the Daskalogiannis Revolution (1770-71).[456] According to the local

legend, the organizer of the great Cretan rebellion, Ioannis Vlachos or Daskalogiannis (1730-1771), invited the same violinist, Triantafyllakis, to attend the meeting
of the local chieftains who were planning the rebellion, and to compose a dance for
them as a symbol of the revolt. That is why the dance has ten steps which commemorate the day of the meeting (October 10, 1769), namely when the people of Sfakia
(south, western Crete), made the decision to go ahead with the revolution against
the Turks, and therefore its music consists of twelve music phrases (parts) in honor
of the twelve leaders of the revolt.[457]

The name of the performance, namely "five stepped dance," is purely symbolic and
stands for the fifth attempt to free Crete from the Turks (even though there are more
steps). Tradition says that, until the early 1960s, the people of western Crete, while
dancing the *pentozalis*, used to call out the name of the captain that corresponded to
each musical phrase, in this way honoring the memory of Daskalogiannis, his chief
comrades and their revolt.[458]

Performing Histories

Such stories should be examined under the lens of oral tradition. Even though
they may not always be supported by historical evidence, the legendary narrations
of the instrument players and the locals contain, to some extent, some truth. What
is significant is the function they serve in the Cretan dancing folklore and the great
degree to which they are propagated in the community; they help to connect the
individual members of the community, who participate in their retelling and in the
relevant music and dance activities, to a greater, grander reality and group identity.
More importantly, those dancing stories have contributed to the way Greeks – and,
by extension, the rest of the world – view Crete since the local group identity has,
throughout the ages, passed beyond the boundaries of the island of Crete, becoming
part of Greek history.

Even today, Ancient Greece and Byzantium are viewed as the progenitors of and
constitute a vibrantly relevant reference point for modern Greek culture, "a gold-
en age since when the purity of the original Hellenic culture had suffered endless
contamination and enfeeblement."[459] When Cretan dances are performed, the legends are being reincarnated, reminding one of the Greek struggles for freedom. In
a sense, they function as a local history lesson, as, oftentimes, elders take time to
explain to the younger audience the deeds of their ancestors, referring to specific names, facts and places. This way, the past unites with the present constituting
the ethics of gallantry (*levendia, palikaria*) and love of honor (*philotimo*), thus the
essence of being Cretan, diachronic. Most of those stories do not remain only on
oral terms, in informal conversations that may take place in such social spaces such
as coffeehouses. In addition, they are used as part of the formal education of the
young; they are proudly presented as authentic in local history books and other

media, such as websites, assuring that the ideals of Hellenism and Christianity will continue to be honored and respected.

Performing Gallantry

Cretans live in today in an era of uneasy globalization; but yet "theirs" relies on a past of many histories and a future of many expectations. As they craft a notion of "Cretanness" for broader and outside consumption,[460] a process of a highly flexible "creative construction of ethnicity is increasingly common."[461]

On the island of Crete, music industry has become a strong and unifying force in the construction and maintenance of a pan-Cretan identity. Dawe argues how Cretan music provides a distinct local sound in a global soundscape, an alternative to the range of foreign goods entering the island as well as a reminder of home to Cretans worldwide.[462] Moreover, Herzfeld identifies the characteristic idiom of Cretans to be able to adjust to the necessities of the times and calls for "a poetics of tourism," a term he justifies by the fact that "through their adjustment, Cretans grasp and steal the change from the teeth of the commercial shark."[463]

Theoharis Xirouhakis, Professor of Physical Exercise, Dance Instructor and Choreographer, founded in 1978 the first School for the instruction of Cretan Dances in Chania-Crete under the name "Crete: Giving birth to gallant men" (*Levendoyenna Kriti*). As he states, this attempt of his "sprang out of pure love for the brave dances and the beautiful Cretan traditions."[464] Over 20,000 students, as young as four and as old as seventy, have graduated from this school and have participated as dance teachers and lead dancers in many Cretan associations both in Greece and abroad.

Mr. Xirouhakis was born at the village of Gramvousa in the area of Kissamos-Chania. Since he was a young child, he enjoyed hanging around with old, talented dancers, performing at the weddings and the village feasts. As soon as he joined the University of Athens, he was asked by his Professor to become the leader of the University's dance group, a position he kept till his graduation.

Along with his group members, consisting of both younger and older people, he has given over 1,200 performances at several festivals both in Greece and abroad. He has appeared in many television programs, receiving international acclaim and good critical reviews. Since 1981, many groups from several European countries and the United States have come to Chania every year to attend his dance seminars and become familiar with the cultural heritage of Crete.[465] He, himself, has extensively traveled abroad to promote and teach Cretan dancing at several Cretan Associations. For instance, in 1983, in Florida, he organized the first competition of Cretan dance groups amongst 72 different associations in the United States.

In addition, Mr. Xirouhakis has undertaken the organization, composition and performance of several ceremonies for large national and athletic events, such as, for instance, the closing ceremony of the 1st World Championship of Young Track

Athletes in Athens at the Olympic Stadium, as well as the three opening ceremonies of the international track games called "Venizelia"[466] in Chania-Crete. During the last couple of years, his School has been turned into a traditional association with the aim of promoting Cretan culture and thus he recently participated with some of its younger dancers in the ANT1 television network show "Greece, you have talent," where it received the second place, in an attempt to show that "in Greece not only modern music and dance, acrobatics and magicians exist, but also Greek folk traditions expressed through dancing."

After a great deal of studying and effort and more than twenty years devoted to the dissemination and promotion of "our" heroic dances and cultural heritage, Mr. Xirouhakis created in 1992 two videotapes under the title "The Soul of Crete," which depict the birth and development of Cretan dances throughout history to the present time. Those programs highlight customs and traditions, dances, songs, the natural beauty, archaeological treasures and whatever is the best Crete can show to its guests. The second tape of those series focuses on the teaching and learning of Cretan dances.

During the last two years, Mr. Xirouhakis created two more DVDs and compiled everything into an album of 5 DVDs under the same title, "The Soul of Crete," which includes a variety of features: a) special feasts, such as the godson's celebration that follows the old customs and traditions; b) natural landscapes, such as the Cape of Gramvousa with its enchanting beach of Balos; c) the young dancers, the hope and future of our country performing at various locations such as Kissamos and Falassarna; d) a rich dance show at the Venetian harbor of Chania with dancers of various ages and great artists; and e) young dancers performing several new choreographies at the first international competition of the TV ANT1 "Greece, you have talent" where they won second place, capturing the hearts of all Greeks.

Many Cretan cultural and political authorities speak fondly of Mr. Xirouhakis' work and his contributions to traditional feasts and Cretan ceremonies. Today, his company consists of 70 dancers of various ages from 4 to 30 years old who wear traditional costumes and are ready to perform anywhere they are invited. 12 *lyra* players, 2 *violin* players, 19 distinguished *laouto* players, 95 dancers and 30 Cretan folk singers collaborated in the production of the 5 DVD series. In addition, Mr. Xirouhakis is well-known as a choreographer. Inspired by Cretan history, tradition and folklore, he has created several dances. For the purposes of this study, we will closely examine two of them, "The Battle of Crete" and "The Meraklidikos."[467]

Studying abroad in Crete-Greece: At the Venetian fort of Gramvousa (at an uninhabited island off the coast of northwestern Crete) that kept remaining unconquerable.

The Battle of Crete

"The Battle of Crete" was created in 1991 in order to honor all those who fought and gave their lives in that historical battle that took place on 20 May 1941. Horrifying pictures and reports such as the ones related to the Massacre of Kondomari inspired Mr. Xirouhakis to create that dance. That Massacre refers to the execution of male civilians from the village of Kondomari in Chania-Crete by an ad hoc firing squad consisting of German paratroopers on 2 June 1941 during World War II. The shooting was the first of a long series of mass reprisals on the island of Crete and was orchestrated in retaliation for the participation of Cretans in "The Battle of Crete." Since his childhood, "the historic battle was an event carved in his fantasy mostly due to the narrations he himself heard at the coffeehouses of his village where he also encountered and had the chance to speak with several wounded villagers." Those atrocities were the reason that, when the celebrations for the 50 years from the Battle of Crete took place and a singing competition was established by the Prefecture of Chania, he asked to participate by creating a dance.

On the second DVD of the series "The Soul of Crete," which focuses on the teaching and learning of Cretan dances, "The Battle of Crete" is included. Mr. Xirouhakis views that historic event as "one of global significance and chose to pay tribute to the heroic warriors via his choreography." Let us briefly note here that "The Battle of Crete" took place during World War II and began on the morning of 20 May 1941, when Nazi Germany launched an invasion (the first mainly airborne one in military history) of Crete under the codename "Operation Mercury" (where "parachute rangers" were used on a massive scale).

Crete has great strategic importance in the Mediterranean. The harbor at Souda Bay in Chania, one of the largest in the Mediterranean, has been an ideal base for naval operations. Control of the island was desirable to both the British and Germans as it would give them greater control of the Mediterranean, the northern end of the Suez Canal, and North Africa. Greek and Allied forces, along with Cretan civilians, defended the island. After one day of fighting, the Germans had suffered heavy casualties and none of their objectives had been achieved.

The battle lasted about 10 days and was unprecedented in many ways, but mostly because it was the first time the German troops encountered mass resistance from a civilian population. In fact, because of the heavy casualties suffered by the paratroopers, Adolph Hitler forbade further large scale airborne operations. His strategic plan was interrupted by a small island in the Mediterranean while his master plan to invade Russia before the coming of winter had to be postponed, which caused thousands of Nazi soldiers to lose their lives as they were not prepared to survive the harsh Russian winter.

The dance devoted to the aforementioned historical event has been performed on several occasions, usually "Battle of Crete" anniversaries, in both Crete and abroad, in Germany, Australia and the United States; places where Cretan diaspora communities reside. Mr. Xirouhakis based the dancing figures on moves he "witnessed in mountainous villages where tradition is kept authentic." While choreographing, he spoke and danced with old, outstanding dancers, and collaborated with folklorists, university professors and specialists in teaching folk dances. He utilized all of those resources and simultaneously added his own, personal character, "embodying it to the dance meter, ethos and style."

The dance depicts the spontaneous resistance of the Cretan people to the German parachutists, the hand-to-hand fighting, but also the victory feast. At the same time, it provides the message of that great battle: Cretan people were born free; always to live, fight and give their blood for their freedom. The music of the dance is composed by young Cretan music artist Dimitris Vakakis[468] and its lyrics, in the traditional *mandinades* format, by Mr. Xirouhakis:

> Black birds have covered the Cretan sky and old Mt. Psiloritis has roared.
> All together, the brave ones of Crete, old men, women and children, burst
> forth like lions for the sacred idea, in order to show to the barbarians that

Crete cannot be taken over, and that, even when burnt by enemies, its soul remains invulnerable. So as to spread out to the whole world the message that the Cretan neck does not bend to foreign rule; it was born free and will live free, so hear this well in both East and West!

The "Battle of Crete's" melody starts slower and becomes faster when the lyrics repeat. This allows the creation of a dance that is both dragging and leaping. Several dancing figures take place such as the so-called "cuttings or little heels," namely when the music cuts off and the dancers hit the heels of their shoes, the high jumps, the turns and the plain slaps on legs. Its choreography consists of three parts. Part one is called "attack and defense" and shows the spontaneous resistance of the Cretan people who used whatever they could find in order to fight. During the battle scene, the dancers do not hold hands so as to show "readiness for attack, alert." Part two is the "body-to-body fight." As a wild animal reacts to an enemy which approaches its lair and threatens its young by stamping its legs and attacking with fury, similarly the Cretans react to the all-powerful enemy who approaches and threatens their existence: they stamp three times so as to frighten it. With loud cries, the body-to-body fight follows and, finally, the destruction of the enemy ensues. Lastly, the warriors make two turns in order to check and see whether more of the enemy appears.

As soon as the warriors realize that the danger is over, they celebrate their triumph in the third part, with fast, *pyrrichean* (in the mood of a war) steps, one turn and a frantic moment of jumping movements which takes place on the spot. This is the way the choreographer, Mr. Xirouhakis, chose to depict the celebration of the Cretan soul's victory that did not succumb to the war's fury. According to him, "oftentimes, the body may have been proven weak to the Germans who knelt before a number of major European powers, but the soul of the Cretans did not break; it rather struggled, remained straight and thus won." On the DVD series, Mr. Xirouhakis concludes "his-story" with the following: "Till the sun rises and strikes Mt. Psiloritis, Crete will stand up, fight and feast… I am from Crete, an island that does not bend, does not age, and, when enslaved, it will always be free in order to offer freedom lessons."

The Meraklidikos

Meraklis in the local, Cretan dialect stands for the happy enthusiast who shows affection to his object, in other words, the satisfied connoisseur who also embodies artistry in every action. In 2009, Mr. Xirouhakis created the "Meraklidikos" dance to portray joy and *kefi*. The dance, which is part of the 3rd DVD of the series "Soul of Crete," is filmed at the Church of Santa Irene at his native village of Gramvousa and Mr. Xirouhakis conceives of it as a manifestation of "all who love Cretan tradition and its gallant dances."

"Meraklidikos" is a rhythmic, pleasant dance, conducted in small and sharp, jumping steps. In combination with its music accompaniment, a joyful and "high spirited" temperament is created. Its steps are simple and easy so that anyone can perform it. The dance has many vivid musical turns and figures such as the "little heel," the "high strikes and jumps," the "dimension" and the unique "*meraklidiki*," which, after all, gave its name to the dance. All movements accentuate the grace and the gallantry of the dancer who, in order to execute them well, needs to pay careful attention to the details of the dance. Another goal of this dance is to excite the first dancer and thus create the mood for improvisation.

The music of the dance is composed by *lyra* player Alexandros Xirouhakis[469] and the lyrics mostly by his uncle-choreographer, Mr. Xirouhakis[470]:

> When the *meraklis* is born, God gives him the grace, thus no one can ever deprive him of it. The *meraklis* always distinguishes himself because of his dancing steps: they are modest, gallant, as if he is painting! The *meraklis* gives joy and makes a table-feast proper: he is always the first in manners and ethics, a bastion of the heart. The eagle and the *meraklis* do not cry when suffering; instead, they turn their pain into song and perform it.

While the first dance, the "Battle of Crete," refers to a historical event, the second, the "Meraklidikos," wishes to embody the spirit and the scent of Crete. In both dances the handhold position resembles the letter W. Comparing them to the ways that gave creation to the *sirtos* and the *pentozalis* we realize how the performing myth-making tradition repeats itself even several years after. It is to the hands of the future, now, to judge how well these "new" dances will fit in and whether they will disseminate in the years to come.

Cretan Dance Poetics

"Islands and islanders can serve as subjects with a clearer (though still in their own way messy) relationship with local identity and the external order."[471] Cretans see themselves as more Cretan than Greek. They see Crete as an island nation and the uniqueness of their dance performances reinforces this ideal, by negotiating notions of space, place, ethnicity and identity.[472] As a result, cases like the Cretan one, attest to the significance of history for islanders, as legends of the past are being reborn through carefully executed music and dance performances, which reaffirm the intrinsic connection with "our" islands.

The above performances remind us that history repeats itself and it is in the past, therefore, that one needs to look before proceeding further. By insisting on performing Cretan dances, locals conscientiously revisit their roots. Moreover, by creating new dance forms that converse with history in ways that are not sterile but, rather, cross-fertile, they manage to bring together the past with both the present and the future. This results to the creation of a dancing poetics that clearly speaks of Cretanhood.

Chapter 5

Greek Literature and the Other Arts

Beyond *Zorba* and *Captain-Michael:*
Music Tradition and Globalization through the Work of Nikos Kazantzakis

Introduction

Nikos Kazantzakis (1883-1957) is Greece's most translated writer and philosopher. His work and spirit have inspired many composers. This entry focuses only on Greek composers who have set Kazantzakis' works to music. In the 21st century and over 55 years after Kazantzakis' death, the significance of studying those music compositions that are inspired by and based on his works is important. The conditions under which they were created, the questionings posed and the composers' motivations are parallel to the Kazantzakian wanderings and ideals, which are diachronic and universal, in opposition, for instance, to their film representations that have distorted the writer's view. [473]

Kazantzakis & Music

In a book on Kazantzakis by Alexiou (his first wife's sister) we read that he performed passionate *amanedes* (vocal improvisations evolving around the word *aman*, "woe is me"), swaying his bent head: "Those *amanedes*, my lady," Kazantzakis commented referring to his mother-in-law, "I learnt the time that I, as a young boy, traveled to Constantinople..."[474] In a 1903 letter to his friend and classmate Harilaos Stefanidis, we read: "Wagner's Lohengrin was performed (...) Its music is dreamlike, something fantastic! You forget the whole world, all the pain, and, seduced, you let your soul be surrounded by harmony waves..."[475] From other sources we learn that, since birth, Kazantzakis had been influenced by the folk music of his native island, Crete, and that Byzantine Greek Orthodox chanting enabled him to unite with God.[476]

The impact of Greek folk songs in Kazantzakis' *Odyssey* is significant and proves his knowledge of that music-poetic genre. Moreover, similarly to the Greek folkloric literature writers,[477] Kazantzakis embodies in his writings Cretan *mandinades* not so as a proof of a cultural continuity but rather due to the proverbial wisdom they powerfully bear.[478]

In his Report to Greco, Kazantzakis notes: "Do you want to outdo Titian and Tintoretto? Don't forget what the Cretan mandinada teaches: 'You're building your nest too high and the branch is going to break on you.'"[479] Ball argues that, even today, Kazantzakis is a source of inspiration for the Cretan folk poets who are engaged mostly with the philosophical component of the Cretan-born writer. Thus, Cretan folk poets transform the Kazantzakian prose into poetry, particularly inspired by the bipolar opposition "heart rebelling" against "day-in-day-out, sober rationality."[480]

Kazantzakis believed in the power of poetry when turned into song. In his novel *Freedom or Death* the schoolmaster, instead of answering to questions of the sort "where do we come from and where do we go to," he grasps the Cretan *lyra* on his knee and plays. The dying grandfather-Sifakas experiences disembodiment, as the voice of the music instrument recalls his deeds and experiences, to be transubstantiated later into the soul which abandons his mortal body but eases him into paradise.[481]

While living abroad, Kazantzakis' music preferences were classical. In Antibes, he listened to the radio. He admired the *Brandenburg's Concertos* by the "divine," as he used to call him, J. S. Bach. He was passionate with Monteverdi, and expressed special preference to Handel's *Oratorios* and Mozart's works.

Indeed, we know that he attended the opera *Don Giovanni* in Salzburg, conducted by Bruno Walter. In letters, he mentions the great music life of Vienna, the sounds of Beethoven, Brahms and Strauss, and the Viennese dances. It is there that he listens to music by Richard Strauss, Busoni and Schoenberg conducted by directors such as Erich Kleiber, Bruno Walter, Otto Klemperer and Alexander von Zemlinksy.

Kazantzakis preferred the "more human" voices, as he would call them, the "clearer and simpler," such as the mezzo-soprano or the contralto. He loved Japanese music, the traditional theaters Noh and Kabuki along with the dance that accompanied them, which he preferred over Chinese music performances. Amongst dance forms, he distinguished the ones that were associated with religious exaltation.[482] In Assisi, he was impressed by the bells, and characteristically noted that he "prefers the silences only specific music may express."[483]

Kostas Sfakianakis (1890-1946), musicologist and Director of the Greek Conservatory, composer and Byzantine music historian, was Kazantzakis' close friend. [484] Alexiou narrates how, while on vacation at Heraklion, the capital of Crete, both of them would spend their afternoons playing music, Beethoven's and Mozart's violin and pianos sonatas. [485]

There is testimony proving that Kazantzakis was in contact with Spanish composer Manuel de Falla (1876-1946). Also, through Kazantzakis' correspondence, we know his relationship with the Czech composer Bohuslav Martinů (1890-1959) whose opera, *The Greek Passion*, based on the Kazantzakis 1954 novel *Christ Recrucified*, was his swan song.

Kazantzakian Music Stereotypes

In 1964, the film "Zorba the Greek" was released, directed by Michael Cacoyannis, its popular soundtrack composed by Mikis Theodorakis. The popularity of that theme led to the production of a Theodorakis ballet, first presented in 1979 by the National Opera of Greece in Lorca Massine's choreography. In 1987, it was even expanded into a ballet in 2 acts and 22 scenes, enriched with more Theodorakis' songs, which would emphasize the national identity of the main character, the writer and the composer.[486] In 1968, a Broadway musical was produced, with a book by Joseph Stein, lyrics by Fred Ebb, and music by John Kander.

Mikis Theodorakis has composed music for two more theatrical plays by Kazantzakis, *Christopher Columbus* (1975) and *Kapodistrias* (1976). It was the soundtrack for the movie "Zorba the Greek," however, that became the expression of a very specific Greek class: that of Greece in the early 60s. Due to its popularity, Zorba is considered mostly as an ethnic work: Is there any publication that does not have on its cover a dance scene? [487]

In *The Anatomy of Music*, Mikis Theodorakis comments that the film's music has been turned into a myth. For the composition of the famous Zorba dance, the *sirtaki*, the composer relied on already existing material borrowed from the local Cretan tradition, more specifically, the *Armenohorianos Sirtos* by Giorgos Koutsourelis,[488] composed around 1949-1950, for Cretan lute and vocals. Because it was both born and perceived as an exportable product of Greekness, namely a required music-dance accessory, the new dance, *sirtaki*, became not only its trademark but, more significantly, its transubstantiation.[489]

Nikos Mamangakis has also set to music a Zorba excerpt for 4 protagonists (4 voices and 10 instruments; 1959-1960). In 1984, the same composer wrote music for and published basic excerpts from Kazantzakis' *Odyssey*. His music idiom is based partially on Greek folk elements. Influenced by the tradition of the Cretan rhyming couplets, he attempted to find methods for using the texts in a way that the language could be sung faithfully to its prosody and rhythm.[490] "His" *Odyssey* was performed in 1984 both at the Athens Festival and Heraklion-Crete.[491]

In 1966, wanting to converse with Nikos Kazantzakis, Manos Hadjidakis did not hesitate to set poems to music to the prose of Kazantzakis for the play *Captain Michael* (in English known as *Freedom or Death*). Songs such as "That was not an island," "Giorgos' red-nosed wife," "My lady of the vineyards" or "How beautiful Crete is" are popular amongst Greek music lovers. Hadjidakis' music which "dresses" those *Freedom or Death* excerpts is lyrically and realistically Greek. Via the powerful melodies, messages for one's home, family and freedom are conveyed.

To the category of artistic Cretan productions the Moundakis' works also belong. In 2003, Manos Moundakis set *The Odyssey* prologue and first rhapsody into music, a composition which incorporated elements of music that can be found on Crete. Kostas Moundakis, his father, had already collaborated with him toward the production of the 1976 *Report to Nikos Kazantzakis* disc (otherwise known as *Offering to the Great Cretan*), with composition titles such as "Immortal Island," "Exquisite Freedom Stands," "Hail-Hail to Freedom," "The Responsibility of being Cretan" and "Zorba's Dance," where the following lyrics from: "Boss, in history, include my own theory too; World is a mess, Alexis Zorbas"!

Kazantzakis & the Theater

Kazantzakis perceived of himself as a theatrical writer, but the conditions in Greece during his time did not allow for his plays to be extensively acted. He believed his era was dramatic due to the prevailing controversies, revolutions, sarcasm and agony. He chose to write theatrical dramas because, through them, he felt he could better express the contemporary man's fears and hopes. Even in his novels he becomes theatrical.[492] For example, he believed that his play *Kouros* should be an opera. According to Georgousopoulos, "if we add music to the Kazantzakian form, we will come across the oratorio *Joan of Arc* by Claudel-Honegger."[493]

Kazantzakis aimed at altering modern Greek play-writing theory by attempting to escape the traditional plausibility when representing characters and situations.[494] In his plays, he dealt with his era's problems adjusted at ancient Greek and mythical scenarios. Simultaneously, he expressed the hopes of those who suffer by believing in a better future.[495] His motivations were ideological and ethical, and his theater philosophical.[496] Contemporary scholars of his work support that a great chapter in Kazantzakis' theatrical presence are the adaptations of his dramas and novels into operas or musicals.

Kazantzakis & Kalomiris

Poulakidas supports that Manolis Kalomiris had suspected the operatic elements in the early novels and theatrical plays by Kazantzakis.[497] In 1915, Kalomiris turned the first Kazantzakis play into a music tragedy, *The Masterbuilder*. The Athenian audience warmly welcomed it as, "in the original Greek music drama, it found an echo of itself."[498] The Greek National Opera first staged it in 1943 while a most recent production premiered at the Athens Concert Hall in 2008.

Kalomiris detected the artistic and particularly the music value of the work (as the University committee also did) and decided to use it in the context of his ambitions to create national opera in parallel with the ethnic drama.[499] The composition lasted four years and Kalomiris acknowledges it as the one that he identifies mostly with. It is the only Kazantzakis theatrical play – along with *Kapodistrias* – which takes place in contemporary Greece.

In 1944, Kazantzakis, inspired by the life and deeds of the last Byzantine emperor, wrote *Constantine Palaiologos*. He reworked the play in 1946 and came up with its last format in 1951. The tragedy's theme evolves around the eve of the Fall of Constantinople. Along the simile City-Capture which stands for Hellenism-Fall, Kazantzakis added another dimension as well: the Human Being-Palaiologos versus every human's struggle to go over the perishable scenery of the moment and gain meaning and purpose in life.[500]

In 1953, the tragedy was published in the journal *New Hestia*[501] with the subtitle

"The ethnic legend of the Fall." The work is divided in two acts and four scenes. It is written in a 13-syllable rhyme and parts of it are in prose. As soon as Kazantzakis published the text, he urged to donate it to Kalomiris,[502] who narrates: "I could not keep my tears… I kept constantly being shaken by the melodies, the harmonies, the themes and the motifs, similarly with the good times when his *Masterbuilder* had enchanted me…"[503] The performance took place in 1962, after Kalomiris' death, by the National Opera of Greece, at the Herodes Atticus Odium.

The music language of the work represents the most refined and sophisticated version of Kalomiris' personal meta-Wagnerian, national idiom. All the music springs from one central thematic source. Byzantine hymns and the rhythms and modes of Greek folk song are intertwined in it. The use of Byzantine hymns seems all the more impressive because they seem to retain their monophonic purity within a complex polyphonic counterpoint.

Melissa & Periander

Kazantzakis got engaged with great, tortured souls who suffered a lot in life, loved and resisted blatantly to God and Fate. As he… "reports": "I was struggling to pull them from Hades, so as to exalt the pain and the struggle of the human being, of the living man."[504] In the Kazantzakian works, both the mythological and the historic figures change characteristics. They revolt based on ethical criteria, thus their struggle is being promoted as part of a spectacle that carries larger ecumenical meaning. Their struggle puts up front a positive philosophy: A series of purposeful changes will produce social harmony.[505]

Kazantzakis' *Melissa* belongs to his most mature theatrical plays.[506] It was written in 1937, during a tough, turbulent epoch,[507] but was not performed until 1962.[508] The dictatorship that prevails in Greece and the civil war in Spain influence Kazantzakis deeply. The writer derived material for this tragedy from Greek history and mythology. Amongst the messages the play conveys are also the various generation battles (similar to those exhibited in *Freedom or Death*).

Theodore Antoniou's composition *Periander: Scenes from the Life of a Tyrant*, an Opera in Two Acts was also based on the theatrical play *Melissa* by Kazantzakis. The opera narrates episodes from the life of the second tyrant of Corinth. Antoniou, in a lyrical way, combines with sensitivity sounds and mild timbres, paying particular attention to the way by which the chorus is being handled. *Periander* is Spartan in words. Its political ideology, the tyrant and the concept of necrophilia, the Oedipus complexes, the dictatorship and the authoritative mentality, the people who revolt, all these are topics that "upset" the composer.

Kazantzakis & the World

The political vision which, since the old times and according to Plutarch, was attributed to Alexander the Great, has always been an existential problem for Kazantzakis, as East and West consisted one of the many binary oppositions he struggled to unite within him, one more pair of the big dialectic game of the antitheses that governed his philosophy.[509] His constant quest was a synthetic vision of Greece that synthesized its cultural history: Archaic, Classical, Hellenistic, Byzantine and modern, including its ties to the East and the West. He called that comparative, syncretic gaze "Cretan glance." How can we combine our eternal battle with nature? Is eastern destiny indeed dough in the hands of occidental men?

Cafe Antarsia is a neo-folk opera which takes place in Turkish-occupied Crete around 1889. At the play, *Karagiozis*, the main character of the Greek shadow-puppet theatre, is given human dimensions as a local Greek-Turk, and is able to move in both sides, so as to literally light up fire to the warriors of independence during the period of the last revolts. The music is a mixture of Balkan, Greek and rock sounds. Live recordings in New York combine clarinet *taximia* (instrumental improvisations) with the Greek bouzouki and *laouto* sounds, along with a variety of melodies performed on both the Cretan and the Pontic *lyras*.

The Greek-Texan composer, Nikos Brisco, explained to me that "the work and life of Kazantzakis reflects what it means to be Greek and to a greater extend humane…" He further commented that, "while composing *Cafe Antarsia*, which is based on Kazantzakis' *Freedom or Death*, he felt not only proud for his ancestry and history, but was essentially challenged to abandon the security of the western compositional style and notation, and grasp on his hands and heart the ethnic instruments of Crete, the *lyra* and the *laouto*."

The libretto is written by Ruth Margraff whose goal was to create a world folk opera, thematically inspired by Kazantzakis. In the United States, Margraff is known as a visionary of a new operatic music movement. In a message of hers she argues that the *rembetika*, what used to be the music of the underworld of Greece, along with the songs of the *Cafe Aman Aman* and the Cretan libertarian, rebel songs known as "songs of the table," particularly those belonging to the late Ottoman period, are intrinsically operatic in style. Thus, her desire is both to make modern Greek history known abroad, something which has not been emphasized enough compared to the ancient Greek drama and mythology, and to underline the co-existence of eastern-European elements on Greek music, due to the country's proximity to the Balkan areas.

Lastly, in March 2006, in Australia, at Sydney's "Parade Theater," a contemporary adaptation of *The Masterbuilder* by the Greek-Australian composer Constantine Koukias took place. Australian Cretologist Alfred Vincent was the dramaturgist and Christine Kanellakis the choreographer. The emphasis of that work focused on the love-career, personal happiness and social offer conflicts. According to the program, the goal of the performance was to give the Australian (and Greek-Australian) public a chance to enjoy a branch of modern Greek culture which is not so well known. Kazantzakis *Masterbuilder*'s story is timeless and open to many allegorical interpretations while Kalomiris' music heightens the inherent drama.

Finale

In the 21st century Nikos Kazantzakis and the music interpretations of his work should be appropriately recognized, because his writings, despite their local character, are versatile due to the universality of his ideas, which inspire, even today, Greek composers all over the world. If globalization means that we recognize the same human values in things of different form, then music works based on or inspired by Nikos Kazantzakis work are not only a strong advocate of an artful creation but also a model for creative imitation. Therefore, one of the ways, according to which the Kazantzakian voice could be better and with no dissonance heard is through its music arrangements. After all, Kazantzakis, who thought of himself as a bow, would force the music composers himself, not only to stretch him so as not to go rotten, but to extend him further, even under the danger of breaking him apart.[510]

The *Masterbuilders*

The *Masterbuilders* Kazantzakis & Kalomiris

Nikos Kazantzakis is arguably the most important and translated Greek writer and philosopher. He was born in Crete on February 18 1883, when the island was under the Ottoman Empire. After obtaining a law degree in Athens-Greece, he studied philosophy under Henri Bergson in Paris and traveled widely in Europe, Asia and the Soviet Union. During the Balkan Wars (1912-1913), he volunteered and served with Special Services in the Greek Premier's office. Intensely poetic and religious, Kazantzakis wrote many plays and a variety of historical and philosophical works of fiction, poetry and travel writing. He also translated many classics into modern Greek. He died on October 26 1957, in Freiburg- Germany.[511]

Manolis Kalomiris was born in Smyrna in 1883, his family being from the Greek island of Samos. He is perceived as the founder of the National Music School of Greece and his numerous works are deeply associated with Greek folk tradition. At a young age, he attended primary School in Athens, and in 1899, High School in Constantinople. He then left to Vienna where he studied music. Upon the completion of his coursework, he moved to Kharkov (then Russia, now Ukraine) where he taught till 1910, when he permanently settled in Greece as a teacher of piano and advanced theory music classes at the Athens Conservatory. In 1919, he founded the Hellenic Conservatory, which he administered till 1926, the year he also founded the National Conservatory. He died in Athens in 1962.[512]

Composer Kalomiris is regarded as an artist of similar stature and a well-matched ideological companion to writer Nikos Kazantzakis. His first, 1915 opera, *The Masterbuilder (O Protomastoras)* was based on Kazantzakis' tragedy *The Sacrifice (I Thisia)*, which Kazantzakis wrote in Paris around 1910, initially under that title and the pen name Petros Psiloritis (Psiloritis being another name for Mount Ida). The composer saw the artistic and musical significance of this play and used it to realize his ambition of creating a national opera: *The Masterbuilder* was the piece he held closest to his heart.

The Sacrifice received a prize at the 1910 "Lassanis Drama Competition" and was then also published at the *Panathenaea* magazine. As an opera, it was completed in the fall of 1915 and presented for the first time in Athens the year after. Kalomiris had difficulties setting to music Kazantzakis' poetic prose and therefore created the libretto himself aided by poet friends. He developed the lyrical element, but otherwise kept close to the text by Kazantzakis, focusing on the heroine's devotion.[513] The music score, a music tragedy in two parts and one intermezzo, was published in 1939 by Gaitanos. *The Masterbuilder* premiered in Athens on March 11 1916, at a production at the Athens Municipal Theater. Kalomiris conducted the orchestra, while the stage director was Miltiadis Lidorikis. A reworked version was then presented in 1930 at the Olympia Theater under the baton of world-famous Greek conductor Dimitri Mitropoulos.

The folk legend about the bridge of Arta forms the core of the plot. Despite the gloomy predictions made by the builders and villagers, the bridge is completed, and the masterbuilder is sure it will not collapse. When the noble asks him what reward he would like, he seeks permission to build a house in the center of the village and to marry his beloved. At the same moment, a young woman arrives with news that the bridge is about to collapse. A wise prophetess then appears and announces that the bridge will not stand unless the masterbuilder's lover is sacrificed. She does not, however, reveal the woman's name, since, if the magic is to work, the masterbuilder and his lover must confess of their own accord. Unaware that the woman in question is his daughter Smaragda, the noble swears to hand her over in person. The masterbuilder remains silent; as night approaches, the builders decide to sacrifice him. Smaragda then confesses that she is the lover, and self willingly descends into the bridge's foundations.[514]

Western Prototypes, Eastern Aspirations, National Goals

Both Kazantzakis and Kalomiris studied in Europe, where they became involved in the European intellectual debate, which also extended to western music. They witnessed the revival of ancient Greek tragedy in the philosophy of Nietzsche and the music of Wagner. In 1908, Kazantzakis completed his thesis on "Friedrich Nietzsche on the Philosophy of Right and the State." For Kazantzakis, who was much influenced by Nietzsche's asceticism at that time, *Lohengrin's* music was "something out of a dream."[515]

Both artists were eager to write tragedies and melodramas, as it can be seen in the numerous tragic elements found in their works. Theater critic Kostas Georgousopoulos commented that, "if we scratch *The Masterbuilder's* form, we will eventually meet with Wagner's *Parsifal*."[516] In Kalomiris' work the mature principles of Wagner were applied in the spirit of the romantic idea of fusing music and poetry, while his compositions are characterized by national romanticism, influenced mostly by Wagner, Strauss and the Russian School, also relating a lot to Debussy's as well as to the expressionists' and the neoclassicists' beliefs.[517]

In his 1910 essay *For Our Youth*, Kazantzakis salutes "prophet" Ion Dragoumis, or Ida (after Mount Ida), a Greek diplomat, writer and revolutionary, to whom he also dedicated his tragedy *The Sacrifice*. His early political beliefs were profoundly influenced by Dragoumis' ideology. As he characteristically said, "fully touched and fiery, he was going through nationalism. Ion Dragoumis was a shadow he felt by his side."[518] Besides, true friendship united both men. Kazantzakis also devoted to Dragoumis his Canto "Alexander the Great" (*Tertsines*, 1960). That same year, the writer also became a founding member of the Educational Society which supported the use of modern Greek language (*Demotic Greek* or *Demotiki*).

In a parallel motion, this was one of the most inspiring and productive periods of Kalomiris' life, something reflected in the density of his music. The elections were won by a Cretan, Eleftherios Venizelos, whom the composer saw as "The master-builder of modern Greece" and "the lighthouse of his spiritual life." That is why, in *The Masterbuilder*, he included the traditional Cretan (*pentozalis*) melody to honor his great idol. Later, he also composed a march and a song devoted to that politi-cian.[519] Kazantzakis also admired Venizelos, whom he had the chance to experience closer while he was voluntarily serving during the Balkan wars at his private office. He considered him capable and worthy to realize the Great Idea (meaning the resti-tution of Greece's former borders), and thus, in 1919, he served as a General Direc-tor at the Ministry of Relief under the Venizelos government.[520]

Tragedy and melodrama convinced the Greeks during 1908 to 1910 – a time when Greece, in the turmoil of the Balkan Wars and World War I, was torn between the Liberal Party of Venizelos and the royalist supporters of King Constantine – that they were capable of overcoming their defeatism and of rebuilding their country. Both works exalt Greece, modern Greek language, the Great Idea as well as Greek national identity. In the 1920s and 1930s, music critics were certain that Kalomiris would develop into a leading national musical figure, that he would become "the Venizelos and Palamas" of Greek music.

It is important to stress that, from 1803 onwards "Greekness" characterized every aspect of Greek cultural output. During the waning days of the Turkish Occupation and in the early years of the newly-established Greek state, Greek literature and mu-sic had to be equal to the great traditions of Europe. Just like Greek authors wrote under the shadow of Homer, Sophocles and Plato, music composers lived over-whelmed by the legacy of Beethoven and Wagner. Anthropologist Michael Herzfeld analyzed the intense attempts toward the formation of a Greek, national identity, the general speculation in the 19th century Balkan region and the European trends of beautification and romanticism. He illustrated how Greek folklore was (and is) a cultural weapon, an ideology, in other words, which promises cultural continuity and uninterrupted, unsullied national unity from antiquity to today.[521]

Since the last decades of the 18th century, folk songs had been recognized by the patriarchs of the nationalistic movement as one of the basic axis of a nation's col-lective identity. The oral poetry of modern Greeks was embraced by the European romantics in their enthusiastic quest of unadulterated sources of humane literary expression. It was affectionately embraced by foreign wise men and won the public admiration of even great Goethe. Kalomiris himself affirmed that, in *The Master-builder*, he used the "Forty apprentices" folk melody.[522] Definitely, he was not the first Greek who embodied Greek folk songs into classic, western-like music. His *Masterbuilder*, however, functioned as a factual manifesto of the Greek National School's ideology as he purposefully used a popular melody as a familiar recognition point by the audience. Consequently, having demoticism as an ideal, both Kazantzakis and Kalomiris created their own idiolect and became word makers of a "colloquial Greek language" (*romeiki*), something analogous to what Greek national poets Solomos and Palamas in literature did.

Similarly to how Kazantzakis sang passionate *amanedes*,[523] in his 1946 speech Kalomiris, among others, mentions: "I, personally, in my childhood, had never heard an opera aria, a lied or a romantic song. I had heard, however, my grandmother, my *nene*, as we called her in Smyrna, to perform songs such as "Lygos the Brave the Master Brigand" and "Forty Gallant Men from Livadia." I had also listened to Tsatsa Marouka. Tsatsa Marouka was the Muse of my childhood (…) She sang her own songs, which she offhandedly made, both the verses and the melody."

In order to achieve their goal, Kazantzakis and Kalomiris use the popular legend of the bridge of Arta. The human sacrifice theme and the sacrifice motif that is their main concern, the story of the "walled-up woman" toward the successful creation of a building, is part of the oral tradition of other countries, such as Albania, Turkey, Romania, Bulgaria, Bosnia, Serbia and Hungary.[524] The building may not be a bridge, but a monastery or a castle. Simultaneously, the same myth is found elsewhere in Europe, in the Caucasus, even in India. Folklorist Georgios Megas has recorded and documented 333 Greek variations of that Greek song in which the bridge may be that of Larissa, of Adana, of Spercheios, of Pineios, or the fountain of Arachova, the aqueduct of Derka, etc.[525] On the island of Crete, specifically, it is entitled "The wife of the Masterbuilder" but also as "The Arch of Mesara," a place where still one of the very few arcaded bridges of the island is located.

The political dimension of the Kazantzakis and the Kalomiris works is not only unequivocal, but – viewed via prophetic lenses – identified with any "great idea" and "great personality" capable of transcending one's self toward Hellenic, ecumenical ideas and ideals. Moreover, Manolis Kalomiris is considered to be a national composer, but also the creator and the founding father of contemporary Greek music. On June 11 1908, he organized in Athens the first concert which consisted exclusively of his compositions. This is regarded as the official first event of the so-called National School of Music whereas the accompanying liner notes written by the composer are considered as its "manifesto." In *The Masterbuilder*, traditional folk songs are used as part of the plot, as an element of folk culture. Those well-known melodies are also used as familiar recognition points for the listener.[526]

During that time, the composers of the National School of Russian music were acting respectively. According to Kalomiris, "they shaped their music language by the songs of the folk people who live in villages and steppes simultaneously inspired by the poems of Pushkin and Lermontov."[527] Similarly to how national poet Solomos believed that, "if we shut Greece in our soul, we will feel all majesty," in the same spirit Kalomiris in his manifesto proclaimed that "this must be the scope of any genuinely national music, to build the Palace where the National Soul will be enthroned!" In addition, he firmly believed that music composition means – above any theoretic and technical issue – one thing: Poetry. Prior to becoming a musician, the composer must be a poet."[528]

As it has already been mentioned, the subject and motif of human sacrifice both artists examine is significant in the Balkans and Asia but also in the world at large. In Albania, for instance, Ismail Kadare's novel *The Three-Arched Bridge* (1978) is very popular.[529] In Greece, however, "sacrifice" is addressed over and over again through time; From Iphigenia to the Biblical Abraham and Isaac, all the way to the modern-day "God, the Masterbuilder" of Nobel Laureate poet Odysseas Elytis, as well as in *The Dream of Nikitas, the Masterbuilder* of Aris Fakinos.

It is worthy to mention that, part of the soundtrack of the 1957 movie *Christ Re-crucified* directed by Jules Dassin and music by Georges Auric, which is based on the homonymous novel by Kazantzakis, is the folk song "The Bridge of Arta." Therefore, it looks like this legend was indissolubly connected with Hellenism and functioned as a point of recognition for Greekness and Greek identity. As the composer himself declares, "he chose a free creation founded on a popular, folk legend, because he believes that the legend only, the legend of the ancient tragedy, welcomes, and asks for, on top of everything, the music processing."

Both artists found their answer in Nietzsche's Übermensch, the manly "Master-builder" who dreams without overlooking the Darwinian nature of life. Although he is propelled by passion, he controls and directs his urges with rigid rationality. This is how he defeats destiny itself and is prepared to go for the next practical achievement of the impossible (maybe... taking back Constantinople?). He knows how savage the battle for survival is and brings back fearlessness to the Greek nation. Both Kalomiris and Kazantzakis identify with their hero, who is given the role of the exceptional individual in the history of their nation, [530] as well as with the meaning of the Nietzschean and Christian self-sacrifice, namely for the common good instead of the individual one.[531]

To that end, they both greatly reduce the supernatural element. The spirit of the river does not appear, and a rational explanation is suggested for the repeated collapse of the bridge. Emphasis is placed on the psychology of the master-builder and other main characters, as well as the interplay between the various individuals and groups.[532] A basic feature of the Kazantzakis plot, which Kalomiris adopts, is that the required victim is not the wife of the master-builder but his secret lover, the beautiful daughter of the village's landlord, who has to confess her love publicly.

We must, however, take a few moments to consider a different approach to the main themes of the works under examination. By giving his tragedy the title *The Sacrifice*, Kazantzakis focuses on the act that constitutes the core of Christianity and on his metaphysical preoccupations which clearly dwell in his writings and for which he was harshly criticized, regardless of the fact that, in reality, he revered Christ and his teachings.[533] His tragedy reveals a religious uplifting (in the sense of man being an upward-looking, a "homo erectus" being), something we also find later in Kalomiris' opera *Constantine Palaiologos*, the work where, for the second time, in 1953, Kazantzakis attempts to "exploit" folk tradition through the legend of the Marble King. It is his basic conviction, however, that "the only way to save yourself is to fight to save the others," and, therefore, commands "his" masterbuilder: "If you want to solidify the bridge, tear off your breast, take your heart out and lay it as a foundation for the bridge." But is it, after all, the sacrifice of the masterbuilder or the sacrifice of Smaragda and the Greek (or any other for that matter) state, that is at the core of both Kazantzakis' and Kalomiris' concerns?

Kazantzakis warns the Greeks that without a clear, manly look at the broader future, they will never be able to survive as a nation. The woman-Greece fulfils the society's demand for self-sacrifice, thus becoming immortalized in history. The "old man-river," the masculine element, is the source of nationalist desire. Kalomiris dedicates a good deal of space and time to his heroine. Indeed, the piece could easily have been entitled "Smaragda" (like Strauss' *Salome*). Human sacrifice – flesh for the soul – is for both artists a prerequisite for creation and an act of love, and it is female in gender.

Kalomiris' agonies, however, are more ethnic than existential. The hard building of the bridge symbolized for the composer the making of Great Greece with Eleftherios Venizelos as the masterbuilder. Let us not forget that the victorious Balkan Wars of 1912-14 had preceded along with the overtone of Pinelopi Delta's *Tale with No Name* (1910). In those ethnic contexts human sacrifice is legitimate, namely the supersession of personal happiness versus the tough struggle of the individual to learn how to serve the general social interest along with the importance of the heroic sacrifice of the woman-Smaragda as an action of love.

The Kazantzakis Text & the Kalomiris Libretto[534]

If we compare the text and the libretto of *The Masterbuilders*, we will conclude that Kalomiris follows the structure of the 1908 Kazantzakis' text both in words and spirit.[535] Approximately 80% of the final poetic text of the opera (which was 90% in its first version) fully corresponds to the literary text. In both works, the main roles remain the same: Lord, Old man, Masterbuilder, Mother, Lord's daughter (Smaragda), Singer, Builders, Harvesters, Gypsy women and Woman. Potentially, the idea of such a close adaptation is related to the text's copyright issues "in support of the composer," something obvious on the accompanying notes of the 1916 libretto publication.[536] This fact annoyed Kazantzakis, who, because his percentages were withheld by Kalomiris, called him "musical donkey."[537]

An essential, structural difference is that Kalomiris divides the first part of the work in two parts (first and second scenes), expressing in writing his desire not to have a break between them, exactly because the scenery does not change. Several parts of his opera are in prose or reciting style, faithful to the grandiloquent Kazantzakian sayings, exactly because the writer's style is comprehensible and relatively plain in relation to his future theatrical plays, such as, for instance, the adaptation of his novel *Christ Recrucified* into the opera *Greek Passion* by the Czech composer Bohuslav Martinů.

"Keys" to the understanding of the opera remain the over 18 "Wagnerian" leitmotivs, which symbolize roles and concepts, such as those of the Masterbuilder, the Gypsies, the Singer (a and b), the Forty Apprentices, the river, the hatred between the old man and the Harvesters, fate, Smaragda, love (a and b), the Builders and the work (a and b), the Lord, the bridge, the firmed bridge, the Mother, paternal affection and Smaragda's funeral.[538] Similarly to how "Wagnerian" is the music atmosphere that the composer wishes to create, so "Wagnerian" both those leitmotivs and the analogies of his heroes are (for instance, the Mother remotely reminds one of Erda in Wagner's tetralogy).

Kalomiris provides his singers-actors with more scenic instructions, such as, for example, the Old man "with uncontrollable hatred," the Harvesters' wives "frightened," which, however, do not oppose to what Kazantzakis had in mind; later, in the unfinished manuscript, the "second 1916 version," as the writer calls it, he adds on notes that refer to the symbolism of the roles. A characteristic example is the instruction for the green, potentially "hopeful" dress of Smaragda,[539] a detail that does not exist in Kalomiris but which was used by the recent performance of the National Greek Opera at the Athens Concert Hall.

When Kazantzakis imagines music and describes it in words Kalomiris instrumentates it with tambourines and castanets, so that it actually sounds, for example, "gypsy." At the same time, he frequently "rhymes" the text with verses, so that it could be properly set to music. The scene which he musically develops at the end with the builders' hammers to sound rhythmically while underlying the tragic character of human sacrifice and Smaragda's agony, attests to his composing abilities and is the result of a common adaptation of theatrical prose into music theater.

In other words, music, as a means, allows Kalomiris to transform verbal meanings, even pauses, into music episodes – for instance, the Kazantzakis' intermezzo, and it is exactly here that all of his effort to compose an opera based on western prototypes lies. The endless melodies are distinct for their intensely ornamenting character whereas significant words in the text are given emphasis through long durations, preferably at the higher ranges of each voice's "tessitura."[540]

In relation to the text per se, it has already been highlighted how both *Masterbuilders* strongly defended demoticism. In addition, they are both word makers. Kazantzakis, however, remains faithful to the language of his native island, namely Crete, and we can see that in a) words he chooses, b) grammatical deviations and c) the intense use of proverbial speech.[541] In opposition, Kalomiris, by "popularizing" Kazantzakis' language, undoubtedly becomes more ecumenical since "his" *Master-*

builder it acquires a panhellenic readership.

In general, Kalomiris preserved all the elements that served his goals, whereas he removed others based on either music-dramatic or ideological criteria. For instance, Kazantzakis had devised characters that Kalomiris did not incorporate in his opera, such as "Dimitris," "pale woman," "another woman," "three girls" (which, as a role, existed in the first performance but was later removed), "Eleni," "Mariyitsa" as well as some other yet smaller and non-talking roles such as "Andreas," "Barba-Tasos" and "Tasoula." At the same time, Kalomiris depicts more intensely the difference between villagers-gypsies as well as the fact that the gypsies mentally relate to the masterbuilder.

For the Singer's role, Kalomiris sees "a young, delightful man up to sixteen years old" thus he arranges for a female voice (even though at his second manuscript the composer for the same role reports "soprano or lyric tenor"). Kalomiris' master-builder is a tenor; therefore a baritone or bass would have been excluded for the role of the young man. A contra-tenor – a "sopranist," indeed! – would have been ideal. However, that is a quite rare voice range, hence the woman-soprano was preferred throughout all the performances of the opera.

In relation to the Singer, Kalomiris leaves out the episode at which the chorus doubts and accuses him of being "lazy," someone who "very unfairly is even given food." Many other comments are missing from the libretto, such as the ones that humiliate the Kazantzakian bard who "dies" out of love for Smaragda, degrading his masculinity, since "a hair of hers is worthy more than all bridges" while "it is better to sit at the waterside devastatingly crying till Smaragda through a smile heals him." Here the composer's criteria are possibly ideological and relate to the social acceptance of the music profession during his era.

For dramaturgical purposes, the conspiracy scene against the Masterbuilder is totally missing. Only one of its phrases is being used by the Harvesters: "Why wouldn't his body get saturated so as to feel for us and our children?" Another point which Kalomiris does not embody in his libretto is when, with evilness, the Old man foresees the upcoming misfortune. Obviously, the composer does not wish to decrease the surprise from the moment the disaster is actually going to come, desiring, therefore, to increase, instead, the dramatic quality of his tragedy.

Let us not forget that Kalomiris characterized this work as "music tragedy." In his foreword to the 1916 libretto publication he explicitly highlighted that "it is not opera, as people use to commonly call the music drama." He desires "through all the expressive means that the art of music possesses to empower the tragic impression that is born out of the drama. In addition, his music has the ambition to manifest (…) the Greek soul." On the cover of his play, Kazantzakis notes the subtitle "Tragedy" and, as a result, his work is obviously targeting to reviving an ancient Greek drama due to its a) structure – for example, the use of the chorus, b) context – intense hubris, and c) general goal – negotiation of a popular for the audience subject that aims to catharsis and guidance.

Structurally comparing both works with the ancient Greek tragedy, one observes the use of the chorus (Gypsy women and Builders, Harvesters and their Wives). In Kalomiris, the "voices" are collective and express the two contradictory ideas of "love and creation."[542] In opposition, the Kazantakian ones are divided into weak/female (e.g. the three women) and strong/male elements (e.g. the harvesters). The female element of the Kalomiris' chorus acquires "weak" voice only in the role of the Gypsies. Moreover, at this melodrama, the chorus has a double role, both vocal and scenic, whereas it is not about one but two groups of choruses, which may co-exist or even collide (for example, Gypsy women and Builders with Harvesters and Women).

The works' 1st part refers to the rebuilding and the 2nd to ways of progress.[543] In addition, Kazantzakis divides the chorus in two parts, namely the weak-minded and conservative Harvesters and the wanting to change, innovative, free and democratic Builders.[544] In Kalomiris' opera, the orchestra represents a third chorus, off stage, which comments on the scenic action of the tragedy via rich counterpoint and elaborate contours.[545] At the intermezzo, which as a form takes us back to the Cretan Renaissance and reminds us of both an ancient Greek choral but also the play *Erofili*, Kalomiris juxtaposes the Gypsy women to the Wives (of the Harvesters) most likely in order to achieve a richer vocal participation.

The conflict between roles in two levels is also a "classic," tragic element. Apart from the "superficial" clashes between the Masterbuilder and the Lord, the Masterbuilder and the Mother, Smaragda and the Lord, and so on, there are also "inner" conflicts: when the Lord collides with himself, as a father, he is forced to soften. When Smaragda clashes with the notion of the sacred duty, she chooses the most magnanimous sacrifice, even though in the beginning she sounds split and uncertain.

At the play by Kazantzakis, the Masterbuilder's hubris towards God is more intense. He does not admit gods and fates, he neglects destiny, and proceeds remaining faithful to the superhuman Nietzschean powers. More specifically, for Kazantzakis, God is "That" whereas for Kalomiris "This." In addition, Kalomiris leaves out the blasphemy scene that negotiates the relationship between human-God while, by adding the last part of the folk song instead, he enforces and projects the importance of Smaragda's magnanimous sacrifice.

In both works, the audience knows before the Lord does that Smaragda, who, in opposition to the folk song is not the wife but the Masterbuilder's lover, is not chaste. And it is exactly here where the tragic irony that brings both works closer to an ancient Greek tragedy lies. The Lord, as if he were Oedipus, proceeds painfully and tryingly toward self-awareness and acceptance of his own role, which requires that he decides based not on personal and egoistic criteria but rather by sacrificing the part of himself that is devoted to his beloved daughter.[546]

Kazantzakis gets inspired by the "myth" of the popular folk song but Kalomiris is the one who includes word by word its lyrics. He even "plays" by improvising with its verses in folkish style. He also develops its finale, embodying the dramatic episode with the curse that Smaragda delivers and the Masterbuilder asks her to alter, something that does not even bother Kazantzakis. As a result, the folk song is Kazantzakis' idea, which he embodies as a folk legend, and which, in continuation, Kalomiris "exploits" more fully in terms of structure, poetry, music and dance.

More specifically, Kalomiris did not intervene at the Kazantzakis text, but only in parts where he felt it was important so as to secure coherence and dramaturgical continuation. In three parts, he asked assistance from poet friends: a) The Singer's aria "Oh! Your hands," which was modified by Nikos Poriotis, b) the duet "What are you bringing to me, after all?" by Agnis Orfikos (nickname for Georgios Stefopoulos) and c) the verses of the Masterbuilder's aria "One Palace Lord" by Myrtiotissa (nickname for Theoni Drakopoulou-Pappa).

In particular, the erotic dialogue between Smaragda and the Masterbuilder musically disguises into a "fifteen-syllable" duet. Stefopoulos chose some key-phrases from the Kazantzakis' text (for example, "how much I love your hands") and developed them further. In every two of the Masterbuilder's verses he borrows, he adds on four of his own, whereas, right after, Smaragda responds with approximately the same text. For purely music purposes, the duet "It's getting dark again, my love…" follows, through which the composer intertwines the voices of the lovers via a canon's counterpoint technique. This duet with minor changes is being repeated at the second part, during the farewell scene.

Strangely, the composer himself does not precisely clarify the aforementioned parts. In the "thank you notes" of the first 1916 version, however, he nominally refers to his three friends-men of letters, who assisted him in the prose's adaptation into verses. Moreover, he acknowledges the professor of Byzantine music at the Athens Odeum and scholar of the Greek folk song, Constantinos Psachos, who informed him on two folk songs on the bridge of Arta and, finally, Spuros Theodoropoulos (Agis Theros) for the mourning song from the region of Mani which he sang for him and thus became the basis for the Singer's dirge at the third part (namely the second part of the final version).

Furthermore, the composer testifies that, in his *Masterbuilder*, he used the following folk melodies: a) The "Forty Apprentices" at the beginning of the opera and the second part but also while Smaragda is being immured at the foundations, b) "A Little Bird at Dawn" at the ballet of the first part, a little bit after the Lord's entry and c) the "Pentozalis" at the end of the first scene of part one. "All the other music themes and motifs are purely a product of his inspiration even when based on modes and scales of our folk songs or gypsy melodies."[547]

Let us keep in mind that, in the opera by Kalomiris, Smaragda extensively participates also at the intermezzo, emphasizing the importance of true love. She is less sarcastic when, for instance, she talks with the Singer. The dance does not "accuse" her, her father does not consider of her as "unashamed" while she, herself, sings "openly," without hiding her love. All in all, the lengthy music and melodic arrangements of the composer which focus on the main heroine, Smaragda, in combination with the profoundly erotic lyrics added by the three poets, tend to magnify at the opera the meaning of the female sacrifice.

Bridging Arta with Beijing

Manolis Kalomiris' *The Masterbuilder* had not been performed since 1950. The Greek National Opera first staged *The Masterbuilder* on February 19 1943, with Antonis Delendas and Anna Remoundou in the leading roles. It is important to observe that *The Masterbuilder* is the only Greek opera that Maria Callas ever sang in 1943, in the intermezzo, and then again in 1944 in the role of Smaragda, at the Odeon of Herodes Atticus, conducted by Kalomiris himself. A new production premiered at the Athens Concert Hall on January 2008, as a co-production of the Greek National Opera and the Athens Megaron, with Thomas Moschopoulos as the stage and Elias Voudouris as the music directors (sponsored by "Ellaktor," a construction and renewable energy group of companies). Smaragda was performed by Kerri Marcinko and the masterbuilder by Avgust Amonov. The opera was going to represent Greece during the Cultural Olympiad of Beijing 2008. Greece's Minister of Culture, at that time, did not authorize the mission, even though that work had been chosen precisely due to the diachronic nature of its messages whereas also excerpts of it had already been presented at concerts by the Thessaloniki State Orchestra in both Thessaloniki and Beijing on October and December 2007 respectively.

The Cultural Year of Greece in Beijing-China, which officially began on October 17 2007, offered the Chinese the chance to become acquainted with the customs, traditions and art of the Greek culture and civilization. According to a statement by the Greek President Karolos Papoulias: "Both Greece and China are heirs to an immense legacy, which rests on the ideals and achievements of two major civilizations with universal ecumenical importance. Moreover, the Olympic ideal expresses mankind's desire to build a world based on the rules of fair play, humanism, reconciliation and tolerance." Therefore, it was not coincidental that *The Masterbuilder* was chosen to represent Greece. Not only Kazantzakis is so popular in China, but the work itself is emblematic. Though written in the early 20th century, the ideas it carries are diachronic, and very well portray the bridging of the East with the West. According to a greeting statement from Sun Jiazheng, China's Minister of Culture: "China and Greece have long-standing histories and brilliant civilizations. The Chinese and the Greek people share traditions of prolonged friendship (…) The Cultural Year of Greece is a bridge for understanding and friendship that will enhance the relations between our two peoples."[548]

Captain Michael[549]

Nikos Kazantzakis' *Captain Michael* (1953a) inspired fellow Cretan Manos Hadjidakis (Op. 24, 1966) to compose a homonymous song cycle the lyrics of which are based on original phrases from the Kazantzakis' novel – a work that was also theatrically adapted. Both the writer and the composer have influenced cultural and musical life in modern day Greece. The soundtracks of *Zorba the Greek*, a film based on the homonymous novel of the first, and *Never of Sunday*, which won an Academy Award, by the latter, gave them international fame back in the 1960s.

Kazantzakis was born in 1883 in Heraklion, the capital of Crete, when the island was still under Ottoman Occupation whereas Hadjidakis, of Cretan descent, was born in 1925 in Xanthi, a town in northern Greece of dense Balkan and Ottoman cultural texture. Thus, both creators had lived within and firsthand experienced multi-cultural co-existence, something evident and prominent on their work.

Captain Michael, known in English by its subtitle, *Freedom or Death*, celebrates the glory of Crete and its oppressed people. Though it is essentially a historical novel, it is not only the struggle of the Cretans, for which the hero dies at the end, but the absolute dedication to any cause, which inspires human beings to self-assertion and self-sacrifice on a superhuman scale.

In 1966, the famous Cretan actor Manos Katrakis asked Hadjidakis to write music for the theatrically adapted by Gerasimos Stavrou and Kostas Kotzias play *Captain Michael* (7 ballads and 4 instrumental pieces). The songs composed were initially performed by Giorgos Romanos at the Athens Festival. That vocal cycle is well-known to Greeks throughout various interpretations due to its folk and popular elements as well as the high poetic value of its lyrics-identical phrases from the homonymous book.

Kazantzakis became a founding member of the Educational Society that supported the use of modern Greek language. He was much interested in the linguistic problem and thus created a demotic language with high appreciation of folk culture. So, his ideology coincides with his narrative style resulting to the creation of both an epic and a folkish narration.

In a parallel motion and in addition to his work as a composer, Hadjidakis was one of the initiators of a movement for the recognition and dissemination of contemporary music and of the work of Greek composers. He wanted to preserve local tradition with a natural and unforced way – to which extend he used the Cretan example – so as to save and promote the real cultural identity of a people or ethnic group.

Both creators worked with antithesis as well as with synthesis, trying on the one hand to stress oppositions and on the other to attempt some sort of synthesis or even a kind of transubstantiation by transforming matter into spirit. The co-existence of a "Belle Époque" style along with authentic Turkish minarets added color and content to a society-medley from all the corners of Greek earth that accidentally happened to live in at border-lined regions and yet dance tangos at public squares.

For both men, memory on the island of Crete seems dramatically present. Kazantzakis' comparative, syncretic "Cretan gaze" is well-respected by Hadjidakis: both men's vision is of a Greece that synthesizes its cultural history as an existential problem, a political vision and a continuous quest. Hadjidakis' composition transforms the Kazantzakian East-West "play" into sounds.[550] For example, the first theme of the "Circassian" song is based on a Byzantine-*rembetiko* mode[551] which the composer processes through western harmonies and techniques.

Several of the Hadjidakis' melodic lines are rooted more in the modes of the *rembetiko* than in the major and minor scales of western music, although he often transcends them in a way that brings to mind the abstraction of the West. Still, his deviations from the dominant mode do not sound like the modal combinations of learned Byzantine and Turkish musicians, because they cannot be explained as abstract mathematical combinations of two or three scales. By using Cretan popular melodies, such as the one of the "Erotokritos" in the introduction to *Captain Michael*, Hadjidakis is plumbing the Greek "collective unconscious."

Manos Hadjidakis' music "dresses" Freedom or Death excerpts powerfully and faithfully to Kazantzakis' ideas, conveying messages for one's home, family and freedom. Both creators carry a duty to their ancestors, which translates to every human's inner, rallying cry for freedom, independence and return to the land through an orientation to the landscape, the customs and the folk people of Greece.

Captain Michael focuses on the co-existence of Greeks and Turks during the 19th century Ottoman-occupied Crete. Its 2007 music instrumentation by musicologist Yannis Samprovalakis uses traditional instruments in order to represent those two parallel worlds, similarly to the living conditions of the basic heroes, the Christians and the Muslims. The Cretan *lyra*, for instance, and the *santouri* represent correspondingly the Greek and the Ottoman elements, colliding in fight or creatively co-existing.

This way, both the folk-popular becomes artful and the western compositions "dress" with ethnic costumes, eulogizing their marriage to the East. The co-existence of a symphonic orchestra with traditional instruments that the Orchestra of Colors commissioned for the 13th anniversary upon the composer's death and which was performed at the Athens Concert Hall (June 2007), was embodied by the Thessaloniki State Symphony Orchestra to concerts dedicated to the 50th anniversary of Nikos Kazantzakis' death in both Greece (October 2007) and Beijing (December 2007). The performances were based on a rationale initiating from the ideological ground of the Kazantzakian work. Subsequently, the Hadjidakis music through the use of instruments such as the Cretan *lyra* also supported the evolution of such ideas.[552]

The orchestrator "plays" nicely with sounds performed on string instruments, such as the viola, the Cretan *lyra*, the cimbalom and the harp. Various sound levels co-exist similarly to how in Crete heterogeneous cultural elements (for example, Arabic and Venetian) were met in the same society. Each element moves independently but yet relates to other ones in antagonistic, peaceful, even "in love" relationships. This way, similar to how Christians and Muslims lived parallel lives in Crete, the Cretan *lyra* (that represents the Greek element) and the *santouri* (that represents the Otto-man element) creatively co-exist or even "argue" with each other.

Hadjidakis' preoccupation with the elevation of this musical form led to the development of a unique genre of Greek art songs and established his reputation as the Schubert of Greece.[553] For him, the art of song is a social service, because songs unite us within a common myth. Similarly, for Kazantzakis, the narration of endless national struggles constitutes meaningful stories that contain within them the history and the beliefs of all Greek people, in the same manner that folk songs do.

Kazantzakis believed that poetry can substantiate all pain and fight into dream and immortalize as much as of the ephemeral as possible by turning it into song.[554] This was also crowned by the composer who perceived Crete as the mermaid of the Mediterranean with an important cultural but also "syn-cretic" role. Both creators, namely, spoke of "freedom" suggesting "world peace."[555] Therefore, their message is timely, diachronic and ecumenical.

Captain Michael either as a novel or a music composition manages to penetrate the folk masses. The driving force behind it is the desire to create a mythical-poetic space. The problematics and thematics are indigenously Greek whereas the creators' aim is to define a field of poetic communication that touches upon both eternal and contemporary myths articulated with an expressive language that would connect the immediacy of present experience to Greek cultural memories. Both classically-trained Kazantzakis and Hadjidakis write from "inside" Greek culture whereas they also stand "above" that culture and consciously create from the "outside." Hadjidakis transforms Kazantzakis' textual amalgams into soundscapes that explore issues of cultural identity in relation to a shared past targeting to a harmonious dialogue in the present through echoes of a common future.

Melissa & Periander

The libretto of Theodore Antoniou's opera *Periander* is based on the Kazantzakian tragedy *Melissa*. The Cretan in descent composer, deeply impressed by his compatriot, creates his musical theater, approximately 40 years after. Which are, however, the conditions, the questionings and his motivations, and how parallel are they with the Kazantzakian wanderings?

Historically, Periander was the son of Cypselus, the first tyrant of Corinth. He had a personal guard of 300 armed soldiers and was violent with everyone. Either by kicking or by pushing down from a staircase, he killed his own wife, Lysidice, whom he called "Melissa" (namely bee), the daughter of the Epidaurus tyrant Procleus. Next, he burnt his mistresses alive, because they unjustly had accused Melissa and which, thus, via infuriating him, turned him into a murderer. Periander had two sons with Melissa, Cypselus and Lycophron.

Despite the enforcement and the preservation of his power through excessive wildness, Periander was an illuminated leader and, during his era, Corinth flourished greatly. He applied rules that relieved social tensions, he protected the small peasants by enforcing local economy, he created an aquaduct and he also constructed Diolkos, a road useful for transferring boats from the one side of the isthmus to the other, utilizing, this way, the ports of the Corinthian and the Saronic gulfs and increasing the Corinthian naval power and commerce.

Theodore Antoniou

Theodore Antoniou was born in Athens in 1935. His works are innumerous and various. They include operas, symphonic and choral compositions, concerts, chamber and soloist music, as well as music for the movies and the theater. Specifically for his contribution to the field of theater music he was in 1998 awarded the "Karolos Koun" prize (in fact, he was the first to receive it). For his opera *Oedipus at Colonus* he received the "Music Price 1998" by the Greek Union of Theatrical and Musical Critics.

In his compositions, Antoniou adopts "serial" techniques combined with avant-garde, ancient, byzantine and Greek folk music elements. He considers himself as a par excellence dramatic composer of abstract programmatic music. His rhythms are mature and his music language intensively and expressively tonal. He, himself, considers composing as a mission to the service of humanity.

His opera *Periander*, inspired by Kazantzakis' *Melissa*, moves into three parallel temporal levels: past, present and future. This way, time for Antoniou functions synchronically, creating parallel surfaces that coexist, lending to the present equal meaning both with the past and the future. Corinth, as a space, is central, while dominant in the work's plot is a type of a detective mystery, similar to that of a

Hitchcock movie.[556]

Purposefully, the opera is not loaded with words because, while released from the text, it allows the music to fill in any gaps. Therefore, its text is prudent, as in an opera, by definition, the rhetorical aspects of the language subject harmonically both to the music sound and the dramatic acting. However, this does not mean that *Periander's* speech is not concise, deliberate, precise and carefully chosen. For instance, at the eighth episode of the opera, grandfather-Procles advises grandson-Lycophron on power matters reminding him that he should not torture the people and deprive them of wheat but feed and empower them instead.

Morphologically examining the two works we conclude that *Periander* uses conclusions-epilogs from the authentic Kazantzakian text and that its libretto is more poetic rather than a word-by-word translation of *Melissa*. The opera's music dresses the words and turns them into theatrical acts through not description but texture. The frequent absences of words that are substituted by theatrical action contribute to the composition's tragic quality and add on a symbolic emphasis to the absence of a group in taking decisions during tyrannical regimes.

Generally speaking, the Antoniou central ideas and meanings do not differ from the Kazantzakian ones, the libretto, however, is not as thick as the Kazantzakian text. The composer's interest focuses on the liberal and democratic vision with which the compatriot writer also agrees. While Antoniou condenses Kazantzakis' word into teachings and proverbial key-phrases, Kazantzakis, through his distinct, juicy writing, attempts to amplify the use of "folk" language (the so-called movement of demoticism), something that had always been a serious part of this literary acquisitions.

This way, Antoniou manages to make language and music partners that "harmonically" conspire to a didactic result. Music and text meet in his opera, but not always. The "textual silence" also has an important role, as, for example, in the sixth episode, when Periander pulls his sword to kill Lycophron. Then his father, Cypselus appears whom Periander embraces and kisses on the mouth, and whose presence seems to calm him down momentarily, since Periander hands the sword over to Lycophron's wife, Myrto, so as to avoid the homicide.

Antoniou's sounds have their roots on the second Viennese School, particularly to the work of Alban Berg. The composer sensitively selects smooth contours, paying special attention to the way through which he treats the chorus. His music composition is constituted by singers, narrators, actors, dancers, chorus and orchestra, and is scenically very interesting, with visual projections. The music of the opera also includes electronic music elements, namely production of fragments of properly processed and shaped both natural and artificial sonic effects. More specifically, in *Periander*, there are speakers and tape music for the repetitive, reproductive production of sounds, something like a "drone." Let us note here that Antoniou is considered as a pioneer Greek composer in such techniques.

Lastly, the composer adds on a narrator, as Stravinsky does in his *Oedipus*.[557] While, however, in Stravinsky's case the narrator explains the scenario in French, because the Latin libretto by Cocteau is obscure, Antoniou's narrator epigrammatically comments and underlines aphorisms and cases to avoid or to imitate. Periander's fury is such, however, that, during the penultimate episode, he even strangles the narrator, namely the voice of consciousness!

Melissa & Periander

Kazantzakis' *Melissa* consists of three acts, with correspondingly three, five and one scenes. *Periander: Scenes from the Life of a Tyrant*, an Opera in Two Acts by Antoniou is bilingual, with an English libretto by George Christodoulakis, translated in German by Peter Kertz. It was written between 1977 and 1979,[558] commissioned by the Staatstheater am Gaertnerplatz of Munich,[559] and was performed on February 6 1983. The two acts of the opera consist correspondingly of six and four episodes.

Kazantzakis admired Plutarch and Herodotus and mainly derived by them the materials for his tragedy on Periander and the tragic family of the Cypselids.[560] Most likely, his 1937 itinerary throughout the Peloponnese influenced him toward that direction, even though Periander is absent from his reports.[561] *Melissa* takes place in Corinth and Epidaurus during the end of the 6th century, and so does Antoniou's *Periander*.

However, Kazantzakis transforms the inherited material and adjusts it to his own preferences, including himself. According to a letter of his, "he took a popular theme, he renewed, adapted and gave it a new depth and wider meaning."[562] In his turn, Antoniou bases his opera on the theatrical play *Melissa* but uses the ancient topic with fidelity to the historical accuracy, in an attempt to give a) diachronic credit to his work through projecting the ancient Greek culture and b) Greek identity to his creation.

For instance, Antoniou, in the fourth episode of the opera, presents Periander accepting the faithful man he had sent to the tyrant of Miletus Thrasyvoulos so as to ask his advice in terms of succeeding in his dictatorship. Thrasyvoulos then, upon leading the man to a field with crops and without uttering anything, starts with a stick hitting and seizing all larger and robust seeds. Upon his return to Corinth, the sender narrates to Periander this event, who, imitating the way the tyrant of Miletus governs, kills all of his potential competitors. That story inspired the opera's poster which, according to Antoniou's descriptions, depicted a field with crops and a suspending sickle, a scene projected at the very beginning of the opera.

Let us not forget that one of Antoniou's composition professors was Manolis Kalomiris, who obviously influenced the composer in terms of his desire to continue through music supporting "our" national identity. Overall, also within the general terms of neoclassicism, many are the composers who get inspired by Greek tragedies and create operas that target to the interpretation of archetypal forms and the influence they have exercised on the western world and civilization.

In Kazantzakis' *Melissa*, the most tragic person is Periander, a wild, uncompromising soul. His inner drama, his solitude, shocks the spectator. The writer chooses to give a feminine title to his work but also his own ending to the tyrant's life, who, exalted, kills the only keeper of his name, namely his son Lycophron. Antoniou, however, chooses a masculine name for his opera: *Periander*.

According to history, Periander died in Corinth, in his eighties, either by committing a suicide disgusted by his own life either by natural death. Lycophron, his son, accepted to return to Corinth only when his father promised he would take over his position in Corfu. When this became known, however, the inhabitants of Corfu killed Lycophron.

In Kazantzakis' play, Lycophron visualizes a plan that reverses the direction of the Oedipodean parricidal: Periander informs him he has taken poison and asks for his forgiveness but the young man is adamant and, in a quite harsh manner, tells him that Melissa hated him throughout her whole life. Frenetic, Periander kills him with a golden knife. He then passes away in the palace, which, according to his last command, is being set on fire by the guards. In Antoniou's *Periander*, however, two men from the army of Lycophron, in presence of the people of Corinth, kill the tyrant.

It is worthy to emphasize that, historically, Melissa's real name was Lysidice (or Lucide) but Periander called her caressingly "Melissa," namely… bee, a name sweet as… honey, an affectionate nickname which means that, nearby her, he continuously enjoyed a "honey-moon." In both works Melissa is omnipresent. Even when dead, she always goes around as a remorse, one of the Furies. Antoniou achieves this by the simultaneous appearance of Melissa's character on the roles of the singer, the dancer and the actress.

In addition, the selection of voice types for each one of the roles is not accidental. The tyrant, the messenger and the dignitary are baritones, namely "the voices of power," while Lycophron and Cypselus tenors, voices that "subject to" the "base" presences of the grandfather-Procles and the commentator-narrator. Lastly, Melissa is a mezzo and Myrto a soprano, feminine contours surrounded by plural, masculine presences.

Kazantzakis ignores the "wise" elements of the tyrant's personality and his contributions and prefers to distribute his plot amongst different moral characters. Antoniou, at the same time, really… tyrannizes Periander. Even in his first episode, he refers to the building of a bridge, obviously that of Diolkos, the road, namely, that was used so as to transfer ships from the one side of the isthmus to the other. In our personal conversation, the composer underlines that, every time he crosses the Isthmus of Corinth, Periander comes to mind.

Other differences in the plots of *Melissa* and *Periander* are the name of Lycophron's fiancé, Alka in Kazantzakis and Myrto in Antoniou, as well as the fact that, in

Periander, Myrto, who already has a baby with Lycophron, is also a victim of Periander's sharp sword. In addition, Kazantzakis neither alludes to, at least obviously, to the Oedipodean complex of the tyrant and his mother Krateia, nor to the necrophilia scene between Periander and Melissa. In opposition, Antoniou refers to all of those events in an obvious manner as he describes both the Oedipodean complex in the introductory prelude of the second act and the necrophilia on the second episode of the opera. Interesting also is that the necrophilia act is being represented by the dancers in the fifth episode.

Besides the fact that the composer brings to life the historic part of the tyrant's personality, all of the aforementioned elements enforce the idea of the authoritarian character, constituting Periander even more hateful and, at the same time, victim of his own destiny. In the already discussed second episode of the first act, Antoniou uses several "Melissas," besieging the spectator with the intensively feminine presence that, even as a ghost, through multiple presences, is being victimized and shocked by the necrophilia tensions of her husband.

One may conclude that Kazantzakis seems to have with "Melissa" a more personal relationship while Antoniou wants "Periander" to dominate in his opera as a tragic, tyrannical character, whose God is solitude and whose condemnation is guilt. This agrees with the studies by Zografou and Petrakou that approach the Kazantzakis' tragedy psychologically,[563] asserting that it reveals the writer's personal experiences and castration by his totalitarian father. That is why Kazantzakis, in an attempt to take revenge, fabricates Lycophron in a way so as to take care of his own matters with the inner self.

Peter Bien and others have approached Kazantzakis' *Melissa* in political terms. They have analyzed the fact that Kazantzakis lived in a difficult era: Hitler and Mussolini were in Europe, dictatorship in Greece, civil war and the death of Lorca in Spain.[564] His hometown, Heraklion, was a communist cell expecting a folk uprising.[565] The political ideology, the ancient Greek tyranny and repression which urges people to revolt, the variance, namely, is undoubtedly the reason which for Antoniou chose Periander. This opera of his is "apparently a commentary on the political events that take place during that time."[566] Music is not a decorative art but a means he uses so as to reflect on what upsets him out of everything that happens around him.

If then, according to Bien, Kazantzakis is providing us with political teachings,[567] a similar goal Antoniou's opera also has. At the closing of the work, the composer embodies an identical text-excerpt from the first ode by Aeschylus' *Agamemnon*. The insistently repetitive last phrase is of a monumental dimension and, of course, symbolic character: "Because the Gods are not indifferent to those who have shed rivers of blood."

Diachrony in Kazantzakis

The theatrical play *Melissa* by Nikos Kazantzakis has musically inspired other composers as well. In 1957, it was broadcasted by the radio, arranged by Nikos Gatsos, accompanied by the Symphonic Orchestra of the National Broadcast Foundation, in music composed by George Kazasoglou. Argyris Kounadis wrote the music for the theatrical adaptations of the play directed by Alexis Solomos in 1962 and 1964. Lastly, in Romanian translation, at the Municipal Theater in Bucharest, *Melissa* was accompanied by jazz music composed by Harry Tavitian.

To my question why he chose this specific theatrical play, Antoniou's response was not his Cretan descent or strong personal and professional connections with Crete, but the fact that "Kazantzakis is an international chapter that belongs to the whole world."[568] Let us add here that Antoniou, for his composition degree thesis, under the supervision of composers Antiochos Evangelatos and Marios Varvoglis, created a cantata for voice and music ensemble, the Kazantzakis "*Tertsina* (Tercet)-Christ," to his opinion, "a superb and unknown poem."

All in all, Kazantzakis and Antoniou opted for a topic that is not that well known as Sophocles' *Oedipus*, for instance, but which however, is adequately and culturally rich. This way, they both contributed to bolstering the diachronic significance of Greek culture by moving from the personal level and the family story of the hegemon to the general cry against every form of tyranny that leads to anguish.

Amor Fati

The work *Amor Fati* has been George Koumendakis' guide to life. Koumendakis (b. 1959) is regarded as one of the most influential, contemporary Greek composers "with a work encompassing a wide range of musical idioms, constantly evolving in new directions."[569] In 2007, he composed *Amor Fati* commissioned by the Thessaloniki State Symphony Orchestra specifically for the 50 years upon Nikos Kazantzakis' death anniversary.

The following thoughts by Irvin Yalom became the inspiration for *Love of Fate*, "an optimistic work," according to the composer, perhaps his "first with a positive impulse for life":[570]

> I much prefer a Nietzschean life-celebratory, life engagement, amor fati (love your fate) perspective (…) Those individuals who feel they have lived their lives richly, have fulfilled their potential and their destiny, experience less panic in face of death. Therapists have much to learn from Nikos Kazantzakis, the author of so many great life-celebratory works of art (…) I love the advice he offers for life: "Leave nothing for death but a burned-out castle." It's not a bad guideline for our life.[571]

Koumendakis attempted to see Kazantzakis' work through contemporary lenses, without the usual folkloric dimension – which he believes "is mistaken and restrictive in terms of the true essence of his creation, his philosophical and ideological substance."[572] Since 1994, when awarded the Nikos Kazantzakis prize in Heraklion, he had been considering the composition of a work inspired by the author's writings and personality.[573] The work consists of three, consecutive movements and a long coda, all in one and only tempo. The musical core and the basic theme are derived from Cretan musical phrases (*condylies*) whereas the pitch is based on the sounds of the Cretan *lyra, thiaboli* (wooden flute), *mandoura* (a processed reed in the shape of a flute) and *askomandoura* (bagpipe). Out of the brass, he only used the horn, for sound economy, in order to avoid excessive tensions and impressions.

In *Amor Fati*, George Koumendakis approaches Cretan music via an abstractive orchestral script, without using any traditional Greek instruments. The composer keeps in mind the Cretan music atmosphere and makes a free paraphrase of its general idea, that being the main characteristic of his personal style of writing. The quotation is distant and abstract, thus not profound at all. This way, Koumendakis purposefully chooses to work on a second creative level, keeping in mind the tradition, always with love and respect to its roots.

The inaugural soloist lines on the violins refer to Cretan *condylies* witnessed in Swiss musicologist Samuel Baud-Bovy's transcriptions; brief musical phrases, in other words, initially performed on a piece of reed between two consecutive nodes (*condyles*), and which, later on, also applied to string instrument music (*lyra*, violin).

As each bow has many turns-embellishments, similarly the composer improvises, evolving around a pentatone, such as the notes that correspond to the "fingers" of the node.

The use of three vibraphones rhythmically accompanied by the strings represents the distinctiveness of the Cretan lute as a par excellence accompanying "percussive" instrument. The string melodies converse with the wind sounds as a Cretan *thiaboli* or *mandoura* would give space to the performer who is simultaneously the singer to vocalize half, one, one and a half or two fifteen-line rhyming couplets (*mandinades*). The patterns stemming out from the composer's transcriptions of bird chirpings sound on the woodwinds that intermingle with the strings in a Cretan dialogue or improvised rhyming couplets composition (*mandinadomahia*). The synthesis integrates the dancing dimension, as required by the Greek, traditional triptych "melody-word-motion" in syncopated and "asynchronous" accents which, combined with the rhythms of the "percussive" strings, realize a slow dance.

The balance between the Dionysian sounds on the winds, on one hand, and the Apollonian strings, on the other, immediately alludes to the Nietzschean ideas that Nikos Kazantzakis adopted and the composer crowns via the naming of this work: the "tragic" co-existence of spirit and flesh, reason and passion, love of fate and the dual substance of man. The work's message is undoubtedly auroral: the passion of the cross is followed by the Word's up-heaval, something annunciated by the resurrectional "bells"-vibraphones, whilst during the last meters of the work, the composition's vibration remains peaceful and meditative.

All in all, *Amor Fati* reveals a spiritual approach, which we could trace on the catharsis targeted to at the end of this composition. Koumendakis makes particular instrumental choices to illustrate his ideas by avoiding brass and percussion and including bird chirping (a *Messianic* influence) of actual recordings as well as a soprano saxophone and a piccolo clarinet. He is not making use of traditional, Cretan or other Greek instruments, even when he implies dancing rhythms. He shows a strong preference for the chordophones and the aerophones and relies on them to perform several variations of the lyric parts but also for conversing while improvising on basic melodies.

Philosophically, Koumendakis' composition is characterized by mature mellowness. His work reflects ideals of what it means to be a Cretan through esoteric meditation, something natural for a Cretan-born musician who, in a way, via this composition is re-connecting with his roots.

Cretan *thiaboli* (wooden flute) performed by Giannis Rompogiannakis.
Photo by Yiannis Bromirakis.

Iphigenia's Sacrifices

Prelude

The central thread of this treatise is the meaning of sacrifice and its literary, theatrical, music and dance transformations, in other words, sacrifice in daily life as both "Logos" and "Event." The centripetal force is the Greek folk song "The Bridge of Arta" and radii of the circle the first opera by Manolis Kalomiris *The Masterbuilder*, which is based on the theatrical play by Nikos Kazantzakis *The Sacrifice*, as well as the soundtrack of the movie *Iphigenia* by Mikis Theodorakis and the choreodrama *Iphigenia at the Bridge of Arta* by George Koumendakis. The goal is to examine the ideology of the play, the opera, the film and the choreodrama, the similarities but also their differences, specifically because of the various means of expression in use. Driving force is the comparative study in the aforementioned stories of a) the roles' conflict, b) the embodiment of the folk myth elements and the ancient, "Euripidian" tragedy and c) their contemporary, timely, bridging dimensions. Is the emphasis, after all, on the tragic, Nietzschean, "superhero," on the Christian self-sacrifice or on the female heroine? Is it a variation of Iphigenia, of Smaragda, of Greece, or of the "homo erectus" being?[574]

The Bridge of Arta

The nucleus of the story all works under study narrate and negotiate is based on the popular Greek folk ballad "The Bridge of Arta," of which over three hundred orally transmitted versions that differ widely in detail have been collected from many parts of the Greek world. The song is associated with the northwestern town of Arta because many versions refer to the fine old bridge which still stands just outside the town. That song belongs to the "Akritic Cycle," part of a series of epic songs that emerged around the 9th century. Such songs take us back to the days of the Byzantium and celebrate the heroic exploits of the Akrites, the frontier guards (from the Greek word *akra*, thus, "edges").

The song lyrics focus on the establishment of a bridge via human sacrifice. According to it, numerous builders and apprentices – under the masterbuilder, are trying to construct a bridge, which daily, however, collapses. A bird with human voice announces to them that, in order for the building to remain standing and thus solidify, the masterbuilder must sacrifice the woman he loves (usually his wife), a fact that is realized after a series of curses that turn into wishes. Moreover, the term "bridge of Arta" is a contemporary Greek idiomatic expression used for works that not only require collective labor, but also take a great deal of time to complete. Greeks say, for instance, "like the bridge of Arta," "as if it were the bridge of Arta," "the way it progresses looks like a contemporary bridge of Arta," etc.

It is worthy of mention that Greek stone bridges comprise unique samples of folk architecture. The builders-creators have been utilizing the natural laws, assembling small but strong stones, through a special technique, so as to give to the bridge the appropriate arcaded shape, within the vertical level, and to avoid the development of drawing powers and the sliding of the stones. That structural deterioration did not lead to impoverishment of the bridges' aesthetic. In opposition, the intense variety of the bridges and architectural composition emphasizes each builder's-creator's yearning and reinforces the bridges' emotional language as elaborate monuments of people's needs for communication in the previous centuries.[575]

The roots of human sacrifice take us back to pre-Indo-European times. In the Greek world, we trace them at the cult of Zalmoxis, a legendary, social and religious reformer, who, as Herodotus informs us, was the only God of the Dacians in Thrace who turned humans into immortal.[576] Even today, in the Greek world, when builders dig so as to lay the foundation of a house, a black cock by preference is usually being slaughtered, because, due to popular belief, the soul of the "victim" moves its existence into the foundation and continues to live "walled-up" within its new, architectural body. This way, the foundation is being solidified, through the sacrificed soul, which attains supernatural power, since it is being saved from the body, while it turns into a "phantom," protector of the building, saving it from dangers and punishing the ones who attempt to harm it.

The Tragic Iphigenia

The story of human sacrifice is mostly known to us through the times of Iphigenia, a myth that connects two traditions, of the Trojan war and the house of the Atreides, as well as two worlds, the political cosmos of Agamennon – as the leader of the Greeks in the Trojan war – and his family world, where the crimes of the Atreus family take place. It is worthy to note that in *The Iliad*, Agamemnon has one daughter, who is called Iphianassa, but none named Iphigenia. Even though there is no direct reference to Iphigenia's name, there are indications showing that Homer knew about the sacrifice in Aulis. It is possible, therefore, that Iphigenia's myth pre-existed in oral tradition for a long period before it actually appeared in literature.

As we learn via ancient Greek tragedies, to sacrifice virgins, was a way to obtain fame. Young girls could not fight at the war, but their blood was being spilled so that male society might survive. In ancient Greek tragedies, there are also several examples of virgins which for death meant marriage, such as Antigone, Cassandra, and, lastly, Iphigenia. All these are Hades' brides. If we consider that a) a wedding determines the relationship between a woman and a man and b) a sacrifice the relation between God-human and human-victim, we can then easily realize how great the symbolism between those two ceremonies is.

All three, great, tragic poets have written works related to the sacrifice of Iphigenia. According to "Agamemnon," the first part of the trilogy *Oresteia* ("Agamemnon-Choephori-Eumenides") by Aeschylus, goddess Artemis is furious because of two eagles that devoured a doe and its unborn fawns, and therefore asks for the sacrifice of the king's daughter. Iphigenia is grasped by slaves and brought to the altar whereas via the herald we learn that Iphigenia was sacrificed – without mentioning how last minute the sacrifice was avoided.

In *Electra*, Sophocles reminds us of Iphigenia's tragic fate. Here, the heroine informs us that Agamemnon entered the sacred woods and killed a doe bragging that he won the goddess in archery. Therefore, Artemis delayed the armada in Aulis, prohibiting them to depart to Troy and asked for Iphigenia's sacrifice as redemption for Agamemnon's deeds. Potentially, Sophocles considered the conformity to the oracle by Agamemnon as an inevitable need. In his *Electra*, Iphigenia's sacrifice was executed, though it is not clear by whom, Agamemnon or soothsayer Calchas.

The substantial differences between the aforementioned two tragic poets relate to Artemis' rage as the cause of the sacrifice. Euripides, the third, great tragic, differentiating himself by all, uses another outcome for the myth: in Iphigenia's place, a doe is being sacrificed. According to his version, the cause for Artemis' rage is the following incident: Agamemnon insulted the goddess and promised to redeem by offering her as a sacrifice the most beautiful thing blossoming on earth that year. It was then, however, that his daughter Iphigenia was born, whose fate, therefore, never escaped her father's oath.

The differences amongst Aeschylus, Sophocles and Euripides are influenced by the view that human fate merely depends on human beings themselves. Time-wise, the story unfolds right before the departure of the Greek fleet to Troy as they are anchored in Aulis. Dead calm does not allow them to sail. Diviner Calchas foreshadows that gods will send a tail wind to their sails only if Agamemnon sacrifices his daughter Iphigenia. Agamemnon is forced to invite his daughter from Argos under the excuse that she is on her way to marry Achilles.[577]

Mikis Theodorakis & the Ancient Myth[578]

One of Greece's most significant composers, Mikis Theodorakis, was born in 1925. Under scholarship, he studied at Paris music analysis with Olivier Messiaen as well as orchestra conducting with Eugène Bigot. He is known for several classical music compositions, though poetry set to music is usually perceived as his most significant achievement. His compositions have been interpreted by world famous artists while popular are his movie soundtracks as well. Based on traditional Cretan music, he created the most internationally acclaimed Greek rhythm, the *sirtaki*-"Zorbas." Theodorakis is also known for his intensely political work, since he has served as a politician, minister as well as activist, honored by the "Lenin Peace Prize."

On November 1977, the movie *Iphigenia* premiered in the United States. The film, based on the homonymous tragedy by Euripides, was directed by Michael Cacoyannis and came with a soundtrack by Mikis Theodorakis. Tatiana Papamoschou acted as Iphigenia, Irene Papas as Clytemnestra, Kostas Kazakos as Agamemnon and Costas Carras as Menelaus. The movie received the "Best Film Award" at the 1977 Thessaloniki Film Festival, where Tatiana Papamoschou also received the "Best Leading Actress Award."

That film is the third and only one in color in the "Euripidean" trilogy by Cacoyannis that Theodorakis composed music for (after the release of *Electra* in 1962 and *The Trojan Women* in 1971). The soundtrack consists of 11 suites, namely music themes that contribute to the imposing atmosphere of the Cacoyannis' cinematography. The composer used basic symphonic instruments for his melodies, namely human voices, recorder, flute, oboe, clarinet in C, horn, trumpet, trombone, piano, *santouri*, percussion, violins, viola, violoncello and contrabass. He considers this composition as "one of the best he has composed for the cinema."[579]

In an attempt to underline the diachronic futility of wars, Cacoyannis chose Euripides because of his antiwar messages and the psychological liveliness of his characters. Theodorakis fully agreed with that spirit. For example, in the beginning of *Iphigenia*, soothsayer Calchas announces the oracle in the presence of Menelaus and Odysseus. Agamemnon, infuriated for the sacrifice that he is forced to offer, he threatens he will dismiss the army. Then, ingenious Odysseus assembles the Greek army outside his tent so as to applaud him. As soon as Agamemnon sees them, similarly to how Helen's beauty seduced Menelaus, the men sing a cappella a triumphant song which is nothing else but an abbreviated paraphrase of the Euripidean choral by Iphigenia on verses 751-800:

> Fast ships, engraved with mermaids, move by the wind so as to conquer Troy!
> Let's capture the round walls of Priam, while inscribing by our weapons circles, channels of blood.
> Blood that is thick, barbarian, shed by Greek hands.

Similarly to the director, the composer also makes use of the modern Greek language so as to give coherence and emphasis to the irrational passions for a woman, power, gold and slaughter. Substantially, the hero is the victim and a new heroism comes on the surface since Iphigenia emerges out of both the degradation of politics and the personal desire, choosing to die unselfishly and proudly for an ideal, "our" Greece. After all, in full accordance with the Euripidean spirit, people are responsible for their misery, while the irony, after all, is that the bravest, that will also get glorified, is a female child, namely Iphigenia. In this context, at the film, the music technique employed by Theodorakis moves in parallel rhythms with the movie, since it comments on what the images tell, adding, at the same time, a diachronic nuance to the film's message.

George Koumendakis at the Bridge

The composer of the Olympic Games *Athens-2004* George Koumendakis was born in Rethymno. He took his first music classes at the Rethymno Odeon and the Athens Hellenic Odeon. Later, he attended composition seminars and lessons with professors such as Pierre Boulez, György Ligeti, Iannis Xenakis, etc. He has composed several works that have been performed at hundreds of concerts internationally by famous music groups and top musicians. He is a "Prix de Rome" recipient and has been a "host composer" at several parts of Greece and abroad, while, in 1994, he was honored by the "Nikos Kazantzakis" award. Much anticipated in 2014 is his opera *The Murderess* (based on the homonymous novel by Alexandros Papadiamandis) commissioned by the National Opera of Greece.

Iphigenia at the Bridge of Arta (1995) by Koumendakis for the "Edafos Dance Theatre," commissioned by The Athens Concert Hall, a work for soprano, trumpet and sampled piano, in a serious yet playful mood, bridges the ancestral myth with the folk song, placing emphasis onto its dancing dimension as well. The work is a mocking comment on the combination of those two myths, ancient and folk. After a long in time cartoonist persecution by her sacrificers, Iphigenia suddenly stops, and along with her every music and motion stops as well. Exhausted, and in full silence, she peacefully offers to her persecutors the stones by which they will entomb her, a scene quite unforeseen and intensively, emotionally effective. This way, *Iphigenia* functions timely, bridging collectively the past with the present, at eras of global dynamics and turbulence, as a "micro-tragedy," through which catharsis on a personal level is achieved.

The composer's goal is the tragic spirit through a humorous mood under the hope that humor will counterbalance his speculations. The piano accompaniment to silent films was the initial idea for the way Koumendakis wanted his music to accompany *Iphigenia at the Bridge of Arta*. Iphigenia urged him not to forget her Greek ancestry thus he also left his composition wander in Pontic Greek and Cretan rhythms. This way, in "modes that very much move him, Pontus knotted with Jazz and Crete with Renaissance." In addition, because his story should be told clearly, he mobilized the soprano at the role of the bird with human voice and the trumpet as the announcer.[580]

The first music image of this work refers to the building-demolition. The bird with the human voice crowns the tragedy of fate which, as the stone, remains stable, but also the marriage of darkness and beauty, as the stones roll. The nightmare of Iphigenia is her destiny, which she is reminded to exorcise through dance. This cathartic dancing nuance prompts to the role of dance in ancient Greek tragedy but also in Kazantzakis' hero of the homonymous novel, Zorbas, who uses dance movement rather than speech as a pioneer method of psychoanalysis. The chasing of the deer-victim, which is eventually captured, follows. The moored boat is unlocked and sails for the "fires that do not listen."

The composition is crowned by the song "Stone the heart is," dedicated to Greek composer Manos Hadjidakis, the Koumendakis' "Masterbuilder," who, in his own way, bridged antiquity with contemporary, folk Greece, in verses co-written with the choreographer and founder-soul of the Edafos Dance Theater, Dimitris Papaioannou. This composition recaps history with references to Troy and the narrows where blood falls like water and pain is big and frosty. This is an abstractive space, where the folk song locations of the rivers Danube and Euphrates meet, where the streams of time from antiquity to today reverberate with expeditions (and where expansionist plans-campaigns between East and West still exist). Characteristically, the bird narrates:

> Hot blood, what blood does it bring, count.
> Blood like a chain, like a river,
> my generation's stamp: killing.
> If you love me, the paternal tombs
> will have a gold deer to reside.

Iphigenia at the Bridge of Arta speculates the role of human beings as marionettes of destiny. Iphigenia-bride, mute to her fate, throws the bouquet before being walled-up while, throughout the composition, special stress is being placed on the action of building, the persistence for life, despite of all the vicissitudes, and the reminders-prophecies of the bird-fate, something that is being perceived through music-dance via the reminding, repeated music-rhythmic motifs: As if youth is trying to escape everything that looks out for enclosing it in the closet of time and which, at the end, devours everyone. This composition re-examines the world's value system as it is being defined by hegemonic traditions in combination with the will of the marginal to belong to a society where the terms are being reversed. In other words, Koumendakis' work doubts the "sovereign convictions" that present themselves as "fair" and "right" to current conditions and situations that are "unfair" and "inferior." Shouldn't, after all, in the 21st century, the society embody and embrace otherness?

Moreover, the correlation of human ambition, will and struggle is faced as a path full of nightmares, shadows of death and Sisyphuses. Human vanity is underlined whereas the faith that axioms and honors are a "fake beauty" is deified. Lastly, it is recognized that, in love, which is being possessed by deep passion and not mediocrity, the price is large. Those who dare to proceed there where no one has ever arrived, those who go over avarice and egoism, will be tortured in their biological substance, arguing for a place in social memory. The brief, but comprehensive in meanings composition, bears long catharsis since it repeats the eternal conflict between superior powers and mortals: Will redemption exist?

From History to Her-story

How, then, do Kazantzakis' *Sacrifice* with Kalomiris' *Masterbuilder* but also Theodorakis' *Iphigenia* and Koumendakis' *Iphigenia at the Bridge of Arta*... bridge with each other? The ideologies of the theatrical play, the movie's soundtrack, the opera and the choreodrama present more similarities rather than differences. Let us pay attention, for a moment, to their titles.

According to the Greek language, the feminine in gender, abstract notion of "sacrifice," turns into a concrete male noun for the "masterbuilder," so as to return, again, to its feminine, yet specific, "woman-Iphigenia" nouns and the neutral word for "bridge." The weight, thus, is being transposed, from the ancient thought and the daughter that is being sacrificed, to the people who offer the wife for the sake of its bridge, to Kazantzakis where the sacrifice gains more Christian extensions, to the Masterbuilder-Kalomiris where the scapegoat is the Greek for Greece, to Theodorakis where a new, female heroism emerges and, lastly, to the Iphigenia-young daughter of Koumendakis, life itself, namely, that constantly demands adjustments and sacrifices. In other words, the offspring becomes wife, crucifixion, nation and, lastly, panhuman goal. In all cases, central questioning constitutes the relationship between gods and humans throughout the crucial moment of significant and almost unlikely decisions as well as the sacrifice for a superior, sociopolitical target that conflicts with the family sphere of the heroes (father-daughter, men-women, children-siblings, con-panions).

For all the works studied here, it is characteristic that exact time and space information is absent. The creation of a building-world out of the body of a woman is bridging, through the female body as the mediator. Moreover, that mediation is usually realized through the wedding, thus the moment a woman abandons childhood by "being built" into spousal life. If we consider, moreover, the walled-up for almost a year pregnant woman, then the "sacrifice" in question illustrates well whom mother-nature offers her body to for further creation under whatever cost that bears.[581]

In other words, in Greek tradition, sacrifice insists... femininely. The name "Iphigenia" itself symbolizes she who becomes strong (from the Greek words *ifi*, strongly, powerfully, and *gignomai*, to become). A woman, even today, sacrifices her flexibility and is being trapped in marriage in an attempt to balance career and family. Fertilization and motherhood, inherent female powers, conquer the impetuous, masculine, rivers under the price of their personal life due to their flexibility and adjustability. As the Greek word for "bridge" (*gefiri*) is of neutral grammatical gender and does not belong to neither one of the two banks it unites, similarly a woman creates life from her body, bridging the past with the future, being a symbol of human struggle for survival. It is the foundation of society itself, the Greek woman-mother Virgin Mary, the wife or daughter who tames the man-river and brings honor to the *ecos* (home-household), even if asked to dynamically mediate between the world of the living and the dead.

Consequently, the story we examined shows the elasticity of tradition since it keeps re-appearing from antiquity to today. It is also diachronic because the motif of sacrifice is necessary as myth-history toward the building of national ideology-propaganda. It may be that the diviner becomes a bird but the message exists to remind us that "it is impossible to escape destiny." The largest difference of the Greek version and the ones we meet in other parts of the world is that, in Greece, myths are both being sung and danced. Therefore, unifying bridge amongst all works, from antiquity to today, is the existence of a whole ritual and not a purely poetic text, something that enables their reincarnation into a classic tragedy of folk, artistic and dancing dimensions, with ultimate goal a catharsis.[582]

For instance, the dragging dance in three-time "Arch" (*Kamara* or *Kamarahti*), performed on the islands of Skiathos, Samos and Euboea, in a two-beat rhythm, is performed to the song "The Bridge of Arta" during Easter, on the second day upon Resurrection Sunday, thus on Monday, usually the day of St. George. At this dance, the whole village participates, in a big circle. The leader of the group sings a strophe of the song that the dancers repeat along a *tsakisma* (interpolation, usually couplets that praise love). The hands unite arm-in-arm, in the shape of an X. The significance of the dancing dimension of such a tragic song verifies the particularity of Hellenism to be simultaneously mythic and lyric, and not only epic and narrative. The frequently met opposition of happiness versus sorrow seals the Orthodox meaning of *harmolipi* (joyous grief) through a ritual way that harmonically is being expressed via the traditional triad word-sound-motion.

Essential is also to highlight the environmental dimension of the aforementioned myth as it could (and should) be used toward sensitizing the communication for the protection not only of the natural but also the constructed environment. Potentially, an announcement of the sort "Married… masterbuilder is sought!" is well-timed today as several historic, Greek bridges suffer due to rainfalls but also leaks. Can, at the end, human beings tame nature with their bridges? How can "we" interfere with "our" natural environment? What are the results of bridging countries that are located north and south of the Mediterranean, according to the paradigm of the "Union for the Mediterranean (UfM)," but also the popular, yet debatable, construction of a port at the Greek town of Timpaki, south on the island of Crete, a project which aims at uniting Africa/Asia-East with Europe-West?

The arcaded arches bring discord-disunity and the rivers' conflux confluence-meeting. Therefore, an establishment of political and cultural bridges is particularly desirable. The ancient poet Euripides underlined to both Agamemnon and Menelaus that "the discord and the logomachy between brothers is a great mischief." Toward that bridging direction moves the "Kokkalis Program" at Harvard University, for instance, underlying the necessity for southeastern synergies,[583] and so does also each building by famous Spanish architect Santiago Calatrava, who envisions bridges even at New York's "Ground Zero-World Trade Center" area. In those contexts, the relatively recent collapse of Berlin's Wall could also be placed, an action that under-lies bridging and not isolating, thus the need for a connecting passage between the old and the new world, as a transit hub (*plimni*, in Greek).

All the stories talk about humans' choice to exist mobilized or immobilized, namely for two attitudes toward life that stress the existence of borders and their transgression. For all "Masterbuilders," though the mythical dimension is very clear, the geographic dimension is absent. Their timelessness and essence are found in the unifying bridge and the sacrifices it demands in order to bridge every distance, locked in a constant battle between the old and the new. Symbolically, this could also be seen as the passage from this world to the afterlife (similarly, in the Muslim faith a bridge leads to paradise). Let us also not forget the ancient Epirotic river of Acheron (etymologically, from *achon reon*, namely "the growl carrier"), which, according to the myth, led to the gates of Hades. It is also interesting to note that it is a bridge which is (almost always) built rather than an arch or a wall (even though, according to Leontis, there were…no bridges during the time of the construction of the actual Arta one!).[584]

Consequently, Kazantzakis, Kalomiris, Theodorakis and Koumendakis "build" literary and musical bridges, linking the past to the present, "walling up" the past in order to achieve a "rudimentary" bridging with a "constructive" present. Maybe, after all, the healthiest aspect of a nation is to be found in societies that are destroyed over and over again, that remain fields of sacrifice and struggle, as well as in the flexibility of traditions and their cultural bridges.

So, if, according to the Kazantzakis *Masterbuilder*, "only pain teaches the secrets of life," then, let the desire of the Kalomiris worker be a wish: "the Fate of each laborer of our country, the rush for the big works, the beautiful, the time and the people, those two monsters, let us all alone to build our bridges!" And if, as wise Euripides remarks and Theodorakis agrees with, "there is none in this world to be absolutely happy till the end and none was born without a sorrow" because "the deeds of the Gods are unexpected to the humans but those whom the Gods love they do save from misfortune," then, let us "be happy through our sacrifices," making our hearts stone, according to Koumendakis, in the boat of life, to the journey toward Ithaca, with love as our pennon, since, as genuine Greeks, "we would already have understood what those Iphigenias mean!"[585]

Chapter 6

Tasty Greece

A Hungry Bear Does Not Dance

Imagine a gypsy wandering around with a bear. He would ask it to stand on its two hind feet and perform dancing movements. Today, although that type of entertainment at local fairs is – thank God for the poor bears – almost extinct, the old Greek proverb is very alive confirming the idea that, for a dance event to be accomplished, food is necessary. In the same spirit, Greek folk music lyrics ask "the lords" to "eat and drink," because dancing won't start before everyone's stomach is well fed.

Greek cooking mostly relies on its produce of the country: fresh, seasonal fruits, vegetables, grains, pulses, legumes, goats and sheep, fresh fish, and, of course, the ever present olive oil. Cheeses, yogurt and honey are also fundamental. All of this is enhanced with fresh, young wine from the patchwork of vineyards that quilt the Greek landscape, and digested with the ubiquitous presence of other "white" spirits (such as *ouzo, tsipouro, raki*). Most Greeks in rural areas have their own olive grove and vineyard, even a pergola of hanging grapes shading their porch, with fruit trees, gardens for vegetables, wild berries covering the property fences on their land, and a profusion of flowers.

It is in Greece where one becomes the beneficiary of Zeus' virtue, the lavish and frequent *philoxenia* (hospitality). Village rules deem that one who enters the coffeehouse must treat those already present. Treating (*kerasma*) with drinks and nuts or fruit is still common in most of the public places of the Greek towns, but also among neighbors in the tiny side streets. Several times in a week, neighbors will share some of their cooking, bringing a plate of their day's lunch. Denying any food or drink that Greeks may offer you may offend traditional rules and even get you into trouble.

Greek cookbooks have been and are still being published in many languages. The roots of Greek cooking, as it is practiced still in the villages, are believed to stem from the Homeric, the Minoan and the Hellenistic times of several millennia ago. Enriched with Mediterranean and Oriental recipes, it presents a varied and plentiful fare. Cultural continuing through cooking is a widespread belief as the Greek language itself borrows expressions from food. All in all, Greek food, like everything Greek, is certainly "big" and "fat."

Baked Realities

Starter: "Bread and Patience"[586]

One food is indispensable at any Greek meal: Bread. It is an omnipresent food item, and more than any other material dish, "it evokes memories, feelings and identities that are both vast and individual."[587] Greeks of all ages and social status crave a piece of fresh bread, a basic taste at the heart of the age-long relationship between man and the earth.

Greeks have the highest level of bread consumption in Europe. Greek bread is mainly made with wheat flour, save the barley which is used mostly for dry bread, or more precisely rusk or biscuit, called *paximadi*.[588] In agricultural areas, people still use domestic ovens to make bread. At Greek bakeries, a variety of daily breads is displayed in large, straw baskets on the floor, so that everyone can see, reach, hold, smell and shop for their loaves.

Grain has been a symbol of the continuity of life for thousands of years. Humans have always used, praised, created iconic symbols of and made gods in the name of wheat, barley and corn for generations, and they continue to use them in ceremonial rituals.[589] Symbolic meanings attached to Greek bread are pervasive. Like myths, the Greek perception of bread can almost be a guide for life, because food choices often define who we are.[590]

Greek bread, an example of material folklore, represents something people make using their hands. The study of bread makes a tasty case-study in terms of its position in Greek culture and folklore across time.[591] Customs, beliefs and traditions make up a large part of why Greeks eat bread and when. For Greeks, bread is surrounded by strong religious and superstitious beliefs and functions as folk medicine.

All in all, Greeks attribute great value to bread, as they identify it with nutrition of both body and soul. Their use of bread is tied to basic rites and stages of human life, such as weddings, births, deaths, various religious celebrations as well as social and political activities. The significance of Greek bread is also witnessed in several oral and verbal performing arts.

As Lévi-Strauss proposed, "food is not only good to eat, but also good to think with."[592] Thus, in the crumbs which follow, I chew on why bread plays such a role in the Greek ecosystem by entering Greek bakeries, ovens and households. I bake the influences Greek bread continues to have on today's lore in order to better understand how that type of food has shaped Greek cultural identity. My goal is to knead dough which illustrates how, through a loaf of Greek bread, we may discover the leaven of our essence.

Old Breads: "There is Still Lots of Bread for Me to Eat"

Bread is one of the oldest prepared foods. Over fifty kinds of bread existed in ancient Greece made by a variety of flours – predominantly wheat, barley, rye, dried lotus root, millet, spelt and rice. In Minoan Crete, we find important information regarding the history of Greek bread. The Minoan palaces had storerooms – the so-called magazines – where they hoarded large quantities of wheat. These long, narrow rooms can be seen at the ruins of the Palace of Knossos, where large storage jars known as *pithoi*, filled with olive oil, wine and other agricultural products, were kept. Each *pithos* held about 50 gallons (227 liters) and there was room for as many as four hundred of them.

From the time of Homer, the Greeks have been preoccupied with defining what makes man a civilized being and what sets off the human world from the non-human which surrounds it and sometimes bids to engulf it. Lévi-Strauss' antithesis of the raw and the cooked is a fruitful way of approaching the Greeks' attempt to understand their own culture, for they often distinguished between nature and culture in just these terms.[593]

Homer, the eight-century B.C. epic poet, mentioned bread throughout his works, calling it the "marrow of man's bones." In *The Iliad*, he poetically described the plowing of a field of wheat.[594] In *The Odyssey*, he identified humanity and civility (thus Greekness) with bread-eating to distinguish it from the inhumanity of the Cyclopes[595] and called human beings "bread eaters."

Hesiod and Herodotus spoke of "wheat-eaters" as well; thus, people who farmed the land and knew how to sow and reap as well as how to prepare bread. These people were cultivated versus the "meat-eaters," who were considered savage.[596] All in all, for the Greeks since antiquity, the cultural level of a group of people has often been determined by whether they know how to consume and how to prepare bread. Pelasgus, who appears as a sort of remote culture-hero and is credited with the invention of bread, is also said to have "changed men who were bestial into a tamer state."[597]

Ancient Greek philosophers spoke of the classical elements – fire, earth, air and water – as representing the realms of the cosmos.[598] All these elements meet in bread and thus make it the "perfect" food. Diogenes Laertius referred to the wheat of philosophy. Plato and his followers emphasized the wheat of philosophy, comparing it to the barley of rhetoric. Such philosophical metaphors depict how crucial life meanings are blended together in organized groups, the same way flour, water and yeast mix in a baked loaf.[599]

In Greek antiquity, a wide variety of breads was available. Clay effigies of bread have been found in several places in Greece, such as at the temple of Demeter in Acrocorinth.[600] According to Greek mythology, a mortal once helped Demeter, the goddess of harvest and the grain. Let us not forget that Demeter is Ceres in the

Roman world, thus the root for the word… cereal![601] As a reward, Demeter taught him how to plant and harvest wheat and gave him seeds, a wooden plough and a chariot drawn by serpents to travel the world and teach the rest of mankind the art of agriculture.[602] The lyric poet Orpheus, in his hymns, called Demeter wheat-bearer (*stahiotrofos*) and wheat-giver (*sitodotra*), among other things. In the visual arts, Demeter is depicted crowned with ears of corn and holding a sheaf.

For the Athenians, cereals, wheat and barley were the basis of every meal. *The Deipnosophists* (*deipno* meaning "dinner" and *sophistes* "the wise ones") is variously translated as *The Banquet of the Learned or Philosophers at Dinner* or *The Gastronomers* or *Banquet of Scholars* and is a work of approximately 15 books (some complete and some surviving in summaries only) by the ancient Greek author Athenaeus. Chrysippus of Tyana, a learned writer on the art of making bread, is recognized by Athenaeus. Chrysippus' work entitled *Bread-Making (Artokopikos)* is a first-century B.C. Greek cookbook which includes recipes for many varieties of breads and desserts, such as cheese bread, spiced wine cake, pine nut cake and nut chews.[603] Pontianus, another character in Athenaeus, describes a classification of bread by ingredients which he has read in *Plant Life* by the Alexandrian writer, Tryphon.[604]

Athenaeus further analyzes some of the breads, cakes, cookies and pastries available in the classical world. Among the breads mentioned are griddle cakes, honey-and-oil bread, mushroom-shaped loaves covered in poppy seeds and the military specialty of rolls baked on a spit. The type and quality of flour used to produce bread could also vary, as noted by Diphilus when he declared "bread made of wheat, as compared with that made of barley, is more nourishing, more digestible and in every way superior."[605] In order of merit, the bread made from refined (thoroughly sieved) flour came first, followed by bread from ordinary wheat, and then unbolted bread, made of flour that had not been sifted.

Thus, Greeks were the first to show how mixing various flours tasted better. They were also the first to add grains and nuts to their breads as well as other ingredients such as cheese, honey and olives. They were also pioneers in building public bakeries and the first professional bread cooperatives, by applying formal regulations for the evening working hours. That is why, in ancient Greece, bakers were considered revolutionary: they offered shelter where enemies of the state could gather at nights.

The tradition of bread making, and of a cuisine in which bread played a major part of every meal, continued through Hellenistic and Byzantine times even into the four centuries of Ottoman Occupation (1453-1821), when specific parts of the towns existed where the bakers would locate the necessary flour so as to produce the essential amounts of bread necessary for the enslaved population. Today, to be a certified baker requires specific state accreditations imposed by the bakers' corporation. Bakers must sell clean and well-baked bread, work daily, serve bread morning till night, accept inspections and keep track of the weight of the bread they produce.[606]

Bread-and-Butter: "Greece and… Dry Bread!"

Morton demonstrates how the English language has appropriated dozens of food-related words and put them into new and often strange use.[607] For example, "dough" and "bread" have both been used as slang equivalents for "money," the former since the mid-nineteenth century and the latter since the 1940s. "Dough" possibly came to denote money because we "knead" it. For many people in the 19th and 20th centuries, bread and dough were simply what money was typically exchanged for. The famous philologist Eric Partridge suggested that "bread" is a clipped form of "bread and honey," which is cockney rhyming slang for "money."[608]

Greek is a poetic language, evolving and playing around metaphor and symbolization. In Greek, emphasis is placed on food words, which reveals that the language structure evolves around the culture of eating.[609] The Greek word for bread comes to us with an interesting linguistic background. On Linear B script tablets, wheat and barley are depicted with special symbols. In Pylos and Mycenae we see the word "baker" (*artokopos*) on various signs. As Herodotus informs us, *artokopos* stems from the Indo-European root "pek" or "pok" which means "to bake" (Voutsina 2000, 14). *Artos*, thus, is the older form of the modern Greek word for bread, *psomi* that comes from *psomos*, which meant "morsel" in ancient Greek.

The Greek word "bread" stands for a hard day's labor, and if someone does not have any bread then starvation is on its way. A Greek who works hard to win his bread is someone who is making a living and, knowing that a man can not only live by bread, he accompanies bread with cheese and olives, symbols of plain, healthy diet. Good Greek friends have eaten together bread and salt and swear to the bread they eat. Greeks are not only of a good generation but of a good… batch! Let us not forget that in the word "companion," the Latin term *panis* (bread) is hidden, meaning that companions are the ones who have eaten and are still eating bread together. In Greek, companion is *syndrofos*, thus the one who eats with you.

Bread as food identifies with adequacy, and its deficiency with hunger. It is always present on the Greek traditional table during big feasts and significant moments in life, along with various customs, superstitions and beliefs. He who despises bread "steps on bread," he is, in other words, ungrateful and unfaithful (namely, *psomopatis*). In *Christ Recrucified* (else known as *Greek Passion*) Nikos Kazantzakis uses the expression "get lost *psomopati*." In addition, Kostas Kristallis (1868-1894) has written a poem (259 verses long) entitled "Psomopatis."

In the Old Testament bread is not only a daily staple but a moral indicator as well: the sinner eats "irreverent" or "false" and the lazy "idle" bread. Similarly, in the English language, bread serves as a metaphor for basic necessities and living conditions. A "bread-winner," a word that dates back to the early nineteenth century, stands for the household's main economic contributor and ties with the phrase "putting bread on the table." A remarkable or revolutionary innovation is often referred to as "the greatest thing since sliced bread."

As he gets older, a Greek is actually eating his own bread. Greek women continuously complain about their little breads and not… love handles. When they get tired, it is as if they had just finished kneading. In the Greek worldview, bread is a symbol of continuity and healthy life, and many Greeks carry the profession "baker" as their last name (*Fournaris*). Greeks pray for the daily bread. A Greek in a relationship is mature or convinced, because he has been baked. When they earn money, Greeks are making their own bread, sometimes even through sweating. To procrastinate is to fail to blend the bread ingredients and to keep sifting and sifting. The hungry dreams of bread loaves and may even eat the tablecloth, whereas the greedy wants both the dog fed and the pie untouched. Interestingly, there is also a village in the Serres district called *Psomotopi* ("Breadland").[610]

Many kinds of verbal folklore refer to foods, including folk speech, proverbs and even slogans.[611] Although cooking, sharing and eating food with family and friends are matters of physical survival as well as personal and community identity, foods are sometimes abstracted to carry other meanings. The verbal language of food, according to Mason, is a "food speech" which encodes messages for others to decipher and which demonstrates our need to lend literal substance to elusive thoughts and feelings.[612]

The study of food and food-related metaphors in folk speech offers the researcher important clues to the perceptual, cognitive and affective phenomena represented in our use of these traditional expressions.[613] Because there are so many bread phrases sandwiched into everyday Greek conversation, Greek bread acquires a semantic role which is socially recognized: it affirms hospitality and the sharing of it translates to brotherly love.

Greek families sit around the table. One blesses the meal; the father grasps the loaf and carefully removes its crusts and places it back to the basket. Someone cuts the bread and grasps a piece. The father, the backbone and breadwinner of the family, has the right to taste the crust, which is considered a special part: whoever gets to eat it is considered cherished by her or his in-laws.

In the section on bread starters Maria and Nikos Psilakis advise: "At this point we should remember to keep a small ball of dough to use as a starter the next time we make bread or to lend it to another housewife, who will return it to us when she makes bread."[614] According to Eric Ball, passages like the above promote an ethic of culinary sociability, of sharing with one's friends and neighbors, as opposed to consumer convenience:

> The fact that this cookbook is comprised of recipes collected from various Cretans whose names and hometowns are included in the text need not be interpreted as a strategy for demonstrating traditional authenticity only, but also for proposing an ethos of sharing (of the recipes and other knowledge) mediated by print.[615]

Artopolis[616]: "For a Piece of Bread"

Economic historian Fernand Braudel draws upon statistician Paul Ladame and calls wheat, rice and corn the "plants of civilization" that "profoundly organized man's material and spiritual life" and have exercised the "determinism of civilization over the world's peasantry and human life in general."[617] Bread has been associated with crucial political, social and financial moments. In ancient Rome and during the French Revolution, the price of bread controlled the relationship between the folk and the authorities – the way the price of oil does today. In the 1862 novel by Victor Hugo, *Les Misérables*, which is set in the Parisian underworld, the protagonist, Jean Valjean, is sentenced to prison for 19 years for stealing a loaf of bread.

The Lawrence Strike of 1912, which united dozens of immigrant communities under the leadership of the Industrial Workers of the World in Massachusetts, was led to a large extent by women. It is commonly known as the "Bread and Roses Strike" and the women's signs read "We want bread, but we want roses, too," the word "bread" symbolizing financial security, and "roses," the quality of life.[618] Similarly, in Greece, the term "bread" was associated with the protests at the Athens Polytechnic School in 1973, during the military junta, when the students called for "bread, education and freedom" – an indignation embraced by the whole of society.

Food is related to cultural identity, continuity, security, validation, economics and social control, and for many it serves a comforting escape.[619] In hard times in Greece, bread kept people alive. During the Turkish occupation, bread was usually made from coarse flour, mainly from barley, and thus the saying "barley bread was the first creation of God" was coined. In his long poem "The Free Besieged," which refers to the period of occupation, the national poet of Greece Dionysios Solomos (1798-1857), accurately portrays hunger when describing the image of a chirping bird, which grasps a grain while a hungry mother jealously stares at it.

During a Greek meal people take great care that the bread basket is never empty. The use of a piece of bread to dunk in the sauce or wipe a Greek plate is interpreted as a compliment to a good and successful meal, and a freshly baked loaf best serves this purpose. The Greek belief that plates should be fully emptied accompanies that action and recalls the straitened times in Greece, when people were starving and thus did not have enough bread to eat.

The symbolic bakery is an integral part of the Greek economy, politics and society. Publicist Tzimitras talks about how Greek politicians eat bread and salt as they develop diplomatic relationships but, as often happens in a bipolar political system, their struggle is for the same loaf.[620] Communism, that may deprive people of their daily bread, and capitalism, that may take the workers' bread from their own mouths, has become a "bread and cheese" fear for Greek politicians. Systemic problems in the Greek economy or political structure are like butter on each other's bread. Meanwhile, Greek governments tend to ignore the Third World where people hope not for "bread" but just a "little piece of it."

Tzimitras[621] continues by reflecting on the revolution in international affairs since the break-up of the eastern bloc, when one half of the old unity "had the bread and the other the knife." Furthermore, the new republics that emerged from the USSR could not survive on their own because "the bachelor's bread is eaten by his dog and his collar by louse" and, all in all, "their breads would be moderate." Thus, according to the English proverb, "they had to know which side their bread was buttered on," and, therefore surrendered to the opposite system, in their attempt to secure the foundation of a new, global house, thus their bread, wine and olive-oil. Many states joined the European Union as an action to bring them bread: "capitalism and dry bread!"[622] On the contrary, "those who had not eaten sweet bread for years" and "were thus dreaming of breads," realized eventually that the bey's bread had always been white (*hasiko*). White bread is called hasiko, a word taken from a group of villages in Chalkidiki (*Hasika*). There white bread was mostly eaten as the villagers were historically wealthier, had more privileges and paid less taxes.[623]

In the past, Greeks of lower social status consumed mostly black bread, wheat bread, or bread made with flour which was a mixture of wheat, barley, rye or maize. The dough of the latter was harder as maize is heavier, and Greeks were ashamed to admit that they were eating maize bread.[624] Even today, white bread signifies high status, and is identified with something good and innocent. Celebratory breads are always white,[625] whereas contemporary Greek bakeries call bread that is white and fluffy "luxurious" to distinguish it from "rustic," which is darker and harsher. The rhyming couplet (*mandinada*) by famous Cretan musician Psarantonis affirms this: "My lad, fluffy as white bread, when you smile, your cheeks have dimples."

Offering bread is to offer financial support, at least in the concept of traditional Greek society and particularly for people who do not have the money to afford basic needs. Greeks consider meals made of bread, such as sandwiches – however substantial they may be – to be merely light snacks. Greeks wish to work "for a piece of bread" knowing that "they have to eat lots of it" in order to feel satiated. The word "bread" carries with it the problem of unemployment as well as the lack of benefits and allowances. In the current global financial situation, Greeks are currently wondering whether bread will once more be considered a sign of opulence.

Today, Greeks are not sure how they can speak of globalization when a large part of the earth's population is "frothing for bread" (*psomolisso*) or is "living on bread alone" (*psomozo*). Tzimitras[626] wonders what one can do, when for many countries bread is at the mouth of the lion and the developed North offers only breadcrumbs: "a starving belly cannot even take bread." Promises of amelioration are not enough because "words satiate thus bread is useless."

Conclusively, and as Homenidis argues, the future is being baked in the today's oven using ingredients of the past. Furthermore, he comments on Obama's attempt to present himself as the Kennedy of the 21st century and compares it to what contemporary Greek politicians do. According to him, "the former prime minister of Greece, Constantine Karamanlis (1907-1998) still brings you the bread. Others may have added butter and marmalade to it, but he is the one responsible for it." [627] Reality proves that today few are the ones who will be happy with just some bread and olives. What can a Greek do other than claim that "bread is the warp as everything spins in the belly along with wine which silences the critics" and proceed to "swear to the bread he eats"?

Daily Breads: "Church and Bakery do not Ruin"

Korsmeyer supports the idea that tastes convey meaning and hence have a cognitive dimension which is often overlooked.[628] She goes further to observe that foods are employed in symbolic systems which extend from the ritual ceremonies of religion to the everyday choice of breakfast. "Perhaps most obviously, eating is an activity with intense social meaning for communities large and small, and the values and meanings of tastes, foods and eating are all around us and are readily revealed by reflection upon life, practices and habits."

Bread has not only been a dietary staple for Greeks since antiquity but a devotional item as well. Generally speaking, bread is the food of the soul and the body. It is a symbol for unity because it consists of multiple seeds. In Greek culture, it represents shared but united life. Mystic, ceremonial breads are usually small and round. Cutting and delivering them symbolizes sacrifice, acceptance and participation.

A representation on a sarcophagus found in the area of Agia Triada in the valley of Mesara depicts a basket of bread next to a bird and the sacred tree of the Minoan period. The bread, made from the new crop of seeds, represents a valuable offering of Cretans to the gods: a custom that survives in Greece to this day, drawing its origins from ancient Greece, when the Greeks made bloodless offerings or sacrifices to the gods, such as Demeter, during the celebration of the "Grand Breads" (*Megalartia*).[629] In the centuries that followed this practice was incorporated into Christian rituals – in the form of consecrated bread – and has survived to this day.

Freud's "bread investigation" is rooted in religion as well: "the bread that was the god (primitive identification), and the breaking of the loaf that was the god's body (totemism), and then the sharing of that broken bread in a communal meal commemorated with different Christian masses (sacrifice of the father imago)."[630] Freud also observes how in the German language the same word-sound stands for body (*Leib*) and loaf (*Laib*), as if an over-refined loaf equals an instinct-less body.[631] Parts of Greek religious breads, the so-called offerings, are cut into pieces and shared to the believers who did not receive the Holy Communion ("the Gift"), thus they are called "the anti-gifts" (*antidoro*).

The reason bread is closely associated with religion is due to the "miraculous" fact of rising. Bread was considered "magical" from the moment a housewife witnessed its dough risen and interpreted the process as "divine." The Parable of the Leaven was given by Jesus in the New Testament: "The kingdom of heaven is like yeast that a woman took and mixed with three measures of wheat flour until the whole batch was leavened."

In Greek contemporary society, leaven symbolizes the fermentation of the human society as a whole and for each person as an individual. According to the Greek calendar, sourdough is made on September 14, the day of the Exaltation of the Holy Cross. The preparation lasts for nine days, with holy water being added to the flour every three days. Fresh basil is used for blessing the water, the plant which, according to the Greek Orthodox belief, grew at the place where St. Helen "discovered" the Holy Cross. Exceptionally, sourdough can also be made during any ritual which involves sanctification of the water, such as, for example, on January 6, the day of the Epiphany and the eve of Christ's baptismal anniversary. That dough is then used continuously as leaven and the housewife keeps each time a piece of it for the making of the bread to follow.

According to Welsh, foods in historical and contemporary life transcend simple nourishment; they carry with them clear implications for the body and soul.[632] In other words, foods are not only used for sustenance but can also be both culturally symbolic and useful for spiritual and physical mending. For Greeks, who are predominantly Greek Orthodox, wheat symbolizes the human nature of Christ, who was born in Bethlehem, the town which means "house of bread" in Aramaic.

In the Gospels, we find many references to the symbolic use of bread, and several are miracles of Christ which involve bread. Bread was the means by which Jesus demonstrated his divine nature when a few loaves were miraculously made sufficient to feed thousands. Christ in his teachings used words such as "seeding," "sower" and "bread" and characteristically reported: "I am the bread of life: he that cometh to me shall never hunger; and he that believeth in me shall never thirst."[633]

During the Last Supper, Christ cut and shared the bread which was then transformed into His body, creating the basis for the mystery of Eucharist. If wine is the godly ecstasy, then bread is the visible substance of the spirit which dies and gets reborn.[634] The ancient Greeks used to have for breakfast the so-called *akratisma*, thus wine with dipped pieces of bread. This continued during the Byzantine times and was called *voukakraton*.[635] As manna which saves people from hunger, Christ is the bread from on high that saves us all. That is why the Tsatsaronakis bakery (located at the village of Platanos in Chania-Crete) which produces many varieties of Cretan rusks – the most popular being the barley ones – exporting them even to the United States, is called "The Manna."[636]

Everyone understands bread is essential to life and, just as bread is vital to mortal life, so Jesus is essential to everlasting life. In the same way we consume bread so as to live, Christ, as if he were bread, died so that we may live: "And as they were eating, Jesus took bread and blessed it, and broke it, and gave it to the disciples, and said, take, eat; this is my body."[637] The eating of bread, therefore, that symbol of the body of Christ, is something that discerning disciples of Christ do regularly in obedience to his command.

Through speech (*logos*), a linkage between Jesus and the flesh, bread and *Logos* (knowledge) is being established. By eating the "bread," one can enter into a special relationship with the divine.[638] Born in the mouth, in a dark but yet secure space, wise words, having been prepared and cooked, digested and assimilated, come out in the shape of a sage message and a philosophic mission, so as to be spread to the world.

Waldenberger[639] illustrates how the stories of the Bible have delineated the relationship between food and sanctity. She examines contemporary breads and how they are often promoted as healthy and organic, showing how bread can hearken back to a healthier and purer time. A traditional *meze* (appetizer) or light meal on the island of Crete, is *dakos*, a piece of dry bread softened by water and olive-oil, served with spices (oregano, salt and pepper) as well as fresh tomato juice and white cheese, otherwise known as the "owl": a symbol of wisdom as the sacred bird of goddess Athena.[640]

Korsmeyer maintains that one of the most significant roles of food is social: eating is part of the rituals, ceremonies and practices that knit together communities.[641] This process takes place over time and the temporality of a narrative permits extended reflection upon the ways eating serves communities. Because of their narrative form, stories lead the reader imaginatively to a discovery availed through a taste, an act of eating or a reflection upon food.

During summer luncheons, I recall my aunt Androniki sharing with me information about the protector of the Greek bakers, St. Spyridon. According to Cretan legend, while under Ottoman Occupation (around 1870) the Turkish Aga had asked his servant to use the lower part of a Byzantine icon depicting St. Spyridon as a tray for molding the dough and carrying the bread to the Fountoulakis bakery. The loaves, though unleavened, kept miraculously rising. The smart baker suspected something was going on, made the "holy" discovery and self-exiled himself to escape the Aga's anger.[642]

According to my mother, the *fanouropita* will satisfy Fanourios, the Greek "lost and found Saint." Once my luggage was delayed for two months and thus considered "lost" my mom prepared a *fanouropita* and... guess what, the luggage arrived. The story of this bread is contained in two sources; both events take place in Crete around 1500-1600.[643] Interestingly enough, this saint is not amongst those mentioned in Byzantine sources, which tells of how rich the religious element in Greek folk traditions is. The St. Fanourios pie consists of an odd and changeable group of ingredients, which may include flour, sugar, olive oil, orange juice, raisins, walnuts, cinnamon and cloves. It is considered "poor" or Lenten fare.

The religious legend concerns the mother of St. Fanourios, who was wicked and did not give alms to the poor. Only once in her life had she given an onion skin to a beggar. When she died, she went to Hell and was boiled in a cauldron filled with tar. The saint, who had gone to Heaven, upon seeing his mother in Hell, pleaded with God that her sins might be forgiven. God gave him permission to pull her up with an onion skin. As her son pulled her up, other damned women also grabbed the onion skin in an attempt to get to Heaven. But the woman pushed them down, and in doing so she committed a much graver sin. Thus the rope was cut and she, too, fell back down into Hell.[644]

After this event, the Saint asked that people offer nothing to him but bread so that the sins of his mother would be forgiven. In return, he would reveal whatever they had lost. Traditionally the *fanouropita* is made once a year, on the eve of the St. Fanourios day, on 26 August. Today, many people bring *fanouropites* for blessing throughout the year and not just on the saint's day. It is brought to the church of St. Fanourios with a lighted candle. Women write on small pieces of paper the names of those among the living they wish to be remembered. These are read aloud by the priest, who blesses the breads during the religious ceremony.

After the Mass, the breads are cut and eaten. During the sharing of the bread, it is a common practice among the faithful to repeat the invocation "May God forgive the mother of St. Fanourios." The psychological function of religious folklore is evident here: the comforting tradition of the service of "lost and found," the burial customs and beliefs concerning life after death, as well as the constant quest of the living to foresee their fortune.

Greeks prepare ceremonial breads (*prosforo* and *artos*) and have them blessed in church, wishing that their goods will multiply and their land will be fertile the same way as Christ miraculously multiplied the loaves of bread. These breads usually have a symbol marked on top – the result of pressing the dough with a large seal. Usually this reads "IC XC NIKA," in a cross-form. The first letters are abbreviations for the name Jesus Christ, whereas NIKA is a Greek verb that means "conquers" – in the sense of "being victorious."

Korsmeyer speaks for food which is crafted to look something other than itself and calls it "representational":[645] "The cognitive significance of food is an effect of reference, representation, expression, exemplification and the social conditions of its preparation and serving."[646] Not all eating has much significance, but any ceremonial meal possesses it in abundance. Could one then refrain from perceiving Adam and Eve as providential loaves of wisdom?

Country-Style Breads: "All the Crooked Breads are the Bride's Fault"

Food obviously sustains life, but, beyond survival, the creative relationships established between people and food carry metaphoric and symbolic meanings.[647] Deftereos illustrates in detail the symbolic, magical and religious role of bread in Greek culture, specifically at birth, weddings and death.[648] Maria and Nikos Psilakis provide, apart from cultural insights, Greek recipes of all the bread-lore they examine.[649]

Many are the Greek customs around the "grain culture" and its sowing, flowering and harvesting. Bread, a symbol of procreation, health and prosperity for the Greek society, marks important events throughout the calendar year. It is the focal point of several foodways, of the things people do, their festivals and celebrations.[650] Places that produce bread function as spatial, orienting references; a common Greek response when asking for directions would relate to the proximity of a bakery.

Greeks have a soft spot for ceremonial breads. Bread is offered as blessing on rites of passage and during holidays. Specific sweet breads are made during Easter (*tsoureki* and *lambrokoulouro*) and at Christmas (*christopsomo* and *vasilopita*). During the 40 days of Lent, Greeks consume *lagana*, a sort of unleavened bread. At Cretan weddings, the round bread (*koulouri* or *gamokoulouro*) is decorated by dough as if it is "embroidered" to look like a traditional piece of cloth (*ploumisto*).

Cretan wedding bread, a piece of art. Around it, almonds with honey, sugared almonds (*koufeta*) and traditional fried pastry treats with honey (*xerotigana*).

These are masterpieces of bakery and art, bearing a universe of symbols. There is much love that goes into the process of kneading, a process carried out in the context of tradition and faith that results in richly ornamented loaves of bread. The decorative elements are fashioned in dough to resemble crosses, flowers, trees, fruits, birds, ploughs, animal yokes, music instruments and bells for sheep and goats. In some regions, bread decorations include an imitation of a small tree laden with fruit, all made of dough, direct reference to the worship of trees in Crete in prehistoric times. [651] Bread decoration is an art and is practiced by experienced women, the *xobliastres*, whose skills pass from one generation to the next.

At the core study of foodways is the specific relationship between people and their food practices. Food carries many different meanings for people, universal or not. Many foods represent religious and folkloric traditions, suggesting that they carry both overt and covert meaning for a group.[652] The cutting of the New Year's *vasilopita*, the only food that embodies a non-taxable monetary gift, is made to commemorate St. Basil every 1 January: the person whose piece includes the hidden coin is considered the lucky one for the ensuing year. The way the pie is cut is itself a ceremony; the first piece goes to Christ and then the household and its members follow.

Bread functions as a means to predict and presage death in the various shapes taken by its dough. In the event a Greek feels the presence of an evil spirit, a Greek should throw pieces of bread to cause the spirit to disperse. A Greek soul will not rest if it did not respect bread while alive,[653] and Greeks bury crosses and bread loafs with their dead to please them. Additionally, *koliva*, which consists of boiled wheat with sugar and several herbs and spices, is a popular dish prepared for funerals and memorial services.

Bread protects the dead while it also satisfies the souls who maintain a positive influence on the living. During burial, Greek priests spread bread – which they cut with their own hands – on the casket as an offering, as well as sprinkling wine, an action that recalls ancient Greek death rituals. The reason Greeks do not use a knife to cut the bread is because it conjures up the image of Archangel Michael with the sword – the angel of Death who transports the souls from the earth to the skies.[654]

After the burial, breads, symbols of consolation and peace, are shared. A common idea is that the dead still need food. A mourning song, recorded on the island of Rhodes, talks about the mother who loses her son and is thus asked to "put wine in a glass and bread in a basket, call the neighbors over to comfort her and the orphans to eat and bless her." At the house of the deceased, there are all kinds of bread products, from salty to sweet, daily bread to biscuits. In some parts of Greece a table is set on the ground, with no tablecloth, symbolizing that the dead can share a meal with the living.[655] This explains, why, according to Greek belief, "no bread piece should go wasted." Oftentimes, the first bread piece is sunk into wine.[656] Similar bread rituals follow when the bones are transferred to a charnel-house as well as during the memorial services.[657]

In the past, Greeks used to knead their bread secretly, as they thought it was better prepared alone. This belief relates to the idea of the evil-eye: the notion that some-one's mean look (or thought) can cause trouble not only to human beings but also to the objects that relate to them, such as food. Bread is particularly sensitive and has an inclination to "the eye" – it may not rise or turn out too sour if it is afflicted. This is a popular belief particularly for the type of bread called "self-rising" [(e)*ftazimo*]. Some Greeks would incense the bread to make sure "it will not get the eye," or would also cut a piece of it and give it to a passer-by, assuring that their food is shared and, thus, blessed. Even though in general each housewife would make her bread at home, at times of festivity several women would gather together at one house in order to make buns, cookies and festive breads.

Greek bread is used as a gift in social relationships.[658] When I left Greece to pursue graduate studies in the United States, I was presented with a loaf made by my grand-mother Eleni, as, according to her, I was going to "exile." Breads are exchanged be-tween family members as well as amongst best-men and godparents. Engaged men will send breads as gifts to their future wives and as tokens of faith during Christmas and Easter. The future groom will send bread to his future bride, and she will reply by sending him a loaf back.

Breads were traditionally used as wedding invitations, which a young boy would deliver from house to house. The Greek proverbial question "did they send you a *koulouri* (bread roll) and thus you came?" which is nowadays used to mark the pres-ence of a non-invited, non-desired guest, stems from this tradition. Lastly, wealthier Greeks would usually offer several breads to the church, which would then distrib-ute them to the poorer members of the society.

Greeks also attribute medicinal qualities to bread. Warm bread enables kids with underdeveloped linguistic skills (*bradylalia*) to speak faster and clearer; as bread enters the children's body, it gives the power and ability to talk. At the same time, warm bread, particularly at nights, attracts witches to it, and thus is kept away from, for example, the house of women who have just given birth. Bread also heals chick-enpox and sleep-walking and is present when the first tooth appears and the nails are cut for the first time, as well as when the baby first walks.[659] The "magic," healing qualities of bread assist pregnant women in guessing the gender of a baby.[660]

Hippocrates, Galen and Dioscorides, three famous ancient Greek doctors, stud-ied and practiced the medicinal attributes of flour mixed with water or mashed wheat. They spoke of them as dietary, nutritious supplements, which enabled prop-er digestion and assisted possible intestinal and rheumatic conditions. According to Dioscorides, mashed barley, in particular, functioned both as a stimulant and a poultice for dog bites, skin diseases and dysentery, whereas Galen supported wheat is the best calefacient, i.e. warm food.[661]

A famous physician and gifted writer of the Byzantine era, Aetios Amidinos (502-574 AD), used bread for cancer treatment.[662] During those times, bread – when mixed with water, olive-oil or butter and baked – was also recommended for in-flammations. Deftereos shows how these therapeutic attributes have passed into contemporary Greek culture by subconsciously influencing the connection between bread and life.[663] Greek women, for instance, will still make and consume special breads in order to heal infertility, secure a safe delivery, have strong descendants and produce adequate milk during breast-feeding.

Arty Breads: "Bread and Circuses"[664]

Representative foodways carries symbolic meanings in literature, fine and folk art. Performances are often rich with food metaphors and analogies.[665] "The variety of meanings we find assigned in visual art to taste, food, eating and appetite is more than matched in the narrative arts, further attesting to the complexity of what we might label 'gustatory semantics.'"[666] In other words, because eating is a daily necessity, one finds scenes of food distributed liberally about the plots of stories.

A tale I recall my grandmother Christina sharing with me is about a king who was unhappy because he could not find any tasty bread. A wise old man showed him that "The Sweetest Bread of the World" is the one that we, ourselves, have made – the product of our hard work and elbow grease.[667] Many Greek writers have used bread at the core of their writings as a symbol of essence and importance. Paganos illustrates how "bread" has naturally become a core topic in Greek literature since the Greeks "fight" for bread every day and, when they do not have it, they are miserable and desperate (2004). He examines the work of several writers, including Ptohoprodromos – dating back to the 12th century – as well as Alexandros Papadiamandis (1851-1911), Georgios Drosinis (1859-1951), Grigorios Xenopoulos (1867-1951), Angelos Sikelianos (1884-1951), Alexandros Kotzias (1926-1992) and Miltos Sachtouris (1919-2005). All of them treat bread nostalgically, as a home-made substance, which sets a seal on Greek life by being such a strong presence in religious and folk traditions.

Greece's Nobel price laureates George Seferis (1900-1971) and Odysseus Elytis (1911-1996) make use of bread imagery in their works as well. Seferis, in his "An Old Man at the Riverbank" (1942) speaks of men, "the patient dough of a world which throws us out and kneads us, caught in the embroidered nets of a life that it was as it should be," whereas in the "Heroic and Elegiac Song of the Lost Second Lieutenant of Albania" (1943) Elytis describes how in the war bread drips blood and how death is a tasteless bread.

Korsmeyer claims that food performs many of the same symbolic activities as works of art, and that visual art indicates the potential for foods and flavors to assume an enormous diversity of meanings.[668] Pavlopoulos speaks of Greek bread in art asserting that, in the Byzantine iconography, bread had a transcendental meaning, being identified with the body of Christ, whereas in contemporary Greek art bread is either the major topic in still-life paintings or a complement to larger stud-ies.[669]

One of the Greek painters who gave bread thematic autonomy is Nikolaos Gyzis (1842-1901) with two oil-paintings on canvas dating from the same period (1876-1885): "Breads" and "Easter bread."[670] Another is Theofilos Hatzimihail (1867/1870-1934) who painted bakeries. One works portrays the inner part of a bakery with the baker in the front, removing the cooked loaves, while two women are waiting to get bread, and in the background workers are weighing bread prior to cooking it. In-deed, as Pavlopoulos emphasizes, there is an anecdote about this painting: Theofilos was asked why the bread loaves are upright and thus may fall over. He responded that only real breads fall.[671] Lastly, Hector Doukas (1885-1969) has painted a boy holding a worn piece of bread staring at his mother breast-feeding.

In 1998, the sculptor Thodoros Papayannis (1942) presented a personal exhibit on bread in both Athens and Ioannina. He prepared a whole clay installation which represented bread creation in an environment that included human beings as well. According to Pavlopoulos,[672] the result was astonishing as it memorialized the ex-perience of life in the country in a meta-war Greece. Painter Christos Bokoros (b. 1956) approached bread religiously as an offering and through a dual symbolism "in favor of health" and "in favor or relief." In his 1997 work "For Living and Dead I" Bokoros focused on bread as sacrifice and as part of the Holy Communion, de-picting a loaf wrapped in a white cloth as a ritual offering, symbol and vehicle of a strong collective memory.

Lastly, photographers have focused on Greek bread. Voula Papaioannou (1898-1990) captured daily bread making during the years Greece was trying to recover and rebuild after the devastation of the world wars. Dmitri Kessel, a photo-essayist for *Life* magazine, has taken an incredible picture of a Greek family eating their noon meal of bread during the Greek civil war era (January 1948) and John Phillips, a photographer known for his war images, captured two young Greek boys eating bread and tomatoes around that same era (December 1947).

Folklore offers to food studies a conception of food as more than "just what we eat." It is, rather, the aesthetic domain of activities and practices surrounding it. The performance of food is a system in which all activities bear upon each other, and meaning emerges out of those relationships.[673] Peter Schumann views theater and all forms of art as absolutely essential. He describes theater – in its ideal form – "like bread," "like a necessity."[674]

Shadow-theater or puppetry is a popular Greek form of entertainment, its name, *Karagiozis*, borrowed from its main hero, a black-eyed, hunchbacked, poor Greek man. Various shadow-theater performers have invented scenarios, one of which in-volves *Karagiozis* as a baker. "Karagiozis the Baker" was first performed by Mimaros (thus, Dimitrios Sardounis, 1865-1912). In the adaptation of that play by Evgenios Spatharis, *Karagiozis* performs songs about "Christmas and Easter breads." This was performed in February 2009, on Crete, by the Athanasiou Company, who presented *Karagiozis* commenting on the current financial situation and the fact that people today can afford less and less bread.[675]

Bread has been the topic of movies, such as "Bread and Chocolate" (*Pane e Cioccolata*; 1973) and "Bread and Tulips" (*Pane e Tulipani*; 2000). "Cloudy Sunday," one the most popular Greek songs by Vassilis Tsitsanis, was the soundtrack to a 1959 film originally titled *For Bread and Love*. In fact, "Cloudy Sunday" is performed in a *zeibekiko* dance, a composite of "Zeus" and "*bekos*," thus, "bread." As a dance, *zeibekiko* relieves the spirit, the soul and the body. Mourrais-Velloudios maintains that another name for that dance was *artozinos* (thus, living bread) and, therefore, symbolically and religiously it serves and relieves the spirit, the soul and the body, while the dancer releases possible inner pressure.[676]

Dionysis Savvopoulos, Greece's Bob Dylan, composed a song called "Zeibeikiko": "In this world, whoever believes in God's words and hence loves, eats dirty bread." Other well-known Greek composers have set lyrics to music which include strong "bread metaphors," such as Stavros Xarchakos with the popular "Kaisariani" song that talks about "home, warm and sweet bread," and how violent death makes that taste "bitter." The same lyricist, Lefteris (Eleftherios) Papadopoulos, in another popular song set to music by Xarchakos speaks of the "Heartless Life" being the one which deprives one of a single piece of bread.

Renowned Mikis Theodorakis speaks of "Love's Bread" (lyrics by Kostas Tripolitis), "The Bread is on the Table" for everyone to flavor and share (lyrics by Iakovos Kambanellis) and how "My Bread is Sweet" (lyrics by Manos Eleftheriou). Mimis Plessas (lyrics by Kostas Rouvelas) composed "Bread and Tear" and Stelios Kazantzidis performed "The Bread of the Exile is Bitter," "dry and worse than home's bread and olives" (music by Yannis Vasilopoulos, and lyrics by Vaggelis Atraidis and Nakis Petridis).

Sumption and Ashbrook describe how one of their favorite sports is to ask a group of friends the following: "If you were exiled to a remote island where a boat would call once a week to leave you necessary supplies and if, while you were there, you had to live exclusively on three foods, which three would you choose?" They conclude that, after discussing and revising their lists, in the end all come back to bread, realizing that given only three foods bread would be the one necessity.[677]

As a child in Greece I grew up listening and performing the song "Buns" (*koulourakia*) which conveyed information on how to make bread rolls using my two hands. It also highlighted the scent of freshly made cookies which I would then take to school with me and share with my friends. Growing up on an island, I would spend hours with my peers practicing our skills at the beach, playing "little breads" by throwing stones onto the surface of the sea and marking the concentric ripples that tracked across the surface. Since then, "there have been times when I bit off more than I could chew, but through it all when there was doubt, I ate it up and spit it out, I faced it all and I stood tall and learnt how to do it my way."[678]

Ecological Breads: "You Reap What You Sow"

Food is a good vehicle for teaching a whole range of subjects because of its inter-relatedness to the notion of "home," which makes everyone feel very connected to it. According to Pollan,[679] food should be taught in schools as an academic subject: "You can't learn about food without learning about ecology, without understanding co-evolution and Darwin, without understanding the carbon cycle and the energy cycles and what links us to the sun. You learn about chemistry, biology and you learn about physics, plus you learn about history and anthropology." In 2006, at the Greek village of Rizo in Pella, teachers used "bread" as a way to teach students at the elementary school level to create puzzles, acrostics, crosswords and brain teasers, as well as mathematics – by applying bread transactions to mathematic operations – and English – by translating and creating a vocabulary consisting of "bread" words and phrases.[680]

Consideration of foods and of eating can be central to an increased understanding of the role of bodily experience.[681] In 1996, the Historical Museum of Crete presented the educational program "The Circle of the Bread" designed by ethnologist Eleni Tsenoglou and museum educators Olga Berdiaki and Fani Kampani. Through it, children discovered the production of bread via interactive activities, music and games, while observing the folklore collection of tools used for bread production as well as hearing about, learning how and even baking their own bread. As the webpage explains,[682] the goal of this project was to make children conscious about the bread they daily eat and of the labor and the agony required of the Greeks in order to secure such a basic, nutritional meal. An inspiring part of the project is the dough-decoration activity.

Bread is the substance of life: it fills our stomachs and our souls too, and its history takes us deeply back in time as it was consumed over than 8,000 years ago. Today, in Greece, bread is the most basic and one of the healthiest, nutritious foods. A bread roll (*koulouri*) makes for a tasty and nutritious snack. The *koulouri* from Thessaloniki, in particular, has conquered Europe as it is also affordable. In Thessaloniki people daily consume approximately 150,000-200,000 rolls, re-introducing simplicity in our eating habits. CNN has been promoting the Greek diet through documentaries that show how Greeks, particularly those from the island of Crete, hold records for longevity due to the well-known "Mediterranean diet." Researchers have discovered that Cretans have the lowest rate of heart diseases and cancer. They describe the high consumption of the Cretan rusk (*paximadi*) as one of the secrets of the miraculous Mediterranean diet.

Counihan uses bread as a lens for analyzing contemporary social and economic change in the town of Bosa in the Italian island of Sardinia. Once, men grew wheat and women baked bread together in their homes. The bread circulated through kin and friendship channels and was consumed communally. Now Bosan people no longer grow wheat; they buy bakery bread which is distributed according to the principles of the marketplace and they consume it ever more individualistical-ly. Counihan[683] concludes that Bosa's situation is characteristic of "modernization without development" which leads to an increasing atomization of social relations.

Greek bread is the memory of a strong connection with the land and the taste of earth. Greeks daily experience this in the communal subconscious and insist on consuming "wonder breads" that will help them reconnect with their primal roots. By making their own breads, Greeks are responsible for baking their own reali-ties. If they are careful in the process, they will relish sharing and caring. In today's world, I suggest that we consider re-introducing bread making into our lives, so that we both strengthen our community ties and become more sustainable. A kneading housewife is involved in an effort to work with nature and to bring nature into her confidence, in order to maintain the foundations of her family and, therefore, the substance of her ecosystem.

Greek bread evokes nostalgia for past times and sustaining memories are nour-ishing to the spirits as a warm loaf on a blustery winter night. After all, the first food a baby will chew on right after ablactation is a piece of bread, a smooth transition to a whole new world. The ceremony of preparing bread is part of the Greek world. As a mother is a model to her children, who persistently wander in her kitchen, looking for security in her apron, and crane their necks to see what is baking in her pantry-world, so the study of Greek bread can open pathways to the understanding of life-and-death-matters.

Now, more than ever, we may consider becoming the bakers of our own breads, of resurrecting our rolling pins and baking pans, in an attempt to integrate everyday encounters with our leavened nature. My goal has not been to offer you a recipe. But advice I do have: if you want a future that is not an illusion, get yourself a fresh loaf of Greek bread.[684]

We Speak What We Eat: My Big Fat Greek Language

Greeks do not spend but eat time. They eat their years studying and working, but also their liver, when they try hard to achieve what they want. Greeks eat their words, when they forget, are stressed or say fat lies. They eat rain, when wet, their moustaches, when they intensively argue, their tongues, when they do not mean what they just said, cabbage and straw, when they easily believe, and noodles, when the ones they love set them aside. They may even eat you as onion-stew, unless they like you so much, and thus crave for you.

Greek clocks do not waste but eat minutes. Greek noses, when curious, eat you. If Greek hands are hungry, you will soon get money, or be beaten. In Greece, too much work does not harm but eats you; you are not being scolded but eaten, you are not getting a boot but being eaten or even… eating wood (namely, get beaten with a stick), your head is not itching, but eating, and you are not searching thoroughly but you are eating the world, hoping you won't be eaten by the woodworm. Not only you have to be aware of eating someone with your eyes, but also not forget that getting older you are actually eating your own bread.

Ancient Greeks seemed to know the dialectics between language and food. Pindar offered food via his poetry, and thought of his lyric works as refreshing drinks and his melodies sounding sweet as honey. Several literary species in classical Greece were expressed via cooking metaphors: satyr was the "sampler dish" whereas the farce functioned as an interlude, "stuffing" amidst a serious performance. The general idea was that both books and men of letters were technicians producing pleasant mixtures for the mouth or the mind so as to satisfy the hunger of the word-eaters (*lexifagos*).

For ancient Greeks, "the beginning and the root of each good was the pleasure of the abdomen," or, as Greeks today say, even "love goes through the stomach." The ancient Greek "table" became the word for the modern Greek "bank" (*trapeza*). Greeks still speak of the Epicurean feast, a sumptuous meal, and the Meal of Lucullus. They recall the famous symposia, the thirty sophists who sat around a dinner table to discuss a wide range of topics in the *Banquet of Scholars* by Athenaeus and "the dining philosophers problem," which combine learning with… eating.

A central life concept, time (*chronos*), is a word which etymologically relates to Cronus. According to mythology, Cronus was the rather unaffectionate father of Zeus, who ate his children, in an effort to give himself more authority time. The great tragic poets of Greece attributed to Zeus adjectives such as caterer (*trofodotis*), alimentary (*Trophonius*), fructuous (*epikarpios*), of the apples (*milosios*) and of the figs (*sykasios*). In addition, the word diet (*dieta*) stems from the Greek name for Zeus, namely, Dias. Even the word nutrition, *diatrofi*, is a composite of the words "Dias" and "trofi," thus, Zeus and food. In that context, nutrition is the proper diet, the one Zeus had, that consisting of dittany tea (*diktamo*), honey (*meli*) and goat milk (*gala*).

Greek words may be sweet, as sugar, coming out of a mouth as a river of honey. They may be silent as a fish or as a pillar of salt, or calm as yogurt. When Greeks speak rudely, elders put pepper on their tongues. But when they get angry, they need to swallow vinegar. "Good appetite!," "To your health!" and "Good digestion!" are frequently used expressions in Greek, absent from English.

In Greek, "language" and "tongue" are one word: "glossa." "In the beginning was the Word," the "*Logos*," something born in the mouth. The Annunciation is nothing else but a verbal conception: as the Virgin Mary absorbs the words of the Holy Ghost, she becomes pregnant, and gives birth to Christ. Words, thus, using the human body and brain as transportation vessels, are getting into the mouth, down the larynx to the pharynx and the esophagus, to be devoured and assimilated.

A closer look at the anatomy of the body tells us that Greek men have the Adam's apple. In general, Greeks grow almond trees instead of tonsils whereas they may get barley on their eyes (but not a sty). In their brains they have almonds – and not cerebellums, and on their skin olives – and not spots.

Synaesthetically, Cretans "hear" the smell, and Greeks "flavor" colors. Tints may be of the rotten apple, the orange, the carrot, the eggplant, the cabbage, the plum and the fish; the green of the olive, the cabbage and the pistachio; the brown of the chocolate, the hazelnut, the coffee and the cinnamon; the white of the milk; the cherry red; the yellow of the lemon, the corn and the honey. When sunburned, a Greek looks like a dark-fired frying pan or pot.

Greek wine (*krasi*) is the nectar of gods. The grape (*stafili*) is a symbol of fertility. "Wine and children speak the truth," a Greek proverb says, whereas – inspired by the Aesop fable – "the grapes the fox cannot reach it calls them sour." Ancient Greeks rarely drank wine waterless. Thus, *krasi* stands literally for wine mixed with water and the phrase "I put water in my wine" means compromising. Lastly, to a Greek, *oinops pontos*, what Homer called the "wine-dark sea," makes perfect sense.

Greece's ethnic identity is recognized in its language. Bean soup is Greece's national food. When beans insist on being raw, they behave like the country's old-time enemies, the Turks. During Lent, bean soup reminds Greeks of sacrifice and restraint. This legume may be giant (*gigandes*), elephants (*elefandes*), or black-eyed (*mavromatika*). Another legume, yellow split peas (*fava*), may get married when mixed with onion and tomato, and, if you mash it and make a hole in its middle, then, be careful, because there might be something wrong with or a hindrance in your life.

Speaking of condiments now, salt is a necessary ingredient for human nourishment, and a symbol of duration, concord and devotion. When Greeks throw salt to someone else's plate, they are interfering into other people's business. Stingy Greeks don't even give you a grain of salt. Greeks who have eaten bread and salt together are like brothers and sisters. The family man is the salt of the household.

Fruits, like the pomegranate (*rodi*) and the apple (*milo*), symbolize fertility. According to Greek mythology, the pomegranate sprang from the blood drops of Dionysus and symbolized Hades. Pluto, the god of the underworld, gave Persephone, Demeter's daughter, pomegranate seeds to eat, so bind her to the underworld. Traditionally, Greeks, for good luck, would break a pomegranate in front of their doors upon reentrance to their houses on New Year's.

Apple is a symbol of good luck, fertility and fruitfulness. It symbolizes devotion of the one partner to the other, particularly at weddings. It also stands for the acquisition of knowledge, heritage and progress. As a Greek proverb says, illustrating Newton's discovery and imaginativeness, "the apple will fall under the apple-tree." It is a purely erotic fruit. In Greek mythology, the apple-tree is the gift of the Earth to Zeus' wedding. Paris offers an apple to Aphrodite as the winning prize of a beauty contest – the apple of discord. Its name is also associated with beautiful Milos, who hanged himself from a tree, when he found out about Adonis' death. Upon Milos' death, Aphrodite converted him into a seed, which was named … *milo* (apple).

Food expressions also mark Greek cultural ideals. The wise person's children cook before they get hungry. The pot rolls around until it finds its lid. Too many cooks slow down the cooking process and spoil the broth. The guest and the fish stink after the third day. When a Greek brags about many cherries, bring along a small container, and if you get burnt at the pumpkin, blow even the yogurt.

On Greek months which do not contain an "r" into their names, Greeks must put water in their wine. Everything is seasonal, thus Greeks consume mackerel in August. Most Greeks have generous hearts as artichokes. Mean Greeks may profit fat out of a fly or milk out of the male goat. Old Greek women are rich in broth, because they have eaten the sea by the spoon, whereas wealthy Greeks even own the bird's milk.

You may think what I have been sharing with you is zucchinis (*kolokithia*), squash words (*kolokithokouvendes*) or vegetable marrow pies (*kolokithopites*). But I will teach you how many pears fit in the sack, so let's call the figs figs and the washtub washtub. By the way, did you know that in ancient Greece figs were very important in cooking and whoever stole a fig from someone else's tree was immediately accused as *sikofantis* (slanderer)? So, please, don't hide behind the leeks, as I may catch you, and, as a Greek, dance you on the roasting pan.

Greeks do not put on layers of clothes, they, instead, dress themselves as… onions. They are so hospitable; they may prepare a whole meal out of an onion only. Greeks should not eat like pigs, even if they are hungry as wolves. Eating light, as a bird, is the best, especially with golden spoons.

Food is a basic societal need. As Greeks claim, "appetite comes by eating" and "if the pot boils, friendship lives." Sharing a meal is the most common Greek social activity. Perhaps fast-food was invented to house the lonely and to save them faster: the faster the process, the shorter the sense of solitude. We may drink alone, but food presupposes companionship, exchange of understanding. Perhaps that is why, unconsciously, Greeks always speak to their babies when they feed them: to accustom them to the sociality of food.

Take for example the Greek word *nostimo* (tasty), which shares the same root with the word nostalgia. *Nostos* means the return, the journey, while *anostos* means without taste. Nostimos, thus, is the one who, from the Homeric Odysseus to the contemporary Greek, has journeyed and arrived, has matured, ripened and is, therefore, tasty, and, in extension, useful.

I have tried to nibble on this spicy, meaty, juicy honey of a topic in order to savor and relish. I asked you to feast your eyes on the veritable potpourri of mushrooming food expressions that grace the table of Greek language and season your tongue. As I chewed the fat about the food-filled phrases that are packed like sardines and sandwiched into everyday Greek conversations, I have tried to sweeten the pot with some tidbits of food for thought guaranteed to whet your appetite.

I hope this essay was food for thought. In that case, I don't need to eat my words. (Otherwise, I'm ready to eat my hat.) After all, Greeks speak what they eat, and their big fat Greek vocabulary could make Greek a piece of cake!

A Sample Greek Meal

The following recipes I chose because they take a reasonable amount of time to be prepared. As a Greek in the States, I was many times asked to prepare a meal. For the dishes I have selected to describe, I was able to find "abroad" all the necessary ingredients. So, after a while, the combination of those dishes became, more or less, a standard meal for guests or parties. In addition, they can also please vegetarians, as they offer lots of variety for people with different tastes. Lastly, you may add bread, cheese and olives, just because those three things almost always accompany a typical Greek meal (bread and water being offered for free at all restaurants in Greece).

Menu

Avgolemono (Egg-Lemon Soup)
Melitzanosalata (Eggplant Salad)
Maroulosalata (Lettuce Salad)
*Kotopoulo sto Fourno me Patate*s (Baked Potatoes and Chicken)
Halvas (Sweet Semolina Pudding)

Cooking Process

Put the eggplants in the oven to bake. Prepare the *halva* first. Get the chicken in the oven, then prepare the soup and do all the preparation work for the *melitzanosalata*. Make the salad, but don't dress it until ready to serve. When the eggplants are done, remove from the oven and cut open immediately to cool faster.

The Recipes

Avgolemono (Egg-Lemon Soup)

1 medium yellow onion
1 c. rice
2 eggs
1-1/2 lemons
Salt
Pepper

In a saucepan, bring 10 c. water to a boil with 1 chopped onion. Add 1 t. salt and 1/2 t. pepper. Add 1 c. rice, cover the pan, reduce heat to simmer and cook it until tender, about 20 minutes. In a separate bowl, beat the eggs, while adding the lemon juice from 1-1/2 lemons. Slowly add (in parts) the boiling soup and continue beating. Remove the saucepan from the heat and stir in the egg mixture. The rice will absorb most of the water. Taste, adding more water and lemon juice if necessary to keep it as a soup. Stir for a few more minutes; the soup will look frothy.

Melitzanosalata (Eggplant Salad)

2 eggplants
2 cloves garlic
1/4 c. parsley
2 tomatoes
1-2 T olive oil
1 T lemon juice
Salt
Pepper

Cut deeply into 2 eggplants (4" long scores on all sides), then wrap them in aluminum foil and bake for 30-40 minutes at 350°F until soft. Remove from the oven and allow them to cool, then mash with a fork in a bowl or pulse briefly in a food processor. Chop two cloves of garlic and 1/4 c. parsley into small pieces. Finely chop 2 tomatoes. Add the eggplant, garlic, parsley, tomatoes, some olive oil (enough to lightly coat the mixture), salt and pepper to taste, and one T lemon juice. Garnish the spread with fresh parsley and olives. Chill and serve with slices of bread.

Maroulosalata (Lettuce Salad)

1 head lettuce
2 cucumbers
1/2 bunch fresh dill
2 T olive oil
1 T red wine vinegar
Salt
Pepper

Wash, slice, and mix 1 head of lettuce, peel and slice 2 cucumbers and 1/2 bunch of fresh dill (to taste). Add olive oil, red wine vinegar, salt and pepper to taste.

Kotopoulo sto Fourno me Patates (Baked Potatoes with Chicken)

5 cloves garlic
4 potatoes
3/4 c. olive oil
2 T dried oregano
2 lemons
Salt
Pepper

Chop 5 cloves of garlic into small pieces. Peel and slice 4 potatoes (1/2" thick), then place them in a roasting pan with the garlic. Add 3⁄4 c. olive oil and 2 T oregano (enough to lightly coat everything), salt and pepper. Add the juice of 2 lemons and enough water to cover the bottom of the pan. Wash and place the twelve raw chicken pieces on top. Bake them at 350°F until tender (approximately 1-1/2 hours). Broil for the last few minutes, turning once so that the chicken is nicely browned.

Halva (Sweet Semolina Pudding)

1/8 c. walnuts or almonds
1/2 c. sugar
1 lemon
2 cinnamon sticks
4 whole cloves
1/4 c. olive oil
1/3 c. semolina (2/3 coarse and 1/3 fine-ground)
1/8 c. raisins
1 t. ground cinnamon

Make the syrup first. Chop 1⁄8 c. walnuts or almonds (blanched and peeled) into small pieces. Heat 3/4 c. water in a saucepan. Add 1/2 c. sugar, orange and/or lemon peel from 1 lemon, 2 cinnamon sticks and 4 cloves. Bring to a boil. Remove syrup from heat and cool to room temperature. In a deep saucepan, place 1/4 c. olive oil and cook till it begins to smoke, then add a little over 1/3 c. semolina (preferably 2/3 coarse and 1/3 fine). The mix should swell; keep stirring. When the semolina turns brown, add the syrup slowly while continuing to stir. Add the chopped nuts and 1/8 c. raisins. Continue adding as much syrup as it needs to become a jellied mixture. Place in a bowl, sprinkling cinnamon powder on the top. Let it cool at room temperature.

Chapter 7

Re-Discovering Greece

The Amphitheater "Greece"[685]

Why "Greece" in the 21st century? Why a book with essays on Greek culture, after all? Coming almost to an end, I feel I owe you, the readers, an apology, namely a sense of how I perceive of my own country which, particularly during the recent years, has been undergoing a rather unfair treatment by all sorts of global media.

Undoubtedly, Greek language has a diachronic value. Many are the ones who have realized its essence and therefore strived to learn it. The founding fathers of the USA were amongst those believers. For example, Benjamin Franklin argued how one can explain English by Greek whereas Thomas Jefferson asserted that the Greek language constitutes the basis of good education and that its knowledge is indispensable to fill up the character of a free, well-educated man.

Several places bear Greek names, such as Ithaca, where I used to teach in upstate New York, or Philadelphia, where I moved at right after, the so-called American Athens or City of Brotherly Love. However, though the advantages out of Greek language learning are remarkable, it is not merely that part of "our" culture one could benefit from. In either case, the best way to go about studying Greece is by living it, in other words, via an experiential, empirical way of learning.

Where does this educational method come from? In ancient Greece, Socrates believed that the teacher facilitates learning thoughtfully assessing where the student is at and prompting the student's own discovery, what we usually refer to as the "Socratic method." Believe it or not, Greeks associated school with leisure, Plato's "Academy" being an exemplar: learning can, and should, be enjoyable, according to the great philosopher. Lastly, even Aristotle identified two significant spheres within experience which foster growth in general: the shared life and practice.[686]

As mentioned in the beginning of this book, the best way to go about studying one culture is through the method of participant observation. When life is shared, virtue is learned through community, namely the threads established by family, education and friendship networks. However, when amongst those Greek nets, one will immediately go through quite a… shock: privacy is lacking. Even the wealthy Greek language has no word for it. So, what happens when everyone knows everyone else's business? A feeling of connection and security, perhaps? Potentially, lack of privacy puts a check on people who do not want to be caught or who are in the process of doing something that would embarrass their family. In fact, in Greece, there is less crime, not because of good policing, but because of the risk of shaming. Plus, even if you are antisocial, you will never be entirely alone!

Social structure is another key element of the Greek world. Socialization is achieved through extreme hours spent over coffee drinking even though, interestingly, traditional Greek coffee cups are tiny when compared to the time it takes to consume them. Folk practices, such as the famous evil-eye or dancing, are advocates of communal democracy, balance and harmony, as no one should claim being better than the other, whereas, at the same time, everyone is welcome to join hands and perform united in a circle.

Such social practices bring a catharsis, which, along with intensive chatting that takes place even through modern ways of communication (such as facebook, for instance), a form of daily psychotherapy takes place. This way, a Greek only needs to jump in a taxi should she/he wish to go over a psychoanalytical session, as the driver will most likely be all ears to her/his problems and existential wanderings or, even better, visit a village and start finding out more about it via its older inhabitants. Gossiping can be therapeutic, after all!

Undoubtedly, Greek food holds high dietary health benefits. Is it only what you eat, however, or how you eat it? Take a look at a Greek family, that focuses its life around the kitchen spaces, how it substantially relaxes and enjoys every meal in the company of whomever it is with as well as in combination with conversation. Moreover, ask around to find out how many Greeks do follow what Hippocrates said: "Let medicine be thy food, and food be thy medicine."

When in Greece, a main question to ask one's self is whether it is worthy to work in order to live, or to live in order to work. For example, Greeks take it easier than Americans do. Napping is one of their frequent habits. Even if they cannot really sleep, half an hour or so with their body lying down and their eyes closed, they manage to relax their heart rhythms by also providing themselves with more energy to keep them going for the rest of the day. Older family members are kept engaged in the community and in extended-family homes, adding their wisdom to the younger ones and, at the same time, more years to their lives as they do not feel the existential pain of not belonging.[687]

Keeping one's self active, as lots of Greek do, either because they use their cars less, or because they work more in the fields, is definitely a plus on one's lifestyle. Although unemployment is high, almost everyone has access to a family garden and/ or livestock. And, yes, you may hear that Greeks might arrive late to an appointment, but isn't it better to never feel the simple stress of not making it "on time"?

All in all, the Greek ecosystem allows for a healthier both body and soul to be built. Greek culture develops a strong sense of belonging which provides one with a purpose in life. Even following the Greek Orthodox faith offers Greeks an escape that comforts their souls. The Church, having embodied elements from Greek life since antiquity and by being more open, manages to bring a group closer, potentially through the so-called placebo effect of believing as well.[688] Greek nature has its role toward that direction too: tall mountains, abrupt hills, harsh landscapes, abundance of islands, aggressive waves, all these have contributed to a nation feeling self-sufficient and tough.

Recent studies on a uniquely Greek ideal, that of *philotimo*,[689] explain how it stems from the pride people take in their lives and their homeland (something that explains why they are also famous for their hospitality, *philoxenia* in Greek). There is no word like it in English. Literally, it translates to "love of honor." "Money and beauty and power can have nothing to do, have no place when *philotimo* is involved, because *philotimo* is about offering of yourself, expect nothing in return, and only because you want to create, perhaps, beauty or a wonderful moment for somebody because you're inspired to do it."[690]

So, we, Greeks, are still known as "the Zorba Nation" and, instead of saying things, we would rather dance them for you. This is why I have purposefully chosen to focus on the performed aspects of the our culture, mostly because I wanted to emphasize that, via performing, you just forget to… die, in an effort to live life to the fullest, revisiting Yalom's words, so as to "leave nothing for death but a burnt-out castle"![691] Or, in the words of the Cretan, contemporary folk poet Mitsos Stavrakakis as expressed through one of his *mandinades*, because "the only way to encounter Death, when He comes, is by being worthless."[692]

As Socrates said, "an unexamined life is not worth living." This is the advice offered to you by someone who identifies with what Nikos Kazantzakis said back in 1955 hoping that, after having read this book and through those wise words, not much will be Greek to you any more:

> The further away one is from one's country, the more one thinks of it and loves it (…) From afar (…) one has more freedom to create an image of the country worthy of true love (…) Far away from Greece I am better able to grasp her essence and her mission in the world, and thus my own humble mission. Something special happens to Greeks who live abroad. They become better. They take pride in their race, they feel that being Greeks they have the responsibility to be worthy of their ancestors. Their conviction that they are descended from Plato and Pericles may perhaps be utopian, it may be an act of autosuggestion going back thousands of years. But once this autosuggestion becomes faith it exercises a fertile influence on the modern Greek soul. It was thanks to this utopia that the Greeks survived. After so many centuries of invasion, slaughter and famine they should have disappeared. But the utopia, which has become faith, does not let them die. Greece still survives; I think it still survives through a succession of miracles.[693]

Endnotes

1. Herzfeld 1992.

2. Dimou 1997: 26-27.

3. Herzfeld 1987.

4. Herzfeld 1986: 215-33.

5. Hnaraki 2011a.

6. Kazantzakis 1969: 325-26.

7. Herzfeld 1987: 7.

8. Magrini 2002.

9. Petrides 1989: 151-57.

10. Herzfeld 1986: 228.

11. Tsarouchis 1978: 31.

12. In opposition to the ancient Greek saying "moderation is best," that is, "avoid extremes."

13. Dimou 2001: 41-42.

14. This story along with its performing dimensions is further explored in Chapter 6 compared to Iphigenia and her... *Masterbuilders*.

15. Hnaraki 2011a.

16. Based on the 2012 paper "From Field to Archive: An Ethnographic Approach to the Study of Cretan Folk Music" presented at the University of Prince Edward Island (co-sponsored by the *Island Studies Program* and the *Advancing Interdisciplinary Research in Singing Project*).

17. This may be explored by music pieces such as the famous 4'33" by John Cage, a controversial composition and by far the best-known of the many musical works that consist mainly of silence.

18. Namely a narrative with reflections, interpretations and "thick" descriptions of a culture that uses, amongst others, approaches borrowed from anthropology, folklore, oral history, conversation analysis and ethnopoetics.

19. Glassie 1989.

20. Such as fieldnotes, technological media (e.g. audio-visual recording devices), photographs, documents (e.g. diaries, journals, administrative records, newspapers, registration data, TV programs, concert brochures), census taking, mapping, genealogizing, feedback and collaboration, informal conversation (gossiping), interviews (unstructured; structured), and so on.

21. Kolovos 2010.

22. This information derived from the following sources: Hnaraki 2010c; Andrikopoulos 2006; Alexatos 2010.

23. Based on my participation at the project "Computational Comparative Analysis of the Folk Songs of Crete" funded by the John S. Latsis Public Foundation-Greece, with Dr. Christina Anagnostopoulou as its principal researcher (2009).

24. The database was annotated by area (4 regions), hyper-area (East/West), genre and hyper-genre (dance or non-dance).

25. The results of that study showed distinctive music patterns of each type of music piece,

hyper-type, area, hyper-area which Conklin and Anagnostopoulou have described in detail (2011).

26. Magrini 2002.

27. Herzfeld 1984: 439-54.

28. Herzfeld 1987.

29. Herzfeld 1992.

30. Herzfeld 1985: xi.

31. Hnaraki 2007: 53.

32. Hnaraki 2007: 48.

33. The Arabs had no reason, political, religious, or financial, to convert all Christians into servants, and, in fact, they did not do that in any of the countries they conquered. Older speculations that the Arabs engaged in mass killings, promoted violent conversions, and brought disaster on the Cretans are no longer accepted, at least not to the degree that they had been in the past (Hnaraki 2007: 48).

34. Hnaraki 2007: 48.

35. The "Partitio terrarum imperii Romaniae" ["Partition of the lands of the Roman (Byzantine) Empire"], a treaty signed after the sack of Constantinople by the Fourth Crusade in 1204, established the Latin Empire and arranged the partition of Byzantine territory among the participants of the crusades. In the process, the Republic of Venice became the chief beneficiary (Hnaraki 2007: 48).

36. Panagiotakis 1987: 366.

37. Panagiotakis 1987: 134.

38. "Document: 1862 Crete (…) Ambassador" 2001.

39. Panagiotakis 1987: 139.

40. Panagiotakis 1987: 346.

41. Even the conversion of the Arabs who remained in Crete after its liberation was a problem for Istanbul (Panagiotakis 1987: 401).

42. Panagiotakis 1987: 347.

43. Panagiotakis 1987: 143.

44. Panagiotakis 1987: 189.

45. Hnaraki 2010f.

46. Panagiotakis 1987: 387.

47. Daly 2000: 40-43.

48. Babiniotis 2002.

49. Alexakis 1995: 9, 16.

50. Glassie 1999.

51. Magrini 2002.

52. Shiloah 2002.

53. The main idea in Glassie 1989.

54. Hortatsis 1996.

55. Hortatsis 1996 (161-64).

56. He chose Jewish-Arabic names for his characters (Hortatsis 1996).

57. Hortatsis 1996: 42-43.

58. This continued on several levels until the last third of the sixteenth century (Hortatsis 1996: 56).

59. 1994.

60. Kazantzakis 1953b.

61. Kazantzakis 1985.

62. Similar is the main idea in Hobsbawm and Ranger (1983).

63. Holst-Warhaft 1998: 111.

64. Psilakis 1997: 19-26.

65. See, for instance, Kazantzakis 1953a and 1954.

66. Kazantzakis 1953a.

67. 1971: 83-4.

68. Medieval epic hero; the biracial knight of the *akro* (border), *dighenis* (of two races, *dio* "two," *gheni* "races"); son of an Arab chieftain and an aristocratic Greek lady; the topic of the second part of Kazantzakis' *Odyssey*.

69. Herzfeld 1991b.

70. Herzfeld 1991b: 24.

71. Herzfeld 1991b.

72. Herzfeld 1991b: 55.

73. "I do not accept Crete (…) without dance…" 2001: 76-77.

74. Caraveli 1985; Feld 1989; Blacking 1995.

75. Hnaraki 2007: 66.

76. Makreas 1979.

77. Cretans dance the *sousta* (spring), a couple dance with a man and woman facing each other, and, occasionally, the *balos*, a Greek folk dance, mainly performed on the islands, also in pairs. Both words are also Italian.

78. *Mandinades* are further examined in Chapter 3 as "songs of the plains."

79. More on how Daly "bridges the local with the *glocal*" in an upcoming Chapter 2 essay.

80. Skoulas 2001.

81. Psarantonis 2001.

82. Due to a nationalistic policy of purism which relates to what Clifford (1997) calls "navigating roots of locality, identity, xenophobia" and "routes of mobility and hybridity."

83. Even though the ancient Greek *lyra* has structurally nothing to do with the Cretan one.

84. Magrini 2002.

85. Idea based on Hobsbawm and Ranger (1983).

86. Dimou 1997: 99.

87. Kallergis 2001.

88. The title of the first song in this CD is "The murder's knife," essentially a love song that speaks of a man who will commit a murder with an old knife, if not married to the girl he is in love with.

89. Explored by Baldacchino 2011.

90. Williams 2002.

91. Williams 2002.

92. Williams 2002.

93. 2002.

94. Bien talks about Kazantzakis' activism and the transubstantiation of life into art (1974: 129) by quoting *Zorba the Greek* (1953b).

95. Daly 1994.

96. Based on the unpublished paper "Turkish-Cretan Folk Musicians and Dancers" that was presented with Dr. Agisilaos Aligizakis, Dr. Emmanuel Chnarakis and Mr. Andreas Yakoumakis at the 11th International Cretological Congress, Rethymno-Crete, Greece, on October 27 2011.

97. "Wake up Rodinos, and play the *lyra* sweetly, to raise the dead who are deep in their graves" (*mandinada*)! Rodinos was born in the town of Rethymno in 1912. At the age of sixteen, he formed his own group. He had a passion for the *lyra* and performed at fairs and other social events without compensation. On the day of his funeral, all people in Rethymno closed down their businesses to attend the ceremonial procession. Rodinos was a great performer, creator, and master of folk music. He created a school which modern Cretan artists respect and follow (Aerakis 1994).

98. Known as Harilaos the *Kritikos* (Cretan), Piperakis was born in 1894 or 1895 in Xirosterni, Chania. He started learning the violin but soon switched to the Cretan *lyra*. In 1912 or 1913 he traveled to the United States, where he lived most of his life, and died in 1978. He founded his own record company under the name *Faros* (Lighthouse). In the United States he was known as the "god of music," in the East as the "Big Satan," and in Athens as "the Paganini of *lyra*" (Aerakis 1994).

99. Foustalierakis was born in 1911. He lived in the town of Rethymno and owned a small watch repair shop. He created his own school in Cretan music, using the *boulgari* as a melodic, solo instrument and not merely for accompaniment. After the 1922 catastrophe, he often collaborated with musicians who came to Crete from Asia Minor (Aerakis 1994).

100. Williams 2002.

101. Hnaraki 2007.

102. Magrini 2002.

103. Williams 2002.

104. Daly 2001.

105. Daly and Stavrakakis 1982.

106. Daly 2001.

107. Skordalos was born in 1920 in the village of Spili. At the age of nine, he got his first *lyra*. Seven years later, he made his professional debut in Athens. A large segment of his long professional career was devoted to performances abroad for Cretans of the diaspora. He has been characterized as the "Beethoven of Cretan music" because his music personality reminds one of the great European composers. Along with Nikos Xylouris and Kostas Mountakis, Skordalos completes the triad of the three "immortal" *lyra* players of the younger generation (Aerakis 1994).

108. Williams 2002.

109. Detorakis 1977.

110. Vardakis 2001.

111. Petrakis 2005.

112. Such as Demir aga, a 1900 famous *lyra* player from the Kastelli village at the Pediada region.

113. Based on the unpublished paper "The Contribution and the Influence of Eustratios Kalogerides on Cretan Music" that was presented with Mr. Konstantinos Atsalakis, Dr. Agisilaos Aligizakis, Mr. Andreas Yakoumakis and Dr. Emmanuel Chnarakis at the 11th International Cretological Congress, Rethymno-Crete, Greece, on October 27 2011.

114. Aligizakis 2011.

115. Aligizakis 2011.

116. Aligizakis 2011.

117. Amargianakes, Fragoulis and Kalogeridis 1985.

118. Based on invited presentations that were given in 2009 and 2010 respectively at the University of Pennsylvania's Modern Greek Language Program as well as The Houston-Texas Cretan Association.

119. For a biography of Nikos Xylouris (1936-1980): http://www.creteonthe.net/xylouris-nikos-en.htm.

120. Daly 2000.

121. Daly 2000.

122. Hnaraki 2007: 150.

123. Based on the 2011 unpublished paper titled "Zeus Performed: Greek Mytho-Musicologies" presented at "Revisiting the Past, Recasting the Present: The Reception of Greek Antiquity in Music, 19th Century to the Present," in Athens-Greece, at the Michael Cacoyannis Foundation. Organized by the BASEES Study Group for Russian and Eastern European Music, the *Polyphonia Journal* and the *Hellenic Music Centre*.

124. Schnapp 1996: 18.

125. Nora and Kirtzman 1996: 18.

126. Nora and Kirtzman 1996: 15 and 18.

127. Della Dora 2008: 220.

128. McColley 2007: 62.

129. Rackham and Moody 1997: 275.

130. Hnaraki 2004: 68-75.

131. Hnaraki 2007: 94.

132. Herzfeld 1991b.

133. Hadjidakis 1958.

134. Psarantonis 1999. http://intotherhyth.blogspot.com/2011/05/psarantonis-i-reckon.html.

135. Lagoudianaki 2011.

136. Hulot 2007.

137. Kazantzakis' "Cretan glance" (1965: 445).

138. Paschalides 2010.

139. Hatziantoniou 2010.

140. Daly "Kelly Thoma."

141. Daly 2010.

142. Thoma 2009.

143. Minas I. Alexiadis: http://www.theatre.uoa.gr/didaktiko-dynamiko/melh-dep/mhnas-i-ale3iadhs.html.

144. "Music Wagon: The Abduction of United Europe": http://totrenostorouf.gr/gr/music/europe.

145. 2007: 169.

146. This feeling toward a place where locals "duel" landscapes and "sing" places Solomon thoroughly investigates (1997).

147. Based on a 2011 paper that was presented with musicologist Yannis Samprovalakis as "Traditional Cretan Rhyming Couplets at Greek, Artistic Compositions: From D. Mitropoulos Cretan Feast (1919) to G. Koumentakis's *Amor Fati* (2007)" at the International Musicological Conference "Crossroads: Greece as an Intercultural Pole of Musical Thought and Creativity" organized by the Aristotle University of Thessaloniki-Department of Music Studies.

148. More on the composer's biography in Trotter (2000), Sadie (2001) and Kostios (1985).

149. Kostios (2010). Garoufalis-Xanthoudakis 2011: 16.

150. Papaioannou: "Dimitri Mitropoulos: A Greek Sonata (orig. Eine Griechische Sonate)."

151. Trotter 2000: 55. Also, Garoufalis-Xanthoudakis (eds.) 2011: 16 and 57.

152. In 1917, he gave a concert for the soldiers who were fighting including his new composition *Skinai apo ton Stratona (Scenes from the Barracks)* (Trotter 2000: 56-7).

153. Apostolakis, "The *mandinada* of soldier Dimitri Mitropoulos."

154. He received his piano diploma in 1919 with a distinction for his exceptional performance ("Andreas and Iphigenia Siggros Prize"). Kostios: "Dimitri Mitropoulos: Life part (a): What? Where? When?"

155. Trotter 2000: 60.

156. Apostolakis: "The *mandinada* of soldier Dimitri Mitropoulos."

157. During 1910-1920, namely when Mitropoulos studied at the Athens Conservatory, Marios Varvoglis had already composed the Symphonic prelude *Santa Barbara* (1912), the *Greek capriccio* for violoncello and orchestra (1914) and the Symphonic poem *The Feast* (1909-19). Kostios: "Dimitri Mitropoulos: The composer."

158. Apostolos Kostios, "Dimitri Mitropoulos: The composer."

159. Apostolos Kostios, "Dimitri Mitropoulos: The composer."

160. George Lambelet, *Proia*, 2nd of March (1926).

161. Alex Thurneyssen, *Bradyni*, 6th of June (1926).

162. Kostios, "Dimitri Mitropoulos' *10 Inventions*."

163. Such was also the case with his work *Skinai apo ton Stratona (Scenes from the Barracks)* whereas Mitropoulos also liked Glazunov's (1865-1936) *Opus 3: Overture No. 1 in G minor for orchestra "On Greek Themes"* (1882) (Trotter 2000: 58).

164. Pianist Danae Kara has included that work in her CD *Dimitri Mitropoulos: Piano Works and Nikos Skalkottas: 3 Pieces* (Italy: AGORA,' 1997), AG 099.

165. Distinguished Greek actor and director Alexis Minotis wrote four days after the composer's death: "Dance and music regained their Hellenic character, and I cannot think of how that could have happened, in due time, without Mitropoulos." Kostios: "D. Mitropoulos' Music for Euripides' *Hippolytus*."

166. Hadjidakis 1958.

167. Hadjidakis 1958: 119-120.

168. *En Chaniois 4* (Chania, 2010).

169. In parallel ways, Koumendakis' *Amor Fati* (2010) also proceeds.

170. It is said that people queued for 3 days to get tickets for her debut in Bellini's *Norma*.

171. Daly 2001.

172. Daly 2001.

173. Daly 2001.

174. Daly was brought up in England, North America (San Francisco mainly) and Japan.

175. Daly 2000: 40-43.

176. Daly 2001.

177. Daly, interview, Houdetsi-Crete, 13 July 2001.

178. Daly 2000: 40-43.

179. Dawe 2008: 139.

180. Daly 2001.

181. Hetherington 1997.

182. Hannam, Sheller, Urry 2006: 13.

183. Daly 2001.

184. Magrini 2003: 19.

185. Plastino 2003: 1-36.

186. Daly and Halkias 2000: Disc 2, Track 5.

187. Daly "About Music."

188. Levin (with Süzükei) 2006: 210.

189. Shelemay 2000: 19.

190. Levin (with Süzükei) 2006: 51.

191. Daly 2008.

192. Levin (with Süzükei) 2006: 125.

193. Levin (with Süzükei) 2006: 27.

194. Levin (with Süzükei) 2006: 76-77.

195. Sayan Bapa associating Tuvan music with Buddhist animism in Levin (with Süzükei) 2006: 225.

196. The Cretan lyrics of the *White Dragon* (2008) homonymous track talk about birds – such as the nightingale, the blackbird and the wild pigeons – as love messengers.

197. Levin (with Süzükei) 2006: 124.

198. Alexakis 1995.

199. Stokes 1994: 4.

200. Plastino 2003: 25.

201. Shelemay 2000: xiii-xv.

202. Marranchi 2002: 578.

203. Whatmore 2002.

204. Calliope, Euterpe, Polyhymnia, Terpsichore, Clio, Urania, Thalia, Erato, Melpomene.

205. Herzfeld 1981.

206. Ball and Lai 2006: 270.

207. Ball and Lai 2006: 270.

208. This is track 15 on the Hnaraki 2007 accompanying the book CD.

209. This phenomenon refers to a long procession of visions that consist of a group of shadows walking or riding, armed with weapons. Legend has it that this group of people are Greek fighters that died during the Battle of Frangokastello (17 May 1828) and since then they appear as supernatural beings in the area.

210. http://www.cretaquarium.gr/indexen.php.

211. Other terms for ecopoetry are ecopoetics, environmental literary criticism, green cultural studies. The prefix "enviro" is anthropocentric and dualistic, implying that we, humans, are at the center, whereas "eco" implies interdependent communities, integrated systems, and strong connections among constituent parts (Glotfelty and Harold 1996: xx).

212. Gilcrest 2002: 7.

213. Rueckert 1996: 111.

214. 1999: 80-1.

215. Scigaj 1999: 78-9.

216. "Mesara, the Home of Europe" 2001: 2; and Panagiotakis 1987: xv.

217. Hnaraki 2010b: 99.

218. Magrini and Leydi 2000.

219. Besides specific natural images, traditional Cretan lyrics also talk about the protection of pastoralism and life on the mountains (Manouselis 2003: 182-195).

220. Lord 1960.

221. "Teacher John wholeheartedly wished Crete to be Greek" reads the 10th line of "The Daskalogiannis Song" (1947: 15).

222. Llewelyn 1965: 81.

223. Llewelyn 1965: 82.

224. Llewelyn 1965: 83.

225. League, "Rewriting Unwritten History (…) Cretan Violin."

226. League, "Rewriting Unwritten History (…) Cretan Violin."

227. Notopoulos 1952: 228-9.

228. Daskalogiannis was imprisoned for about a year and was put to death in June 1771.

229. Llewelyn 1965: 86-7.

230. In 1888, Emmanuel Vardidis edited that work again whereas, in less than a year, the song was re-edited in Athens by Pavlos Fafoutakis, followed by Bortolis (in 1939). Lastly, in 1947, Vasilios Laourdas offered us the first autotelic publication of that song (Kapsetakis 2007: 4-5), something that proves its literary value (also explaining why we have primarily used this publication for our study).

231. Petropoulos 1954: 231-2.

232. It is the longest gorge in Europe (15km), an internationally recognized "sight" which was declared a National Park in 1962, with a reputation since the antiquity. It placed Crete on the international environmental maps and, as a tourist attraction, has contributed significantly not only to the growth of the economy of Sfakia but of the whole prefecture.

Humans have lived within and around the gorge, developing an almost self-sufficient economy with activities that have resulted in the natural protection of the park and sustainable development (Papavasileiou 2008: 70).

233. More on this by the German linguist and archaeologist Deffner (130-1) who also believed that, "whoever walks in the mountains and the gorges, will turn into a gallant man and love freedom" (101).

234. Chaniotaki-Smyrlaki 2008: 129.

235. Papavasileiou 2008: 70.

236. Kapsetakis 2007: 3.

237. Barba-Pantzelios 1947.

238. Chaniotaki-Smyrlaki: 131.

239. Morgan 1960: 35.

240. Morgan 1960: 36.

241. Morgan 1960: 37.

242. Indeed, Morgan attributes such poetic virtues to Aristophanes (1960: 41).

243. 2006: 31-32.

244. 2006: 38-9.

245. 1993: 382.

246. 1959: 10.

247. 1964: 45.

248. The addition of the epilogue (something unusual as most oral heroic poetry is anonymous) technically known as *sphragis* is a quite regular feature in Cretan poetry observed in the 16th-17th centuries paintings of the Cretan-Venetian school (e.g. by El Greco; Notopoulos 1952: 235).

249. Notopoulos 1952: 249.

250. Hnaraki 2011e: 180.

251. 1994.

252. Hnaraki 2007: 64.

253. Ball 2006b: 275.

254. Apostolakis 1993: 18-19; Morgan 1960: 28-29 and 34.

255. Morgan 1960: 33.

256. 2006: 180.

257. Tuan 1991.

258. Dreese 2002: 8 and 69.

259. Baud-Bovy 1960: 83.

260. 1960: 83.

261. 2000: 446.

262. Hnaraki 2006c.

263. Herzfeld 1985.

264. 2004: 1.

265. Baud-Bovy 1960: 83.

266. Levin (with Süzükei) 2006: 73-124.

267. 1958: 114.

268. Kaloyanides 1975: 21 and Hadjidakis 1958: 113-4.

269. Ball 2006b: 298.

270. Kaloyanides 1975: 23. Hadjidakis (1958: 111) argues how this song is old because it does not rhyme: rhyming was introduced to Crete in the 15th century.

271. Morgan 1960: 25-29.

272. 1960: 25.

273. Morgan 1960: 26.

274. Hay 2006: 31.

275. Wilson 2006.

276. Smith 1994.

277. Ball 2006b: 294.

278. Cohen 2001.

279. One of his many fans is Nick Cave, who invited him to perform at the "All Tomorrow's Parties" international rock festival he staged in Australia in 2009.

280. More on how Psarantonis performs... "mountain" Zeus on Chapter 2.

281. CD liner notes.

282. Clifford 1997.

283. Koumendakis, personal communication, April 25 2010.

284. Hnaraki 2007: 103-4.

285. Aligizakis 2005.

286. Unpublished paper "Traditional Folk Musicians and Dancers of the Pediada Province (1900-1970)." Presented with Dr. Agisilaos Aligizakis, Dr. Emmanuel Chnarakis, Mr. Andreas Yakoumakis, Mr. Gregoris Fragoulidakis and Mr. Konstantinos Fysarakis at the 11th International Cretological Congress, Rethymno-Crete, Greece, on October 27 2011.

287. Beaton 2004: 35-57.

288. Hnaraki 2007: 94.

289. Caraveli 1985.

290. Erdener 1987: 3-5.

291. Erdener 1987: 7.

292. Erdener 1987: 81.

293. Erdener 1987: 299.

294. Unpublished paper "Serenade in Eastern Crete." Presented with Dr. Agisilaos Aligizakis, Mr. Konstantinos Atsalakis, Mrs. Lydia Aligizaki, Mr. Emmanuel Stratakis, Mr. Andreas Yakoumakis and Dr. Emmanuel Chnarakis at the 11th International Cretological Congress, Rethymno-Crete, Greece, on October 27 2011.

295. On this topic, one may read further the following interview transcripts part of the "Digital Crete: Musical Routes Program": http://digitalcrete.ims.forth.gr/MusicalRoutes/index.php?view=articleandid=2080%3A%CE%9C%CE%AD%CE%BB%CE%B1%CE%BC%CF%80%CE%B5%CF%82+%CE%9D.+%CE%A1%CE%B5%CE%B8%CF%8D%CE%BC%CE%BD%CE%B7%CF%82andtmpl=componentandprint=1andpage=andoption=com_content

http://digitalcrete.ims.forth.gr/MusicalRoutes/index.php?option=com_contentandview=articleandid=2423andtype=andoriginPage=expanded

http://digitalcrete.ims.forth.gr/MusicalRoutes/index.php?option=com_contentand-
view=articleandid=2469andtype=andoriginPage=expanded

296. More works are currently in progress.

297. Based on the 2011 paper "Singing the Tree: The Olive Oil Culture in Cretan Folk Poetry" presented at the University of Toronto and the Canadian Institute of Mediterranean
Studies conference on the Olive Oil Culture in the Mediterranean.

298. Hnaraki 2007: 95-6. Sykäri's 2011 study is thoroughly informative on both the performative and the compositional aspects of that Cretan poetic form.

299. Oftentimes, symbols of local cultural identity are certain flowers or plants. For instance, the metaphorical use of the wild flower signifies that a woman's unruliness makes
her more difficult for a man to conquer erotically, yet also more attractive to him than tamer
women who are symbolized by cultivated flowers (Ball 2006b, 289).

300. 2007: 678.

301. Meneley 2007: 683.

302. Psilakis 1996: 264.

303. 2011.

304. 1999.

305. 2008: 31-2.

306. Perhaps, the naming of Popeye's, the sailor's wife, cartoon character Olive Oyl (a "cor-
ruption" of olive-oil) is not accidental either.

307. Krochmal 1955: 228. Homer coins the olive-oil as "liquid gold."

308. Boardman et. al 1976: 188.

309. Boardman et al. 1976: 188 and 193.

310. For more information on the topic of olive cultivation and production see Vallianou-Hatzi 2003.

311. http://www.terracreta.gr/index.html.

312. Vasilakis 2003: 56-8.

313. Notopoulos has compared the Homeric epics with Cretan folk balladry (1952, 1959
and 1964).

314. Stathis 2004: 84-5.

315. 2001: 101.

316. 2001: 102.

317. Sutton 2001: 102.

318. Apostolakis 1993: 234-5.

319. On a side note, Aristotle studied the olive-tree and turned its cultivation into a whole
science. According to him, whoever uprooted or destroyed an olive tree, particularly of the
ones around the "sacred" Athenian areas, should be confronted with a death penalty.

320. Father Philotheos 2003: 31.

321. 2007.

322. 2004.

323. Hnaraki 2011e: 180-2.

324. Paraphrasing verses from the poem *Astyanax* by Greek Nobel Laureate George Seferis

(*Mythistorema 17*, translated By Edmund Keeley and Philip Sherrard: http://www.poetry-foundation.org/poem/181958.

325. *Communication*: 36.

326. Based on fieldwork conducted between 1998-2002 and past experiences from active participating in wedding feasts because of my origin.

327. Stroebel 1979.

328. Sugarman 1997.

329. Cowan 1990.

330. Kaeppler 1995.

331. Petrides 1961.

332. Hnaraki 2006c.

333. Herzfeld 1985.

334. Kazantzakis 1965: 445.

335. Orfanos 2006.

336. Dimiroulis 2007: 45.

337. Torp 1992: 207.

338. Theodorakis 1990: 223-4.

339. Bien 2000.

340. Bien 2001: 312.

341. Merrill 1975: 104.

342. Hartocollis 1974: 209.

343. Hartocollis 1974.

344. Hartocollis 1974: 206.

345. For more information on that see Philippides 2005: 182-3.

346. Zografou (1960) and Petrakou (2005) have applied psychological analyses to Kazantzakis' works and talk about his relationship with his father and how it has influenced his writings. For Kazantzakis' own thoughts on his father see *Report to Greco*: 31-33.

347. Kazantzakis 1965: 445.

348. Philippides (2005) meditates more on those "bipolar" Kazantzakian notions (spirit-body, mind-material, abstinence-sensuality, laziness-action, logos-action, high style-folk style: 158).

349. Bien 1965.

350. Bien 1974: 131-33.

351. Kazantzakis 1965: 486 and Hnaraki 2007: 45.

352. More on those political connotations in Bien 1965 and Kastrinaki 2006: 151-62.

353. Bien 2000: 164.

354. Farinou-Malamatari 1998: 173-4.

355. According to Orfanos, "Myths can be like mirrors" (2006: 8).

356. Kazantzakis 1965: 458-9.

357. Papaioannou 1983: 80-1.

358. Yialourakis 2007: 33-34.

359. Matthias 1998: 242-3.

360. Papanikolaou 2006: 92.

361. Bien 1965: 159.

362. Holst-Warhaft 1997: 233.

363. Kazantzakis 1983: 567.

364. For a more detailed discussion on the relationship of the folk and the authentic in Kazantzakis' work see Philippides 1997.

365. 1995.

366. Philippides 2005: 177-183.

367. Dimou "Dialogues: The Metaphysics of 'Grinia.'"

368. After all, quoting… Zorba, "life is trouble, only death isn't"! Kazantzakis 1953b.

369. Kazantzakis 1965: 454-5.

370. Bien 1989: 20.

371. Philippides 2010.

372. Based on the 2008 paper "The Cultural Significance of Isadora Duncan in the 21st Century: Raising Ecological Awareness through Dance" presented at the "Cultural Significance of Delphi in the 20th century" organized by Stockton College at the European Cultural Center in Delphi-Greece.

373. Terry 1963: 57.

374. Duncan 1956: 47-50.

375. Terry 1963: 35.

376. Terry 1963: 27.

377. Daly 1995: ix. Seroff also comments on how his biography is objective whereas Duncan's biography is fictional and romancing (1971: 13 and 21).

378. *Isadora Duncan*: 1987.

379. Terry 1963: 112-3.

380. Rosemont: xv.

381. Mazo 2000: 65.

382. Duncan 1927: 103.

383. Jowitt 1985: 5.

384. Steegmuller 1974: 84.

385. Jowitt 1985: 7.

386. Durham 2006: 102-3.

387. Sheroff 1971: 55.

388. 1975: 211.

389. Bien 2005.

390. Rothstein 2004.

391. Terry 1963: 65.

392. Duncan 1927: 47.

393. Terry 1963: 154.

394. Rosemont 2001: 51.

395. Daly 1995: 90-91.

396. Rosemont 2001: 33.

397. Rothstein 2004.

398. Duncan 1956: 119.

399. 1956: 92.

400. Daly 1995: 95.

401. Seroff 1971: 58.

402. LaMothe 2006: 114; Terry 1963: 34. Duncan 1927: 88.

403. Ted Shawn in Terry 1963: 166.

404. Jowitt 1985: 7.

405. Jowitt 1985: 7.

406. 1995.

407. One could observe sound similarities on Duncan's and Kazantzakis' work. Both have profound religious- and freedom-oriented wanderings and are strongly influenced by Nietzsche, whom they perceived as the first dancing philosopher.

408. Reid 2008.

409. Lesson Plan #1: 2004.

410. Lesson Plan #1: 2004.

411. Duncan 1927: 14.

412. Rosemont 2001: 45.

413. Lowenthall 1993: 5.

414. Durham 92-3 2006.

415. Terry 1963: 31.

416. Jowitt 1985: 8.

417. Duncan 1956: 102.

418. Duncan 1956: 91.

419. Preston 2005: 277.

420. Preston 2005: 282.

421. Steichen 1959.

422. Rosemont 2001: 109.

423. Kurth 2002: 42.

424. Daly 1995:100.

425. Daly reconstructs Duncan's body in landscape (1995: xiii and 3).

426. Daly 1956: 79.

427. Daly 1995: 101.

428. Ball 2006b: 287.

429. Paraphrasing… Ball 2006b: 290.

430. *Soul Speed*, as they introduce themselves, is a dance and theatre troupe from Whaingaroa, Waikato. They are trying to raise awareness through performance about the critically endangered Maui Dolphin, the *popoto*. Motivated and responsive to current local and global issues, this time surrounding the Whaling Moratorium, *Soul Speed*'s next project is a work about the southern right whale, the *tohora* (Barbour 2005).

431. 2007.

432. Halprin 2000: 96.

433. Hnaraki 2006c.

434. 1983: 1.

435. 1996.

436. 1987: 7.

437. 1988: 7-8.

438. What Bottomley (1992) terms as "the spirit of resistance": 86.

439. Riak 2007: 52.

440. Hanna 1979: 4-5.

441. Hnaraki 2007: 101.

442. 2004: 4-5.

443. Sachs 1937.

444. Makreas 1979: 18-22.

445. Hadjidakis 1958.

446. Riak 2003: 213.

447. Magrini 2000: 455.

448. 1990.

449. Hnaraki 1998: 42-43.

450. One may also notice the wordplay between *zala* (steps) and *zali* (dizziness).

451. Hnaraki 1998: 43-44.

452. Petrides 1961.

453. Tsouhlarakis, "The traditional dances of Crete."

454. League, "Rewriting Unwritten History (…) Cretan Violin."

455. The "Greek War of Independence," also known as the "Greek Revolution" was a successful war of independence waged by the Greek revolutionaries between 1821 and 1832.

456. "The Daskalogiannis Song" is also studied in Chapter 2 as "Homeric poetry" in relation to "Cretan balladry."

457. Tsouhlarakis, "The traditional dances of Crete."

458. Among those who took part in the Daskalogiannis Revolution was the great war-chief Iosif Daskalakis or Sifodaskalakis from the village of Ambadia, Rethymno. Sifodaskalakis survived the revolt but was crippled in his left leg. According to tradition, some years later, Captain Sifis wanted to dance the *pentozalis*. The musicians and dancers adapted the rhythm of the dance steps to that of a lame man. This performance became part of the tradition of the Amari-Rethymno province as "koutsambadianos" or "ka(r)tsimba(r)dianos" (Tsouhlarakis, "The traditional dances of Crete").

459. 1982.

460. Hnaraki 2007: 131.

461. Stokes 1994: 16.

462. 2007: 153-154.

463. 1991: 78.

464. All quotes associated with Mr. Theoharis Xirouhakis relate to personal communication I had had with him during June-September 2011.

465. For instance, the cultural part of the educational program of the Pancretan Association

called "Dias" (Zeus).

466. Named in honor of Eleftherios Venizelos (1864-1936) from Chania, an eminent statesman as well as charismatic leader in the early 20th century (the Athens International Airport is also named after him).

467. Another choreography by Mr. Xirouhakis is that of "The Young Zorbas," based on the popular soundtrack of the 1964 film "Zorba the Greek," which "continues to spread the aroma of Crete" (Xirouhakis, 2011).

468. He was born in Chania in 1974 and expressed his interest in Cretan music when he was two years old.

469. On the DVD, on the Cretan lute, Manolis Balomenakis performs.

470. Except the first verse, which is traditional, and the last one, which is composed by Mr. Nektarios Leounakis (Xirouhakis, 2011).

471. Baldacchino 2011: xxix.

472. Dawe 2004: 73.

473. Bien 2000.

474. Alexiou 2007: 22.

475. Petrakou 2005: 52.

476. Girard 1995, Prifti 1991 and Papaioannou 1983.

477. Beaton 1994.

478. Ball 2006b: 291.

479. Kazantzakis 1965: 493 and 504.

480. Ball 2006b.

481. Beaton 1988: 14.

482. Papaioannou 1983.

483. Girard 1995.

484. He wanted him to compose music for this theatrical play *Nikiforos Fokas* (Petrakou 2005: 284-5).

485. Alexiou 2007: 22.

486. Papanikolaou 2006: 105-6. The "Zorba" music theme had already been employed by Theodorakis for his composition at the Iakovos Kambanellis' theatrical play *Neighborhood of Angels* as prelude for the popular Greek song "Strose to stroma sou yia dio" ("Make your bed for two").

487. Papanikolaou 2006: 105.

488. Hnaraki 2007: 121-131 and Holst-Warhaft 1997.

489. Papanikolaou 2006: 100.

490. Chrysostomou 2006: 201.

491. Petrakou 2005: 48.

492. Kazantzakis 1976:115-121.

493. 1984.

494. Constantinidis 1997: 33-34.

495. Kazantzakis 1976:115-121.

496. Petrakou 2005: 632.

497. Petrakou 2005: 64 and Poulakidas 1983.

498. Papahatzaki-Katsaraki 1985: 40. Critic Alkis Thrylos comments on how "a lyric song turned into prose was looking for music" and how "Mr. Kalomiris, a creator of new rhythms and eternal melodies, emphasized harmony." *Noumas* 12-3-1916: 59.

499. Petrakou 2005: 210.

500. Papahatzaki-Katsaraki 1985: 92-3.

501. Volume 54 (630), October 1 1953.

502. Petrakou 2005: 534.

503. Kalomiris 1959.

504. Kazantzakis 1965: 447 and 542.

505. Constantinidis 1997: 45.

506. Kazantzakis 1964.

507. Papahatzaki-Katsaraki 1985: 173.

508. More information on Petrakou 2005: 325-6.

509. Kazantzakis 1965: 548 and 591, and Philippides 2005.

510. Paraphrasing a prayer in "his" *Report*.

511. http://www.kazantzakis-museum.gr/index.php?pre_id=623andid=623and level=0andpre_level=0andaction=andsearchKey=andlang=en.

512. http://www.kalomiris.org/.

513. Vincent 2005: 119.

514. http://www.kazantzakis-museum.gr/index.php?id=804andpre_id=1009andlevel=4andpre_level=5andlang=en.

515. From a letter to his friend and colleague Charilaos Stephanides, dated March 10, 1903 (Aposkitou-Alexiou 1978).

516. 1984.

517. Frangou-Psychopaidi 1990.

518. Kazantzaki 1984.

519. Kalomiris had clearly dedicated the 1st 1917 version of the work for voices and piano to Venizelos, a dedication which he, however, removed from the 2nd 1939/40 version, most likely due to the censorship applied by the Metaxas dictatorship.

520. http://www.stigmes.gr/gr/grpages/articles/kazantzakis.html.

521. Herzfeld 1982.

522. One may look at Maliaras 1995 for more information on folk songs in Kalomiris' music.

523. 2007: 22.

524. Dundes (1996) offers eighteen essays devoted to the folkloric ballad about the immurement of women within a structure to ensure its successful construction, the so-called "foundation sacrifice" motif in folklore.

525. 1971.

526. On June 22 1958, in a speech on the radio, Kalomiris spoke of lifetime inspirations: "My childhood was haunted by our folk songs, by the melodies and rhythms of our people, by our legends and traditions, by Byzantium, its mythical kings and its haunted monasteries. Along with them, by Greek poetry... I found my inspiration in modern Greece and tried

to sing primarily and mainly for the Greeks."

527. Kalomiris 1946.

528. Kalomiris 1946.

529. The collection *Mythistory and Narratives of the Nation in the Balkans* illustrates how such stories are written at crucial historical periods in the Balkans as well as how the sacrifice motif is central when it comes to structuring a nation (Aleksić: 88).

530. Bien 2007: 19-20.

531. The masterbuilder-sacrifice relationship Kazantzakis negotiates in *Kapodistrias* as well (1971).

532. Vincent 2005: 122.

533. Classic examples are his play *Buddha* (1956) and the novel *The Last Temptation of Christ* (1960).

534. The present study concerns the third and last version of *The Masterbuilder* 1942 libretto by Kalomiris, compared to the 1908 text by Kazantzakis, on which Kalomiris was based to compose his homonymous music tragedy in three acts between Easter of 1913 and October of 1915.

535. According to Glytzouris (2008), when we talk about the Kazantzakis *Masterbuilder* we must keep in mind three versions, the 1908 drama in two-acts *Sacrifice*, the 1910 tragedy *Masterbuilder* as well as the unfinished 1916 second 1916." However, Kalomiris did not take into consideration the "second 1916 version," hence, without ignoring it we do not take it into consideration in the present study.

536. "Only Manolis Kalomiris, who composed and adapted this music work, holds the right to publish it and to allow its theatrical performance by either professional actors or amateurs."

537. Petrakou 2005: 211.

538. The Hellenic Music Centre (http://www.hellenicmusiccentre.com/) is planning on publishing the opera's music score which will include an appendix of all its leitmotifs.

539. Petrakou supports that the writer's green connotations refer to nature (2005: 208-9).

540. Leotsakos 1986: 30.

541. Specific examples one may find in Hnaraki and Samprovalakis 2010: 489.

542. Leotsakos 1986: 31.

543. Bien 2001: 20-21.

544. Papahatzaki-Katsaraki 1985: 37.

545. Leotsakos 1986: 21.

546. Petrakou 2005: 204.

547. Maliaras 2001: 37.

548. Mu Quian 2007.

549. This essay was illustrated by audio-visual examples and was presented by Musicologist-Orchestrator Yannis Samprovalakis at the conference titled "The Ottoman Past in the Balkan Present: Music and Mediation" which took place at the University of Athens on October 2 2010.

550. Hadjidakis 2007.

551. Andreopoulos 256-9.

552. Aggelikopoulos 1997: 18-21.

553. Miralis 2004: 51.

554. Kazantzakis 1965: 98.

555. Hadjidakis 1988: 34-5.

556. Personal interview with the composer: 18 January 2007.

557. Bauschatz 1991.

558. Around that time Antoniou creates his own style of notation, mixing traditional and contemporary techniques, while in 1979, the year, namely, he finished composing *Periander*, he becomes a full professor at Boston University.

559. The reason for that was the success of his cantata "Nenikikamen" ("We have won") he has been commissioned to compose for the Munich 1972 Olympic Games.

560. More information on Papahatzaki-Katsaraki 1985: 102-116.

561. More information on Petrakou 2005: 319-320.

562. Papahatzaki-Katsaraki 1985: 114.

563. Petrakou 2005: 319.

564. Papahatzaki-Katsaraki 1985: 173.

565. Bien 1992 and 1997: 157-8.

566. Personal interview with the composer: 18 January 2007.

567. Bien 1997: 160.

568. Personal interview with the composer: 18 January 2007.

569. More on the composer's biography in Hellenic Music Centre, "George Koumendakis." In: http://www.hellenicmusiccentre.com/index.php?option=com_virtuemartandpage=shop.browseandcategory_id=18andItemid=57andlang=enandvmcchk=1andItemid=57.

570. Koumendakis 2010.

571. Yalom 2002.

572. Koumendakis 2010.

573. "It was the Thessaloniki State Symphony Orchestra and Myron Michailidis with their commission that acted as a catalyst toward the fulfillment of my desire, and that for I thank them warmly." Koumendakis 2010.

574. The etymology of the Greek word *anthropos*, namely human being, is a composite of the Greek words *ano* (up) and *throsko* (I look, watch upwards). Thus, human heads stand erect toward the heavens, human eyes look upward. The Greek word for religion, *thriskia*, etymologically relates to that word.

575. More on Greece's stone arch bridges in Grassos 2007.

576. Eliade 1972.

577. On the Iphigenia myth as dealt by the three ancient Greek tragic poets see also Jovanovic 2007: 2-4 and 6-8.

578. This essay is based on the 2012 paper "Harmonizing the Iphigenia Sacrifices: Music Approaches of the Ancient Myth by M. Theodorakis and G. Koumendakis" delivered at a meeting on "Stage Music and Ancient Drama" dedicated to the memory of Georgios Amargianakes, at the Department of Philosophy-University of Crete; Division of Theatre Studies and Musicology.

579. http://entertainment.in.gr/html/ent/497/ent.37497.asp.

580. Based on personal communication (e-mail) with the composer.

581. Mandel (1983) examines how the story of a woman sacrificed and immured symbolically reproduces Greek cosmogony and notions of culture and nature.

582. Alexiou's chapter "Myth in Song" is enlightening on that matter (2002: 172-210).

583. http://www.hks.harvard.edu/kokkalis/index.html.

584. 1999: 648-9.

585. Paraphrasing and alluding to Cavafy's *Ithaca*: "(…) And if you find her poor, Ithaca did not deceive you. As wise as you'll have become, with so much experience, you'll have understood, by then, what these Ithacas mean."

586. Phrases in quotation marks are familiar Greek proverbs.

587. Thursby 2008: 155.

588. Milona 2004: 306.

589. Thursby 2008: 164.

590. Paraphrasing Thursby 2008: 155.

591. Thursby 2008: vii.

592. Quoted in MacClancy 1992: 2.

593. Segal 1974: 289-290.

594. Segan 2004: 183.

595. Odyssey: 9, 121, 135 and 212.

596. Psilakis 2001: 34-36.

597. Segal 2004: 297.

598. Plato characterizes the elements as being pre-Socratic in origin from a list created by the Sicilian philosopher Empedocles (ca. 450 BC). Empedocles called those the four "roots."

599. Rigotti 2008: 109-11.

600. Brumfield 1997. Nikos and Maria Psilakis speak for the breads of the gods (2001: 21-24) and provide the readers with more information on ancient Greek bread (2001: 125-140).

601. Thursby 2008: 157.

602. Segan 2004: 179.

603. Segan 2004: 210.

604. Milona 2004: 306.

605. Tannahill 1973: 91.

606. For further information one may read the "Federation of Bakers in Greece (OAE)" webpage: http://www.oae.gr/index2.htm.

607. 2005.

608. Morton 2005.

609. Hnaraki 2008.

610. Hnaraki 2008.

611. Thursby 2008: 1.

612. 1982.

613. Mason 1982.

614. Psilakis (Nikos and Maria) 1997: 233.

615. Ball 2003: 24. Ball views such publications as a way to facilitate the exchange of cooking

knowledge among members of the Cretan community and beyond.

616. The Greek word "*artos*" means bread and "*polis*" town. *Artopolis* was created "to bring a true European style cafe to Chicago": http://www.artopolischicago.com/.

617. McCracken 2001: 116.

618. Watson 2005.

619. Thursby 2008: x.

620. 2004.

621. 2004.

622. Tzimitras 2004.

623. For further information on the "bread whiteness" one may look at Jones (2007: 145) and Voutsina (2000: 10).

624. Voutsina 2000: 15.

625. Voutsina 2000: 19.

626. 2004.

627. 2008.

628. 2002: 4.

629. Riglis 2005: 43.

630. Hillman 1985: 176.

631. Hillman 1985: 175.

632. 1971: 167.

633. John 6.35-40.

634. Voutsina 2000: 118.

635. Koukoules in Voutsina 2000: 183.

636. Here is the bakery's webpage: http://www.tomanna.gr/en/history.cfm?menu_id=1.

637. John 6.54-58.

638. Rigotti 2008: 31-27 and 100.

639. 1995.

640. Hnaraki and Papoutsaki 2012.

641. 2002: 9.

642. "Historic Notes" 2007 and Psilakis 2001: 107-8.

643. Kaplanoglou 2006.

644. Kaplanoglou 2006.

645. 2002: 118.

646. 2002: 136.

647. Thursby 2008: x.

648. Deftereos 2000.

649. Psilakis (Nikos and Maria) 1997.

650. Thursby 2008: 4.

651. Riglis 2005: 27-28.

652. Thursby 2008: ix.

653. Deftereos 2000: 136-139.

654. Deftereos 2000: 141.

655. Deftereos 2000: 178.

656. Deftereos 2000: 183.

657. Memorial services according to the Greek calendar take place on the 3rd, the 9th and the 40th day after death, as well as after the 6, 9 and 12 months, and during the so-called "Saturdays of the souls."

658. Deftereos 2000: 211-219.

659. Saritas has researched the celebration of teething in Turkish culture (2011).

660. Deftereos 2000: 108-109.

661. Varella 2004.

662. Voutsina 2000: 68 and 164.

663. 2000.

664. From the Latin "panem et circenses."

665. Thursby 2008: 155.

666. Korsmeyer 2002: 185.

667. Antonakis 2002.

668. 2002: 7.

669. 2004.

670. In one of Gyzis' letters, dated March 29 1876, we read that his wife, Artemis, liked homemade bread. Pavlopoulos 2004.

671. 2004.

672. 2004.

673. Long 2009: 7.

674. 1968: 35.

675. Milona 2009.

676. 1966.

677. Sumption and Ashbrook 1941: 11.

678. Paraphrasing Frank Sinatra and Paul Anka's (lyrics) "My Way" (1970).

679. 2008.

680. For more information, http://dim-rizou.pel.sch.gr/ergasies/psomi/page01.html.

681. Korsmeyer 2002: 10.

682. For more information, http://www.historical-museum.gr/programmata.html.

683. 1984.

684. Paraphrasing Freud in Hillman 1985: 177.

685. This entry is based on the 2012 paper "The amphitheater 'Greece': Re-discovering experiential education in the 21st century" presented, upon invitation, at the National Hellenic Student Association (NHSA) Philadelphia Convention.

686. Stonehouse, Allison and Carr 2009.

687. Buettner 2012.

688. Sternberg 2012.

689. See, for example, Katerinakis 2012.

690. Katerina Taiganides de Ezcurra in Shapiro 2007.

691. Yalom 2002: 316.

692. *Mandinada* excerpt from "Demon," the first song in Stavrakakis (Mitsos and Vasilis) 2001.

693. Interview on the French radio about Greece: http://www.youtube.com/watch?v=9fvf-bhZFrJ0.

Bibliography

[GR] stands for works that have been published in Greek.

Aerakis, Stelios. 1994. *Cretan Musical Traditions: The Masters; 1920-1955, Original Recordings.* Aerakis, Cretan Musical Workshop. S.A. CD 540.

Alexakis, Manolis. 1995. "Ross Daly: Through Music We Discover Humanity." *Ostria* 1: 9, 16.

Aggelikopoulos, Vasilis. 1997. "Hadjidakis Autobiographed." *Diphono* 21: 18-21. [GR]

Aleksić, Tatiana (ed). 2007. *Mythistory and Narratives of the Nation in the Balkans.* Newcastle: Cambridge Scholars Publishing.

Alexatos, Gerasimos, 2010. *The Greeks of Görlitz: 1916-1919.* Kyriakidis Publications. [GR]

Alexiou, Elli. 2007. *In Order to Become Great.* Athens: Kastaniotis. [GR]

Alexiou, Margaret. 2002. *After Antiquity: Greek Language, Myth, and Metaphor.* Ithaca, NY: Cornell University Press.

Aligizakis, Agisilaos. 2011. *The Violin's Music Odyssey at the Big Castle 2000+.* Heraklion-Crete. [GR]

____. 2005. *Cretan Dance: Art & Physical Education.* Heraklion-Crete: Sistron. [GR]

Amargianakes, Georgios, Fragoulis K. and Kalogeridis E. 1985. *Cretan Music.* Vikelaia Municipal Library. Heraklion-Crete. [GR]

Andreopoulos, Andreas. "Imago Poetae: The Aesthetics of Manos Hadjidakis." *Journal of Modern Greek Studies*: 255-268.

Andrikopoulos, Konstantinos. 2006. *The Miracle of Görlitz.* Documentary.

Anemoyannis, Yorgos. 1997. "Music at the Works by Kazantzakis." *Lexi*: 276-283. [GR]

Antonakis, Yorgos. 2002. *The Sweetest Bread.* Athens: Akritas. [GR]

Antoniou, Theodore. 1983. *Periander: Mixed-media Opera for Singers, Dancers, Actors, Narrator, Choir, Orchestra and Tape.* Munich: Baerenreiter Verlag.

Aposkitou-Alexiou, Martha. 1978. "Unknown Nikos Kazantzakis' Letters." *Amalthea* 9 (34): 122-123. [GR]

Apostolakis, Sakis. "The *Mandinada* of Soldier Dimitri Mitropoulos." Retrieved March 5, 2013, from http://www.enet.gr/?i=issue.el.home&date=04/03/2010&id=137942. [GR]

Apostolakis, Stamatis. 1993. *Rizitika: The Folk Songs of Crete.* Athens: Gnosis. [GR]

Babiniotis, Georgios. 2002. *Dictionary of the Modern Greek Language.* Athens: Kentro Lexikologias. [GR]

Baldacchino, Godfrey. 2011. "Editorial" in *Island Songs.* Lanham MD: The Scarecrow Press: xix-xli.

Ball, Eric. 2006a. "Folkism and Wild(er)ness: Observations on the Construction of Nature in Modern Greek Culture." *Journal of the Hellenic Diaspora* 32 (1-2): 7-43.

____. 2006b. "Guarding the Wild: Place, Tradition, Literature and the Environment in the Work of a Cretan Folk Poet." *Journal of American Folklore* 119 (473): 275-300.

____. 2003. "Greek Food after *Mousaka*: Cookbooks, 'Local' Culture, and the Cretan Diet." *Journal of Modern Greek Studies* 21: 1-36.

Ball, Eric and Lai, Alice. 2006. "Place-Based Pedagogy for the Arts and Humanities." *Pedagogy: Critical Approaches to Teaching Literature, Language, Composition and Culture* 6 (2): 261-287.

Barba-Pantzelios (ed. by Vasileios Laourdas). 1947. *The Song of Daskalogiannis.* Heraklion: Mourmel. [GR]

Barbour, Karen. 2005. "We are Not Struggling, We are Thriving." *Danz Quarterly* 1. Retrieved March 5, 2013, from http://www.danz.org.nz/Magazines/DQ/Sept05/soul-speed.php.

Baud-Bovy, Samuel. 2006. *Musical Recordings in Crete: 1953-54.* Center for Asia Minor Studies: M. Merlie M.F.A.

Bauschatz, Paul. 1991. "Oedipus: Stravinsky and Cocteau Recompose Sophocles." *Comparative Literature* 43 (2): 150-170.

Beaton, Roderick. 2004. *Folk Poetry of Modern Greece.* Cambridge: Cambridge University Press.

_____. 1998. "Of Crete and Other Demons: A Reading of Kazantzakis' Freedom and Death." *Journal of Modern Greek Studies* 16 (2): 195-220.

_____. 1994. *An Introduction to Modern Greek Literature.* Oxford: Clarendon Press.

Bien, Peter. 2007. *Kazantzakis: The Politics of Spirit* (Volume II). Heraklion: Crete University Press. [GR]

_____. 2005. "Inventing Greece: The Emergence of Greek National Identity." *Journal of Modern Greek Studies* 23 (2): 217-234.

_____. 2001. *Kazantzakis: The Politics of Spirit (Volume I).* Heraklion: Crete University Press. [GR]

_____. 2000. "Nikos Kazantzakis' Novels on Film." *Journal of Modern Greek Studies* 18: 161-170.

_____. 1997. "*Melissa*, an Indication of the Kazantzakian Future." Scientific Proceedings *Nikos Kazantzakis: 40 Years from his Death*: 155-162.

_____. 1992. "Kazantzakis' 'Melissa.'" *Journal of Modern Greek Studies* 12: 34-44.

_____. 1989. *Nikos Kazantzakis Novelist.* Bristol.

_____. 1975. "Kazantzakis' *The Masterbuilder* with an Additional Note on *Kapodistrias.*" *The Literary Review* 18 (4): 398-411.

_____. 1974. "The Mellowed Nationalism of Kazantzakis' Zorba the Greek." *Review of National Literatures: Greece: The Modern Voice* 5 (2): 113-136.

_____. 1965. "Zorba the Greek, Nietzsche, and the Perennial Greek Predicament." *Antioch Review*, Spring.

Blacking, John. 1995. *Music, Culture, and Experience.* Chicago: University of Chicago Press.

Boardman, John, Kathleen M. Kenyon, E. J. Moynahan and J. D. Evans. 1976. "The Olive in the Mediterranean: Its Culture and Use." *Philosophical Transactions of the Royal Society of London*; Series B, Biological Sciences 275 (936): 187-196.

Bottomley, Gillian. 1992. *From Another Place: Migration and the Politics of Culture.* Sydney: Cambridge University Press.

Brumfield, Allaire. 1997. "Cakes in the Liknon: Votives from the Sanctuary of Demeter and

Kore on Acrocorinth." *Hesperia* 66 (1): 147-172.

Buettner, Dan. 2012. "The Island Where People Forget to Die." *New York Times*, October 24.   Retrieved March 5, 2013, from http://www.nytimes.com/2012/10/28/magazine/the-island-where-people-forget-to-die.html?pagewanted=all&_r=0.

Caraveli, Anna. 1985. "The Symbolic Village: Community Born in Performance." *Journal of American Folklore* 98 (389): 259: 286.

Chaniotaki-Smyrlaki, Argyro. 2008. "Chapter 3: The Role of the Samaria Gorge in History." Emmy Papavasileiou ed., *The Gorge of Samaria: Shelter for Life, Den of Freedom*. Samaria National Park Management Body: Prefectural Administration of Chania: 129-39.

Chrysostomou, Panos. 2006. *Nikos Mamangakis: I Hear Music, I Understand Life*. Athens: Agyra. [GR]

Clifford, James. 1997. *Routes: Travel and Translation in the Late Twentieth Century*. Cambridge MA: Harvard University Press.

_____. 1986. "On Ethnographic Authority." In James Clifford and George E. Marcus *Writing Culture: The Poetics and Politics of Ethnography*. Berkeley: University of California Press: 21-54.

Cohen, Sara. 2001. "Popular Music, Gender, and Sexuality." In S. Frith, W. Straw and J. Street (Eds.), *The Cambridge Companion to Pop and Rock*. Cambridge: Cambridge University Press: 226-242.

Communication, Cultural Newsletter 4 (Embassy of Greece in Beijing, Press and Communication Office). Retrieved March 5, 2013, from http://www.minpress.gr/minpress/cultural_newsletter_english_text_vol.04.pdf.

Conklin, Darrell and Christina Anagnostopoulou. 2011. "Comparative Pattern Analysis of Cretan Folk Songs." *Journal of New Music Research* 40: 2.

Constantinidis, Stratos. 1997. "The Appeal of Modern Greek Drama and Its Future in the English-speaking World." *Journal of Modern Greek Studies* 15 (2): 175-186.

Cooke, Mervyn (ed). 2005. *The Cambridge Companion to Twentieth-Century Opera*. Cambridge: Cambridge University Press.

Counihan, Carole. 1984. "Bread as World: Food Habits and Social Relations in Modernizing Sardinia." *Anthropological Quarterly* 57 (2): 47-59.

Cowan, Jane. 2000. "Greece." In *The Garland Encyclopedia of World Music*, edited by Tim Rice, James Porter and Chris Goertzen. New York: Garland (2): 1007-1032.

_____. 1990. *Dance and the Body Politics in Northern Greece*. Princeton: Princeton University Press.

Dalianoudi, Renata. 2010. *Manos Hadjidakis and Folk Music Tradition*. Athens: Embeiria Ekdotiki. [GR]

Daly, Ann. 1995. *Done into Dance: Isadora Duncan in America*. Middletown, Connecticut: Wesleyan University Press.

Daly, Ross. "About Music." Retrieved March 5, 2013, from http://www.rossdaly.gr/en/texts-recommendations/64-about-music-by-ross-daly.

_____. "Kelly Thoma." Retrieved March 5, 2013, from http://www.rossdaly.gr/en/projects/43-kelly-thoma.

_____. "Anamkhara by Kelly Thoma." 6/2/2010. Retrieved March 5, 2013, from http://www.

rossdaly.gr/el/news/99-kelly. [GR]

_____. 2008. *Ross Daly: White Dragon*. Sistron. CD.

_____. 2001. Interview, Houdetsi-Crete, 13 July.

_____. 2000. "Cretan Traditional Music: Ross Daly." *Welcome Crete* 5: 40-43.

_____. 1994. *Traditional Music Instruments: Music Instruments from Greece, Middle-East, North Africa, Central Asia and India*. Municipality of Patras. [GR]

_____. 1992. *Ross Daly & Labyrinth: Mitos*. Eurasia (8): World Network. CD.

Daly, Ross and Halkias, P. 2000. *Greeks and Indians*. Saraswati. SARA002. CD.

Daly, Ross and Stavrakakis, Mitsos. 1982. *Dreamlands*. Producer: Stelios Aerakis.

Dawe, Kevin. 2007. *Music and Musicians in Crete: Performance and Ethnography in a Mediterranean Island Society*. Lanham, Maryland; Toronto; Plymouth, UK: The Scarecrow Press.

_____(ed.). 2004. *Island Musics*. New York: Berg. "I do not accept Crete without *lira*, feast, without dance…" 2001. *Hyper-X* 26: 76-77. [GR]

Deffner, Michael. 1927. *Travel Impressions from Western Crete with Several Pictures*. Syllogos pros Diadosin Ofelimon Vivlion: Athens.

Deftereos, Angelos. 2000. *Bread at Greek Customs: Its Symbolic and Magic Use by Modern Greeks*. Athens: Legato. [GR]

Della Dora, Veronica. 2008. "Mountains and Memory: Embodied Visions of Ancient Peaks in the Nineteenth-century Aegean." *Transactions of the Institute of British Geographers* 33 (2): 217-232.

Dermitzakis, Emmanuel. 2008. *Based On What I Recall from the Old Big Castle*. Heraklion: Dokimakis. [GR]

Detorakis, Theoharis. 1977. "Observations on the Memetaka's Songs." *Amalthea*. [GR]

Dreese, Donelle. 2002. *Ecocriticism: Creating Self and Place in Environmental and American Indian Literatures*. New York: Peter Lang.

Diktakis, Athanasios. 1999. *Folk Musicians From Chania That Do Not Exist Anymore*. Kastelli-Kissamos. [GR]

Dimiroulis, Dimitris. 2007. "Everything Looks Magnified." *The Tree*: 155-156. [GR]

Dimou, Nikos. "Dialogues: The Metaphysics of 'Grinia.'" Retrieved March 5, 2013, from http://www.ndimou.gr/dial_7.asp.

_____. 1997. *Apology of an Anti-Hellene*. Athens: Opera. [GR]

_____. 2001. *Ironic Modern Greek Dictionary*. Athens: Patakis. [GR]

"Document: 1862 Crete, Under Turkish Rule, through a Letter by the American Ambassador." *Patris*: 6 November 2001. [GR]

Dontas, Nikos. 2008. "With the Vision of a New World." *Masterbuilder: Manolis Kalomiris*. Athens: Greek National Opera.

Dubisch, Jill (ed.). 1986. *Gender and Power in Rural Greece*. Princeton: Princeton University Press.

Dundes, Alan. 1996. *The Walled-Up Wife: A Casebook*. Madison: University of Wisconsin Press.

Duncan, Isadora. 1956. *The Art of the Dance*. New York: Theatre Arts Books.

____. 1927. *My Life*. New York: Boni and Liveright.

Durham, Valerie. 2006. "Isadora Duncan: Child of the Romantic, Rebel of the Victorian, Consummate Artist of the Modern." Retrieved March 5, 2013, from http://www.duncandancers.com/romanticism.html.

Economakis, Elias. 2008. *The Struggle for the Music of Eastern Crete*. Athens. [GR]

____. 2004. *Stratis Kalogeridis: His Music Work; His Contribution to the Music Tradition of Eastern Crete*. Athens. [GR]

Eliade, Mircea. 1972. *Zalmoxis, the Vanishing God: Comparative Studies in the Religions and Folklore of Dacia and Eastern Europe*. Chicago: University of Chicago Press.

Erdener, Yildiray. 1987. *Dueling Singers: Interaction Processes and Strategies among Turkish Minstrels*." Ph.D. dissertation, Indiana University.

Euripides. The Project Gutenberg EBook of *Iphigenia in Aulis*, by Euripides. Retrieved March 5, 2013, from http://www.gutenberg.org/catalog/world/readfile?fk_files=915468.

Farinou-Malamatari, Yeorgia. 1998. "Kazantzakis and Biography." *Nikos Kazantzakis Chania November 1997 Scientific Two-Days' Proceedings*: 163-178. [GR]

Father Philotheos (Abbot of the Toplou Monastery). 2003. "The Olive-tree and the Oil in Christian Religion." *Proceedings of the International Symposium on the Olive and Olive-Oil in Crete*. Sitia-Crete (SEDIK): 22-31. [GR]

Feld, Steven. 1989. *Sound and Sentiment*. Philadelphia: University of Pennsylvania Press.

Ferrario, Sarah. 2005. "Greek Tragedy and Opera: An Interdisciplinary Undergraduate Seminar." *Classical World* 99 (1): 51-66.

Fournarakis, Konstantinos. 1929. *Cretan Turks*. Chania: Yiannakoudakis. [GR]

Fragou-Psychopaedi, Olympia. 1990. *The National School of Music: Ideology Problems*. Athens: Institute of Mediterranean Studies. [GR]

Geertz, Clifford. 1988. *Works and Lives: The Anthropologist as Author*. Stanford University Press.

____.1973. "Thick Description: Toward an Interpretive Theory of Culture" and "The Politics of Meaning." *The Interpretation of Cultures*. New York: Basic Books: 3-32 & 311-326.

George, Sarah. 2009. *The Bridge of Arta as a Source for the Masterbuilder by Nikos Kazantzakis*. M.A. thesis, Department of Greek-Latin; Ghent University-Belgium.

Georgousopoulos, Kostas. 1984. "One Opera." *Ta Nea*, July 1. [GR]

Gilcrest, David. 2002. *Greening the Lyre: Environmental Poetics and Ethics*. University of Nevada Press.

Girard, Philippe. 1995. "Nikos Kazantzaki et la Musique." *Le Regard Cretois* (11) : 27-40.

Glassie, Henry. 1999. *The Potter's Art*. Bloomington: Indiana University Press.

____. 1989. *The Spirit of Folk Art: The Girard Collection at the Museum of International Folk Art*. New York: Harry N. Abrams, Inc., and Santa Fe: The Museum of New Mexico.

Glytzouris, Antonis. 2008. "The Masterbuilder's Mendings." *Ariadne* 14: 167-180. [GR]

Grassos, Yiorgos, ed. 2007. *Greece's Stone Arch Bridges*. Makrinitsa-Mt. Pelion: The Makrinitsa Center for Environmental Education. [GR]

Hadjidakis, Manos. 2007. *The Comments of the Third Program: A Modern Greek Mythology*.

Athens: Exandas. [GR]

_____. 2006. *Captain Michael*. MINOS-EMI. CD.

_____. 1988. *The Mirror and the Knife*. Athens: Ikaros. [GR]

Hadjidakis, Yeorgios. 1958. *Cretan Music: History, Music Theory, Songs and Dances*. Athens: Unpublished. [GR]

Hamilakis, Yannis. 1999. "Food Technologies/Technologies of the Body: The Social Context of Wine and Oil Production and Consumption in Bronze Age Crete." *World Archaeology* 31 (1): 38-54.

Hanna, Judith. 1979. *To Dance is Human: A Theory of Nonverbal Communication*. Austin and London: University of Texas Press.

Hannam, Kevin, Sheller, M., Urry, J. 2006. "Mobilities, Immobilities and Moorings." Editorial Introduction to *Mobilities* 1 (1): 1-22.

Haralambous, Christos. 2003. *Nikos Xylouris: Through the String of the Lira*. Athens: Exandas. [GR]

Hartocollis, Peter. 1974. "Mysticism and Violence: The Case of Nikos Kazantzakis." *International Journal of Psycho-Analysis* 55: 205-210.

Hatziantoniou, Natali. "Cretan in Spirit, but not Literally." *Eleftherotypia*, 3/2/2010. Retrieved March 5, 2013, from http://www.enet.gr/?i=news.el.article&id=128235.

Hay, Pete. 2006. "A Phenomenology of Islands." *Island Studies Journal 1* (1): 19-42.

Herzfeld, Michael. 1992. *The Social Production of Indifference: Exploring the Symbolic Roots of Western Bureaucracy*. Oxford: Berg.

_____. 1991a. "Performances of Masculinity in Mountain Crete." *Archaeology 41*: 72-78. [GR]

_____. 1991b. *A Place in History: Monumental and Social Time in a Cretan Town*. Princeton NJ: Princeton University Press.

_____. 1987. *Anthropology through the Looking-Glass: Critical Ethnography in the Margins of Europe*. Cambridge: Cambridge University Press.

_____. 1986. "Within and Without: The Category of 'Female' in the Ethnography of Rural Greece." In *Gender and Power in Rural Greece*, ed. J. Dubisch. Princeton: Princeton University Press.

_____. 1985. *The Poetics of Manhood: Contest and Identity in a Cretan Mountain Village*. Princeton, N.J.: Princeton University Press.

_____. 1984. "The Horns of the Mediterraneanist Dilemma." *American Ethnologist* 11: 439-54.

_____. 1982. *Ours Once More: Folklore, Ideology and the Making of Modern Greece*. Austin: University of Texas Press.

_____. 1981. "Performative Categories and Symbols of Passage in Rural Greece." *The Journal of American Folklore* 94 (371): 44-57.

Hetherington, Kevin. 1997. "In Place of Geometry: The Materiality of Place." *Ideas of Difference*. Oxford: Blackwell.

Hillman, James. 1985. *Freud's Own Cookbook*. New York: Harper Collins.

"Historic Notes." 21-26 December 2007. *Kriti Press* 90: 8. [GR]

Hnaraki, Maria. 2012a. "Cretan Identity through its Dancing History." *Papers in Ethnology and Anthropology* 19 (8): 65-86.

____. 2012b. Co-published, prefaced, edited and translated *Folk Musicians from Crete-Giorgis Mathianakis or Psaros & Manolis Mathianakis or Alagnianos: Eastern Crete-Pediada County No. 5*, 2 audio CDs accompanied by booklet, published by the Municipality of Minoa-Pediada.

____. 2012c. Co-published, prefaced, edited and translated *Folk Musicians from Crete-Yannis Fragoulidakis or Skarpathiotis: Eastern Crete-Pediada County No. 4*, 2 audio CDs & DVD, accompanied by booklet, published by the Municipality of Minoa-Pediada.

____. 2012d. "Maria Callas." *Greek Ethos* 14. Greek Olympic Society, Columbus: Ohio.

____. 2011a. "Are Greeks Really European?" *IBT Times*, by Palash R. Ghosh, November 09: Retrieved March 5, 2013, from http://www.ibtimes.com/are-greeks-really-european-212891.

____. 2011b. Co-published, prefaced, edited and translated *Folk Musicians from Crete-Giorgis Maravgakis-Droseros: Eastern Crete-Pediada County No. 3*, audio CD & DVD, accompanied by booklet, published by the Municipality of Minoa-Pediada.

____. 2011c. Co-published, prefaced, edited and translated *Folk Musicians from Crete-Manolis Chaniotakis: Eastern Crete-Pediada County No. 2*, audio CD accompanied by booklet, published by the Municipality of Minoa-Pediada.

____. 2011d. "From Homeric Poetry to Cretan Balladry: The Daskaloyannis Song." *Papers in Ethnology and Anthropology* 18 (7): 123-132.

____. 2011e. "Iphigenias Walling-up Bridges: Sacrifice as Music Performance." In *PAX SONORIS: History and Today* (4). Astrakhan: Russia: 167-179.

____. 2011f. "Music Passports and Customs: Ross Daly and the Cretan *Lyra* Transcending Borderlines." *Thematic Journal: Tradition-Folklore-Identity*. Sremski Karlovci: 41-68.

____. 2011g. "Souls of Soil: Island Identity through Song." In Godfrey Baldacchino (ed.) *Island Songs*. Lanham MD: The Scarecrow Press: 171-185.

____. 2011h. "Roman the Melodist." *Greek Ethos* 12. Greek Olympic Society, Columbus: Ohio.

____. 2010/11. "Eastern and Western Traffic Lights: Cretan Cultural Crossroads."
Modern Greek Studies Yearbook 26/27: 157-188.

____. 2010a. "Baked Realities: Big Fat Greek Breads." *Petis Propos Cullinaires* 89: 35-66.

____. 2010b. "Big Fat Green Rhymes: Unfolding the Environmental Clue of Cretan Songs." *Papers in Ethnology and Anthropology* 16 (5): 96-105.

____. 2010c. "Collectors and Scholars of Cretan Folktales: A Tale by a Cretan World War I Survivor at the Gorlitz Concentration Camp." Co-presented with Emeritus Professor Theoharis Detorakis. Conference on "The Cretan Tale." Kastelli-Pediada, Crete-Greece. September 24. [GR]

Hnaraki, Maria. 2010d. "Foreword." George Koumendakis' Full Score *Amor Fati*. Hellenic Music Centre.

____. 2010e. Co-published and edited *Iraklis Stavroulakis 1919-1997: The Master Violinist, a book accompanied by 3 CDs & 1 DVD*. Municipality of Episkopi, Heraklion-Crete, Greece. Prologue and English summary as well.

_____. 2010f. Audio-edited and co-published the audio CD *Sophocles Venizelos Funeral: Chania, February 9, 1964*. National Research Foundation "Eleftherios K. Venizelos." Chania-Crete, Greece.

_____. 2009a. "Classical Masterpieces: Nikos Kazantzakis's *Melissa* and Theodore Antoniou's *Periander*." *Conference Proceedings: Greek Music for the Opera and Other Forms of the Performing Arts in the 20th Century*: 220-228. The Friends of Music Association: The Athens Concert Hall-Greece & The Music Library of Greece "Lilian Voudouri." [GR]

_____. 2009b. "Ross Daly, the Cretan *lyra* and Tuvan throat singing." In *East and West: Ethnic Identity and Traditional Music Heritage as a Dialogue of Civilizations and Cultures*. Materials of the International Scientific Congress. State Folklore Center. Astrakhan Russia: September 2008: 203-209.

_____. 2009c. "Speaking without Words: Zorba's Dance." *Bulletin of the Institute of Ethnography SANU LVII* (2): 25-35.

_____. 2009d. "We Speak What We Eat." *The Smart Set*. November 13, 2009. Retrieved March 5, 2013, from http://www.thesmartset.com/article/article11130901.aspx).

_____. 2008a. "Beyond Zorba and Captain-Michael: Music tradition and globalization through the work of Nikos Kazantzakis." *Greek Artistic Music Creation: Tradition and Globalization* Conference Proceedings: 26-33.

_____. 2008b. "Bridging Kazantzakis' *The Offering* and Kalomiris' *The Masterbuilder*." *Masterbuilder: Manolis Kalomiris*. Athens: Greek National Opera: 59-62.

_____. 2007. *Unraveling Ariadne's Thread: Cretan Music*. Athens: Kerkyra Publications.

Hnaraki, Maria. 2006a. "Greece." In Sean Williams (ed.) *The Ethnomusicologist's Cookbook*. New York: Routledge Press: 240-245.

_____. 2006b. "Greek Folklore." In William Clements (ed.) *The Greenwood Encyclopedia of World Folklore and Folklife*. London: Greenwood Press: 493-501.

_____. 2006c. "Speaking without Words: Cretan Dance at Weddings as Expression, Dialogue and Communication." *Folklor Edebiyat* 45 (1): 93-106.

_____. 2004. "Is King Zeus Alive? Dance Mythomusicologies in the Mountainous Crete." *Archaeology & Arts* 92: 68-75. [GR]

_____. 1998. *Speaking Without Words: Cretan Dance at Weddings as Expression, Dialogue and Communication*. M.A. thesis, Department of Folklore & Ethnomusicology; Indiana University.

Hnaraki, Maria and Papoutsaki, Evangelia. 2012. "Twice-Baked Bread: Dakos." *A Taste of Islands: 60 Recipes and Stories from Our World of Islands*. Island Studies: University of Prince Edward Island Press: 105-7.

Hnaraki, Maria and Samprovalakis, Yannis. 2013. "The Masterbuilder's Bridges: 'Logos' in Kazantzakis' theatrical play and Kalomoiris' opera." *Manolis Kalomoiris: 50 Years After, an Anniversary Volume*. Athens: Fagotto Books: 105-122.

_____. 2010. "Kazantzakis-Kalomiris: Two Greek Masterbuilders." *Tradition and Modernization in the Modern Greek Theater: 3rd Panhellenic Theater Conference Proceedings*, eds. Antonis Glytzouris and Konstantina Georgiadi. Heraklion: Crete University Press: 487-96. [GR]

Hobsbawm, Eric and Terence Ranger. 1983. *The Invention of Tradition*. Cambridge: Cambridge University Press.

Holst-Warhaft, Gail. 1998. "Rebetika: The Double-Descended Deep Songs of Greece." In *The Passion of Music and Dance: Body, Gender and Sexuality*, ed. William Washabaugh. Oxford: Berg: 111-26.

_____. 1997. "Song, Self-Identity, and the Neohellenic." *Journal of Modern Greek Studies* 15 (2): 232-238.

Homenidis, Christos. 08/03/2008. "Constantinos Karamanlis: Karamanlis Brings You the Bread." *E-tipos.com*. [GR]

Homer. 1996. *The Odyssey*. Translated by Robert Fagles. New York: Viking/Penguin.

Hortatsis, Georgios (ed. Stylianos Alexiou and Martha Aposkiti). 1996. *Erofili: Tragedy*. Athens: Stigmi. [GR]

Hulot, M. "Psarantonis!" *Lifo* 24/5/2007. Retrieved March 5, 2013, from http://www.lifo.gr/mag/features/78. [GR]

_____.1974. "Daskalogiannis' Revolution in Sfakia." *Istoria tou Ellinikou Ethnous* (11): 76. Athens: EKDOTIKE ATHENON. [GR]

Isadora Duncan: Movement from the Soul. 1987. A Geller/Goldfine production. DVD.

Jones, Michael Owen. 2007. "Food Choice, Symbolism, and Identity: Bread and Butter Issues for Folkloristics and Nutrition Studies." *Journal of American Folklore* 120 (476): 129-177.

Jovanovic, Jelena. 2007. *Iphigenia's Myth in Z. Racine, Y. Ritsos and Contemporary Poetry*. M.A. thesis, Department of Theatre Studies; University of Patras-Greece. [GR]

Jowitt, Deborah. 1985. "Images of Isadora: The Search for Motion." *Dance Research Journal* 17 (2): 21-29.

Kaeppler, Adrienne. "Theoretical and Methodological Considerations for Anthropological Studies of Dance and Human Movement Systems." 1992. *Ethnographica* 8: 151-157. The Peloponnesian Folklore Foundation.

Kallergis, Mihalis. *Aroma of Crete*. 2001. Heraklion, Crete: Aerakis, Cretan Musical Workshop.

Kalomiris, Manolis. 1988. *My Life and my Art*. Athens: Nefeli. [GR]

_____. 1959. "Constantine Palaiologos." *New Hestia* 66: 1290. [GR]

_____. 1957. "From 'The Masterbuilder' to 'Constantine Palaiologos.'" *Ethnos*, November 13. [GR]

_____. 1946. "The Unknown Music Composer of Our Folk Song." *Academy of Athens Proceedings* 21. [GR]

_____. 1939/40. *The Masterbuilder: Music tragedy in Two Parts and an Intermezzo*. Athens: Gaitanos. [GR]

_____. 1916. "*Masterbuilder's* Prologue." Athens. [GR]

Kaloyanides, Michael. 1975. *The Study of Cretan Dances: A Study of the Musical Structures of Cretan Dance Forms as Performed in the Heraklion Province of Crete*. Unpublished PhD thesis, Wesleyan University.

Kaplanoglou, Marianthi. 2006. "The Folk Cult of St Phanourios in Greece and Cyprus, and its Relationship with the International Tale Type 804." *Folklore* 117 (1): 54-74.

Kapsetakis, Lambis. 2007. "The Poetry in the Memory of Daskalogiannis." *Apopsis* (2). Retrieved March 5, 2013, from http://lyk-aei.reth.sch.gr/yliko/ekdoseis/apopseis2/Apopseis2_kapsetakis.pdf. [GR]

Kastrinaki, Angela. 2006. "'Greek Wild Carry-ons and All That': Zorba, an Internationalist during Occupation." *Nikos Kazantzakis 2004 University of Crete Conference Proceedings*: 151-62. [GR]

Katerinakis, Theodoros. 2012. "The Atypical Case of Cooperative Banking: Cooperative Bank of Chania." In Spitzeck, H., Pirson M., and Dierksmeier C. (eds.) *Banking with Integrity: The winners of the financial crisis?*. Palgrave Macmillan, New York: 91-106.

Kazantzaki, Eleni. 1984. *Four-hundred Letters of Kazantzakis to Prevelakis*. Athens: Kazantzakis Publications. [GR]

_____.1983. *Nikos Kazantzakis: The Uncompromising*. Athens: Kazantzakis Publications. [GR]

Kazantzakis, Nikos (trans. Kimon Friar). 1985. *The Odyssey: A Modern Sequel*. New York: Simon and Schuster.

_____(trans. Peter Bien). 1976. "Drama and Contemporary Man." *The Literary Review* 19 (2): 115-121.

_____. 1969. *Traveling: Italy, Egypt, Jerusalem, Cyprus, the Morea*. Athens: Eleni Kazantzaki. [GR]

_____. 1965. *Report to Greco*. New York: Simon and Schuster.

_____. 1964. *Tragedies with Ancient Themes (Theater): Prometheus, Kouros, Odysseus, Melissa*. Athens: Kazantzakis Publications. [GR]

_____. 1960. *Tertsines*. Athens-Greece. [GR]

_____. 1954. *The Greek Passion*. New York: Simon and Schuster.

_____. 1953a. *Captain Michael*. Athens: Mavridis. [GR]

_____. 1953b. *Zorba the Greek*. New York: Simon and Schuster.

_____(as Petros Psiloritis). 1910. *The Masterbuilder: Tragedy*. Athens: Panathenaea Magazine Publications. [GR]

Kolovos, Andy. 2010. *Archiving Culture: American Folklore Archives in Theory and Practice*. Ph.D. dissertation submitted to the Department of Folklore and Ethnomusicology, Indiana University.

Kornaros, Vitsentzos (ed. Stylianos Alexiou). 1994. *Erotokritos*. Athens: Hermes. [GR]

Korsmeyer, Carolyn. 2002. *Making Sense of Taste: Food and Philosophy*. Ithaca-NY: Cornell University Press.

Kostios, Apostolos. "Dimitri Mitropoulos: Life part (a): What? Where? When?" Retrieved March 5, 2013, from http://www.dimitrimitropoulos.gr/index.php?option=com_content&view=article&id=19&Itemid=32&lang=en. [GR]

_____. "D. Mitropoulos' Music for Euripides' *Hippolytus*." Retrieved March 5, 2013, from http://www.dimitrimitropoulos.gr/index.php?option=com_content&view=article&id=90%3Agiaapkostioshmousikigiatonypolytoeyripidiaggliko&catid=15&Itemid=51&lang=en. [GR]

_____. "Dimitri Mitropoulos' 10 Inventions" (trans. Demetrios Lekkas). Retrieved March

5, 2013, from http://www.dimitrimitropoulos.gr/?option=com_content&view=article&id=53%3Agia9dm10inventions&catid=15&Itemid=51&lang=en. [GR]

____. 2010. "Dimitri Mitropoulos as composer (1) & (2)." *Polytonon* 41 & 42: 33-38 & 33-36. [GR]

____.1985. *Dimitri Mitropoulos*. Athens: National Bank Cultural Foundation. [GR]

Koumendakis, George. 2010. *Amor Fati*. Athens: Hellenic Music Centre in Collaboration with the Thessaloniki Symphony Orchestra.

____. 1995. *Iphigenia at the Bridge of Arta: For Soprano, Trumpet and Sampled Piano*. Commissioned by The Athens Concert Hall. Greece: Label O.E.S.19. CD.

Krochmal, Arnold. 1955. "Olive-Growing in Greece." *Economic Botany* 9 (3): 228-232.

Kurth, Peter. 2002. *Isadora: A Sensational Life*. Back Bay Books.

Lagoudianaki, Lina. 2011. "Psarantonis: The Lyre is the Instrument of God." *Stigmes* January-February: 16-20. [GR]

LaMothe, Kimerer. 2006. *Nietzsche's Dancers: Isadora Duncan, Martha Graham, and the Revaluation of Christian Values*. New York: Palgrave MacMillan.

League, Panagiotis. "Rewriting Unwritten History: Folklore, Mass Media, and the Ban of the Cretan Violin." Retrieved March 5, 2013, from http://chs.harvard.edu/wa/pageR?tn=ArticleWrapper&bdc=12&mn=4885.

Leontis, Artemis. 1999. "The Bridge between the Classical and the Balkan." *The South Atlantic Quarterly* 98 (4): 633-654.

Leotsakos, George. 2006. "Theodore Antoniou." *The New Grove Dictionary of Music and Musicians*. Edited by Stanley Sadie and John Tyrell. Oxford: Oxford University Press.

____. 1986. "*The Masterbuilder*, 'Masterpiece' in Greek music." *Musicology* 1. [GR]

"Lesson Plan #1: The Bouncy Run; Atlanta and the Golden Apples." 2004. *Isadora and the Ancient Greeks*. New York: Isadora Duncan Foundation.

Levin, Theodore (with Valentina Süzükei). 2006. *Where Rivers and Mountains Sing: Sound, Music, and Nomadism in Tuva and Beyond*. Bloomington, IN: Indiana University Press.

Llewelyn, Michael. 1965. *The Great Island: A Study of Crete*. London: Longmans.

Long, Lucy. 2009. "Introduction." *Journal of American Folklore* 122 (483): 3-10.

Lord, Albert Bates. 1960. *The Singer of Tales*. Cambridge, MA: Harvard University Press.

Loukatos, Dimitrios. 1977. *Introduction to Greek Folklore*. Athens: MIET (Educational Foundation, National Bank of Greece). [GR]

Loule, Litsa. 2010. *Nikos Xylouris*. Athens: Diaplasi. [GR]

Lowenthal, Lillian. *1993. The Search for Isadora: The Legend and Legacy of Isadora Duncan*. Pennington, NJ: Princeton Book Company; Dance Horizons.

MacClancy, Jeremy. 1992. *Consuming Culture: Why You Eat What You Eat*. New York: Henry Holt.

Magrini, Tullia. 2003. "Introduction: Studying Gender in Mediterranean Musical Cultures." *Music and Gender: Perspectives from the Mediterranean*. Chicago: Chicago University Press: 1-32.

____. 2002. "Repertories and Identities of a Musician from Crete." *Ethnomusicology on Line* (EOL) 3. Retrieved March 5, 2013, from http://www.umbc.edu/eol/3/magrini/index.

html.

_____. 2000. "Manhood and Music in Western Crete: Contemplating Death." *Ethnomusicology* 44 (3): 429-459.

Magrini, Tullia and Roberto Leydi (eds.). 2000. *Vocal music in Crete (CD with booklet).* Washington, D.C.: Smithsonian Folkways Recordings SFW CD 40437.

Makreas, Mary Ellen. 1979. *Cretan Dance: The Meaning of Kefi and Figures.* M.A. thesis, Indiana University.

Maliaras, Nikos. 2001. *The Greek Folk Song in Manolis Kalomiris' Music.* Athens-Greece: Papagrigoriou-Nakas. [GR]

_____. 1995. "Aegean and Cretan Folk Songs in Manolis Kalomiris' Music." *Mandatophoros* 39-40: 143-170. [GR]

Mandel, Ruth. 1983. "Sacrifice at the Bridge of Arta: Sex Roles and the Manipulation of Power." *Journal of Modern Greek Studies* 1 (1): 173-183.

Manouselis, Yeorgios. 2003. *Small and Big Birds of Our Landscape.* Chania-Crete: Greece. [GR]

Marranchi, Gabriele. 2002. "Sounds Moving Around: Algerian Raï and Rap." *Musica E Storia* X (2): 570-579. Venezia: Fondazione Ugo e Olga Levi.

Mason, Melissa Caswell. 1982. "You Said a Mouthful: Food and Food-Related Metaphors in Folkspeech." *Folklore and Mythology Studies* 6: 29-33.

Masterbuilder. CD. #4998030490. Grant chorus of the USSR state radio-television and state cinematographic orchestra.

Matthias, Susan. 1998. "Prologue to Zorba the Greek." *Journal of Modern Greek Studies* 16 (2): 241-245.

Mazo, Joseph. 2000. *Prime Movers: The Makers of Modern Dance in America.* Hightstown, N.J.: Princeton Book Co.

McColley, Diane Kelsey. 2007. *Poetry and Ecology in the Age of Milton and Marvell.* Great Britain: Ashgate Publishing.

McCracken, Janet. 2001. *Taste and the Household: The "Domestic Aesthetic" and Moral Reasoning.* New York: State University of New York Press.

McDonald, Marianne. 1983. "Cacoyannis and Euripides *Iphigenia at Aulis*: A New Heroism." *Euripides in Cinema: The Heart Made Visible.* Philadelphia: Centrum: 129-191.

_____.1990. "Iphigenia's 'Philia': Motivation in Euripides 'Iphigenia at Aulis.'" *Quaderni Urbinati di Cultura Classica, New Series,* Vol. 34 (1): 69-84.

Megas, Georgios. 1971. "The Song of the Bridge of Arta: A Comparative Study." In *Laographia*: 27: 25-211. [GR]

Meneley, Anne. 2007. "Like An Extra Virgin." *American Anthropologist* 109 (4): 678-687.

Merriam, Alan. 1964. *The Anthropology of Music.* Evanston, IL: Northwestern University Press.

Merrill, Reed. 1975. "'Zorba the Greek' and Nietzschean Nihilism." *Mosaic* 8 (2): 99-113.

"Mesara, the Home of Europe." Patris: 2 November 2001. [GR]

Miller, Henry. 1975. *The Colossus of Maroussi.* New York: New Directions.

Milona, Katerina. 2/7/2009. "Karagiozis Will Always be the Persecuted Who is Asking for

Justice: Karagiozis-Artist Yiannis Athanasiou Reports." *Patris*. [GR]

Milona, Marianthi. 2004. *Culinaria Greece: Greek Specialties*. Ullmann Publishing.

Miralis, Yiannis. 2004. "Manos Hadjidakis: The Story of an Anarchic Youth and a 'Magnus Eroticus.'" *Philosophy of Music Education Review* 12 (1): 43-54.

Morgan, Gareth. 1960. "Cretan Poetry: Sources and Inspiration." *Cretan Annals 14*: 4-68, 203-270 & 379-434.

Morton, Mark. 2005. "Boning Up on Language." *Gastronomica: The Journal of Food and Culture* 5 (4): 6-7.

Mourrais-Velloudios, Thanos. 1966. "Example of a Pyrrichios in 9/8 or 'Artozinos' Namely 'Zeibekikon.'" *Eos* 98-102: 116-125. [GR]

Mu Quian. 2007. "Go Greek and You Shall Find." *China Daily*: 8.

Nettl, Bruno. 1996. "Relating the Present to the Past: Thoughts on the Study of Musical Change and Culture Change in Ethnomusicology." *Music & Anthropology* 1.

Nora, Pierre and Lawrence Kirtzman (eds.). 1996. *Realms of Memory: Rethinking the French Past; Vol. 1: Conflicts and Divisions*. New York: Columbia University Press.

Notopoulos, James. 1964. "Studies in Early Greek Oral Poetry." *Harvard Studies in Classical Philology* 68: 1-77.

_____. 1959. "Modern Greek Heroic Oral Poetry and its Relevance to Homer." Liner notes accompanying Folkways Record FE 4468, *Modern Greek Heroic Oral Poetry*. New York: Folkways.

_____. 1952. "Homer and Cretan Heroic Poetry: A Study in Comparative Oral Poetry." *American Journal of Philology* 73: 225-50.

Orfanos, Spyros. 2006. "Mythos and Logos." *Psychoanalytic Dialogues* 16 : 481-499.

Paganos, Yiorgos. 2/29/2004. "Kneaded with Honey…" *Kathimerini*. [GR]

Panayotakis, Nikolaos (ed.). 1987. *Crete: History and Civilization*. Heraklion-Crete: Syndesmos Topikon Enoseon Dimon ke Koinotiton Kritis. [GR]

Papahatzaki-Katsaraki, Theodora. 1985. *Nikos Kazantzakis' Theatrical Plays*. Athens/Ioannina: Dodoni. [GR]

Papaioannou, John. "Dimitri Mitropoulos: A Greek Sonata (orig. Eine Griechische Sonate)." Retrieved March 5, 2013, from http://www.dimitrimitropoulos.gr/index.php?option=com_content&view=article&id=88%3Agiapapaioanugreeksonatesaggliko&catid=15&Itemid=51&lang=en. [GR]

_____. 1983. "Kazantzakis and Music." *Journal of the Hellenic Diaspora* 10 (4): 79-83.

Papalexandrou, Nassos. 2007. "Constructed Landscapes: Visual Cultures of Violent Contact." *Stanford Journal of Archaeology* 5: 164-182.

Papanikolaou, Dimitris. 2006. *Zorba's Transformations*. Nikos Kazantzakis 2004 University of Crete Conference Proceedings: 91-108. [GR]

Papavasileiou, Emmy (ed.). 2008. *The Gorge of Samaria: Shelter for Life, Den of Freedom*. Samaria National Park Management Body: Prefectural Administration of Chania.

Paschalides, Miltos. 2010. *Xenios*. MINOS-EMI: 5099962808224.

Pavlopoulos, Dimitris. 2/29/2004. "Through Color and Light." *Kathimerini*. [GR]

Petrakis, Savvas. 2005. "A Reference to the Music Tradition of Viannos." *Proceedings of the*

Panviannitiko Conference (1): 429-435. [GR]

Petrakou, Kyriaki. 2005. *Kazantzakis and the Theater.* Athens: Militos. [GR]

Petrides, Ted. 1989. "Greek Folk Dances and Change." In *The Dance Event: A Complex Cultural Phenomenon*, ed. L. Torp. Copenhagen: ICTM STG on Ethnochoreology.

Petropoulos, Dimitris. 1954. "The Songs of Daskalogiannis." *Kritika Chronika* (8): 227-37. [GR]

Philippides, Stamatis. 2010. "Dostoyevsky's Descendants and Kazantzakis." *Kazantzakis in the 21st Century: Nikos Kazantzakis 2007 University of Crete Conference Proceedings.* Crete University Press: 477-520. [GR]

_____. 2005. *Ambivalences: Theses on the Narrative Word of Six Modern Greek Writers.* Athens: Indiktos. [GR]

_____.1997. *Topos: Theses on the Narrative Word of Seven Modern Greek Writers.* Athens: Kastaniotis. [GR]

Plastino, Goffredo. 2003. "Introduction: Sailing the Mediterranean Musics" in *Mediterranean Mosaic.* London/New York: Routledge: 1-36.

Politis, Nikolaos. 1914. *Some Songs of the Greek People.* Athens: Estia. [GR]

Pollan, Michael. 2009. *In Defense of Food: The Myth of Nutrition and The Pleasures of Eating: An Eater's Manifesto.* Penguin.

Poulakidas, Andreas. 1983. "The Operatic Aspects of Kazantzakis' 'Broken Souls.'" *Folia Neohellenica* 5: 157-173. [GR]

Preston, Carrie. 2005. "The Motor in the Soul: Isadora Duncan and Modernist Performance." *Modernism/Modernity* 12 (2): 273-289.

Prifti, Kleopatra. 1999. "Harmonie Musicale dans l' Oeuvre de Nikos Kazantzaki." *Le Regard Cretois* 19: 9-18.

Psarantonis. 2001. Interview, Heraklion, Crete, 15 June.

_____. 1999. *Ideon Andron.* CD: LYRA, ML 4948.

Psilakis, Nikos. 1997. "Crete in the Life and Work of Nikos Kazantzakis: Nikos Kazantzakis' Knowledge of Crete." *Hyper-X* 19: 19-26. [GR]

_____. 1996. *Cretan Mythology.* Heraklion: Karmanor.

Psilakis, Maria and Nikos. 1997. *Cretan Cooking: The Miracle of the Cretan Diet.* Heraklion: Karmanor.

_____. 2001. *The Bread of the Greeks and the Confectioneries of Our Folk Tradition: A Folklore, Gastronomic and Historic Passage Based on Cretan Fermentations (and 450 Recipes).* Heraklion: Karmanor. [GR]

Rackham, Oliver and Moody, Jennifer. 1997. *The Making of the Cretan Landscape.* Manchester University Press.

Raftis, Alkis. 1995. *Encyclopedia of Greek Dance.* Athens: Theater of Dora Stratou. [GR]

Reid, Robin. 2008. "On the Job: Choreographer." *Smithsonian.com*, May 1. Retrieved March 5, 2013, from http://www.smithsonianmag.com/arts-culture/on-the-job-choreographer.html.

Renfrew, Colin and Evi Margaritis. 2011. "Olives: Oiling the Wheels of Civilization." *Current World Archaeology* 48: 46-50.

Riak, Patricia. 2007. "A Cultural Interpretation of Greek Dance." *Journal of the Hellenic Diaspora* 33 (1 & 2): 39-59.

____. 2003. "The Performative Context: Song-Dance on Rhodes Island." *Modern Greek Studies* (Australia and New Zealand) 11: 212-227.

Riginiotis, Theodoros. "Christians and Turks: The Language of Music and Everyday Life." Retrieved March 5, 2013, from http://www.muammerketencoglu.com/imgs/Christian-andTurks.pdf. [GR]

Riglis, Stelios. 2005. *Cretan Healthy Diet*. Athens: Kerkyra.

Rigotti, Francesca. 2008. *Philosophy in the Kitchen: A Small Critique of Culinary Reason*. Athens: Polytropon.

Rosemont, Franklin. 2001. *Isadora Speaks: The Writings and Speeches of Isadora Duncan*. Chicago: Charles H. Kerr Publishing Company.

Rothstein, Edward. 2004. "How the Ancients Became Trendy: The Road From Euripides to Revolution." *The New York Times*: October 29.

Rueckert, William. 1996. "Literature and Ecology: An Experiment in Ecocriticism." In Glotfelty, C. and Harold F. (eds.), *The Ecocriticism Reader: Landmarks in Literary Ecology*. University of Georgia Press: 105-123.

Sachs, Curt. 1937. *World History of the Dance*. New York: W. W. Norton & Company, Inc.

Sadie, Stanley (ed.). 2001. "Mitropoulos, Dimitri." *New Grove Dictionary of Music and Musicians*. London: Macmillan.

Saritas, Suheyla. 2011. "The Importance of Wheat in Teething Celebration in Turkish Culture." *International Journal of Sociology and Anthropology* 3 (4): 120-126.

Savigliano, Marta. 1995. *Tango and the Political Economy of Passion*. Boulder-San Francisco-Oxford: Westview Press.

Schnapp, Alain. 1996. *The Discovery of the Past*. New York: Abrams.

Schumann, Peter. 1968. "Bread and Puppets." *TDR: The Drama Review* 12 (2): 35.

Scigaj, Leonard. 1999. *Sustainable Poetry: Four American Ecopoets*. University Press of Kentucky.

Segal, Charles. 1974. "The Raw and the Cooked in Greek Literature: Structure, Values, Metaphor. *The Classical Journal* 69 (4): 289-308.

Segan, Francine. 2004. *The Philosopher's Kitchen: Recipes from Ancient Greece and Rome for the Modern Cook*. New York: Random House.

Seremetakis, Nadia. 2004. "On the Branches of Memory." *Ode to the Olive Tree*. Academy of Athens-Hellenic Folklore Research Center & General Secretariat for the Olympic Games: Hellenic Ministry of Culture.

Seroff, Victor Ilyitch. 1971. *The Real Isadora*. New York: Dial Press.

Shapiro, Joseph. 2007. "At Home on the Island of Warmth and Hospitality." *NPR*, July 30. Retrieved March 5, 2013, from http://www.npr.org/templates/story/story.php?storyId=12359170.

Shelemay, Kay. 2000. *Soundscapes*. New York: W. W. Norton and Company.

Shiloah, Amnon. 2002. "On Jewish and Muslim Musicians of the Mediterranean." *Ethnomusicology on Line* (EOL) 3. Retrieved March 5, 2013, from http://www.umbc.edu/

eol/3/shiloah/.

Skoulas, Vasilis. 2001. Interview, Anogia, Crete, 1 September.

Smith, Susan. 1994. "Soundscape." *Area 26* (3): 232-240.

Solomon, Thomas. 1997. *Mountains of Song: Musical Constructions of Ecology, Place, and Identity in the Bolivian Andes*. Ph.D. thesis; University of Texas, Austin.

Stathis, Evangelos. 2004. *Greek Folk Songs*. Athens: Sideris Publishing. [GR]

Stassinopoulos, Arianna. 1981. *Maria Callas: The Woman behind the Legend*. New York: Simon and Schuster.

Stavrakakis, Vasilis. 2001. Interview, Ammoudara, Crete, 22 August.

Stavrakakis, Mitsos and Vasilis. 2001. *In the Winds' Vortex*. Heraklion-Athens: Sistron-Music Box International S.A. CD 16555.

Steegmuller, Francis. 1974. *"Your Isadora": The Love Story of Isadora Duncan & Gordon Craig*. New York: Random House & The New York Public Library.

Steichen, Edward. 1959. "My Life in Photography." *Saturday Review*.

Sternberg, Esther. 2012. "The Science of Healing Places." *NPR*, September 27: "On Being" with Krista Tippett. Retrieved March 5, 2013, from http://www.onbeing.org/program/science-healing-places/4856.

Stokes, Martin (ed.). 1994. *Ethnicity, Identity and Music: The Musical Construction of Place*. Oxford/Providence, USA: Berg.

Stonehouse, Paul, Pete Allison and David Carr. 2009. "Aristotle, Plato, and Socrates: Ancient Greek Perspectives on Experiential Learning." In T. Smith & C. Knapp (eds.) *Beyond Dewey and Hahn: Standing on the Shoulders of Influential Experiential Educators*. Wisconsin: Raccoon Institute Publications: 29-41.

Stratigakos, Stavros. 2006. *Nikos Xylouris and Three Poems*. Victory Media A.E. 2 DVDs with liner notes/album.

Stroebel, Margaret. 1979. "Women, Weddings, and Swahili Culture." *Muslim Women in Mombasa, 1890-1975*. New Haven: Yale University Press: 8-21.

Sugarman, Jane. 1997. *Engendering Song: Singing and Subjectivity at Prespa Albanian Weddings*. Chicago and London: The University of Chicago Press.

Sumption, Lois & Ashbrook, Marguerite. 1941. *Breads and More Breads*. Peoria-Illinois: The Manual Arts Press.

Sutton, David. 2001. *Remembrance of Repasts: An Anthropology of Food and Memory*. New York: Berg.

Sykäri, Venla. 2011. *Words as Events: Cretan Mantinádes in Performance and Composition*. Studia Fennica Folkloristica 18. Helsinki: Finnish Literature Society.

Sylivos, Thanasis (ed.). 2010. *Nikos Xylouris: We Sing in Order to Bring People Together*. Athens: Metronomos. [GR]

Tannahill, Reay. 1973. *Food in History*. Penguin Cookery Library.

Terry, Walter. 1963. *Isadora Duncan: Her Life, Her Art, Her Legacy*. New York: Dodd, Mead & Company.

Theodorakis, Mikis. "Iphigenia: Music for Film." Retrieved March 5, 2013, from http://digma.mmb.org.gr/Item.aspx?kkt=TMUSIC000000231. [GR]

_____. 2002. *Iphigenia*. CD: FM Records.

_____. 1990. *The Anatomy of Music*. Athens-Greece: Alfeios. [GR]

Thoma, Kelly. 2009. *Anamkhara*. CD: Aerakis Sistron Music.

Thursby, Jacqueline. 2008. *Foodways and Folklore: A Handbook*. Westport-CT: Greenwood Press.

Tolan, Sandy. 2007. "Olive Oil Season: A West Bank Kitchen Story." *National Public Radio*. Retrieved March 5, 2013, from http://www.npr.org/2007/11/22/16506897/olive-oil-season-a-west-bank-kitchen-story.

Torp, Lisbet. 1992. "Zorba's Dance: The Story of a Dance Illusion and its Touristic Value." *Ethnografika* 8: 207-10.

Tosi, Bruno. 2006. *Maria Callas: La Divina in Cucina*. Trenta Editore.

Trotter, William (transl. Alexis Kalofolias). 2000. *Priest of Music: The Life of Dimitri Mitropoulos*. Athens: Potamos. [GR]

Tsarouchis, Yiannis. 1978. *Between East and West: Five Texts*. Athens: Agra. [GR]

Tsivis, Ioannis. 1993. *Chania 1252-1940*. Chania: Gnosi. [GR]

Tsouhlarakis, Ioannis. "The Traditional Dances of Crete." Retrieved March 5, 2013, from http://www.tsouchlarakis.com/English.htm#Dances.

Tuan, Yi-Fu. 1991. "Language and the Making of Place: A Narrative-Descriptive Approach." *Annals of the Association of American Geographers* 81 (4): 684-696.

Tzimitras, Haris. 2/29/2004. "Histories of Bread and Daily Politics." *Kathimerini*. [GR]

Tziovas, Dimitris. 2003. *Greece and the Balkans. Identities, Perceptions and Cultural Encounters since the Enlightenment*. England: Ashgate.

Vallianou-Hatzi, Despina. 2003. "Olive Cultivation and Production in Crete During Antiquity." *Proceedings of the International Symposium on the Olive and Olive-Oil in Crete*. Sitia-Crete (SEDIK): 86-104. [GR]

Vardakis, Vangelis. 2001. *East of Crete*. Cretan Music Workshop. CD with liner notes.

Varella, Evangelia. 2/29/2004. "Ancient Secrets." *Kathimerini*. [GR]

Vasilakis, Antonis. 2003. "Olive Cultivation and Oil Production in Minoan Crete: Testimonies from Specific Monuments." *Proceedings of the International Symposium on the Olive and Olive-Oil in Crete*. Sitia-Crete (SEDIK): 53-65. [GR]

Vincent, Alfred. 2005. "The Master Builder from Folksong to Opera: The Adaptation of *The Bridge of Arta* by Nikos Kazantzakis and Manolis Kalomiris." *Greek Research in Australia*: 119-156.

Voutsina, Evi. 2002. *Bread*. Athens: Kastaniotis. [GR]

Waldenberger, Suzanne. 1995. "Our Daily Bread: A Look at Bible Breads." *The Digest: An Interdisciplinary Study of Food and Foodways* 15: 17-9.

Watson, Bruce. 2005. *Bread and Roses: Mills, Migrants, and the Struggle for the American Dream*. New York-NY: Penguin Books.

Welsh, Roger. 1971. "'We are What We Eat': Omaha Food as Symbol." *Keystone Folklore Quarterly*, Winter Issue: 165-170.

Whatmore, Sarah. 2002. *Hybrid Geographies: Natures, Cultures, Spaces*. London: Sage.

Williams, Chris. 2002. "Why Does Music Matter? Questions of Identity in Cretan Music."

E-mail communication, 19 February.

Wilson, James. 2006. "Political Songs, Collective Memories, and Kikuyu Indi Schools." *History in Africa 33*: 363-388.

Xirouhakis, Theoharis. 2011. Series of interviews and personal communication during July-August-September. Chania and Heraklion, Crete.

Yalom, Irvin. 2002. "Religion and Psychiatry." *American Journal of Psychotherapy* 56 (3): 301-316.

Yalourakis, Manolis. 2007. "Kazantzakis Told Me…" *The Tree* 155-156: 32-35. [GR]

Zagoris, Stefanos. 2003. "Theodore's Antoniou Music for the Theater." *Epi Skinis*: 47-51. [GR]

Zaimakis, Yiannis. 2008. *Flourishing Dens in Lakkos of Heraklion: Deviation, Cultural Creation, Anonymous Rebetiko (1900-1940)*. Athens: Plethron. [GR]

Zografou, Lili. 1960. *Nikos Kazantzakis: A Tragic*. Athens: Kedros. [GR]

Glossary

Akathist Hymn. One of the most renowned services in the Orthodox Church, attributed to St. Romanos, the *Akathist Hymn* forms an alphabetical acrostic as each of the twelve long and short stanzas begins with a letter of the Greek alphabet, made up of praises and salutations directed to the Mother of God. *Akathistos* means "not seated," which is why, when performed, the audience remains standing.

Akritika Songs. "Akritic Cycle" (*Akritika*) is a series of epic songs that emerged around the 9th century and which take us back to the days of the Byzantium and the heroic exploits of the *Akrites*, the frontier guards (from the Greek word *akra*, thus, "edges").

Aman & Amanes. *Aman-aman* (for mercy's sake!; woe is me!) is an exclamatory expression Greek singers use to denote, among others, sorrow, pain, misfortune. Wonderful melodic improvisations (*amanedes*) develop around the word *aman*. The singing that accompanies such music is definitely of an oriental nature, with a specific and deliberate use of a certain nasal quality, and highly embellished.

Amor Fati. A Latin phrase that translates to "love of fate." According to it, everything that happens in one's life, including suffering and loss, is purposeful. That phrase has been used repeatedly in Friedrich Nietzsche's writings.

Anthropos. *Anthropos,* namely human being, is the one who looks (*throsko*) upwards (*ano*). Thus, humans stand erect toward the heavens, with eyes watching up (hence also the Greek word for religion, namely, *thriskia*).

Andigaermata or apogaermata . Cretan singing technique that elaborates iterative singing. It consists of splitting the lines into fragments while also breaking up words, and repeating incomplete parts of lines in a kind of "stammering."

Armenohorianos sirtos. For the composition of the famous "Zorba dance," the *sirtaki*, Mikis Theodorakis relied on already existing material borrowed from the local Cretan tradition, more specifically, the *Armenohorianos sirtos* by Giorgos Koutsourelis, created around 1949-1950, for Cretan lute and vocals.

Askomandoura. Bagpipe; *askos* (animal skin) and *bandura* [in Italian, a kind of rough flute (pipe) usually out of calamus]. That instrument has been very popular with the shepherds and the inhabitants of the mountainous areas of Crete.

Battle of Crete. Historical battle that took place on 20 May 1941, when Nazi Germany launched an invasion (the first mainly airborne one in military history) of Crete under the codename "Operation Mercury" (where "parachute rangers" were used on a massive scale).

Boulgari. A long-necked lute with a flat soundboard and a hole in the body, essentially very similar to, if not the same instrument as, the *saz*. Under the influence of the Greek *laouto*, it eventually died out. Stelios Foustalierakis played that instrument, and we have many fine recordings of his playing style.

Chaniotis or Chaniotiko(s). A circle, "shuffling" line dance developed in the Chania province, most likely the region of Kissamos, also merely called *sirtos*. It is believed that, in ancient times, the dance served as a necessary means of expression and encouragement in cases of war. There is one characteristic melody labeled as the *protos* (first) *sirtos* (or *Chaniotikos*, or *Kissamitikos*) that is considered to be the original one which from the dance sprung to the rest of the island, composed by Cretan soldiers who participated in the failed defense of Constantinople against the Ottoman Turks in 1453.

Choros. The Greek word for dance, a term standing for the choir which sang, spoke and danced with the purpose of intensifying a mood, an essential part of the ancient Greek theater. Ancient Greeks considered dancing as a high art form, alongside drama, music and poetry, the Muse Terpsichore being its protector.

Choros tis Nifis. The bridal dance; A specific group of people, starting with the close relatives and the family of the bride and the groom "dances" the central and most symbolically elaborate figure in the entire wedding ritual.

Condylia & Condylies. Brief musical phrases initially performed on a piece of reed between two consecutive nodes (condyles), and which, later on, also applied to string instrument music (*lyra*, violin).

Cronus. The father of Zeus; an alteration of the word *chronos* (time).

Crypto-Christians. A population Cretan in origin, language and customs that accepted Islam but secretly kept their Christian faith.

Daskalogiannis Song. A Cretan oral heroic poem that consists of 1,034 lines, all of which are rhyming couplets. It narrates the 1770 Sfakia rebellion against the Ottoman rulers, prompted by promises of Russian aid, and focuses on the treacherous invitation of Ioannis Vlachos or Daskalogiannis (1722 or 1730-1771) to Heraklion by the Pasha, where he was captured and flayed alive.

Demir aga. A 1900 famous *lyra* player from the Kastelli village at the Pediada region.

Dias (Hospites, Philoxenon, Xenios). Jupiter; the amorous father of the twelve gods of antiquity.

Digenis Akritas . Medieval epic hero; the biracial knight of the *akro* (border), *digenis* (of two races: *dio* "two," *geni* "races"); son of an Arab chieftain and an aristocratic Greek lady.

Eleftheria. Freedom; liberty. From the verb *eleutho*, to bring, namely the "deliverer," with an obvious association to childbirth.

Gerakokoudouna. "Hawks-bells," namely small bells added to the bow of Greek instruments in order to further increase the volume and add rhythmic emphasis to the melodies.

Gitsikia Sousta. "Goat" sousta, also known as "Roumat(h)iani." Imposing, leaping dance performed in the region of Palaia Roumata in Kissamos (Chania-Crete).

Glendi & Glendia. Big celebrations; feasts. Events which include dancing, drinking, singing, eating, talking and people in high spirits (*kefi*).

Greek National School of Music. Manolis Kalomiris is perceived as its founder. It drew influences from Greek folk music, poetry and myth, aiming to combine the German Romanticism with Greek motives.

Halepianos amanes. Foustalieris adaptation of the Turkish song, "Ada sahillerinde bekliyorum" (I am waiting at the coast of the island) to the Cretan one, "Everybody asks me why I cry." Obviously, by naming it as such, Cretans refer to Halepa, a region in Chania. However, it is an interesting and intriguing coincidence that this piece comes from Aleppo in Syria and not from Chania.

Harmolipi. The paradoxical yet frequently met opposition of happiness versus sorrow that seals the Orthodox meaning of "joyous grief."

Ideon Cave or Ideon Andron. Cave in the mountain of Psiloritis where, according to tradition, Zeus was born.

Kalamatianos. Popular Greek dance that is believed to have acquired its name from the town of Kalamata in the Peloponnese.

Kamara or Kamarahti. Dragging dance in three-time its name meaning "Arch," performed on the islands of Skiathos, Samos and Euboea, in a two-beat rhythm, to the song "The Bridge of Arta" during Easter, on the second day upon Resurrection Sunday, thus on Monday, usually the day of St. George.

Kantada & Kantades. Serenade performances, namely poetic ways of expression and communication. Etymologically, *kantada* comes from the Latin "cantare," which stands for reciting while singing, praising in verse, performing a role, soothing or enchanting through singing and/or revealing a secret. In ancient Greek, the verb *katado* stood for singing or entertainment through song.

Karagioule Sirtos. Popular melody composed by Cretan-Turkish musician Moustafas Karagioules (1845-1930) from the village of Kallergiana at Kissamos.

Karagiozis & Karagiozides. Figure of the shadow-puppet theater; buffoon; fool. Form of a shadow theater usually performed in open-air theaters on large white screens erected at the far side of the place. The puppets used in Karagiozis are usually made from animal skin and represent figures of history and romance, of nature and fantasy.

Kastrinos Pidichtos. A principal dance form also known as Maleviziotis. Its name derives from the city of Heraklion and its older name Kastro (fortress). It is considered as one of the oldest dances on the island of Crete, stemming from the ancient *orsitis*.

Kefi. High spirits; gaiety.

Kondomari. Village in Chania-Crete known for a massacre that refers to the execution of male civilians by an ad hoc firing squad consisting of German paratroopers on 2 June 1941 during World War II. The shooting was the first of a long series of mass reprisals on the island of Crete and was orchestrated in retaliation for the participation of Cretans in "The Battle of Crete."

Kontakion & Kontakia. A hymnographic form; a long and elaborate metrical sermon, which found its acme in the work of St. Romanos the Melodist (6th century).

Kontaromahies . Live traditions of *mandinada* contests to which improvisatory skills are central. *Kontaromahies* translates to "fights with poles," also known as *drakarismata*, namely "collisions."

Kouritis & Kourites. The ancient Cretan(s).

Koutsambadianos or Ka(r)tsimba(r)dianos. A *pentozalis* dance adapted to the rhythm of the dance steps of a lame (*koutsos*) man, part of the tradition of the Amari-Rethymno province.

Kouzoulos & Kouzouloi. Crazy; mad; insane. From the Turkish *kouzoulou*, which stands for the ewe lamb, because sheep usually proceed in crazy hops.

Kri-kri (Capra aegagrus Cretica). A subspecies of wild goat, large ungulate native to the Eastern Mediterranean, now found only on the island of Crete and three small islands just offshore.

Laographia. Folklore; Ethnography. From *laos* – meaning "nation, people," and the verb *grapho* – meaning "to write."

Laouto & Laouta. Instruments – like most of the large-bodied lutes found in the eastern Mediterranean – related to the very old Arabian lute known as the *oud*. Even the name *laouto* is quite obviously a derivative of the Arabic word *al' oud*, namely, "the wood." They have four double strings, a very low tuning, and are played with long plectrums, originally made from the feathers of a type of buzzard commonly found on Crete. They also have movable frets, indicating that non-tempered intervals must have been in use at some time.

Lefka Ori or Madares. "Bald, bare of any vegetation areas" (*Madares*) is a mountain range located in Western Crete, in the Chania prefecture. *Lefka Ori* (namely, "White Mountains") got their name from the snow that covers their peaks until late in spring.

Levendis & levendes. Gallant; corker. Crete is known as *levendoyenna*, namely giving birth to men of gallantry (*levendia*).

Lyra & Lyras. Pear-shaped, three-stringed, bowed instrument. Instead of pressing the string with the tips of the fingers to produce the different notes, the strings are touched lightly by the back of the nails, producing a very strong, sharp tone, and facilitating a wide range of embellishments which considerably enrich the melodies being played.

Maleviziotis. A principal dance form also known as *Kastrinos pidichtos*. Malevizi refers to a district in the west Heraklion province. It is considered as one of the oldest dances on the island of Crete, stemming from the ancient *orsitis*.

Mandinada & Mandinades. Improvised, fifteen-syllable, in iambic meter, proverbial, rhyming distiches, each divided into an eight- followed by a seven-syllable part, where the fourteenth syllable must be stressed and the fifteenth unstressed. Integral part of the musical tradition of oral composition-in-performance, relying on formulas, thus groups of words under the same metrical conditions that are being repeated.

Mandoura. A processed reed in the shape of a flute.

Melody of Ali. Used for Ross Daly's song "Black Sea" of Ali," originally traced somewhere to the prefecture of Lasithi. Daly asserts that Ali was a Cretan who had converted to Islam.

Meraklis & Meraklides. A man who demands the best and is knowledgeable in the rules of *glendi*, capable of experiencing and conveying true *kefi* and yearning; the happy enthusiast who shows affection to his object, in other words, the satisfied connoisseur who also embodies artistry in every action. In 2009, Mr. Xirouhakis created the "Meraklidikos" dance to portray joy and high spirits.

Moirologia. Mourning songs; dirges. Distinctive by virtue of their special ritual context (funerals, graveside visits and sometimes memorial services), of the behavior associated with them (violent displays of grief), of the performer's sex (almost always female) and of their musical forms.

Mount Juktas. The hill where the tomb of Zeus is located, one of the most significant summit sanctuaries of the Minoan period, a place of worship in the years of Christianity and the Byzantine era as well as during the Turkish period. From a north-west perspective, it resembles the face of a man lying down, looking at the sky, said to be the head of Zeus. Its name derives from a corrupted form of the Roman word "Jupiter."

Palikari & Palikaria. Braves, the human heroes who always stand ready to defy death in order to obtain liberty.

Paniyiri. Big celebration; feast.

Paraloges. Long narratives, "ballads," traced in the last period of the ancient world.

Parea & Parees. Company; gang; party.

Pentozali(s). A popular, line Cretan dance its name meaning five-stepped dance, five dizzying steps or giddy five step rhythm. It is springy and energetic, working up to a great speed. The participants clasp one another's shoulders and perform steps classified as leaping while moving with increasing speed and performing intricate steps on the spot.

Philoxenia. The Greek concept of hospitality, the generosity and courtesy (*philia*) shown to those who are far from home (*xenos-xenoi*).

Pidichtos. Leaping dance.

Pontic Greeks. An ethnically Greek group who lived in the region of Pontus, on the shores of Turkey's Black Sea and in the Pontic Alps, in northeastern Anatolia and the former Russian Caucasus province of Kars, as well as in Georgia. They have distinct customs and speak the Pontic Greek dialect.

Prinianos or Priniotis. Dance from the Ierapetra-Lasithi area. Its name translates to "tree heath-evergreen shrub."

Psiloritis. The tallest (*psilo*) mountain (*oros*) in Crete; also referred to as Ida.

Pyrrichi. War dances of the ancient Greek antiquity.

Rembetiko & Rembetika. The music of the Greek underground. It originated in the hashish dens of Piraeus and Thessaloniki with the forced immigration of 2 million Greek refugees from Asia Minor. It evolved into Greek popular music.

Rizitiko & Rizitika. Songs created by the inhabitants of western Crete who dwell in the White Mountains (*Lefka Ori* or *Madares*) shepherds' lands, in the so-called "domain of *Mousouroi*" areas. Their name derives from the Greek word "*riza*," which means root. Thus, *rizitika* are the "songs of the foothills."

Rodo. The "Rose" dance; a traditionally female dance preserved today at the Chania village of Lousakies.

Samaria Gorge. A UNESCO Biosphere Reserve and a Wildlife Refuge of the EU's Natura network of protected areas. The longest gorge in Europe (15km), an internationally recognized "sight" which was declared a National Park in 1962, with a reputation since the antiquity.

Santouri. Cimbalom; Hammered dulcimer that has a chromatic setup. A type of chordophone composed of a large, trapezoidal box with metal strings stretched across its top.

Sirtaki. The dance of Zorba; a hybrid form, namely a mixture of slow and fast versions of Greek dancing.

Sirtos or Sirto. Dragging dance; movement of the feet over the ground in a dragging or shuffling motion.

Strata Songs. Reserved for parts of the wedding rites other than the banquet, which include the transfer of the dowry to the bridegroom's house, the ceremonial welcome by the bridegroom's mother of the bride, and the gathering of the gifts.

Syncretism. The attempt to reconcile disparate, even opposing, beliefs and to meld practices of various schools of thought. It is especially associated with the effort to merge and draw parallels among several originally discrete traditions, especially in philosophy and religion, thereby asserting an underlying unity. The term owes its meaning to ancient Cretans, who, in spite of their differences among themselves, united in the face of external dangers: the word per se is a compound of *syn* (together) and "Crete."

Synaesthesia. From the Greek syn, "together," and aesthesis, "sensation," is a condition in which stimulation of one sensory or cognitive pathway leads to automatic, involuntary experiences in a second sensory or cognitive pathway.

Tabachaniotiko & Tabachaniotika. Urban type of Cretan music played in years past mostly in coffee shops and restaurants in the harbor districts of Chania and Rethymno, traced to Cretan musician Stelios Foustalieris and, more generally, to the period after the 1923 Treaty of Lausanne.

Tavla Songs. Feast, "table" songs; repertoire reserved for convivial occasions, mainly wedding banquets.

Taximi & Taximia. Freely improvised, unmeasured melody, within a given musical mode, which can occur at the beginning or in the middle of a song.

Thiaboli. Wooden flute; the faithful companion of Cretan shepherds grazing their sheep on the remote mountain slopes of Crete, a word stemming from the Venetian *fiaboli*.

Trichordo Bouzouki. Plucked string instrument with three pairs of strings that used to be part of Cretan music.

Topophilia. Deeply felt sentiment which creates a strong sense of place and belonging, that is not only physically and geographically, but also ideologically specified.

Tourkokrites or Tourkokritikoi. A population that was Cretan in origin, language and customs, but Muslim by faith (Cretan-Turks), who proved to be many times more fierce and harsh than the original Muslim conquerors.

Tragoudo. To sing; scholars have argued how it is a derivative of the classical Greek tragedy.

Tsakisma. Melodic interpolation; usually couplets that praise love.

Viololyra. A type of Cretan *lyra* that shares common traits with the violin.

Vrondolyra. Larger form of the Cretan *lyra*, its name denoting an instrument capable of producing loud as a "thunder" (*vrondi*) sounds.

Transliteration

In this book, we have followed a hybrid transliteration system which combines what both the *ISO 843: 1997 (Information and documentation-Conversion of Greek characters into Latin characters: International Organization for Standardization)* and the *Journal of Modern Greek Studies* (published by the *Johns Hopkins* University Press) suggest. That system approximates the actual pronunciation of modern Greek spelling rather than its grammatical, literary and scholastic rendition. We realize that no system is exhaustive and, therefore, entrusted our longstanding experience in teaching Greek language and culture to non-native speakers (who are expected to be the target audience).

Notes: Double consonants remain as such. Transliterated words do not bear stress accents. Names are in the customary English or foreign form whenever possible. Well-known anglicizations are generally retained but preference is shown for the way that a person cited normally renders her/his name.

A	α	a
	αι	ai
	αυ	af (before y,k,j,p,s,t,f,x,c); av (otherwise)
B	β	v
Γ	γ	g (before a,o,u, & consonants); y (before i,e)
Δ	δ	d
E	ε	e
	ει	ei
	ευ	ef (before y,k,j,p,s,t,f,x,c); ev (otherwise)
Z	ζ	z
H	η	i
Θ	θ	th
I	ι	i
K	κ	k
Λ	λ	l
M	μ	m
	μ π	mp b (initially); mb (medially)
N	ν	n
	ν τ	d (initially); nd (medially)
Ξ	ξ	x
O	ο	o
	οι	oi
	ο υ	ou
Π	π	p
P	ρ	r
Σ	σ , ς	s
T	τ	t
Υ	υ	i
Φ	φ	f
X	χ	ch (if phoneme has long been known in English & after s; h (otherwise)
Ψ	φ	ps
Ω	ω	o

Index

A

Acheron 199
achon reon 199
Acrocorinth 205, 263
Adana 171
Ada sahillerinde bekliyorum 46, 280
Advancing Interdisciplinary Research in Singing (AIRS) 237
aerophones 62, 189
Aeschylus 186, 193
Agamemnon 138, 186, 192, 193, 194, 198
Agia Roumeli 90
Agia Triada 27, 211
agiografia 31
Agrimia 52
Akathist/Akathistos 43, 279
akra/Akrites/akritic/akritika 16, 191, 279
akratisma 212
Akritas, Digenis 34, 35, 280
Alagni/Alagnianos 108, 267
Al-Andalus 46
Aleppo 46, 280
Alexiadis, Minas 57, 58, 242
Alka 185
al-khandaq 28
Amalthea 98, 261, 264
aman/aman-aman/amanes/amanedes 42, 46, 47, 94, 161, 171, 279, 280
Ambadia 251
American Folklife Center at the Library of Congress 21
Amidinos, Aetios 217
Amonov, Avgust 178
Amor Fati 4, 5, 188, 189, 242, 243, 267, 271, 279
Anamkhara 56, 263, 277
Andriopoulos, Elias 52
Anius 110
Anka, Paul 258
Anogia/Anogianos 37, 46, 51, 54, 55, 56
anostos 226
anthropos 127, 255, 279
antidoro 211
Antoniou, Theodore 165, 182, 183, 184, 185, 186, 187, 255, 268, 271, 278
apogaermata/andigaermata 96, 279
Apostolakis, Stamatis 261
Apostolakis, Yannis 91, 108
apple/apple of discord 223, 224, 225
Arachova 171

Archanes (Archbishop of Tirana, Durrës and All Albania) 57
Archives of Traditional Music (ATM) at Indiana University 21
arete 92
Aretousa, Argyris 32, 33, 35
Ariadne 56, 110, 145, 265, 268
Armenohorianos 163, 279
Armenoi 28
Aroma Kritis (Scent of Crete) 39
Arta 169, 171, 172, 177, 178, 191, 195, 196, 197, 198, 199, 265, 271, 272, 277, 281
Artokopikos 206
artokopos 207
Artopolis 257
artos 207
artozinos 220
Askitiki 34
askomandoura 188
Atalanta 140
Athanasiou Company 220
Athenaeus 206, 223
Athens Festival 163, 179
Athens Megaron 178
Athens Odeum 177
Atraidis, Vaggelis 220
Atreides 192
Avgolemono 227
Avlon 113

B

Bacchic 141
baglamas 58
Baka, Spyridoula 72
Balos 152
Barba-Pantzelios 86, 87, 90, 245, 262
Bartók, Béla 61
Battle of Crete 152, 153, 154, 155, 156, 279, 281
Baud-Bovy, Samuel 91, 94, 96, 188, 245, 262
Beethoven 135, 140, 162, 170, 240
bel canto 64
Belilove, Lori 139
Belle Époque 179
Bellini 64, 65, 243
bendir 57, 72
Berdiaki, Olga 221
Bernstein, Leonard 65
Bigot, Eugène 193
Birzeit 113

Blachernae 43
black-eyed 224
Black Sea (Thalassa Mavri) 46, 69, 282
Bokoros, Christos 219
Bonatos, Yannis 90
Bosa/Bosan People 221, 222
Boulez, Pierre 195
boulgari 40, 47, 240
bouzouki 33, 40, 47, 68, 108, 166
bradylalia 217
Brahms 162
Bread and Chocolate (Pane e Cioccolata; 1973) 220
Bread and Tear 220
Bread and Tulips (Pane e Tulipani; 2000) 220
Bread is on the Table, The 220
Brisco, Nikos 166
brostaris 124
Buddha 34, 127, 128, 132, 254
Busoni, Ferruccio 162
byzanchi 73

C

Cacoyannis, Michael 127, 162, 194, 241, 272
Cafe Antarsia 166
Calatrava, Santiago 198
Calchas 193, 194
Callas, Maria (Cecilia Sophia Anna Kalogero-poulou) 3, 5, 64, 65, 178, 267, 276, 277
Caraveli, Anna 36, 239, 246, 263
Carras, Costas 194
Cavafy, Constantine 127, 256
Chalkidiki 210
Chania 29, 30, 45, 46, 56, 68, 69, 108, 146, 149, 151, 152, 153, 154, 212, 240, 243, 252, 263, 264, 265, 268, 270, 272, 273, 277, 278, 279, 280, 281, 282, 283, 284
Chaniotakis, Manolis 108, 267
Chaniotis/Chaniotiko(s) 111, 146, 279
Charles Cros 52
Chemirani Ensemble/Chemriani family members 72
Cherubini, Luigi 64
chiton 136
Chopin 135, 140
chordophones 62, 189
choreodrama 191, 197
choros 83, 123, 135, 280
Christ 44, 132, 212, 213, 214, 216, 218, 224
Christodoulakis, George 184
christopsomo 215

Christ Recrucified 162, 172, 174, 207
chronos 223, 280
Chrysippus of Tyana 206
Circassian song 180
Cloudy Sunday 220
Clytemnestra 194
Colonel Hatzopoulos 21
Columbus, Christopher 139
Comnenus, Alexius I 91
condyles 188, 280
condylia/condylies 48, 50, 105, 106, 107, 108, 188, 280
Koukias 166
Constantine Palaiologos 97, 164, 173, 269
Constantinople 29, 43, 44, 46, 94, 149, 161, 164, 168, 172, 238, 280
Corinth 165, 182, 184, 185
Count Orlov 87
Cretanhood 59, 157
Cretanness 28, 34, 101, 144, 146, 151
Cretaquarium 82
Cronus 54, 223, 280
Cryptochristianoi (Crypto-Christians) 28
Cypselids 184
Cypselus 182, 183, 185
Cythera 89

D

Dacians 192
dakos 213, 268
Dalgas (Antonis Diamantidis) 46
Dalis, Stefanos 98
Damaskenos, Michail 29
daouli 17, 56
Daskalakis, Iosif (aka Sifodaskalakis) 251
Daskalakis, Nikolaos 29
Daskalogiannis 86, 87, 89, 150, 270
Daskalogiannis Revolution 149, 269
Daskalogiannis Song 86, 87, 89, 90, 92, 244, 251, 262, 274, 280
davul 57
Dawe, Kevin 97, 151, 243, 252, 264
defi 17
Deipnosophists, The 206
Delendas, Antonis 178
Demeter 205, 206, 211, 225, 262
Demir aga 241, 280
demotic Greek 12, 47, 179
demoticism 12, 61, 171, 174, 183
Derka 171
Dermitzakis 47, 264

Dew Men (Drosoulites) 82
Diamantidis, Antonis (aka Dalgas) 46
Dias 223, 252, 280
diatrofi 223
dictatorship 165, 184, 186, 253
dieta 223
Digenis Akritas 34, 35, 280
Diktakis 47, 264
diktamo 223
Dimou, Nikos 13, 264
Diogenes 205
Diogenes Laertius 205
Diolkos 182, 185
Dionysus 110, 129, 225
Dioscorides 217
Diphilus 206
dittany 223
Donizetti, Gaetano 64
Dorians 90
Doukas, Hector 219
Dragoumis, Ion 169
drakarismata 104, 281
Droseros (Giorgis Maravgakis) 108
Drosinis, Georgios 218
Drosoulites (Dew Men) 82

E

ecological 7, 56, 80, 81, 82, 85, 92, 94, 100, 109,
    110, 134, 142
ecology 7, 94, 110, 141, 221
ecopoetics 244
ecopoetry 244
ecos 81, 110, 112, 141, 197
Edafos Dance Theatre 195, 196
Efstratios (Stratis Kalogeridis) 48
eftazimo 217
egoismos 124
Eki Attar 73
elea 112. See also elia; See also elies
elefandes 224
eleftheria 122, 280
eleon 112
eleovrytissa 113
El Greco 29, 245
elia 109, 111. See also elea; See also elies
Elias 110
elies 111, 114. See also elea; See also elia
Eligia 90
Ellaktor 178
Ellinas 33
Elytis, Odysseus 172, 218

Emesa 43
Emine 35
Emo 143
environment/environmental 34, 73, 81, 82, 85,
    97, 101, 110, 125, 134, 141, 142, 143, 144,
    145, 198, 219
Ephrem the Syrian 43
epikarpios 223
Episkopi 107
Erofili 31, 32, 33, 176, 269
Eros 131
Erotokritos 32, 33, 35, 37, 51, 87, 106, 180, 270
ethnography 21, 27
ethnopoetics 237
Euboea 113, 198, 281
Euripides 145, 193, 194, 198, 199, 242, 265, 270,
    272, 275
Evangelatos, Antiochos 187
Evangelismos 108
EVIA Digital ArchiveArchive Project: Ethno-
    graphic Video for Instruction and Analysis
    21

F

Falassarna 152
Falla, Manuel de 162
Fanourios 213, 214
fanouropita 213, 214
fava 224
Fermor, Patrick Leigh 46
Fête Crétoise 60
fieldnotes 237
Filedem 46, 47
Fokas, Nikiforos 32, 252
For Bread and Love 220
Forty Gallant Men from Livadia 171
Fountoulakis bakery 213
Fournaris 208
Foustalierakis, Stelios (aka Stelios Foustalieris)
    40, 45, 46, 47, 240, 279
Foustalieris, Stelios. See Foustalierakis, Stelios
    (aka Stelios Foustalieris)
Fragoulidakis, Yannis (aka Skarpathiotis) 108
Frangokastello 82, 244
Fresco, Zohar 57
ftazimo 217

G

gadulka 37
gaida 17
gala 224

galaktoboureko 119
Galen 217
gamokoulouro 215
Gatsos, Nikos 52, 187
gefiri 197
gerakokoudouna 84, 104, 280
gigandes 224
gitsikia 83, 280
Glassie, Henry 20, 237, 238, 265
glendi/glendia 36, 117, 120, 121, 145, 146, 280, 282
glossa 224
Gluck, Christoph Willibald Ritter von 64
Görlitz 21
Gortina 84
Gramvousa 151, 152, 155
grapho 11, 282
Greek National School of Music 61, 280
Greekness 7, 11, 15, 34, 39, 87, 163, 170, 172, 205
Greek Passion 162, 174, 207, 270
Greek Sonata, A (Eine Griechische Sonate) 61, 242, 273
Grinia 249, 264
Gyzis, Nikolaos 219, 258

H

Hadjidakis, Georgios 62, 98
Hadjidakis, Manos 62, 98, 163, 179, 180, 181, 196, 241, 243, 246, 251, 254, 255, 261, 263, 265, 266, 273
Hagia Sophia 43
Halab (Aleppo) 46
Halepa 46, 280
Halepianos amanes 46, 280
Halki 29
halvas (Sweet Semolina Pudding) 227
handaki 28
Handax 28
harmolipi (joyous grief) 198, 281
Harvester Vase, The 27
hasiko/Hasika 210
Hatzimihail, Theofilos 219
Heartless Life 220
Heisenberg, August 21
Hellenic Institute of Byzantine and Post-Byzantine Studies in Venice 21
Hellenic Music Centre 5, 241, 254, 255, 267, 271
Hellenic thesis 12
Hellenism 71, 137, 151, 164, 172, 198

Heraklion 47, 48, 51, 56, 69, 70, 86, 87, 89, 98, 104, 107, 113, 162, 163, 179, 186, 188, 261, 262, 264, 267, 268, 269, 273, 274, 276, 278, 280, 281, 282
Here Nimfi Animfefte! 44
Heretismi 43
heterophonic melodies 94
Hippocrates 217, 233
Homer 7, 85, 91, 92, 111, 114, 127, 132, 145, 170, 192, 205, 224, 247, 269, 273
homophone 94
Homs 43
hondrolia 111
Hortatsis, Georgios 29, 31, 32
Hospites 56, 280
Houdetsi 69
Hugo, Victor 209
Huun-Huur-Tu 72, 73
hybrid/hybridity/hybridization 54, 75, 283, 285

I

ICHTHYS 132
IC XC NIKA 214
Ideon Cave (Ideon Andron) 55, 274, 281
igil 73
Ioannina 219
Iphigenia 172, 192, 193, 194
Iphigenia at the Bridge of Arta 191, 195, 196, 197, 271
Isadora Duncan Dance Foundation 139, 140
Island Studies 237, 266, 268
Ithagenia 47

J

Jiazheng, Sun 178

K

Kaisariani 220
Kalamata 55, 114, 281
kalamatianos 114, 281
Kallergiana 47, 281
Kallergis, Mihalis 39, 239, 269
Kalogeridis, Stratis (aka Efstratios Kalogeridis) 3, 48, 241, 261, 265
Kalomiris, Manolis 61, 164, 165, 167, 168, 169, 170, 171, 172, 173, 174, 175, 176, 177, 178, 184, 191, 197, 199, 253, 254, 264, 268, 269, 272, 277, 280
Kamara 198, 281
Kambanellis, Iakovos 220, 252

Kampani, Fani 221
Kander, John 163
Kanellakis, Christine 166
Kanellos, Vassos 140
kanonaki 17
kantada/kantades/katado 106, 281
Kapetan Mihalis 34
Kapodistrias 163, 164, 254, 262
Kara, Danae 242
Karagioule sirtos 47, 281
Karagiozides 123, 281
Karagiozis 15, 166, 219, 220, 272, 273, 281
Karanou 102
Karatzis 35
Karolos Koun Prize 182
ka(r)tsimba(r)dianos (koutsambadianos) 251, 281
Kastelli 108, 241, 280
Kastrinos pidichtos 104, 108, 281, 282
Kastro (fortress) 51, 104, 281
Katrakis, Manos 179
Kavala 21
Kazakos, Kostas 194
Kazantzakis, Nikos 4, 5, 12, 13, 34, 42, 47, 101, 126, 127, 128, 129, 130, 131, 132, 133, 161, 162, 163, 164, 165, 166, 167, 168, 169, 170, 171, 172, 173, 174, 175, 176, 177, 178, 179, 180, 181, 182, 183, 184, 185, 186, 187, 188, 189, 191, 195, 197, 199, 207, 234, 237, 239, 240, 241, 248, 249, 250, 252, 253, 254, 255, 261, 262, 265, 266, 268, 270, 273, 274, 277, 278
Kazantzidis, Stelios 220
Kazasoglou, George 187
kefi 16, 117, 146, 155, 280, 282
Keftiu 28
kemenche 37, 69, 71
Kennedy, Jacqueline 65
Kennedy, John F. 65, 210
kerasma 203
Kertz, Peter 184
Kessel, Dmitri 219
Kioros (Stefanos Triandafillakis) 149
Kissamitikos 149, 279
Kissamos 47, 108, 149, 151, 152, 264, 279, 280, 281
klarino 17
kleftika 16
Kleiber, Erich 162
Klemperer, Otto 162
klephts 16

koine 75
Kokkalis Program 198
koliva 216
kolokithia 225
kolokithokouvendes 225
kolokithopites 225
kolovi 111
komboloi 16
Konaki 51
kontakia/kontakion 43, 281
kontaromahies 104, 281
Kopanos 136, 138
kopelia/kopelies 111, 114
Kornaros, Vitsentzos 29, 32, 33, 270
Koskinou 16
Kostios, Apostolos 61, 242, 270
kotopoulo sto fourno me patates 227, 229
Kotzias, Alexandros 179, 218
Kotzias, Kostas 179
Koukias, Constantine 166
koulourakia 220
koulouri 215, 217, 221
Koumendakis, George 102, 188, 189, 191, 195, 196, 197, 199, 243, 246, 255, 267, 271
Kounadis 187
Kourites 54, 281
Kouritis 15, 281
koutsambadianos (ka(r)tsimba(r)dianos) 251, 281
Koutsourelis, Giorgos 163, 279
kouzouloi 36, 281
krasi 224
Krateia 186
Kreipe, Heinrich 46
kri-kri 89, 98, 282
Kristallis 207
Kristallis, Kostas 207
Kriti 36, 118, 151
Kritiki Politeia 47
Kritikopoula mou 51
Krumbacher, Karl 21
Kydonies 29
KYR 58

L

La Divina 65, 277. *See also* Callas, Maria
lagana 215
Lambelet, George 61, 242
lambrokoulouro 215
Lambropoulos, Takis 52

laographia 11, 282
laos 11, 282
laouto/laouta 17, 32, 33, 36, 37, 40, 55, 56, 71,
    72, 104, 118, 152, 166, 279, 282
Lasithi 46, 282, 283
Lassanis Drama Competition 168
Lautarchiv: Humboldt-Universität zu Berlin 21
Lavirinthos 69
Lavrangas, Dionysios 61
Leonidas (King of Sparta) 92
Leontaritis, Francisco 29
Leontis, Christos 52
Les Misérables 209
levendia/levendes/levendis 36, 92, 122, 146,
    150, 282
levendoyenna 36, 151, 282
lexifagos 223
libretto 166, 168, 173, 175, 182, 183, 184, 254
Lidorikis, Miltiadis 168
Ligeti, György 195
Linoseli 90
liomazohto 113
Liszt 135
Livadia 171
Lohengrin 161, 169
Lousakies 149, 283
Love's Bread 220
Lucullus 223
Lycophron 182, 183, 185, 186
Lygari, Tatiana 58
Lygos the Brave 171
lyra/lyras 17, 36, 37, 39, 40, 47, 48, 51, 55, 56,
    57, 60, 66, 68, 69, 71, 72, 73, 84, 99, 102, 104,
    105, 107, 108, 111, 117, 118, 152, 156, 162,
    166, 180, 181, 188, 239, 240, 241, 268, 280,
    282, 284
Lysidice (aka Lucide) 182, 185

M

Madares 93, 282, 283
Maleme 30
Malevizi 104, 281, 282
Maleviziotis 104, 281, 282
Mallias, Alexandros 99
Malta 5, 28
Mamangakis, Nikos 163, 263
mandinadologos 104
mandinadomahia 189
mandoura 188, 189, 282
manna 212
Maravgakis, Giorgis (aka Droseros) 108, 267

Marcinko, Kerri 178
Margraff, Ruth 166
Markopoulos, Yannis 47, 52
maroulosalata 227, 228
Martinů, Bohuslav 162, 174
Massine, Lorca 162
Masterbuilder, The 61, 164, 165, 166, 167, 168,
    169, 170, 171, 172, 174, 176, 177, 178, 191,
    197, 199, 254, 262, 264, 265, 268, 269, 270,
    271, 272
Mathianakis, Giorgis (aka Psaros) 108, 267
Matia mou (My eyes) 46
mattinate 36
mazohtres 113, 114
Megalartia 211
Melabianaki, Ourania 51
Melambes 107
Melas, Constantine 137
meli 223
melitzanosalata 227, 228
Melody of Ali 46, 282
Memetakas 47
Meneghini, Giovanni Battista 64
Menelaus 194, 198
meraki 36
meraklides/meraklidiki 36, 156
Meraklidikos 152, 155, 156, 282
meraklis/meraklides 36, 146, 156, 282
Mesara 68, 84, 171, 211, 244, 272
Meskla 95
Messiaen, Olivier 193
Mia mavrofora otan perna 51
milo 224, 225
milosios 223
Mimaros 219
Minos (King of Crete) 110, 118
Minotis, Alexis 242
Mirabello 48
Mirtia 34
mitato 55
Mitos 69, 264
Mitropoulos, Dimitri 3, 60, 61, 62, 63, 169, 242,
    261, 270, 271, 273, 275, 277
mizithra 119
mizithropitakia 119
mobilities 75
moirologia 16, 79, 282
Moschopoulos, Thomas 178
Mouhtaro 108
Mountakis, Kostas 69, 71, 111, 114, 240
Mount Juktas 56, 57, 282

Mouri 86
Mourrais-Velloudios, Thanos 220, 273
Mousouroi 93, 99, 283
multivocality 75
Muses 79
Musical Folklore Archives "Melpo Merlie" 21
Musical Routes: Digital Ethno-musicological Collections of Crete (IMS-FORTH) 21
musica reservata 96
Music Library of Greece 21, 268
muwashahat 46
My Bread is Sweet (lyrics by Manos Eleftheriou) 220
Myrto 183, 185, 186
My Way 221, 258

N

National Opera of Greece 162, 165, 195
na zis' i Kriti! 118
Neighborhood of Angels 252
nene 171
Nenikikamen ("we have won") 255
neokoros 43
Neroutsiko 90
Nevrakis, Nikiforos 62
ney 72
Nietzsche, Friedrich 127, 128, 129, 131, 135, 139, 169, 172, 250, 262, 271, 279
Nobili Veneti 33
nostalgia 73, 103, 110, 222, 226
nostimo 226
nostos 226

O

o choros tis nifis 123
Odeon of Herodes Atticus 102, 178
Odysseus/Odyssean 33, 103, 110, 112, 139, 194, 226
Oedipus at Colonus 182
Oeno 110
ofto 119
oinops pontos 224
Omalos 98, 99
Onassis, Aristotle 64, 65
Oneirou Topoi 69
Operation Mercury 154, 279
oraios, opa-opa leo! 123
Orbecche 31
Oresteia ("Agamemnon-Choephori-Eumenides") 193
Orlov, Count 87

orsitis 104, 281, 282
oud 40, 69, 71, 282

P

Palaia Roumata 280
Palamas 170, 171
Paleoi Skopoi tis Kritis 46
palikari(a)/palikaria 36, 146, 150, 283
Panagia 113
Panathenaea (magazine) 168, 270
Pancretan Association 102, 251
panem et circenses 218, 258
paniyiri 68, 283
Papadakis, Constantine 95
Papadakis, Kostis (aka Kostis tis Papadias) 108
Papadiamandis, Alexandros 195, 218
Papadias, Kostis tis (Kostis Papadakis) 108
Papadopoulos, Lefteris (Eleftherios) 220
Papaioannou, Dimitris 196
Papaioannou, Voula 219
Papamoschou, Tatiana 194
Papas, Irene 194
Papayannis, Thodoros 219
Papoulias, Karolos 178
paraloges 16, 283
parea/parees 36, 96, 105, 107, 283
Paris et Vienne (Pierre de la Cypede) 33
Parsifal 169
Partitio Romaniae 28
Paschalides, Miltos 55, 56, 241, 273
paximadi 204, 221
Pediada 48, 107, 108
Pelalimata 108
Pelasgus 205
Peloponnese 15, 32, 89, 111, 113, 184, 281
Pelops 15
pente 149
Pentelicus (mountain) 138
pe(n)theros/pe(n)thera 80
pentho 80
pentozali(s) 61, 149, 150, 156, 170, 251, 281, 283
Periander 165, 182, 183, 184, 185, 186, 255
perigelastika 16
Pescatore, Enrico 28
Petridis, Nakis 220
Phaistos Disc 40
Phidian 138
philotimo 101, 150, 233, 234
philoxenia 203, 233, 283
Philoxenon 56, 280

pidichtos 54, 56, 104, 108, 146, 282
Pineios 171
Piperakis, Harilaos 45, 240
pithos/pithoi 205
Plant Life 206
Platanos 212
Plessas, Mimis 220
plimni 199
ploumisto 215
Politis, Nikolaos 16, 274
pomegranate 13, 224, 225
Pontianus 206
Pontic Greek 14, 195, 283
Pontic Greeks 14, 283
Portes 90
Priam 194
Princess Europa 57
Pringiponisa 46
priniotis 83, 283
Procles 183, 185
Procleus 182
prosforo 214
Protomastoras 168
Protopappas 87
protos 149, 279
Psachos, Constantinos 177
Psarantonis (Antonis Xylouris) 37, 55, 56, 69, 102, 210, 239, 241, 246, 269, 271, 274
psaria 51
Psaronikos (Nikos Xylouris) 51, 55
Psaros (Giorgis Mathianakis) 108, 267
Psaroyiannis 69
Psiloritis 54, 55, 91, 117, 118, 154, 155
Psiloritis, Petros 168, 270
psomi 207
psomolisso 210
psomopatis 207
psomos 207
psomozo 210
Ptohoprodromos 218
Puccini 65
Pylos 111, 207
pyrrichean/pyrrichi 62, 102, 104, 149, 155, 283

Q

Qadduka 'al-mayyaas (Your flirtatiously swaying figure) 46

R

rabab 68, 69, 72
Rāg Bhairavi 69

raki 14, 117, 118, 120, 203
ratsa 34
ravdistes 113
rembetika/rembetiko 166, 180, 283
Remoundou, Anna 178
Report to Greco 101, 161, 248, 270
Rethi(e)-mniotis (man from Rethymno) 35
Rethymno 34, 35, 45, 46, 107, 195, 240, 241, 246, 251, 281, 284
Rhadamanthus 110
Rhodes 16, 145, 216, 275
rhyton 27
Riadis, Emilios 61
riza 93, 283
Rizites 102
rizitika 52, 93, 94, 96, 97, 100, 101, 105, 283
rizitiko 52, 102, 283
Rizo in Pella 221
rodi 224
Rodinos, Andreas 45, 240
rodo 83, 283
Romanos 3, 5, 43, 44, 179, 279, 281
Romanos, Giorgos 179
Romeic thesis 12
romeiki 171
romiosini 87
rose (rodho) dances 83, 283
roumat(h)iani sousta 280
Rousochoria 28
Rouvelas, Kostas 220

S

Sachtouris, Miltos 218
Samaras. Spyridon 61
Samaria Gorge 89, 90, 263, 283
Samos 168, 198, 281
Samprovalakis, Yannis 180, 242, 254, 268
santouri 17, 33, 72, 131, 180, 181, 194, 283
sarangi 37, 71
Sardounis, Dimitrios 219
sariki 117, 121
sarikopites 119
sarod 69
Saronic gulf 182
Savvopoulos, Dionysis 220
saz 40, 47, 71, 72, 279
Schoenberg, Arnold 162
Seferis, George 33, 218, 247
Serafin, Tullio 64
Serres 208
Sfakianakis, Kostas 162

Sfakia/Sfakian(s)/sfax 86, 87, 89, 90, 91, 92, 98, 150, 244
sheep dance (provatisios horos) 83
Sifodaskalakis (Iosif Daskalakis) 251
Sikelianos, Angelos 33, 218
sikofantis 225
Sinatra, Frank 258
sirtaki 163, 193, 279, 283
sirto(s) 47, 55, 56, 57, 123, 146, 149, 156, 163, 283
sistrum 27
Sitia 33, 48, 50, 106, 108, 265, 277
sitodotra 206
Skalkottas, Nikos 60, 62, 242
Skarpathiotis (Yannis Fragoulidakis) 108
Skinai apo ton Stratona (Scenes from the Barracks) 242
Sklavopoula 28
Skordalos, Thanassis 47, 240
Skordilis, Sifis 86
Skoulas, Vasilis 36, 37, 239, 276
Solomos, Alexis 187
Solomos, Dionysios 33, 171, 209
Sophocles 29, 170, 187, 193, 262, 268
Souda Bay 154
sousta 83, 239, 280
Spatharis, Evgenios 219
Spercheios 171
Spermo 110
sphragis 245
Spili 240
Staatstheater am Gaertnerplatz of Munich 184
Stafidakis, Mehmet Bey 47
stafili 224
stahiotrofos 206
Stamatopoulos, Andreas 58
Stavrakakis, Mitsos 69, 234, 259, 264, 276
Stavrakakis, Vasilis 46, 69, 259, 276
Stavrou, Gerasimos 179
Stavroulakis, Iraklis 107, 267
Stefanidis, Harilaos 161
Stergiou, Andreas 58
Stivaktakis, Christos 36
stivania 121
strata repertoire (songs for the road) 96
Strauss 162, 169, 173
stravomita 111
Strose to stroma sou yia dio (Make your bed for two) 252
St. Spyridon 213
sykasios 223

Symphonic Orchestra of the National Broadcast Foundation 187
synaesthesia/synaesthetically 112, 224, 284
syncretic/syncretism 30, 71, 76, 129, 166, 180, 284
syndrofos (companion) 207
Syria 28, 43, 46, 280

T

tabachaniotiko/tabachaniotika 45, 46, 284
tambouras 47
tambura (or tanpura) 69
tamburello 57
tar 71
tarhu 71, 72
Tavitian, Harry 187
tavla repertoire (songs for the table or "feastsongs") 96
taximi 40, 166, 284
techne 110
Terra Creta 111
Tertsina 187
Tertsines 169, 270
Thalassocosmos (Sea World) 82
thanatos 131
Theodorakis, Mikis 33, 127, 162, 163, 191, 193, 194, 197, 199, 220, 248, 252, 255, 276, 279
Theodore the 2nd, Pope 98
Theodoropoulos, Spuros (Agis Theros) 177
Theophanes the Cretan 29
Theotokopoulos, Domenikos 29
Theotokos 43, 44
thiaboli 188, 189, 284
Thisia 168
Thoma, Kelly 56, 241, 242, 263, 277
Thrapsano 108
Thrasyvoulos 184
thriskia 255, 279
Timpaki 198
topophilia 59, 284
Tourkokrites/Tourkokritikoi 28, 284
Toutoudaki, Spyridoula 36
Traditional Music and Spoken Word Catalog 21
tragoudo/tragodia 79, 284
Train at Rouf Railway Theater, The 57
trapeza 223
Triandafillakis, Stefanos (aka Kioros) 149
trichordo 108, 284
Tripolitis, Kostas 220
trofodotis 223

Trophonius 223
Tryphon 206
tsakisma 198, 284
Tsarouchis, Yannis 237, 277
Tsatsa Marouka 171
Tsatsaronakis 212
Tsenoglou, Eleni 221
Tsiara, Evangelia 58
tsifteteli 13
tsipouro 14, 203
Tsitsanis, Vassilis 220
tsoureki 215
Tsoutsouros 82
Tuva/Tuvan/Tuvans 71, 72, 73, 97, 243, 268, 271

U

Union for the Mediterranean (UfM) 198

V

Vakakis, Dimitris 154
Varvoglis, Marios 61, 187, 242
vasilikos 119
vasilopita 215, 216
Vasilopoulos, Yannis 220
vendema 113
Venerato 51
Venizelia 152
Venizelos, Eleftherios 29, 53, 60, 62, 170, 173, 252, 253, 268
Verdi, Giuseppe 64
Viannos 48, 106, 273
viololyra 108, 284
vlachika 16
Vlachos, Ioannis 86, 87, 150, 280
Vlachos, Michail 98
Vlavianos, Thanasis 58
von Zemlinksy, Alexander 162
Voudouris, Elias 178
voukakraton 212
vraka 121
vrondolyra 84, 284

W

Wagner, Richard 135, 161, 169, 170, 174
Walter, Bruno 162
White Mountains 93, 102, 282, 283

X

Xanthi 179
Xarchakos, Stavros 52
Xenakis, Iannis 195
Xenios 55, 56, 119
Xenopoulos, Grigorios 218
xenos/xenoi 56, 112, 283
Xirosterni 240
Xirouhakis, Theoharis 151, 152, 153, 154, 155, 156, 251, 252, 278
xobliastres 216
Xyloskalo 90
Xylouris, Antonis. *See* Psarantonis
Xylouris, Nikos 3, 47, 51, 52, 55, 62, 69, 72, 99, 240, 241, 266, 271, 276

Y

Ya Daeiti 113
Yalom, Irvin 188, 234, 255, 259, 278
Yeoryios o Kris 29
yia sou! 118
Yotopoulou, Tina 58

Z

Zaffirelli, Franco 65
Zaimakis 47, 278
Zakynthos 29
zala 149, 251
zali 251
Zalmoxis 192, 265
Zambelios, Spyridon 79
zarb 69, 72, 73
zeibekiko 220
Zeus 31, 54, 55, 56, 57, 58
Zorba the Greek 127, 129, 130, 133, 162, 163, 179, 240, 252, 262, 270, 272
zournas 17

About Maria Hnaraki

A professor of anthropology, folklore and ethnomusicology and an accomplished scholar in the field, Maria Hnaraki has extensively researched cultural identity expressions, traditions and customs, such as music and dance events in the Mediterranean, as well as investigated topics in nissology, experiential learning and hybrid educational environments. She favors investigating who people are and how they behave through the arts they create and the customs they observe, coming to the conclusion that "we are all amalgams of many influences and that the same things happen all over the world in different ways."

Hnaraki holds a Diploma of Arts in Music Studies from the National and Kapodistrian University of Athens-Greece (1996), an M.A. in Folklore and Ethnomusicology (1999) and a Ph. D. in Folklore and Ethnomusicology from Indiana University in Bloomington (2002). Additionally, she has a Piano Soloist Diploma from the Hellenic Conservatory of Athens (1997) and degrees in Theory, Pedagogy and Music Education from the National Conservatory of Athens, while she has also received numerous awards, honors and fellowships.

Hnaraki is currently the Director of Greek Studies and an Associate Teaching Professor at Drexel University, Philadelphia. Her wide-ranging circle of activities include, among others, presentations in international conferences on several topics such as contemporary Greek society and its diasporas, cultural identities in the Mediterranean, learning pedagogy, cultural aspects of the Greek language, literature and the other arts, music and dance, publications of book reviews and articles in journals and periodicals, translations, instruction of folk songs and dances, co-organization and performance in music and dance ensembles as well as coordination of various events such as lectures, concerts, theatrical performances, movie showings, and Mediterranean Diet symposia. Due to her almost inherited abilities in researching and using archives, she keeps enriching a patrilineal collection of audio-visual as well as written sources. Last, but not least, she constantly pursues collaborations with multiple organizations and significantly outreaches to innovative Greek businesses.

While at Cornell University, Hnaraki founded a study abroad program in Crete-Greece which she has been expanding and enriching since then. At Drexel University, she has created more than 30 university courses, several of which are unique in the USA, with the educational purpose of implementing an integral, holistic, interdisciplinary, academic approach to the Greek and Mediterranean reality.

Her 2007 book **Cretan Music: Unraveling Ariadne's Thread** has received the "Young Academic Writer and Researcher" price from the Pancretan Association.

About Zorba Press

Zorba Press is an independent publisher of books, multimedia books and audio books (forthcoming), and user-friendly ebooks in many formats. From the gorgeous gorges of Ithaca, New York, we publish the paperback books **The Zorba Anthology of Love Stories**; **The Ithaca Manual of Style**; the anthology **Zenlightenment!**; and a wild comic novel about love and eros (for adults) **Thoreau Bound: A Utopian Romance in the Isles of Greece.**

Currently, we offer about 30 titles – fiction and non-fiction. Recent publications include **The Terrestrial Gospel of Nikos Kazantzakis** by Thanasis Maskaleris; and **50 Benefits of Ebooks: A Thinking Person's Guide to the Digital Reading Revolution**. We publish a number of wonderful books by Michael Tobias in paperback (including his autobiography, **Biotopia**); and the first ebook edition of a modern classic, Tobias's extraordinary novel, **The Adventures of Mr Marigold**.

In 2013 we launched a new line of books about Greece or by Greek authors, including **Sing In Me, Muse, and Through Me Tell the Story: Greek Culture Performed** by Maria Hnaraki, and **The Communal Mind and the Master Artifice** by Helen Sullivan, edited by Amy Mims.

At Zorba Press, we practice what we call "Sustainable Publishing": publishing with a greater sense of awareness and responsibility. Sustainable Publishing is the attempt to bring to the work of publishing a healthy balance between four essential elements: Culture, Commerce, Technology (humanized), and our natural Environment.

Zorba's mission is to promote the innovative ideas and the daring books that nourish children and childhood, point the way to a culture of non-violence, create a sustainable future, and nurture – for every living being – a new world of love, kindness, courage, creativity, sincerity, and peace.

Visit Zorba Press at www.ZorbaPress.com

Made in the USA
Middletown, DE
14 March 2022

62626544R00184